"*Nemesis*, the final volume in the ren..... .... true patriot's anguished and devastating critique of the militarism .uat threatens to destroy the United States from within. In detail and with unflinching candor, Chalmers Johnson decries the discrepancies between what America professes to be and what it has actually become—a global empire of military bases and operations; a secret government increasingly characterized by covert activities, enormous 'black' budgets, and near dictatorial executive power; a misguided republic that has betrayed its noblest ideals and most basic founding principles in pursuit of disastrously conceived notions of security, stability, and progress."

—John Dower, author of
Embracing Defeat: Japan in the Wake of World War II

"Chalmers Johnson, a patriot who pulls no punches, has emerged as our most prescient critic of American empire and its pretensions. *Nemesis* is his fiercest book—and his best."

—Andrew J. Bacevich, author of *The New American Militarism*

"Johnson's book is a sober reminder that the U.S. has become an empire. . . . His most searing commentary to date on the current state of U.S. politics."

—*Financial Times*

"*Nemesis* is a stimulating, sweeping study in which Johnson asks a most profound strategic question: Can we maintain the global dominance we now regard as our natural right? His answer is chilling. You do not have to agree with everything Johnson says—I don't—but if you agree with even half of his policy critiques, you will still slam the book down on the table, swearing, 'We have to change this!'"

—Joseph Cirincione, senior vice president for national security
and international policy, Center for American Progress

"Each of Johnson's erudite chapters both enlightens and disturbs. . . . His writing is often described as 'epolemic,' but that doesn't capture the heartfelt concern that underlies his distress about our country."

—*In These Times*

"The three volumes (*Blowback*, *The Sorrows of Empire*, *Nemesis*) constitute a well-written, detailed, and stimulating display of the radical anti-imperialist critique of American foreign policy. *Nemesis* is particularly good in sounding the alarm. Countervailing reactions are now clearly under way once again, and Johnson's book is a primer on much that needs to be done."

—*The San Diego Union-Tribune*

"*Nemesis* is a five-alarm warning about flaming militarism, burning imperial attitudes, secret armies, and executive arrogance that has torched and consumed the Constitution and brought the American Republic to death's door. Johnson shares a simple, liberating, and healing path back to worthy republicanism. But the frightening and heartbreaking details contained in *Nemesis* suggest that the goddess of retribution will not be so easily satisfied before 'the right order of things' is restored."

—Karen Kwiatkowski, retired U.S. Air Force Lieutenant Colonel

"Last fall a treasonous Congress gave the president license to kidnap, torture—you name it—on an imperial scale. All of us, citizens and noncitizens alike, are fair game. Kudos for not being silent, Chalmers, and for completing your revealing trilogy with undaunted courage."

—Ray McGovern, former CIA analyst;
cofounder of Veteran Intelligence Professionals for Sanity (VIPS)

"Before 9/11, when Chalmers Johnson warned us of Blowback, too few listened. When Johnson then urged us to rethink America's imperial course in *The Sorrows of Empire,* he went deeper, exploring the wages of global American militarism. Now comes *Nemesis,* the third in the trilogy, an urgent warning for a country that, in the words of Dwight Eisenhower, risks 'destroying from within that which it is trying to protect from without.' Johnson is a national treasure. Let's hope we listen this time."

—Eugene Jarecki, director of *Why We Fight,*
Grand Jury Prize Winner, Sundance Film Festival

"Chalmers Johnson's voice has never been more urgently needed, and in *Nemesis* it rings with eloquence, clarity, and truth."

—James Carroll, author of *House of War*

NEMESIS

NEMESIS

THE LAST DAYS OF THE AMERICAN REPUBLIC

CHALMERS JOHNSON

A HOLT PAPERBACK

METROPOLITAN BOOKS / HENRY HOLT AND COMPANY   NEW YORK

Holt Paperbacks
Henry Holt and Company, LLC
Publishers since 1866
175 Fifth Avenue
New York, New York 10010
www.henryholt.com

Distributed in Canada by H. B. Fenn and Company Ltd.

Library of Congress Cataloging-in-Publication Data
Johnson, Chalmers.
Nemesis: the last days of the American Republic / Chalmers Johnson.
    p.   cm.
Includes index.
ISBN-13: 978-0-8050-8728-4
ISBN-10: 0-8050-8728-1
1. United States—Foreign relations—1989–   2. United States—Military policy.
3. United States—Politics and government—1989–   I. Title.
E840.J633 2007
973.931—dc22   2006047200

Originally published in hardcover in 2007 by Metropolitan Books

First Holt Paperbacks Edition 2008

Printed in the United States of America
3 5 7 9 10 8 6 4 2

NEMESIS

In Greek mythology,
the goddess of retribution,
who punishes human
transgression of the natural,
right order of things and
the arrogance that causes it.

Contents

NEMESIS

Prologue: The Blowback Trilogy

Who is Osama bin Laden really? Let me rephrase that. What is Osama bin Laden? He's America's family secret. He is the American president's dark Doppelganger. The savage twin of all that purports to be beautiful and civilized. He has been sculpted from the spare rib of a world laid to waste by America's foreign policy: its gunboat diplomacy, its nuclear arsenal, its vulgarly stated policy of "full-spectrum dominance," its chilling disregard for non-American lives, its barbarous military interventions, its support for despotic and dictatorial regimes, its merciless economic agenda that has munched through the economies of poor countries like a cloud of locusts. . . . Now that the family secret has been spilled, the twins are blurring into one another and gradually becoming interchangeable.

ARUNDHATI ROY,
The Guardian, September 27, 2001

Nemesis is the last volume of an inadvertent trilogy that deals with the way arrogant and misguided American policies have headed us for a series of catastrophes comparable to our disgrace and defeat in Vietnam or even to the sort of extinction that befell our former fellow "superpower," the Soviet Union. Such a fate is probably by now unavoidable; it is certainly too late for mere scattered reforms of our government or bloated military to make much difference.

I never planned to write three books about the decline and fall of the American empire, but events intervened. In March 2000, well before 9/11, I published *Blowback,* based on my years of teaching and writing about East Asia. I had become convinced by then that some secret U.S. government operations and acts in distant lands would come back to haunt us. "Blowback" does not mean just revenge but rather retaliation for covert, illegal violence that our government has carried out abroad that it kept totally secret from the American public (even though such acts are seldom secret among the people on the receiving end). It was a term invented by the Central Intelligence Agency and first used in its "after-action report" about the 1953 overthrow of the elected government of Premier Mohammad Mossadeq in Iran. This coup brought to power the U.S.-supported Shah of Iran, who would in 1979 be overthrown by Iranian revolutionaries and Islamic fundamentalists. The Ayatollah Khomeini replaced the Shah and installed the predecessors of the current, anti-American government in Iran.[1] This would be one kind of blowback from America's first venture into illegal, clandestine "regime change"—but as the attacks of September 11, 2001, showed us all too graphically, hardly the only one.

My book *Blowback* was not much noticed in the United States until after 9/11, when my suggestion that our covert policies abroad might be coming back to haunt us gained new meaning. Many Americans began to ask—as President Bush did—"Why do they hate us?" The answer was not that some countries hate us because of our democracy, wealth, lifestyle, or values but because of things our government did to various peoples around the world. The counterblows directed against Americans seem, of course, as out of the blue as those airplanes on that September morning because most Americans have no framework that would link cause and effect. The terrorist attacks of September 11 are the clearest examples of blowback in modern international relations. In the initial book in this trilogy, I predicted the likely retaliation that was due against the United States, but I never foresaw the terrorist nature of the attacks, nor the incredibly inept reaction of our government.

On that fateful Tuesday morning in the early autumn of 2001, it soon became clear that the suicidal rammings of hijacked airliners into symbolically significant buildings were acts of what the Pentagon calls "asymmetric warfare" (a rare instance in which bureaucratic jargon proved more accurate than the term "terrorism" in common use). I talked with friends and colleagues around the nation about what group or groups might have carried out such attacks. The veterans of our largest clandestine war—when we recruited, armed, and sent into battle Islamic mujahideen (freedom fighters) in Afghanistan against the Soviet Union in the 1980s—did not immediately come to mind. Most of us thought of Chileans because of the date: September 11, 1973, was the day the CIA secretly helped General Augusto Pinochet overthrow Salvador Allende, the leftist elected president of Chile. Others thought of the victims of the Greek colonels we put in power in 1967, or Okinawans venting their rage over the sixty-year occupation of their island by our military. Guatemalans, Cubans, Congolese, Brazilians, Argentines, Indonesians, Palestinians, Panamanians, Vietnamese, Cambodians, Filipinos, South Koreans, Taiwanese, Nicaraguans, Salvadorans, and many others had good reason to attack us.

The Bush administration, however, did everything in its power to divert us from thinking that our own actions might have had something to do with such suicidal attacks on us. At a press conference on October 11, 2001, the president posed the question, "How do I respond when I see that in some Islamic countries there is vitriolic hatred for America?" He then answered himself, "I'll tell you how I respond: I'm amazed that there's such misunderstanding of what our country is about that people would hate us. I am—like most Americans, I just can't believe it because I know how good we are." Bush has, of course, never once allowed that the United States might bear some responsibility for what happened on 9/11. In a 2004 commencement address at the Air Force Academy, for instance, he asserted, "No act of America explains terrorist violence, and no concession of America could appease it. The terrorists who attacked our country on September 11, 2001, were not protesting our policies. They were protesting our existence."[2]

But Osama bin Laden made clear why he attacked us. In a videotaped statement broadcast by Al Jazeera on October 7, 2001, a few weeks after the attacks, he gave three reasons for his enmity against the United States. The U.S.-imposed sanctions against Iraq from 1991 to 9/11: "One million Iraqi children have thus far died although they did not do anything wrong"; American policies toward Israel and the occupied territories: "I swear to God that America will not live in peace before peace reigns in Palestine . . ."; the stationing of U.S. troops and the building of military bases in Saudi Arabia: "and before all the army of infidels [American soldiers] depart the land of Muhammad [Saudi Arabia]."[3] Not a word about Muslim rage against Western civilization; no sign that his followers were motivated by, as the president would put it, "hatred for the values cherished in the West [such] as freedom, tolerance, prosperity, religious pluralism, and universal suffrage"; no support for *New York Times* correspondent Thomas Friedman's contention that the hijackers had left no list of demands because they had none, that "their act was their demand."[4]

The attempt to disguise or avoid the policy-based reasons for 9/11 fed the rantings of Christian fundamentalists in the United States. Televangelist Pat Robertson, later joined by Jerry Falwell, declared that "liberal civil liberties groups, feminists, homosexuals, and abortion rights supporters bear some responsibility for [the] terrorist attacks because their actions have turned God's anger against America," and they launched a hate campaign against all Muslims. Jimmy Swaggart called Muhammad a "sex deviant" and a pervert and suggested that Muslim students in the United States be expelled.[5] The Pentagon added its bit of insanity to this religious mix when army lieutenant general William G. "Jerry" Boykin, deputy undersecretary of defense for intelligence, argued in public in full uniform without subsequent official reprimand that "they" hate us "because we are a Christian nation," that Bush was appointed by God, that the Special Forces are inspired by God, that our enemy is "a guy named Satan," and that we defeat Islamic terrorists only "if we come at them in the name of Jesus."[6]

Because Americans generally failed to consider seriously why we had been attacked on 9/11, the Bush administration was able to respond in a way that made the situation far worse. I believed at the time and feel no differently five years later that we should have treated the attacks as crimes against the innocent, not as acts of war. We should have proceeded against al-Qaeda the same way we might have against organized crime. It would have been wise to call what we were doing an "emergency," as the British did in fighting the Malay guerrillas in the 1950s, not a "war." The day after 9/11, Simon Jenkins, the former editor of the *Times* of London, insightfully wrote: "The message of yesterday's incident is that, for all its horror, it does not and must not be allowed to matter. It is a human disaster, an outrage, an atrocity, an unleashing of the madness of which the world will never be rid. But it is not politically significant. It does not tilt the balance of world power one inch. It is not an act of war. America's leadership of the West is not diminished by it. The cause of democracy is not damaged, unless we choose to let it be damaged."[7]

Had we followed Jenkins's advice we could have retained the cooperation and trust of our democratic allies, remained the aggrieved party of 9/11, built criminal cases that would have stood up in any court of law, and won the hearts and minds of populations al-Qaeda was trying to mobilize. We would have avoided entirely contravening the Geneva Conventions covering the treatment of prisoners of war and never have headed down the path of torturing people we picked up almost at random in Afghanistan and Iraq. The U.S. government would have had no need to lie to its own citizens and the rest of the world about the nonexistent nuclear threat posed by Iraq or carry out a phony preventive war against that country.

Instead, we undermined the NATO (North Atlantic Treaty Organization) alliance and brought to power in Iraq allies of the Islamic fundamentalists in Iran.[8] Contrary to what virtually every strategist recommended as an effective response to terrorism, we launched our high-tech military against some of the poorest, weakest people on Earth. In Afghanistan, our aerial bombardment "bounced the rubble" we had helped create there by funding, arming, and advising the anti-Soviet war of the 1980s and gave "warlordism, banditry, and opium production a new lease on life."[9] In Iraq our "shock and awe" assault invited comparison with the sacking of Baghdad in 1258 by the Mongols.[10] In his address to Congress on September 20, 2001, President Bush declared that the coming battle was to be global, Manichean, and simple. You are, he said, either "with us or against us" (failing to acknowledge that both Jesus and Lenin used the phrase first). His actions would ensure that, in the years to come, there would be ever more people around the world "against us."[11]

As I watched these post-9/11 developments, it became apparent to me that, even more than in most past empires, a well-entrenched militarism lay at the heart of our imperial adventures. It is a sad fact that the United States no longer manufactures much—with the exception of weaponry. We are without question the world's greatest producer and exporter of arms and munitions on the planet. Although we are going deeply into debt doing so, each year we spend more on our armed forces than all other nations on Earth combined. In *The Sorrows of Empire*, I tried to analyze the nature of this militarism and to expose the harm it was doing, not only to others but to our own society and governmental system.

After all, we now station over half a million U.S. troops, spies, contractors, dependents, and others on more than 737 military bases spread around the world. These bases are located in more than 130 countries, many of them presided over by dictatorial regimes that have given their citizens no say in the decision to let us in. The Pentagon publishes an inventory of the real estate it owns in its annual *Base Structure Report,* but its official count of between 737 and 860 overseas installations is incomplete, omitting all our espionage bases and a number of others that are secret or could be embarrassing to the United States. For example, it leaves out the air force base at Manas in Kyrgyzstan, formerly part of the Soviet Union and today part of our attempt to roll back the influence of the Soviet Union's successor state, Russia, and to control crucial Caspian Sea oil. It even neglects to mention the three bases built in tiny Qatar over the past few years, the headquarters for our high command during the invasion of Iraq in 2003, so as not to embarrass the emir of that country, who invited in our "infidel" soldiers. This same kind of embarrassment to the government of Saudi Arabia, not to mention the public displeasure of the Saudi national Osama bin Laden, forced us to move our forces out of that country and to Qatar in the years immediately preceding the assault on Iraq.

The purpose of all these bases is "force projection," or the maintenance of American military hegemony over the rest of the world. They facilitate our "policing" of the globe and are meant to ensure that no other nation, friendly or hostile, can ever challenge us militarily. In *The Sorrows of Empire* I described this planet-spanning baseworld, including the history and development of various installations, the creation of an airline—the Air Mobility Command—to connect them to one another and to Washington, and the comforts available to our personnel through the military's various "Morale, Welfare, and Recreation" (MWR) commands. Some of the "rest-and-recreation" facilities include the armed forces ski center at Garmisch in the Bavarian Alps, over two hundred military golf courses around the world, some seventy-one Learjets and other luxury aircraft to fly admirals and generals to such watering holes, and luxury hotels for our troops and their families in Tokyo, Seoul, on the Italian Riviera, at Florida's Disney World, and many other places.

Americans cannot truly appreciate the impact of our bases elsewhere because there are no foreign military bases within the United States. We have no direct experience of such unwelcome features of our military encampments abroad as the networks of brothels around their main gates, the nightly bar brawls, the sexually violent crimes against civilians, and the regular hit-and-run accidents. These, together with noise and environmental pollution, are constant blights we inflict on local populations to maintain our lifestyle. People who live near our bases must also put up with the racial and religious insults that our culturally ignorant, high-handed troops often think is their right to dish out. Imperialism means one nation imposing its will on others through the threat or actual use of force. Imperialism is a root cause of blowback. Our global garrisons provide that threat and are a cause of blowback.

It takes a lot of people to garrison the globe. Service in our armed forces is no longer a short-term obligation of citizenship, as it was back in 1953 when I served in the navy. Since 1973, it has been a career choice, one often made by citizens trying to escape from the poverty and racism that afflict our society. That is why African-Americans are twice as well represented in the army as they are in our population, even though the numbers have been falling as the war in Iraq worsens, and why 50 percent of the women in the armed forces are minorities. That is why the young people in our colleges and universities today remain, by and large, indifferent to America's wars and covert operations: without the draft, such events do not affect them personally and therefore need not distract them from their studies and civilian pursuits.

American veterans of World War II, Korea, or Vietnam simply would not recognize life in the modern armed services. As the troops no longer do KP ("kitchen police"), the old World War II movie gags about GIs endlessly peeling mountains of potatoes would be meaningless today. We farm out such work to private military companies like KBR (formerly Kellogg Brown & Root), a subdivision of the Halliburton Corporation, of which Dick Cheney was CEO before he became vice president. It is an extremely lucrative business for them. Of the $57 billion that was appropriated for Iraq operations at the outset of the invasion, a good third of it went to civilian contractors to supply meals, drive trucks and buses, provide security guards, and do all other housekeeping work to maintain our various bases.

When you include its array of privately outsourced services, our professional, permanent military currently costs around three-quarters of a trillion dollars a year. This amount includes the annual Defense Department appropriation for weapons and salaries of more than $425 billion (the president's request for fiscal year 2007 was $439.3 billion), plus another $120 billion for military operations in Iraq and Afghanistan, $16.4 billion for nuclear weapons and the Department of Energy's weapons laboratories, $12.2 billion in the Military Construction Appropriations Bill, and well over $100 billion in pensions, hospital costs, and disability payments for our veterans, many of whom have been severely wounded.[12] But we are not actually paying for these expenses. Chinese, Japanese, and other Asian investors are. We are putting them on the tab and so running the largest governmental as well as trade deficits in modern economic history. Sooner or later, our militarism will threaten the nation with bankruptcy.

Until the 2004 presidential election, ordinary citizens of the United States could at least claim that our foreign policy, including our illegal invasion of Iraq, was the work of George Bush's administration and that we had not put him in office. In 2000, Bush lost the popular vote and was appointed president thanks to the intervention of the Supreme Court in a 5–4 decision. In November 2004, regardless of claims about voter fraud, Bush won the popular vote by over 3.5 million ballots, making his wars ours. The political system failed not because we elected one candidate rather than another as president, since neither offered a responsible alternative to aggressive war and militarism, but because the election essentially endorsed and ratified the policies we had pursued since 9/11.

Whether Americans intended it or not, we are now seen around the world as having approved the torture of captives at Abu Ghraib prison in Iraq, at Bagram Air Base in Kabul, at Guantánamo Bay, Cuba, and at secret prisons around the world, as well as having seconded Bush's claim that, as a commander in chief in "wartime," he is beyond all constraints of the Constitution or international law. We are now saddled with a rigged economy based on record-setting deficits, the most secretive and intrusive American government in memory, the pursuit of "preventive" war as a basis for foreign policy, and a potential epidemic of nuclear proliferation as other nations attempt to adjust to and defend themselves from our behavior, while our own, already staggering nuclear arsenal expands toward first-strike primacy.

The crisis the United States faces today is not just the military failure of Bush's policies in Iraq and Afghanistan, the discrediting of America's intelligence agencies, or our government's not-so-secret resort to torture and illegal imprisonment. It is above all a growing international distrust and disgust in the face of our contempt for the rule of law. Article 6 of the U.S. Constitution says, in part, "all Treaties made, or which shall be made, under the Authority of the United States, shall be the supreme Law of the Land." The Geneva Conventions of 1949, covering the treatment of prisoners of war and civilians in wartime, are treaties the U.S. government promoted, signed, and ratified. They are therefore the supreme law of the land. Neither the president, nor the secretary of defense, nor the attorney general has the authority to alter them or to choose whether or not to abide by them so long as the Constitution has any meaning.

Despite the administration's endless propaganda about bringing freedom and democracy to the people of Afghanistan and Iraq, most citizens of those countries who have come into contact with our armed forces (and survived) have had their lives ruined. The courageous, anonymous young Iraqi woman who runs the Internet Web site Baghdad Burning wrote on May 7, 2004: "I don't understand the 'shock' Americans claim to feel at the lurid pictures [from Abu Ghraib prison]. You've seen the troops break down doors and terrify women and children . . . curse, scream, push, pull, and throw people to the ground with a boot over their head. You've seen troops shoot civilians in cold blood. You've seen them bomb cities and towns. You've seen them burn cars and humans using tanks and helicopters. . . . I sometimes get e-mails asking me to propose solutions or make suggestions. Fine. Today's lesson: don't rape, don't torture, don't kill, and get out while you can—while it still looks like you have a choice. . . . Chaos? Civil war? We'll take our chances—just take your puppets, your tanks, your smart weapons, your dumb politicians, your lies, your empty promises, your rapists, your sadistic torturers and go."[13]

In July 2004, Zogby International Surveys polled 3,300 Arabs in Egypt, Jordan, Lebanon, Morocco, Saudi Arabia, and the United Arab Emirates. When asked to identify "the best thing that comes to mind about America," virtually all respondents answered "nothing at all." There are today approximately 1.3 billion Muslims worldwide, some 22 percent of the global population. Through our policies, we have turned virtually all of them against the United States.[14]

Unfortunately, our political system may no longer be capable of saving the United States as we know it, since it is hard to imagine any president or Congress standing up to the powerful vested interests of the Pentagon, the secret intelligence agencies, and the military-industrial complex. Given that 40 percent of the defense budget is now secret as is every intelligence agency budget, it is impossible for Congress to provide effective oversight even if its members wanted to. Although this process of enveloping such spending in darkness and lack of accountability has reached its apogee with the Bush administration, the Defense Department's "black budgets" go back to the atomic-bomb-building Manhattan Project of World War II. The amounts spent on the intelligence agencies have been secret ever since the CIA was created in 1947.

If our republican form of government is to be saved, only an upsurge of direct democracy might be capable of doing so. In the spring of 2003, before our troops could be launched into Iraq, some 10 million people in all the genuine democracies on Earth demonstrated fervently against the onrushing war, against George Bush, and for democracy, including an estimated 1,750,000 people in London, 750,000 in New York, 2,500,000 in Rome, 1,500,000 each in Madrid and Barcelona, 800,000 in Paris, and 500,000 in Berlin.[15] However, the sole victory of this movement came on March 14, 2004, with the election of Spanish prime minister José Luis Rodríguez Zapatero. If democracy means anything at all, it means that public opinion matters. Zapatero understood that over 80 percent of Spaniards opposed Bush's war against Iraq, and he immediately withdrew all Spanish forces. The task of democrats worldwide is to replicate the Spanish achievement in their own societies.

In early 2003, on the eve of the invasion of Iraq, I was putting the finishing touches on my portrait of the global reach of American military bases. In it, I suggested the sorrows already invading our lives, which were likely to be our fate for years to come: perpetual war, a collapse of constitutional government, endemic official lying and disinformation, and finally bankruptcy. At book's end, I advocated reforms intended to head off these outcomes but warned that "[f]ailing such a reform, Nemesis, the goddess of retribution and vengeance, the punisher of pride and hubris, waits impatiently for her meeting with us."

This line inspired poet John Shreffler to pen his conception of such a goddess, American style. In the poem "Neighborhood Girl," he imagines her as an adolescent tomboy from elsewhere, no doubt cruel and merciless when playing the divine role assigned to her but also the niece of Erato, the muse of love poetry. He wrote in part:

> *She's new to the neighborhood, her family just moved in*
> *From Greece or somewhere, she's a great, tall, gawky girl*
> *With braces and earrings and uneven skin:*
> *Hormones and acne, her change is coming in, . . .*

Her name is Nemesis and she's just moved in,
She's new to the neighborhood, she's checking it out.[16]

As the Dutch folklorist Micha F. Lindemans reminds us, "Nemesis is the goddess of divine justice and vengeance. . . . [She] pursues the insolent and the wicked with inflexible vengeance. . . . She is portrayed as a serious-looking woman with in her left hand a whip, a rein, a sword, or a pair of scales."[17] Nemesis is a bit like Richard Wagner's Valkyrie Brünnhilde, except that Brünnhilde collects heroes, not fools and hypocrites. Nonetheless, Brünnhilde's way of announcing herself applies also to Nemesis: "Nur Todgeweihten taugt mein Anblick" (Only the doomed see me).[18]

I remain hopeful that Americans can still rouse themselves to save our democracy. But the time in which to head off financial and moral bankruptcy is growing short. The present book is my attempt to explain how we got where we are, the manifold distortions we have imposed on the system we inherited from the Founding Fathers, and what we would have to do to avoid our appointment with Nemesis, now that she's in the neighborhood.

1

Militarism and the Breakdown of Constitutional Government

Last week, filled with grief and sorrow for those killed and injured and with anger at those who had done this, I confronted the solemn responsibility of voting to authorize the country to go to war. Some believe this resolution was only symbolic, designed to show national resolve. But I could not ignore that it provided explicit authority, under the War Powers Resolution and the Constitution, to go to war. It was a blank check to the president to attack anyone involved in the September 11 events—anywhere, in any country, without regard to our nation's long-term foreign policy, economic and national security interests, and without time limit. In granting these overly broad powers, the Congress failed its responsibility to understand the dimensions of its declaration. I could not support such a grant of war-making authority to the president; I believe it would put more innocent lives at risk.

> —CONGRESSWOMAN BARBARA LEE ([Democrat from California], the
> only member of Congress to vote against the transfer of the war
> power to the president for the invasion of Afghanistan),
> *San Francisco Chronicle*, September 23, 2001

One of the oddest features of political life in the United States in the years since the terrorist attacks is how few people have thought or acted like Barbara Lee. The public expresses itself in opinion polls, which some students of politics scrutinize intently, but there is little passion in the society, certainly none proportionate to the threats facing our democratic republic. The United States today is like a cruise ship on the Niagara River upstream of the most spectacular falls in North America. A few people on board have begun to pick up a slight hiss in the background, to observe a faint haze of mist in the air or on their glasses, to note that the river current seems to be running slightly faster. But no one yet seems to have realized that it is almost too late to head for shore.

Like the Chinese, Ottoman, Hapsburg, imperial German, Nazi, imperial Japanese, British, French, Dutch, Portuguese, and Soviet empires in the last century, we are approaching the edge of a huge waterfall and are about to plunge over it.

If the American democratic system is no longer working as planned, if the constitutional checks and balances as well as other structures put in place by the founders to prevent tyranny are increasingly less operational, we have not completely lacked for witnesses of every stripe, domestic and foreign. General Tommy Franks, commander of the American assault on Baghdad, for instance, went so far as to predict that another serious terrorist attack on the United States would "begin to unravel the fabric of our Constitution," and under such circumstances, he was open to the idea that "the Constitution could be scrapped in favor of a military form of government."[1] The historian Kevin Baker feared that we are no longer far from the day when, like the Roman Senate in 27 BC, our Congress will take its last meaningful vote and turn over power to a military dictator. "In the end, we'll beg for the coup," he wrote.[2]

On October 10, 2002, Senator Robert Byrd (Democrat from West Virginia) asked plaintively about the separation of powers, "Why are we being hounded into action on a resolution that turns over to President Bush the Congress's Constitutional power to declare war? . . . The judgment of history will not be kind to us if we take this step."[3] Nonetheless, the following day, the resolution carried by a 77–23 vote in the Senate and 296–133 in the House of Representatives. The *Berkshire Eagle* editorialized, "The Senate, which was designed by the framers of the Constitution to act as a brake on the popular passions of the day, was little more than a speed bump under the White House steamroller."[4] The libertarian writer Bill Winter conjectured that the problem was "the monarchization of America under Bush."[5] Adam Young, a Canadian political commentator, wondered, "How did the chief magistrate of a confederated republic degrade into the global tyrant we experience today, part secular pope, part military despot, part pseudo-philosopher-king and full-time overbearing global gangster?"[6] Indeed, that is the question for all of us.

Former British foreign secretary Robin Cook noted that "[a]ll the checks and balances that the founding fathers constructed to restrain presidential power are broken instruments." Cook observed the hubris and megalomania that flowed from this in John Bolton, then the number three official at the State Department (subsequently ambassador to the United Nations). When asked about possible incentives that might cause Iran to end its nuclear ambitions, Bolton replied, "I don't do carrots." Cook accurately predicted that members of the Bush administration "will . . . celebrate their [2004] election victory by putting [the Iraqi city of] Fallujah to the torch," as they did that very November.[7]

Marine general Anthony Zinni, General Franks's predecessor as Centcom commander in the Middle East, worried about the way the Pentagon was further expanding its powers at the expense of other agencies of government. "Why the hell," he asked, "would the Department of Defense be the organization in our government that deals with the reconstruction of Iraq? Doesn't make sense."[8] One anonymous foreign service officer supplied an answer to *Los Angeles Times* reporter Sonni Efron, "I just wake up in the morning and tell myself, 'There's been a military coup,' and then it all makes sense."[9] Even the president himself was a witness of sorts to the changes under way, baldly asserting at a White House press conference on April 13, 2004, that he was "the ultimate decision-maker for this country"—a notion that would have appalled the authors of the Constitution.[10]

I believe that George W. Bush and Dick Cheney have led the country into a perilous cul-de-sac, but they did not do it alone and removing them from office will not necessarily solve the problem. The crisis of government in the United States has been building at least since World War II. The emergence of the imperial presidency and the atrophying of the legislative and judicial branches have deep roots in the postwar military-industrial complex, in the way broad sectors of the public have accepted the military as our most effective public institution, and in aberrations in our electoral system. The interesting issue is not the damage done by Bush, Cheney, and their followers but how they were able to get away with it, given the barriers that exist in the Constitution to prevent just the sorts of misuses of power for which they have become notorious.

Historian Carol Berkin in her book *A Brilliant Solution: Inventing the Constitution* argues that the nation's "Founders—including George Washington, Benjamin Franklin, Gouverneur Morris of Pennsylvania and dozens of others—envisioned a supreme legislative branch as the heart

and soul of America's central government. . . . America's modern presidency, with all its trappings, would be unimaginable to men like Madison,
Washington, and Franklin. Of all those historic figures at the 1787 [Con-
stitutional] Convention, perhaps only Alexander Hamilton would relish
today's playing of 'Hail to the Chief.'"[11]

The intent of the founders was to prevent a recurrence of the tyranny
they had endured under Britain's King George III. They bent all their
ingenuity and practical experience to preventing tyrannies of one, of the
few, of a majority, of the monied classes, or of any other group that might
obtain and exercise unchecked power, often adopting institutional precedents from the Roman Republic. Inspired by the French political philosopher Montesquieu's discussion of the "separation of powers" in his *On the
Spirit of the Laws,* published in 1748, the drafters of the American Constitution produced a sophisticated scheme to balance power in a republic.
The most basic structure they chose was federalism, setting up the states
as alternatives to and limitations on the power of the national government. Congress was given that quintessential parliamentary power—control of the budget—without which it would be merely an ornamental
body like the "people's congresses" in communist-dominated countries.
Congress was also charged with initiating all legislation, making the final
decision to go to war, and if necessary getting rid of an unsatisfactory
president by impeachment, something also achievable through periodic
elections. To moderate the power of Congress somewhat, the Constitution
divided it into two quite differently elected and apportioned houses, each
capable of vetoing the other's decisions.

Both houses of Congress must ultimately pass all laws, and the president, who is entrusted with implementing them, is given a veto as well.
The Congress, in turn, can override a presidential veto with a two-thirds
vote, and even when Congress and the president agree on a law, the
Supreme Court, exercising the function of interpreting the laws, can still
declare it unconstitutional. The president and members of Congress must
be re-elected or leave office, but judges serve for life, although Congress
can impeach them. The president nominates the heads of the cabinet
departments, who serve at his pleasure, as well as all judges, but the Senate
must approve them.

Over time, this balance-of-power spirit came to influence other institutions of government that the Constitution did not mention, including

the armed forces, where competition among the services—the army, navy, air force, and Marine Corps—dilutes somewhat the enormous coercive power entrusted to them.[12] To prevent a tyranny of the majority, the Constitution authorizes fixed terms and fixed times for elections (borrowed from the Roman Republic) as a way to interfere with the monopolization of power by an individual, an oligarchy, or a political party.

Unfortunately, after more than two centuries (about the same length of time that the Roman Republic was in its prime), this framework has almost completely disintegrated. For those who believe that the structure of government in Washington today bears some resemblance to that outlined in the Constitution of 1787, the burden of proof is on them. The president now dominates the government in a way no ordinary monarch possibly could. He has at his disposal the clandestine services of the CIA, a private army unaccountable to the Congress, the press, or the public because everything it does is secret. No president since Harry Truman, having discovered what unlimited power the CIA affords him, has ever failed to use it. Meanwhile, the "defense" budgets of the Pentagon dwarf those of the rest of the government and have undermined democratic decision making in the process. Funds for military hardware are distributed in as many states as possible to ensure that any member of Congress who might consider voting against a new weapons system would be accused of putting some of his constituents out of work.

When in May 2005, Secretary of Defense Donald Rumsfeld listed a large number of unneeded domestic military bases that he wanted to close as an economy measure, the affected communities promptly erupted in protest and began frantic lobbying efforts to "save" their particular installations. Advocates of keeping the bases open phrase their arguments in terms of national security, but the true reason is jobs, jobs, jobs.[13] As the philosopher Hannah Arendt wrote at the height of the Cold War, "It is no secret that the billions of dollars demanded by the Pentagon for the armaments industry are necessary not for 'national security' but for keeping the economy from collapsing."[14]

"The price of liberty is eternal vigilance." It is not precisely clear who first spoke these immortal words—Patrick Henry, Thomas Jefferson, or the antislavery abolitionist Wendell Phillips—but during the Cold War and its aftermath, Americans were not particularly vigilant when it came to excessive concentration of power in the presidency and its appendages, and we are now paying a very high price for that. From the founding of the republic to the moment of President Dwight D. Eisenhower's farewell address in 1961, some of our leaders have warned us that the greatest threat to our republican structure of government is war, including its associated maladies of standing armies, a military-industrial complex, and all the vested interests that develop around a massive military establishment.

The classic statement of this threat was by the chief author of the Constitution, James Madison:

> Of all the enemies of true liberty, war is, perhaps, the most to be dreaded, because it comprises and develops the germ of every other. War is the parent of armies; from these proceed debts and taxes; and armies, and debts, and taxes are the known instruments for bringing the many under the domination of the few. In war, too, the discretionary power of the Executive is extended; its influence in dealing out offices, honors and emoluments is multiplied; and all the means of seducing the minds, are added to those of subduing the force, of the people. The same malignant aspect in republicanism may be traced in the inequality of fortunes, and the opportunities of fraud, growing out of a state of war, and in the degeneracy of manner and of morals, engendered in both. No nation can preserve its freedom in the midst of continual warfare. . . . War is in fact the true nurse of executive aggrandizement. In war, a physical force is to be created; and it is the executive will, which is to direct it. In war, the public treasuries are to be unlocked; and it is the executive hand which is to dispense them. In war, the honors and emoluments of office are to be multiplied; and it is the executive patronage under which they are to be enjoyed; and it is the executive brow they are to encircle. The strongest passions and most dangerous weaknesses of the human breast; ambition, avarice, vanity, the honorable or venal love of fame, are all in conspiracy against the desire and duty of peace.[15]

The United States has been continuously engaged in or mobilized for war since 1941. Using statistics compiled by the Federation of American Scientists, Gore Vidal has listed 201 overseas military operations between the end of World War II and September 11, 2001, in which the United States struck the first blow. Among these, a typical example was Operation

Urgent Fury in 1983, "Reagan's attack on the island of Grenada, a month-long caper that General [Alexander M.] Haig disloyally said could have been handled more efficiently by the Provincetown police department."[16] Excluding minor military operations, Drexel University historian and political scientist Michael Sullivan counts only "invasions, interventions, and regime changes since World War II" and comes up with thirty bloody, often clandestine, American wars from Greece (1947–49) to Yugoslavia (1995 and 1999).[17] Neither of these compilations included the wars in Afghanistan (2001–) and Iraq (2003–).

It should be noted that since 1947, while we have used our military power for political and military gain in a long list of countries, in no instance has democratic government come about as a direct result. In some important cases, on the other hand, democracy has developed in opposition to our interference—for example, after the collapse of the regime of the CIA-installed Greek colonels in 1974; after the demise of the U.S.-supported fascist dictatorships in Portugal in 1974 and Spain in 1975; after the overthrow of Ferdinand Marcos in the Philippines in 1986; after the ouster of General Chun Doo-Hwan in South Korea in 1987; and after the ending of thirty-eight years of martial law on the island of Taiwan in the same year.[18] The United States holds the unenviable record of having helped install and then supported such dictators as the Shah of Iran, General Suharto in Indonesia, Fulgencio Batista in Cuba, Anastasio Somoza in Nicaragua, Augusto Pinochet in Chile, and Sese Seko Mobutu in Congo/Zaire, not to mention the series of American-backed militarists in South Vietnam and Cambodia until we were finally expelled from Indochina.[19] In addition, for decades we ran one of the most extensive international terrorist operations in history against Cuba and Nicaragua because their struggles for national independence had produced outcomes that we did not like.

The unintended result of this record of militarism is the contemporary Leviathan that dominates Washington, threatening our nation with bankruptcy, turning many of the organs of our "free press" into *Pravda*-like mouthpieces, and disgracing the nation by allowing our young men and women to torture prisoners picked up on various battlefields or even snatched from city streets in allied countries. In using the term "militarism," I want to distinguish it from defense of country. No one questions the need to raise a citizens' army and the obligation of able-bodied men and women to serve in it in order to defend the nation from foreign aggression. But the wars listed above are virtually all ones that we entered by choice rather than out of necessity. In many cases, they were shrouded in secrecy, while our political leaders lied to Congress and the public about the need to fight them. The launching of the Vietnam and Iraq wars are only the most blatant examples of presidential deception.[20] There are almost certainly several cases currently hidden behind the walls of "classification" in which we secretly fomented the downfall of a government and offered clandestine assistance to the side we favored.[21] Most recently, these may well include the abortive attempt to overthrow President Hugo Chávez of Venezuela in April 2002 and the use of front organizations to bring to power pro-U.S. governments in the former Soviet states of Georgia in November 2003 and the Ukraine in November 2004.

Andrew Bacevich, a West Point graduate and a Vietnam veteran with twenty-three years of service in the U.S. Army, believes, "Americans in our own time have fallen prey to militarism, manifesting itself in a romanticized view of soldiers, a tendency to see military power as the truest measure of national greatness, and outsized expectations regarding the efficacy of force. To a degree without precedent in U.S. history, Americans have come to define the nation's strength and well-being in terms of military preparedness, military action, and the fostering of (or nostalgia for) military ideals."[22]

How did this come about? As a start, we have indeed fought too many wars of choice, starting in 1898 with our imperialist conquests of the Philippines, Guam, Puerto Rico, and our establishment of a protectorate over Cuba, shortly followed by World War I. World War II, while not a war of choice, produced the most complete mobilization of resources in our history and led to the deployment of our forces on every continent. After the victory of 1945, some Americans urged a rapid demobilization, which actually was well under way when the Cold War and the Korean War restored and enlarged our military apparatus. It would never again be reined in, even after the collapse of the Soviet Union. The inevitable result was a continual transfer of powers to the presidency exactly as Madison had predicted, the use of executive secrecy to freeze out Congress and the judiciary, the loss of congressional mastery over the budget, and the rise of two new, extraconstitutional centers of power that are today out of control— the Department of Defense and the fifteen intelligence organizations, the best known of which is the Central Intelligence Agency. I believe we will never again know peace, nor in all probability survive very long as a nation, unless we abolish the CIA, restore intelligence collecting to the State Department, and remove all but purely military functions from the Pentagon. Even if we did those things, the mystique of America as a model democracy may have been damaged beyond repair. Certainly, under the best of circumstances, it will take a generation or more to overcome the image of "America as torturer."[23]

In 1964, Hannah Arendt addressed a similar problem when she tried to plumb the evil of the Nazi regime. Her book *Eichmann in Jerusalem* dealt with the trial of the former SS officer Adolf Eichmann, who was charged with organizing the transport of Jews to death camps during World War II. She subtitled her book *A Report on the Banality of Evil* but used that now famous phrase only once, at book's end, without explaining it further.[24] Long after Arendt's death, Jerome Kohn, a colleague, compiled a volume of her essays entitled *Responsibility and Judgment.* What made Eichmann both evil and banal, Arendt concluded in one of those essays, was his inability to think for himself.

"Some years ago," she wrote, "reporting the trial of Eichmann in Jerusalem, I spoke of the 'banality of evil' and meant with this no theory or doctrine but something quite factual, the phenomenon of evil deeds, committed on a gigantic scale, which could not be traced to any particularity of wickedness, pathology, or ideological conviction in the doer, whose only personal distinction was perhaps an extraordinary shallowness. However monstrous the deeds were, the doer was neither monstrous nor demonic, and the only specific characteristic one could detect in his past as well as in his behavior during the trial and the preceding police examination was something entirely negative: it was not stupidity but a curious, quite authentic inability to think."[25]

Arendt was trying to locate Eichmann's conscience. She called him a "desk murderer," an equally apt term for George W. Bush, Dick Cheney, and Donald Rumsfeld—for anyone, in fact, who orders remote-control killing of the modern sort—the bombardment of a country that lacks any form of air defense, the firing of cruise missiles from a warship at sea into countries unable to respond, such as Iraq, Sudan, or Afghanistan, or, say, the unleashing of a Hellfire missile from a Predator unmanned aerial vehicle controlled by "pilots" thousands of miles from the prospective target.

How do ordinary people become desk murderers? First, they must lose the ability to think because, according to Arendt, "thinking conditions men against evil doing."[26] Jerome Kohn adds, "With some degree of confidence it may be said that the ability to think, which Eichmann lacked, is the precondition of judging, and that the refusal as well as the inability to judge, to imagine before your eyes the others whom your judgment represents and to whom it responds, invite evil to enter and infect the world."[27] To lack a personal conscience means "never to start the soundless solitary dialogue we call thinking."[28]

If an individual's thinking is short-circuited and does not rise to the level of making judgments, he or she is able to understand acts, including evil acts, only in terms of following orders, doing one's duty, being loyal to one's "homeland," maintaining solidarity with one's fellow soldiers, or surrendering one's will to that of the group. This phenomenon is common in some forms of political life, as Arendt demonstrated in her most famous work, *The Origins of Totalitarianism,* published in 1951, but it is ubiquitous in military life, where, in order to prevail in battle, soldiers have been conditioned to follow orders instantly and to act as a cohesive group. In such roles, "Clichés, stock phrases, adherence to conventional, standardized codes of expression and conduct have the socially recognized function of protecting us against reality, that is, against the claim on our thinking attention which all events and facts arouse by virtue of their existence."[29] This is one reason why democratic republics must be particularly vigilant about standing armies and wars of choice if, that is, they intend to retain their liberties.

At Abu Ghraib prison in Iraq, some American soldiers had become so inured to the torture of Iraqi inmates that they made a screen saver of naked Iraqi captives stacked in a "pyramid" with their tormentors looking on and laughing in the background.[30] By contrast, on January 13, 2004, Sergeant Joseph M. Darby of the army's 372nd Military Police Company turned over a computer disk of similar photos from Abu Ghraib of American soldiers torturing Iraqis to the army's Criminal Investigations Division. He said that the photos "violated everything that I personally believed in and everything that I had been taught about the rules of war."[31] Sergeant Darby had not stopped thinking.

No Pentagon civilian or American officer above the rank of lieutenant colonel has so far been prosecuted for the policies that led to Abu Ghraib and other acts of torture and murder in Iraq, Afghanistan, and elsewhere, another proof that, as a consequence of our half century of devotion to war, we unintentionally abandoned our republican checks on the activities of public officials and elevated the military to a position that places it, in actual practice, beyond the law. In so doing, what we have created is a large corps of desk murderers in our executive branch and the highest ranks of our armed forces. These people have replaced their ability to think and judge with "clichés, stock phrases, and adherence to conventional, standardized codes of expression and conduct." For example, Secretary of Defense Donald Rumsfeld shrugged off the defilement and looting of ancient monuments and museums in Baghdad as the American occupation of that country began by saying, "Stuff happens," and then joking that he did not think there were that many ancient vases in Iraq.[32]

It is, of course, natural for political and military leaders to try to put favorable interpretations on their policies. In the wars in Afghanistan and Iraq, however, this has meant making statements that consist of little more than flat contradictions of evidence or specious reinterpretations of law. Attorney General Alberto Gonzales, for example, has tried to legalize the Bush administration's decisions to torture prisoners of war by arguing that a "new paradigm renders obsolete [the Geneva Conventions'] strict limitations on questioning of enemy prisoners and renders quaint some of its provisions."[33] But the allegedly new paradigm is apparent only to Gonzales, and in any case he lacks the authority to nullify a ratified treaty.

Richard Myers, a four-star air force general and former chairman of the Joint Chiefs of Staff, declared categorically to *Fox News*, "One thing we don't do is we don't torture," as if that disposed of the pictures from Abu Ghraib prison.[34] In speaking to our European allies about extensive evidence that the CIA was operating secret prisons and torturing the inmates, Secretary of State Condoleezza Rice said, "With respect to detainees, the United States Government complies with its Constitution, its laws, and its treaty obligations. Acts of physical or mental torture are expressly prohibited. The United States Government does not authorize or condone torture of detainees. Torture, and conspiracy to commit torture, are crimes under U.S. law, wherever they may occur in the world." She mentioned that there had been cases of the "unlawful treatment" of prisoners, but added that "the horrible mistreatment of prisoners at Abu Ghraib that sickened us all . . . arose under the different legal framework that applies to armed conflict in Iraq."[35] She failed to explain what the nature of this different legal framework actually is or how this squares with a ban on torture "wherever [it] may occur in the world."

Commenting on the unauthorized bombing of civilian villages in Afghanistan, former secretary of state Colin Powell said on German TV, "We spent a huge amount of money and we are putting our young men and women on the line, every day, to put in place a form of government that was decided upon by the Afghan people. And we are helping them to rebuild and reconstruct their society. That pattern is the American pattern. We're very proud of it. It's been repeated many times over, and it will be repeated again in Iraq."[36]

As Arendt suggests, it is precisely when such absurdities and flights from reality replace clear thinking that evil enters the picture. What follows are but three illustrations of the consequences of the failure of our political and military leadership to think: the systematic killing of unarmed civilians in Afghanistan and Iraq; the creation of a global network of both known and secret prisons around the world in which our troops or intelligence agents routinely torture the inmates; and the way the military's attitudes at the time of its 2003 assault on Baghdad led to the destruction and desecration of some of the world's oldest known human artifacts.

During World War II in East Asia, the Imperial Japanese Army contrived one of the worst euphemisms ever used to mask criminal acts— namely, "comfort women" (*ianfu*) to refer to the women and girls abducted in occupied countries and sent to the front lines to serve as prostitutes for Japanese officers and soldiers.[37] This phrase will probably haunt Japan until the end of time. A comparable term invented by the United States military is "collateral damage," meaning its killing of civilians and the destruction of private property while allegedly pursuing one or another of its unilaterally declared acts of "liberation."

"Broadly defined," says a U.S. Air Force training manual, "collateral damage is unintentional damage or incidental damage affecting facilities, equipment, or personnel occurring as a result of military actions directed against targeted enemy forces or facilities. Such damage can occur to friendly, neutral, and even enemy forces."[38] This military euphemism has been substituted for plainspoken words that might induce guilt in airmen when they bomb and strafe defenseless communities or in soldiers when they kick down doors of private homes, rush in pointing assault rifles at women and children, and sometimes rob residents under cover of searching for enemies or contraband. The military also certainly hoped that its adoption of such a neutral, inoffensive expression for ones that might offend or suggest unpleasantness would strengthen the resolve of its soldiers and perhaps prevent them from being held accountable for war crimes.

"Collateral damage" is nowhere recognized, or even mentioned, in humanitarian international law. In fact, intentional attacks of any sort on civilians are prohibited under "Common Article 3," which applies to all four Geneva Conventions. The United States has signed and ratified the Geneva Conventions (although it never ratified two supplemental protocols of 1977 that spelled out the international rules of war in greater detail). Common Article 3 prohibits "at any time and in any place whatsoever" violence, including murder, mutilation, cruel treatment, torture, and outrages to human dignity against protected persons—that is, "persons taking no active part in hostilities," such as civilians, the wounded, and prisoners of war. "Such persons are, in all circumstances, entitled to respect for their honor and religion, and must be protected against insults and public curiosity. No physical or moral coercion shall be exercised to obtain information from them or third parties. Reprisals against protected persons and their property are prohibited."[39]

Among the gravest contemporary instances of "collateral damage" were the sanctions enforced against Iraq between 1991 and 2003 and the slaughter of Afghan and Iraqi civilians in the wars waged by the United States after 9/11. On May 11, 1996, the CBS television program *60 Minutes* made famous one of the more notorious statistics in the history of Iraqi-American relations. In an interview with then secretary of state Madeleine Albright, correspondent Lesley Stahl said, "We have heard that a half million children have died as a result of the sanctions [in Iraq]. That's more than died in Hiroshima." Then Stahl asked, "Is the price worth it?" Albright replied, "I think this is a very hard choice, but we think the price is worth it." Osama bin Laden cited just this statistic as one of the reasons al-Qaeda attacked the U.S. on 9/11. In her 2003 memoir, *Madam Secretary,* Albright amended her comment this way: "I must have been crazy;

I should have answered the question by reframing it and pointing out the inherent flaw in the premise behind it. Saddam Hussein could have prevented any child from suffering simply by meeting his obligations."[40] Her clarification, however, was even more disingenuous than her earlier indifference to the deaths of hundreds of thousands of children. As a former ambassador to the United Nations, she was certainly fully informed about the sanctions program and its impact.

During the Gulf War of 1991, the United States drove Iraq from Kuwait but stopped short of invading Iraq itself. Nonetheless, President George H. W. Bush and his national security adviser, General Brent Scowcroft, were determined to do everything in their power to make postwar Iraq ungovernable, to stimulate revolt within the country, and to force Saddam Hussein from office. During the war itself, the United States dropped some ninety thousand tons of bombs on Iraq in the space of forty-three days, intentionally destroying the civilian infrastructure, including eighteen of twenty electricity-generating plants and the water-pumping and sanitation systems.[41] Dr. Thomas Nagy, a professor at George Washington University, analyzed a large number of declassified Defense Intelligence Agency documents on the bombing and concluded that American officials were well aware that the purposeful destruction of Iraq's civilian water sanitation systems would cause increased outbreaks of disease and high rates of child mortality.[42] The primary document, "Iraq Water Treatment Vulnerabilities," dated January 22, 1991, argues that Iraq's rivers "contain biological materials, pollutants, and are laden with bacteria. Unless the water is purified with chlorine, epidemics of such diseases as cholera, hepatitis, and typhoid could occur." Later documents state that the sanctions imposed after the war explicitly embargoed the importation of chlorine in order to prevent the purification of drinking water.

A *Washington Post* analysis of the air war published on June 23, 1991, quoted typical, although unnamed, Pentagon strategists on the bombing campaign, one of whom suggested that "[t]he definition of innocents gets to be a little bit unclear. . . . They do live there, and ultimately people have some control over what goes on in their country." Another air force planner asserted, "We wanted to let people know. Get rid of this guy and we'll be more than happy to assist in rebuilding. We're not going to tolerate Saddam Hussein or his regime. Fix that, and we'll fix your electricity."[43] In

1995, Colonel John A. Warden III wrote in *Airpower Journal*, "[Destruction] of these [electric power] facilities shut down water purification and sewage treatment plants. As a result, epidemics of gastroenteritis, cholera, and typhoid broke out, leading to perhaps as many as 100,000 civilian deaths and a doubling of the infant mortality rate."[44] A team from the Harvard School of Public Health suggested in May 1991 that "at least 170,000 children under five years of age will die in the coming year from the delayed effects" of the bombing.[45]

The bombing itself violated international humanitarian law and made the United States liable to charges of war crimes. Article 54 (2) of the "Protocol Additional to the Geneva Conventions of August 12, 1949, relating to the Protection of Victims of International Armed Conflicts (Protocol 1), June 8, 1977," explicitly states, "It is prohibited to attack, destroy, remove, or render useless objects indispensable to the survival of the civilian population, such as food-stuffs, agricultural areas for the production of food-stuffs, crops, livestock, drinking water installations and supplies, and irrigation works, for the specific purpose of denying them for their sustenance value to the civilian population or to the adverse Party, whatever the motive, whether in order to starve out civilians, to cause them to move away, or for any other motive."[46] As noted earlier, the United States is not a signatory of Protocol 1, but this does not absolve it of the charge that its behavior was profoundly immoral.

The sanctions themselves reinforced and deepened what the bombing began. Jacob Hornberger, president of the Future of Freedom Foundation, quotes State Department officials who helped negotiate U.N. support for our actions as saying that these were the "toughest, most comprehensive sanctions in history."[47] On August 2, 1990, the United States and Britain obtained U.N. Security Council Resolution 661 freezing all of Iraq's foreign assets and authorizing the cutting off of all trade. This embargo lasted until the Anglo-American invasion of 2003. In its history, the U.N. has imposed economic sanctions only fourteen times (twelve of them since 1990), but according to Joy Gordon, the leading authority on the subject, "only those sanctions on Iraq have been comprehensive, meaning that virtually every aspect of the country's imports and exports is controlled."[48] The American and British governments claimed not to have sequestered imports of food and medicine—hence Albright's pretense that all Saddam Hussein had to do was comply with the U.N. to preserve the health of his people—but the two allies so restricted Iraqi exports that it had no money to buy such necessities. Columbia University professor Richard Garfield, an epidemiologist and one of the leading analysts of the effects of sanctions on Iraq, says that "Iraq's legal foreign trade was cut by an estimated ninety percent by sanctions."[49] In particular Iraq was not allowed to import any of the parts it needed to repair its electrical and water purification systems.

The United States and Britain went to extraordinary lengths to keep U.N. documentation of what was happening inside Iraq from being made public. But the United Nations Food and Agriculture Organization (FAO) nonetheless monitored the situation, and in 1995, its researchers wrote to the *Lancet,* the journal of the British Medical Society, that 567,000 Iraqi children were estimated to have died as a result of sanctions. That figure may have been an overestimate, but it led to the U.N.'s "oil for food" program in 1996, which was supposed to remedy shortages of food and medical supplies. It did not work out that way, however, because the U.N. banked the proceeds from the Iraqi oil sales it now permitted in New York and skimmed off 34 percent to pay Kuwaiti claims of war damage against Iraq as well as its own expenses. The United States insisted that a further 13 percent go to the Kurdish autonomous area in the north. There was thus much less money available than the public was led to believe.

In addition, the U.S. government reserved the right to veto or delay any items Iraq ordered, exercising that power often and in secret. As Joy Gordon, who teaches philosophy at Fairfield University and is a prolific writer on the Iraq sanctions, noted, "In September 2001 nearly one third of water and sanitation and one quarter of electricity and educational-supply contracts were on hold. Between the springs of 2000 and 2002, for example, holds on humanitarian goods tripled." Among the items the United States stopped from entering Iraq in the winter of 2001 were dialysis, dental and firefighting equipment, water tankers, milk and yogurt production equipment, and printing machines for schools.[50]

Anupama Rao Singh, the United Nations Children's Fund representative in Baghdad, observed that food shortages were virtually unknown in Iraq before the sanctions, but that from 1991 to 1998, "children under five were dying from malnutrition-related diseases in numbers ranging from a conservative 2,600 per month to a more realistic 5,357 per month."[51] Using his 1999 study, "Morbidity and Mortality Among Iraqi Children," as well as other studies and his own later recalculations, Richard Garfield estimated that, through 2000, the sanctions had killed approximately 350,000 Iraqi children.[52] This is the most widely accepted figure today. When Denis Halliday, the United Nations coordinator in Iraq, resigned in 1998 to protest the effects of the sanctions, he condemned them as "a deliberate policy to destroy the people of Iraq" and called their implementation "genocide."[53] Given that the United States had starved the Iraqis for over a decade and caused the deaths of several hundred thousand of their children, one wonders why former deputy secretary of defense Paul Wolfowitz and others believed American invading forces would be welcomed as liberators.

In the wake of 9/11, a new threat to civilians in Iraq and Afghanistan materialized in the form of random killings by America's often poorly led and unaccountable armed forces. These victims were "shot by snipers, strafed by helicopters, buried under the rubble of their houses by bombs, incinerated by fire, and left to rot in the streets of cities like Fallujah [Iraq] to be gnawed on by dogs."[54] The military keeps no public record on their numbers—what *Boston Globe* journalist Derrick Jackson calls "this atrocity of silence"—but the evidence indicates that in Iraq in the first years after the invasion such killings by Americans amount to between twice and ten times the people slain by insurgents' bombs.

On June 2, 2005, the Iraqi Interior Ministry announced that, over the previous eighteen months, insurgent violence had claimed the lives of some 12,000 civilians, whereas the estimates of the numbers killed by the American military ranged from a low of 21,000 to over 40,000.[55] In July 2005, Dr. Hatim al-Alwani, head of the Iraqiyun humanitarian organization in Baghdad, released his group's estimate that the total number of Iraqis killed from all causes since the U.S. invasion was 128,000, including those who died in the U.S. assaults on Fallujah. A year later, the American public began slowly to awaken to the U.S. military's lax discipline in using lethal force against civilians. Serious cases of out-of-control marines executing the elderly, women, and children at Haditha, Ishaqi, and elsewhere amounted to the equivalent in Iraq of the My Lai massacre during the Vietnam War.[56]

William Langewiesche, a national correspondent for the *Atlantic Monthly*, wrote from Baghdad, "However vicious or even sadistic the insurgents may be, they are acutely aware of their popular base, and are responsible for fewer unintentional 'collateral' casualties than are the clumsy and overarmed American forces."[57] Dahr Jamail, one of the BBC's correspondents in Iraq, reported, "Coalition and Iraqi security forces may be responsible for up to sixty percent of conflict-related civilian deaths in Iraq—far more than are killed by insurgents, confidential records obtained by the BBC's Panorama programme reveal. . . . One of the least reported aspects of the U.S. occupation of Iraq is the oftentimes indiscriminate use of airpower by the American military."[58]

The American press only rarely, and then usually anecdotally, describes the deaths of civilians killed by American troops. American newspapers and television broadcasts routinely remove pictures of noncombatants killed by U.S. forces even though they do not flinch from showing the bodies of people killed by insurgents. One reason may be surmised from an October 2001 set of instructions a Florida newspaper issued to its staff: "DO NOT USE photos on page 1A showing civilian casualties from the war on Afghanistan. . . . DO NOT USE wire stories that lead with civilian casualties. . . . They should be mentioned further down in the story. If the story needs rewriting to play down the civilian casualties, DO IT."[59] The American press has similarly never reported on the nightly use of "flash bombs" fired by Apache helicopters to light up the fields along the Tigris and Euphrates Rivers. These high-tech American bombs have burned thousands of acres of fields and decimated groves of date palms. Hovering helicopters have also made it impossible for Iraqis to sleep on rooftops in the sweltering summertime, as was their custom in order to escape the stifling heat.[60]

There are no "official" statistics on this mayhem because, as former Centcom commander General Tommy Franks put it, "We do not do body counts." (Franks was speaking of the war in Afghanistan but also making policy for the subsequent war in Iraq.) Such a statement signaled to the civilian populations of Afghanistan and Iraq that the United States did not care how many local citizens it killed. However, as Maria Ruzicka, an American peace activist who was killed on April 16, 2005, on the road to Baghdad International Airport, had discovered, it is also a lie. The U.S. military does do body counts, but only publicizes them when they are of propaganda value to the American side.[61]

American soldiers and contractors working in the war zones are authorized to use lethal force at their own discretion whenever they feel threatened. The soldiers are unaccountable for their acts to any authority except their military superiors, and the contractors are, so far as I can ascertain, simply unaccountable. The U.S. military itself invariably conducts its own investigations into any charges of excessive use of force, and these investigations are normally oriented toward covering up what happened. As one knowledgeable human rights observer in Iraq put matters, "The American troops have adopted an atmosphere of impunity. Arrogant and violent behavior goes unpunished and continues."[62] Patrick Cockburn, a journalist for the *Independent* of London with long experience in Iraq, adds, "Every Iraqi has stories of friends or relatives killed by U.S. troops for no adequate reason. Often they do not know if they were shot by regular soldiers or by members of western security companies whose burly employees, usually ex-soldiers, are everywhere in Iraq."[63]

In Afghanistan, there are relatively few unofficial estimates of the numbers of civilians killed by U.S. forces and no official ones. In December 2001, Robert Fisk, the veteran journalist of the Islamic world, reported that high-level bombing of Afghan villages by B-52s had claimed some 3,700 victims.[64] After that time, there were mostly reports of individual deaths, including a Red Cross account of 52 people, half of them children, killed by bombing in eastern Afghanistan on December 29, 2001; 16 villagers killed on January 23, 2002, by U.S. forces at Hazar Qadam; and 14, including women and children, killed when a U.S. jet attacked a vehicle on March 6, 2002, in eastern Paktia province.

On June 30, 2002, a U.S. AC-130 gunship attacked a cluster of six villages a hundred miles north of Kandahar in Uruzgan province. In the village of Karakak, the aircraft sprayed a wedding ceremony being held at night to escape the heat with hundreds of bullets. The Americans repeatedly claimed that their planes had come under antiaircraft fire and that they were only retaliating. However, a U.S. Special Forces investigation on the ground found no antiaircraft gun or expended cannon shells. What they did find were forty-eight bodies, all but three women and children. Afghan officials believed that the United States either relied on intelligence from Afghan informers who were perhaps settling personal scores or were simply shooting up the area in hopes of killing Mullah Mohammed Omar, the leader of the overthrown Taliban regime, who was raised less than a mile from the village. The Americans later admitted the raid was a mistake and promised to build schools, roads, and hospitals and drill wells in the district but there is no evidence that they ever did so.[65] The "independent" Afghan government of President Hamid Karzai has repeatedly asked the U.S. military to obtain Afghan authorization before carrying out attacks, but American officials up to and including President Bush have refused all such requests.[66]

American killings of civilians have been on a far greater scale in Iraq because that country is more populous and urbanized, and the war and insurgency there have proved much more intense than in Afghanistan. On October 28, 2004, physicians and other researchers affiliated with Johns Hopkins and Columbia Universities in the United States and the al-Mustansiriya University in Baghdad published a report in the British medical journal the *Lancet* that concluded, "The risk of death from violence [in Iraq] in the period after the invasion was fifty-eight times higher than in the period before the war. . . . We think that about 100,000 excess deaths, or more, have happened since the 2003 invasion of Iraq. Violence accounted for most of the excess deaths, and air strikes from coalition forces accounted for most violent deaths. . . . Most individuals reportedly killed by coalition forces were women and children."[67]

Some other nongovernmental analysts believe this estimate may be too high. The London-based group Iraq Body Count puts the total of civilians killed by foreign troops at between 34,711 and 38,861 as of May 1, 2006. However, it counts only deaths directly reported by the media or mentioned by official groups.[68] The *Lancet*'s estimate was based not only on an elaborate survey of households but on a comparison of mortality rates in the first nearly eighteen months after the invasion with the almost fifteen-month period preceding it. As the authors note, "The major causes of death before the invasion were myocardial infarction, cerebrovascular accidents, and other chronic disorders whereas after the invasion violence was the primary cause of death." They excluded the city of Fallujah from their investigation because it was too dangerous to do research there. "We estimate that 98,000 more deaths than expected happened after the invasion outside Fallujah and far more if the outlier Fallujah cluster is included."[69]

During the "shock and awe" barrage of cruise missiles and other airborne weaponry that opened the war, Secretary of Defense Donald Rumsfeld and his aides planned to try to kill "high value targets" (HVTs), including Saddam Hussein and General Izzat Ibrahim, Iraq's number two official. According to the plans, Rumsfeld personally had to sign off on any airstrike "thought likely to result in the deaths of more than thirty civilians." The air war commander, Lieutenant General T. Michael Moseley, proposed fifty such raids and Rumsfeld signed the orders for each and every one.

As it turned out, none succeeded. The March 19, 2003, attempt to kill Saddam Hussein and his sons at the Dora Farms compound south of Baghdad was a major fiasco. American intelligence reported Saddam there in an underground bunker that would require particularly large bombs. He was not there, however, nor was any bunker, but the air force killed a lot of Iraqi civilians. Similarly, an April 7 raid in the Mansur district of Baghdad killed only innocent bystanders. The deaths accomplished nothing except to show off America's lethal, high-tech weaponry. Marc Garlasco, a former Defense Intelligence Agency official who headed the "high-value targeting cell" within the Pentagon, described the entire campaign as an "abject failure" and added, "We failed to kill the HVTs and instead killed civilians and engendered hatred and discontent in some of the population."[70]

Jeffrey Sachs, director of the Earth Institute at Columbia University, commented on these and later destructive attacks, "American behavior and self-perceptions reveal the ease with which a civilized country can engage in large-scale killing of civilians without public discussion. . . . The American fantasy of a final battle, in Fallujah or elsewhere, or the capture of some terrorist mastermind, perpetuates a cycle of bloodletting that puts the world in peril. Worse still, American public opinion, media and the [2004] election victory of the Bush administration have left the world's most powerful military without practical restraint."[71]

As a second example of the administration's failure to think and make moral judgments, consider the global network of military prisons it has created in which inmates are routinely tortured. On May 17, 2004, the *Army Times* reported that around the halls of the Pentagon a caustic label had emerged for the enlisted soldiers shown in the infamous Abu Ghraib prison photos: "the six morons who lost the war."[72] I would suggest that there were actually seven morons, not six, and they were not enlisted men. The seven are President George W. Bush; his former legal counsel and subsequently attorney general of the United States Alberto Gonzales; Secretary of Defense Donald Rumsfeld; chairman of the Joint Chiefs of Staff

General Richard B. Myers; Lieutenant General Ricardo Sanchez, commander of ground forces in Iraq until mid-2004; Major General Geoffrey Miller, commander at Guantánamo until April 2004, when he took over Abu Ghraib prison in Iraq; and Senate Armed Services Committee chairman Senator John W. Warner (Republican from Virginia).[73]

These are the people who disgraced the United States and did nothing about it when the details of Abu Ghraib in particular began to be revealed to the public. As the Israeli court that sentenced Adolf Eichmann to death insisted: "The degree of responsibility increases as we draw further away from the man who uses the fatal instrument with his own hand."[74] This is as true in cases of official torture as it is for genocide.

President Bush was directly responsible for removing the legal restraints against torture. On the evening of September 11, 2001, in the wake of the attacks on the World Trade Center and the Pentagon, he returned to Washington and at 8:30 p.m. addressed the nation from the Oval Office. Following his speech, he met with his senior officials concerned with the crisis in the Presidential Emergency Operations Center. According to Richard Clarke, the former counterterrorism chief for both Presidents Clinton and Bush, who was there, Bush entered the room and said, "I want you all to understand that we are at war and we will stay at war until this is done. Nothing else matters. Everything is available for the pursuit of this war. Any barriers in your way, they're gone. Any money you need, you have it. This is our only agenda." In the ensuing discussion, according to Clarke, "Secretary Rumsfeld noted that international law allowed the use of force only to prevent future attacks and not for retribution. Bush nearly bit his head off. 'No,' the President yelled in the narrow conference room. 'I don't care what the international lawyers say, we are going to kick some ass.' "[75] As Timothy Garton Ash has observed, "We got off on the wrong foot on the very first day."[76]

Without question Secretary Rumsfeld heeded what the commander in chief told him. Later that autumn, during the interrogations of John Walker Lindh, our first post-9/11 torture victim, Rumsfeld instructed his legal counsel to order the military intelligence officials to "take the gloves off." In the early stages of his interrogation under torture, Lindh's responses were cabled to the Pentagon hourly followed by return orders to keep up the pressure.

Lindh was then a twenty-year-old, white, middle-class American citizen from Marin County, California, who had converted to Islam, gone to Yemen and Pakistan to study religious texts and Arabic, and traveled to Afghanistan in August 2001, barely a month before the 9/11 attacks. The CIA found him, badly wounded, in a prison of one of the Northern Alliance warlords, our allies in the war against the Taliban.

His American captors stripped and humiliated him, denied him medical treatment, and tortured him for information about the whereabouts of Osama bin Laden. According to Richard A. Serrano of the *Los Angeles Times*, who was shown secret military documents detailing the treatment of Lindh, he "was being questioned while he was propped up naked and tied to a stretcher in interrogation sessions that went on for days."[77] Attorney General John Ashcroft threatened to try Lindh as a traitor but in the end settled for a guilty plea on charges of aiding the Taliban and a twenty-year sentence rather than let Lindh's lawyers seek testimony from captives held at Guantánamo about his torture. As part of his plea bargain, Lindh was forced to sign a statement saying: "The defendant agrees that this agreement puts to rest his claims of mistreatment by the United States military, and all claims of mistreatment are withdrawn. The defendant acknowledges that he was not intentionally mistreated by the U.S. military." As journalist Dave Lindorff observes, Lindh "remains almost certainly wrongfully imprisoned."[78]

Thus began practices that would ultimately infect and contaminate virtually all aspects of the "war on terror." Thanks to the research of Alfred W. McCoy, who has studied the history of U.S. government torture and the CIA's application of it from the early days of the Cold War, its use was not unknown in American clandestine operations.[79] In collaboration with the British, the CIA invented new forms of mental torture that relied on inducing terror, which often did irreversible psychological damage, in addition to such techniques as "water-boarding" or what our Latin American military allies call the "submarino." It involves being held under water until you think you will die. There was, however, great nervousness about using these techniques because laws and international treaties passed and signed during the middle and late years of the Cold War had clearly made torture a crime. Bush and Rumsfeld ordered these restraints removed, and all the old methods were soon back in use in Afghanistan, Iraq, Cuba, and at secret CIA prisons around the world.

Bush's responsibility for legalizing torture came in two key decisions.

The first was his September 17, 2001, Memorandum of Agreement, or "finding"—jargon for a presidential directive authorizing a particular CIA covert operation. This vastly expanded the CIA's activities worldwide, including its payments to the Northern Alliance warlords in Afghanistan to resume the civil war against the Taliban with American air support. Bush also authorized the global pursuit of al-Qaeda "permitting the CIA to conduct covert operations [in some eighty countries] without having to come back for formal approval for each specific operation" and—most important—removed all constraints and safeguards over the CIA's already existing program of "extraordinary rendition."[80]

The latter term is a euphemism for abducting people anywhere on Earth, including inside the United States, and secretly flying them to countries whose police and intelligence personnel are more than happy to torture them for us or where the United States runs its own secret prisons for doing so. Such countries and territories reportedly have included Egypt, Syria, Saudi Arabia, Jordan, Uzbekistan, Thailand, Diego Garcia, Pakistan, and unidentified Eastern European nations. The military or the CIA also run some twenty-five prisons in Afghanistan and seventeen in Iraq.[81] Rendition is a violation of international law, since the U.N. Convention against Torture and Other Cruel, Inhuman or Degrading Treatment or Punishment, adopted December 10, 1984, and ratified by the U. S. Congress in October 1994, specifically says, "No state . . . shall expel, return, or extradite a person to another state where there are substantial grounds for believing that he would be in danger of being subjected to torture." The Geneva Conventions also contain articles stipulating the same prohibition.[82]

Bush's most fateful decision on torture, however, came in a presidential memorandum drafted by John C. Yoo, a University of California law professor who was serving in the Office of Legal Counsel, Department of Justice, and endorsed by Alberto Gonzales, then counsel to the president. Dated January 18, 2002, the memo was (without evident irony) entitled "Humane Treatment of al-Qaeda and Taliban Detainees." On February 7, it was disseminated to the vice president, the secretary of state, the secretary of defense, the attorney general, the director of the CIA, the national security adviser, and the chairman of the Joint Chiefs of Staff. According to the memo, captives from the battlefields of Afghanistan need not be given prisoner-of-war status and the U.S. government would therefore not abide by the provisions of the Geneva Conventions governing prisoners of war.[83] This key decision opened the door to the torture of captives at Bagram Air Base in Kabul, Afghanistan, then at Guantánamo naval base, Cuba, and most infamously at Abu Ghraib prison in Iraq.

Why did Bush do it? It was, in a sense, an admission of guilt. Once he got caught up in his own rhetoric about the "global war on terror" and had issued orders to the CIA and military to act secretly against al-Qaeda and the Taliban, I believe he felt that he had to protect his agents from being charged under the federal War Crimes Act, a 1996 law that carries the death penalty. By declaring captives to be "illegal combatants," a term that does not exist in international law, and asserting that the Geneva Conventions simply did not apply to them, he freed his agents to torture and do as they pleased. As one intelligence official told *New Yorker* reporter Seymour Hersh, "The rules are 'Grab whom you must. Do what you want.'"[84]

Had the president restricted his target explicitly to the terrorist organization al-Qaeda, which had carried out the 9/11 attacks, and moved against it through law enforcement means, the Geneva Conventions would indeed not have come into play and the whole issue of torture could have been avoided. He would have received global cooperation (including from the governments of most Middle Eastern countries) and would surely have been more successful in countering the threat of terrorism than through the route he actually chose. There is widespread agreement among officials in the field, including FBI agents stationed at Guantánamo, that information extracted under torture is usually worthless, that torture largely compels its victims to say what the torturer wants to hear, and that the use of torture precludes building a legal case against a particular captive. Moreover, the people rounded up in Afghanistan usually did not have valuable information, since most of them had been turned over to the Americans by Northern Alliance warlords for the bounties the United States was paying.[85] In October 2004, the deputy commander at Guantánamo, Brigadier General Martin Lucent, said to the press that most of his 550 prisoners had revealed nothing of value: "Most of these guys weren't fighting, they were running."[86]

The president seems to have authorized torture largely for its symbolic value—the desire of his administration and its neoconservative backers to show the world that the United States was indeed a new Rome, that it could act with impunity unchecked by any established norms of international law. It was the first sign of the administration's determination to overawe the world with American power, soon enough embodied in the new strategy of "shock and awe"—the name the military gave its opening cruise missile and bombing salvos against Baghdad in March 2003.[87] Bush himself said to the *Washington Post*'s Bob Woodward, "I had to show the American people the resolve of a commander in chief that [*sic*] was going to do whatever it took to win. No yielding. No equivocation. No, you know, lawyering this thing to death, that we're after 'em. And that was not only for domestic, for the people at home to see. It was also vitally important for the rest of the world to watch."[88]

"There are only two ways to govern," writes Naomi Klein, the award-winning Canadian journalist, "with consent or with fear."[89] Under George Bush, the United States decided to rule Afghanistan and Iraq through fear, and from this naturally followed disappearances without charges, indefinite detentions, torture, and "extraordinary renditions." David Brooks, the right-wing pundit for Rupert Murdoch's *Weekly Standard* and a columnist for the *New York Times,* accurately predicted that after 9/11: "We will care a lot more about ends—winning the war—than we will about means. We will debate whether it is necessary to torture prisoners who have information about future biological attacks. We will destroy innocent villages by accident, shrug our shoulders, and continue fighting. In an age of conflict, bourgeois values like compassion, tolerance, and industriousness are valued less than the classical virtues of courage, steadfastness, and a ruthless desire for victory."[90]

The president's indispensable partner in these operations was his then legal counsel (subsequently attorney general) Alberto Gonzales. In order to protect the president from being charged with illegally ordering the torture of captives, Gonzales gathered around him a remarkable coterie of right-wing lawyers from various branches of the government. These included the Korean-American scholar John Yoo, then assistant attorney general; Timothy Flanigan, deputy counsel to the president; Patrick F. Philbin, deputy assistant attorney general; William J. Haynes, general counsel for the Department of Defense; and Jay S. Bybee, assistant attorney general.[91] With sophistry and ideological fervor these legal specialists prepared briefs—"torture memos"—for the president and the secretary of defense claiming, among other things, that "[i]n order to respect the

President's inherent constitutional authority to manage a military campaign, [the statutory prohibition against torture] must be construed as inapplicable to interrogations undertaken pursuant to his Commander-in-Chief authority. Congress lacks authority under Article I [of the Constitution] to set the terms and conditions under which the President may exercise his authority as Commander-in-Chief to control the conduct of operations during a war."[92] In fact, article 1, section 8 of the Constitution expressly states: "The Congress shall have Power to declare War and make Rules concerning Captures on Land and Water."

As Karen Greenberg and Joshua Dratel, editors of *The Torture Papers* and leading authorities on these machinations, argue, "The 'torture memos' . . . deliberately disregard, even nullify, the balance-of-powers doctrine that has defined the United States since its inception."[93] Harold Hongju Koh, dean of Yale University's law school and a former assistant secretary of state, says, "The notion that the president has the constitutional power to permit torture is like saying he has the constitutional power to commit genocide. . . . It's just erroneous legal analysis."[94] Gonzales's lawyers nonetheless argued for a "unitary executive" theory of presidential power, which essentially suggests that, in time of war (as they also insisted the president's self-proclaimed "war on terror" was), the president as commander in chief has almost uncontestable powers to do more or less as he pleases, whatever Congress or the courts may say.

Perhaps the most shortsighted aspect of this claim to absolute presidential power is that it leads unavoidably to the president's liability under the concept of "command responsibility"—the doctrine that a military commander is legally liable for all abuses and atrocities committed by his troops whether he knows about them or not. After World War II, the United States put Japanese general Tomoyuki Yamashita, the so-called Tiger of Malaya and subsequently commander of Japanese forces in the Philippines, on trial. A U.S. war crimes tribunal found that he had failed to uphold "command responsibility" for his troops, who had massacred thousands of innocent civilians in Manila in early 1945, even though the defense established that he had no knowledge of the crimes. Because Yamashita was tried by a military court, he appealed his case directly to the U.S. Supreme Court, which upheld his conviction by a vote of 5 to 3, thereby establishing the doctrine of command responsibility in American law. Justice Frank Murphy warned in dissent, "In the sober afterglow will come the realization of the boundless and dangerous implications of the procedure sanctioned today. . . . Indeed, the fate of some future President of the United States and his chief of staff and military advisers may well have been sealed by this decision." In other words, American constitutional law already establishes the grounds on which President Bush could be held accountable for his failure to exercise command responsibility in cases of torture at Guantánamo, Abu Ghraib, and elsewhere.[95]

As Justice Murphy suggested, the issue of command responsibility applies equally well to the president's underlings, Secretary Rumsfeld and Generals Myers, Sanchez, and Miller. Rumsfeld's potential liability is, however, greater than just being the highest official in charge of the Department of Defense who failed to stop torture when he learned about it.[96] According to the journalist Seymour Hersh, in late 2001, Rumsfeld personally created a highly secret "special access program" (SAP) that directed American special forces units to kill or capture and, if possible, interrogate high-value targets. Code-named "Copper Green," the SAP "encouraged physical coercion and sexual humiliation of Iraqi prisoners in an effort to generate more intelligence" and was at the root of the Abu Ghraib prison scandal. Both President Bush and General Myers were fully informed about these operations.[97]

In addition, Rumsfeld personally reviewed and signed off on many of the techniques of humiliation, abuse, and torture that would be brought into play at the American prison at Guantánamo. In one case, in a November 27, 2002, memo on acceptable interrogation methods, he personally scribbled in the margins: "I stand for 8–10 hours a day. Why is standing [as a technique at Guantánamo] limited to 4 hours?"[98] Of course, Rumsfeld was not naked and handcuffed when he stood working at his upright desk in the Pentagon.

In December 2003, before army investigators received the first photos of torture practices at Abu Ghraib, now retired colonel Stuart A. Huntington reported to the generals in Iraq that units of Army Rangers, members of Delta Force, Navy SEALs, and other special forces working with the CIA were torturing their detainees. Major General Barbara Fast, the highest-ranking intelligence official in Iraq, had commissioned Huntington, a veteran of the murderous counterinsurgency Phoenix Program during the Vietnam War, which was the model for Rumsfeld's SAP, to look into charges of abuse by Copper Green operatives. Huntington concluded that such measures would imperil rather than aid U.S. efforts to quell the Iraqi insurgency. When Huntington was told by one officer at a high-value-target detention center in Baghdad that prisoners taken by the highly classified units showed signs of having been beaten, he asked whether the officer had alerted his superiors to the problem. The reply was, "Everyone knows about it."[99]

When on May 6, 2004, the press questioned Rumsfeld about his responsibility for widespread military torture in Afghanistan and Iraq, he replied, "My impression is that what has been charged thus far is abuse, which I believe technically is different from torture. . . . Therefore I'm not going to address the torture word."[100] Unfortunately, Rumsfeld's attempt to trivialize what he had authorized did not cause the problem to disappear. It only got worse and ultimately implicated the high command.

All the torture took place during General Richard Myers's term as chairman of the Joint Chiefs of Staff. He knew and approved of everything that was done, including a December 2002 list of new interrogation techniques signed off on by Rumsfeld that were to be used on al-Qaeda captives held at Guantánamo Bay. These techniques included sleep and food deprivation, degrading treatment such as having female soldiers in their underwear grab and kick detainees' genitals and rub their breasts against them, insulting detainees' religious beliefs by having women smear them with fake menstrual blood, and using agonizing "stress positions" to try to get them to talk.[101]

After the torture photos were turned over to army criminal investigators, Lieutenant General Ricardo Sanchez, the senior military commander in Iraq, appointed Major General Antonio M. Taguba to investigate the situation at Abu Ghraib. Given army standards of inspecting itself that prevailed in Iraq at that time, General Taguba conducted an unusually thorough and unbiased examination. He documented numerous incidents between October and December 2003 of "sadistic, blatant, and wanton abuses."[102] General Myers, who was both Sanchez's and Taguba's superior, reacted to the investigation by, first, trying to prevent details of the torture at Abu Ghraib from being released to the American public and then claiming that he had simply been too busy to get around to reading Taguba's report. In April 2004, Myers called Dan Rather, the *CBS News* anchorman,

and persuaded him not to break the story of the Abu Ghraib tortures for
at least two weeks, and in May, four months after Taguba's report had been
completed, Myers told *Fox News* that he had still not read it.[103]

General Myers was certainly aware of another January 2004 internal
army report of abuses committed by the army's 101st Airborne Division
in December in the northern Iraqi city of Mosul. The army kept this document secret until March 25, 2005, when it was released under a Freedom
of Information Act suit brought by the American Civil Liberties Union
(ACLU). The 101st Airborne's behavior is important because it demon-
strates that the acts of abuse and torture going on at Abu Ghraib were
not—in one of General Myers's favorite phrases—the work of a few "bad
apples." The January 2004 report is also among the few internal documents that directly charge the military with using torture. It says, "There
is evidence that suggests 311th MI [the 311th Military Intelligence Battal-
ion] personnel and/or translators engaged in physical torture of the
detainees." The investigating officer, whose name was blacked out of the
released documents, wrote that the guards at the Mosul facility came from
three infantry units of the 101st Airborne and "were poorly trained and
encouraged to abuse prisoners."[104] No one in the division was punished
for the abuses over which General Myers held command responsibility, as
he did for the cover-up that lasted until the ACLU intervened.

Given his overall command of the armed forces, General Myers was
also directly responsible for setting up the torture regime at the Guantánamo prison and then exporting it to Iraq. The first commandant at
Guantánamo after 9/11 was Brigadier General Rick Baccus, an officer in
the Rhode Island National Guard. He ran the facility as a conventional
prisoner-of-war camp, which irritated Pentagon civilian officials, who
wanted to implement a whole list of aggressive new interrogation techniques.[105] In October 2002, General Myers removed General Baccus,
allegedly for "coddling" detainees, and replaced him with Major General
Geoffrey Miller, a former artillery officer who had never before held a post
connected in any way to intelligence work; and yet Miller was now ordered
to increase the flow of "actionable intelligence" from Guantánamo.

In pursuit of this, General Miller introduced direct assaults on prisoners, prolonged shackling in uncomfortable positions, loud music, sexual
humiliation, the threat of dogs, and many other forms of torment. FBI
agents who were assigned to Guantánamo were alarmed by what they

witnessed there and reported back to Washington via classified e-mails (some of which the ACLU was able to have declassified): " 'On a couple of occasions, I entered interview rooms to find a detainee chained hand and foot in a fetal position to the floor, with no chair, food, or water,' the FBI agent wrote on August 2, 2004. 'Most times they had urinated or defecated on themselves, and had been left there for 18 to 24 hours or more.' In one case, the agent continued, 'the detainee was almost unconscious on the floor, with a pile of hair next to him. He had apparently been literally pulling his own hair out throughout the night.' "[106]

The result was that the inspectors of the International Committee of the Red Cross accused the U.S. military of using tactics "tantamount to torture" on captives held at Guantánamo Bay.[107] At the same time, these methods failed to produce good intelligence. Lieutenant Colonel Anthony Christino, an intelligence officer at the Pentagon with twenty years' experience, told David Rose, author of *Guantánamo: The War on Human Rights*, "Most of the information derived from interrogations at Guantánamo appears to be very general in nature; so general that it is not very useful." According to Christino, Guantánamo had not helped to prevent a single terrorist attack.[108]

In August 2003, the Pentagon sent General Miller to conduct a ten-day review of prison facilities in Iraq. While there, he talked directly to junior commanders and gave them copies of a manual of procedures used at Guantánamo. Although he has repeatedly claimed that he instructed American officers in charge of the Iraqi prisons that the Geneva Conventions did apply there, even if not in Guantánamo, much harsher procedures began to be implemented at Abu Ghraib soon after his departure. According to Brigadier General Janis L. Karpinski, then commandant at Abu Ghraib, "Miller came up there and told me he was going to 'Gitmoize' the detention operations."[109]

On September 14, 2003, a month after General Miller had returned to Cuba, General Ricardo Sanchez, the commander of all U.S. forces in Iraq, signed a memo putting Miller's program at Guantánamo into general practice. Sanchez authorized twenty-nine interrogation techniques, including twelve that exceeded limits in the army's own field manual and four that he admitted probably violated international law, the Geneva Conventions, and accepted standards on the humane treatment of prisoners. Sanchez's highly classified memo was released to the public only after a Freedom of Information suit by the ACLU. On the basis of this memo, the ACLU formally asked Attorney General Alberto Gonzales to investigate Sanchez—whom *Hispanic* magazine had just named as 2004's "Hispanic of the Year"—for perjury. In an appearance before the Senate Armed Services Committee on May 19, 2004, General Sanchez had said under oath, "I never approved any of those measures to be used . . . at any time in the last year."[110]

Needless to say, nothing came of the ACLU's request and the army soon exonerated General Sanchez of all responsibility for the horrors of Abu Ghraib. Nonetheless, on May 2, 2006, the ACLU released a new document it had obtained from the inspector general of the Defense Intelligence Agency under a Freedom of Information Act lawsuit. Dated May 19, 2004, the same day as Sanchez's Senate testimony, and marked "secret," the document reports an earlier official investigation into General Sanchez's role in the Abu Ghraib abuses. It says that he had ordered military interrogators to "go to the outer limits" to extract information from prisoners, adding that "HQ [headquarters] wanted the interrogators to break the detainees."[111]

On March 22, 2004, after seventeen months at Guantánamo, General Miller was put in charge of Abu Ghraib prison in Iraq. He did not stay there long, however, because on November 24, 2004, he was reassigned to be assistant chief of staff for installation management for the army, a desk job back in the Pentagon. On July 1, 2004, the Pentagon also relieved General Sanchez after fifteen months as the top general in Iraq and returned him to his old assignment as commander of the army's Fifth Corps in Germany. He was replaced in Baghdad by a four-star general, George Casey. In June 2005, the *New York Times* reported that army superiors believed the Abu Ghraib torture scandal had blown over and were thinking about promoting Sanchez to four stars and giving him the Southern Command in Latin America.[112] However, the possibility of a clash with Congress prevented any further promotions for Sanchez.[113] Meanwhile, General Taguba, who had done the initial investigating at Abu Ghraib, was shunted aside, being transferred to the Pentagon and made deputy assistant secretary of defense for reserve affairs.

Since the publication of the first photos from Abu Ghraib, the Pentagon has conducted at least ten high-level investigations of itself. In April 2005, the army's inspector general issued a report that was intended to be the military's final word on the responsibility of the senior leadership. The entire high command, civilian and military, was exonerated except for Brigadier General Janis Karpinski, a woman and a reserve officer, who was briefly in charge of U.S. prisons in Iraq in late 2003 and early 2004. She received an administrative reprimand and was demoted to colonel.[114] As of the summer of 2006, only seven low-ranking soldiers had been charged with anything.

When the issue of official torture first arose, Senator John W. Warner, chairman of the Senate Armed Services Committee, promised that everyone culpable would be held accountable, but he failed to follow through, thereby earning himself a place among the seven morons who lost the war. The *Washington Post* editorialized, "That the affair would end in this way is even more disgraceful for the American political system than the abuses themselves."[115] But there was still one more disgrace to come. In June 2005, the Senate Republican Policy Committee issued a report claiming that the International Committee of the Red Cross, in daring to criticize U.S. treatment of prisoners in Iraq, in Afghanistan, and at Guantánamo Bay, had "lost its way." The senators of the ruling party recommended that the Bush administration cut off all U.S. funds for the ICRC's operations.[116]

Burton J. Lee III served as a doctor in the Army Medical Corps and, for four years, as presidential physician to George H. W. Bush. He writes, "Today, . . . it seems as though our government and the military have slipped into Joseph Conrad's 'Heart of Darkness.' The widespread reports of torture and ill-treatment—frequently based on military and government documents—defy the claim that this abusive behavior is limited to a few noncommissioned officers at Abu Ghraib or isolated incidents at Guantánamo Bay. When it comes to torture, the military's traditional leadership and discipline have been severely compromised up and down the chain of command. Why? I fear it is because the military has bowed to errant civilian leadership."[117] I believe it is fair to suggest that this civilian leadership is suffering from the same lapses in thinking that afflicted the German desk murderers of the 1940s.

A third example of the administration's inability to think can be found in its criminal attitude toward and treatment of Iraq's greatest cultural treasures. In the months before he ordered the invasion of Iraq, George Bush and his senior officials spoke of preserving Iraq's "patrimony" for the Iraqi people. What he meant by patrimony, at a time when talking about

Iraqi oil was taboo, was exactly that—Iraqi oil. In their "joint statement on Iraq's future" of April 8, 2003, George Bush and Tony Blair declared, "We reaffirm our commitment to protect Iraq's natural resources, as the patrimony of the people of Iraq, which should be used only for their benefit."[118] In this they were true to their word. Among the few places American soldiers actually did guard during and in the wake of their invasion were that country's oil fields and the Oil Ministry in Baghdad. The real Iraqi patrimony, that invaluable human inheritance of thousands of years, was another matter. At a time when American pundits were warning of a future "clash of civilizations," our occupation forces were letting perhaps the greatest of all human patrimonies be looted and smashed.

There have been many dispiriting sights on TV since George Bush launched his ill-starred war on Iraq—the pictures from Abu Ghraib, Fallujah laid waste, American soldiers kicking down the doors of private homes and pointing assault rifles at women and children. But few have reverberated historically like the looting of Baghdad's National Museum—or been forgotten more quickly in this country.

In archaeological circles, Iraq is known as the "cradle of civilization," with a record of cultural artifacts going back more than seven thousand years. William R. Polk, the founder of the Center for Middle Eastern Studies at the University of Chicago, says, "It was there, in what the Greeks called Mesopotamia, that life as we know it today began: there people first began to speculate on philosophy and religion, developed concepts of international trade, made ideas of beauty into tangible forms, and, above all, developed the skill of writing."[119] No other places in the Bible except for Israel have more history and prophecy associated with them than Babylonia, Shinar (Sumer), and Mesopotamia (which in Greek means "between the [Tigris and Euphrates] rivers")—different names for parts of the territory that the British around the time of World War I began to call "Iraq."[120] Most of the early books of Genesis are set in Iraq (see Genesis 10:10, 11:31; also Daniel 1–4; II Kings 24). There was, however, no country of "Iraq" until 1920, when the British combined the three Ottoman provinces of Basra, Mosul, and Baghdad and set up the puppet Faisal dynasty to govern their new domain. Britain dominated Iraqi affairs until 1958, when the last king, Faisal II, was overthrown and executed by Iraqi nationalists.

The best known of the civilizations that make up Iraq's cultural heritage are the Sumerians, Akkadians, Babylonians, Assyrians, Chaldeans, Persians, Greeks, Romans, Parthians, Sassanids, and Muslims. On April 10, 2003, in a television address, President Bush acknowledged that the Iraqi people are "the heirs of a great civilization that contributes to all humanity."[121] Only two days later, under the complacent eyes of the occupying U.S. Army in Baghdad, the Iraqis would begin to lose that heritage in a swirl of looting and burning.

In September 2004, in one of the few self-critical reports to come out of Donald Rumsfeld's Department of Defense, the Defense Science Board Task Force on Strategic Communication wrote, "The larger goals of U.S. strategy depend on separating the vast majority of non-violent Muslims from the radical-militant Islamist-Jihadists. But American efforts have not only failed in this respect: they may also have achieved the opposite of what they intended."[122] Nowhere was this failure more apparent than in the indifference—even glee—shown by Rumsfeld and his generals toward the looting on April 11 and 12, 2003, of the National Museum in Baghdad and the burning on April 14, 2003, of the National Library and Archives as well as the Library of Korans at the Ministry of Religious Affairs and Endowments. These events were, according to Paul Zimansky, a Boston University archaeologist, "the greatest cultural disaster of the last 500 years." Eleanor Robson, a specialist in the history of mathematics in the ancient Near East and a fellow of All Souls College, Oxford, said, "You'd have to go back centuries, to the Mongol invasion of Baghdad in 1258, to find looting on this scale."[123] Yet Secretary Rumsfeld compared the looting to the aftermath of a soccer game and shrugged it off with the comment that "Freedom's untidy. . . . Free people are free to make mistakes and commit crimes."[124]

The National Museum of Baghdad has long been regarded as perhaps the richest archaeological institution in the Middle East. It is difficult to say with precision what was lost there in those catastrophic April days in 2003 because up-to-date inventories of its holdings, many never even described in archaeological journals, were also destroyed by the looters or remained incomplete thanks to conditions in Baghdad after the Gulf War of 1991. One of the best records, however partial, of its holdings is the catalog of items the museum lent in 1988 to an exhibition held in Japan's ancient capital of Nara entitled "Silk Road Civilizations." But as one museum official said to John Burns of the *New York Times* after the looting, "All gone, all gone. All gone in two days."[125]

A single, beautifully illustrated, indispensable book edited by Milbry Polk and Angela M. H. Schuster, *The Looting of the Iraq Museum, Baghdad: The Lost Legacy of Ancient Mesopotamia*, represents the heartbreaking attempt of over a dozen archaeological specialists on ancient Iraq to specify what objects were in the museum before the catastrophe, where they had been excavated, and the condition of those few thousand items that have been recovered.

At a conference on art crimes held in London a year after the disaster, the British Museum's John Curtis reported that at least half of the 40 most important stolen objects had not been retrieved and that, of some 15,000 items looted from the museum's showcases and storerooms, about 8,000 had yet to be traced. Its entire collection of 5,800 cylinder seals and clay tablets, many containing cuneiform writing and other inscriptions some of which go back to the earliest discovery of writing itself, was stolen.[126] Since then, as a result of an amnesty for looters, about 4,000 of the artifacts have been recovered in Iraq, and more than 1,000 have been confiscated in the United States.[127] Curtis noted that random checks of Western soldiers leaving Iraq had led to the discovery of several in illegal possession of ancient objects. Customs agents in the United States found more. Officials in Jordan have impounded about 2,000 pieces smuggled from Iraq; in France, 500 pieces; in Italy, 300; in Syria, 300; and in Switzerland, 250. Smaller numbers have been seized in Kuwait, Saudi Arabia, Iran, and Turkey. None of these objects has as yet been sent back to Baghdad.

The 616 pieces that form the famous collection of "Nimrud gold," excavated by the Iraqis in the late 1980s from the tombs of the Assyrian queens at Nimrud, a few miles southeast of Mosul, were saved, but only because the museum had secretly moved them to the subterranean vaults of the Central Bank of Iraq at the time of the first Gulf War. By the time the Americans got around to protecting the bank in 2003, its building was a burned-out shell filled with twisted metal beams from the collapse of the roof and all nine floors under it. Nonetheless, the underground compartments and their contents survived undamaged. On July 3, 2003, a small portion of the Nimrud holdings were put on display for a few hours, allowing a handful of Iraqi officials to see them for the first time since 1990.[128]

The torching of books and manuscripts in the Library of Korans and the National Library was a historical disaster of the first order. Most of the Ottoman imperial documents and the old royal archives concerning the creation of Iraq were reduced to ashes. According to Humberto Márquez, the Venezuelan author of *Historia Universal de la Destrucción de los Libros*, about a million books and ten million documents were destroyed by the fires of April 14, 2003.[129] Robert Fisk, correspondent of the *Independent* of London, was in Baghdad the day of the fires. He rushed to the offices of the U.S. Marines' Civil Affairs Bureau and gave the officer on duty a precise map locating the two archives and their names in Arabic and English. The smoke, he pointed out, could be seen from three miles away. The officer shouted to a colleague, "This guy says some biblical library is on fire," but the Americans did nothing to try to put out the flames.[130]

Given the black market value of ancient art objects, U.S. military leaders had been warned before the invasion that the looting of all thirteen national museums throughout the country would be a particularly grave danger in the days after they captured Baghdad and took control of Iraq. In the chaos that followed the Gulf War of 1991, vandals had stolen about 4,000 objects from nine different regional museums. In monetary terms, the illegal trade in antiquities is the third most lucrative form of international trade globally, exceeded only by drug smuggling and arms sales.[131] Given the richness of Iraq's past, there are also over 10,000 significant archaeological sites scattered across the country, only some 1,500 of which have been studied. Following the Gulf War, a number of them were illegally excavated and their artifacts sold to unscrupulous international collectors in Western countries and Japan. All this was known to American commanders.

In January 2003, an American delegation of scholars, museum directors, art collectors, and antiquities dealers met with officials at the Pentagon to discuss the forthcoming invasion. They specifically warned that Baghdad's National Museum was the single most important site in the country. McGuire Gibson of the University of Chicago's Oriental Institute said, "I thought I was given assurances that sites and museums would be protected."[132] Gibson went back to the Pentagon twice to discuss the dangers, and he and his colleagues sent several e-mail reminders to military officers in the weeks before the war began. However, a more ominous indicator of things to come was reported in the *Guardian* on April 14,

2003: rich American collectors with connections to the White House were busy "persuading the Pentagon to relax legislation that protects Iraq's heritage by prevention of sales abroad." On January 24, 2003, some sixty New York–based collectors and dealers organized themselves into a new group called the "American Council for Cultural Policy" and met with Bush administration and Pentagon officials to argue that a post-Saddam Iraq should have relaxed antiquities laws.[133] Opening up private trade in Iraqi artifacts, they suggested, would offer such items better security than they could receive in Iraq.

The main international legal safeguard for historically and humanistically important institutions and sites is The Hague Convention for the Protection of Cultural Property in the Event of Armed Conflict, signed on May 14, 1954. The United States is not a party to that convention, primarily because, during the Cold War, it feared that the treaty might restrict its freedom to engage in nuclear war, but during the 1991 Gulf War the elder Bush's administration accepted the convention's rules and abided by a "no-fire target list" of places where valuable cultural items were known to exist.[134] UNESCO (United Nations Educational, Scientific and Cultural Organization) and other guardians of cultural artifacts expected the younger Bush's administration to follow the same procedures in the 2003 war.

Moreover, on March 26, 2003, the Pentagon's Office of Reconstruction and Humanitarian Assistance (ORHA) headed by Lieutenant General (ret.) Jay Garner, the civil authority the United States had set up for the moment hostilities ceased, sent to all senior U.S. commanders a list of sixteen institutions that "merit securing as soon as possible to prevent further damage, destruction, and/or pilferage of records and assets." The five-page memo dispatched two weeks before the fall of Baghdad also said, "Coalition forces must secure these facilities in order to prevent looting and the resulting irreparable loss of cultural treasures" and that "looters should be arrested/detained." First on General Garner's list of places to protect was the Central Bank of Iraq, which is now a ruin; second was the National Museum of Iraq; sixteenth was the Oil Ministry, one of only two places that U.S. forces occupying Baghdad actually defended (the other was the Interior Ministry). Martin Sullivan, chair of the President's Advisory Committee on Cultural Property for the previous eight years, and Gary Vikan, director of the Walters Art Museum in Baltimore and a member of the committee, both resigned to protest the failure of Centcom to obey orders. Sullivan said it was "inexcusable" that the museum should not have had the same priority as the Oil Ministry.[135]

As we now know, the American forces made no effort to prevent the looting of the great cultural institutions of Iraq. Its soldiers, often stationed nearby, simply watched vandals enter and torch the buildings. Professor Said Arjomand, an editor of the journal *Studies on Persianate Societies* and a professor of sociology at the State University of New York at Stony Brook, wrote, "Our troops, who have been proudly guarding the Oil Ministry, where no window is broken, deliberately condoned these horrendous events."[136] American commanders claim that, to the contrary, they were too busy fighting and had too few troops to protect the museum and libraries. However, this seems to be an unlikely explanation. During the battle for Baghdad, the U.S. military was perfectly willing to dispatch some two thousand troops to secure northern Iraq's oil fields, and their record on antiquities did not improve when the fighting subsided. At the six-thousand-year-old Sumerian city of Ur with its massive ziggurat, or stepped temple tower (built in the period 2112–2095 BC, and restored by Nebuchadnezzar II in the sixth century BC), the marines spray-painted their motto, *Semper Fi* (*semper fidelis,* "always faithful"), onto its walls.[137] The military then made the monument "off limits" to everyone in order to disguise the desecration that had occurred there, including the looting by U.S. soldiers of clay bricks used in the construction of the ancient buildings.

Until April 2003, the area around Ur, in the environs of Nasiriyah, was remote and sacrosanct. However, the U.S. military chose the land immediately adjacent to the ziggurat to build its huge Tallil Air Base with two runways, measuring 12,000 and 9,700 feet respectively, and four satellite camps. In the process, military engineers moved more than 9,500 truckloads of dirt in order to build 350,000 square feet of hangars and other facilities for aircraft and Predator unmanned drones. They completely ruined the area, the literal heartland of human civilization, for any further archaeological research or future tourism. They did, however, erect their own American imperial ziggurats. On October 24, 2003, according to the Global Security Organization, the army and air force "opened its second Burger King at Tallil. The new facility, co-located with [a] . . . Pizza Hut, provides another Burger King restaurant so that more service men and women serving in Iraq can, if only for a moment, forget about the task at hand in the desert and get a whiff of that familiar scent that takes them back home."[138]

The great British archaeologist Sir Max Mallowan (husband of Agatha Christie), who pioneered the excavations at Ur, Nineveh, and Nimrud, quotes some classical advice that the Americans might have been wise to heed: "There was danger in disturbing ancient monuments. . . . It was both wise and historically important to reverence the legacies of ancient times. Ur was a city infested with ghosts of the past and it was prudent to appease them."[139]

The American record elsewhere in Iraq is no better. At Babylon, American and Polish forces built a military depot, despite objections from archaeologists. John Curtis, the British Museum's authority on Iraq's many archaeological sites, reported that, on a visit in December 2004, he saw "cracks and gaps where somebody had tried to gouge out the decorated bricks forming the famous dragons of the Ishtar Gate" and a "2,600-year-old brick pavement crushed by military vehicles."[140] Other observers say that the dust stirred up by U.S. helicopters has sandblasted the fragile brick façade of the palace of Nebuchadnezzar II, king of Babylon from 605 to 562 BC.[141] The archaeologist Zainab Bahrani reports, "Between May and August 2004, the wall of the Temple of Nabu and the roof of the Temple of Ninmah, both of the sixth century BC, collapsed as a result of the movement of helicopters. Nearby, heavy machines and vehicles stand parked on the remains of a Greek theater from the era of Alexander of Macedon [Alexander the Great]."[142]

In another example of American indifference to the Iraqi environment, the Marine Corps air base known as "Tikrit South" is located next door to a vast preserve where Saddam Hussein kept a herd of gazelles. The marines shot and ate the gazelles as a supplement to their prepackaged Meals Ready to Eat (MREs). Corporal Joshua Wicksell of Corpus Christi, Texas, declared freshly cooked gazelle to be delicious.[143] And none of this even begins to deal with the massive, ongoing looting of historical sites across Iraq by freelance grave and antiquities robbers, preparing to stock the living rooms of Western collectors. The unceasing chaos and lack of security brought to Iraq in the wake of our invasion have meant that a future, peaceful Iraq may hardly have a patrimony to display. It is no small accomplishment of the Bush administration to have plunged the cradle of the human past into the same sort of chaos and lack of security as the Iraqi present. If amnesia is bliss, then the fate of Iraq's antiquities represents a kind of modern paradise.

THE CIVILIZATION WE ARE IN THE PROCESS OF DESTROYING IN IRAQ IS PART of our own heritage. It is also part of the world's patrimony. Before our invasion of Afghanistan, we condemned the Taliban for their March 2001 dynamiting of the monumental third-century AD Buddhist statues at Bamiyan. Those were two gigantic statues of remarkable historical value and the barbarism involved in their destruction blazed in headlines and horrified commentaries in our country. Today, our own government is guilty of far greater crimes when it comes to the destruction of a whole universe of antiquity, and few here, when they consider Iraqi attitudes toward the American occupation, even take that into consideration. But what we do not care to remember, others may recall all too well.

2

Comparative Imperial Pathologies:
Rome, Britain, and America

In late July [43 BC] a centurion from Octavian's army suddenly appeared in the Senate House. From the assembled gathering he demanded the consulship, still vacant, for his general. The Senate refused. The centurion brushed back his cloak and laid his hand on the hilt of his sword. "If you do not make him consul," he warned, "then this will." And so it happened.

—TOM HOLLAND,
Rubicon: The Last Years of the Roman Republic (2003)

War came naturally enough to the British, after so much experience of it, and empire offered them a more or less perpetual battle-field.

—JAN MORRIS,
Heaven's Command: An Imperial Progress (1973)

The English-speaking peoples are past masters in the art of concealing their selfish national interests in the guise of the general good. . . . This kind of hypocrisy is a special and characteristic peculiarity of the Anglo-Saxon mind.

—E. H. CARR,
The Twenty Years' Crisis (1939)

In 1972, Henry Kissinger, then President Nixon's national security adviser, was in Beijing talking with Zhou Enlai, China's first postrevolutionary prime minister, about normalizing Chinese-American relations. At one point in their conversation Kissinger asked what the prime minister thought was the significance of the French Revolution. Zhou replied, "It's too soon to tell."

Zhou Enlai was not being as enigmatic as this sounds. The two men had been discussing the Chinese revolution of 1949, the most complex revolutionary upheaval in recorded history. A great deal of time will have to pass before we can begin to appreciate its various meanings, if we ever do. Zhou Enlai was also reminding Kissinger that historical significance is an extremely elusive concept and that comparisons, precedents, analyses, and claims of importance derived from history are almost invariably elements of arguments best judged by their contemporary purposes and whether or not they are persuasive, rather than by their claims of accuracy.

The most famous English-language study of ancient Rome is surely Edward Gibbon's *The History of the Decline and Fall of the Roman Empire* (published in six volumes between 1776 and 1788). He contended, among other things, that Christianity brought down Rome because it sapped the Roman spirit, was hostile to Mediterranean culture, and displaced Roman imperial pretensions with monasticism and contemplation. Not many people today would buy that interpretation, particularly since the collapse of the Roman Republic into dictatorship preceded by a century the spread of Christianity. Moreover, Emperor Constantine's conversion to Christianity in 312 AD imposed the autocratic style of Rome on the church as much as it Christianized the Roman empire.[1]

So long as one is not dogmatic, it is perfectly logical to compare aspects of the American republic some 230 years after the Declaration of Independence with ancient Rome and the British Empire. Pundits of all sorts have been doing so for decades. In fourteen speeches to the U.S. Senate on Roman constitutionalism, in 1993, the venerable Senator Robert Byrd (Democrat from West Virginia) observed, "Many, if not most, of the Framers were conversant with Roman history and with the history of England. They were also familiar with the political philosophy of Montesquieu, whose political theory of checks and balances and separation of powers influenced them in their writing of the Constitution. Montesquieu was also influenced in his political philosophy by the history of the Romans, by contemporary English institutions, and by English history."[2]

This is true and a good reason for putting the United States in a class with the Roman Republic as well as the British Empire. But I want to focus on the traditional Roman and British comparisons for other reasons, more germane to our moment. The collapse of the Roman Republic offers a perfect case study of how imperialism and militarism can undermine even the best defenses of a democracy, while enthusiasts for the American empire systematically prettify the history of the British Empire in order to make it an acceptable model for the United States today.

When it comes to the collapse of Roman democracy, Zhou Enlai's dictum probably applies. Not enough time has passed to produce a universally accepted understanding of the events. The problem is not one of new materials, since short of a miraculous archaeological discovery, new sources that could alter our basic knowledge about ancient Rome are unlikely to appear. Writers today have roughly the same sources that Shakespeare consulted in writing his plays *Julius Caesar, Antony and Cleopatra, Coriolanus,* and *Timon of Athens*—primarily, the Greek historian Plutarch. Contemporary historians can also consult remnants from the works of three Roman historians, Livy, Tacitus, and Suetonius. Nonetheless, Rome still inspires utterly contradictory interpretations, providing a classical backdrop for clashing contemporary political projects.

Three contemporary books illustrate the differences of opinion about the Roman Republic's end that are alive and flourishing today. The British classicist Anthony Everitt's *Cicero: The Life and Times of Rome's Greatest Politician* is a worthy example of what might be thought of as Western historical orthodoxy: the view that Julius Caesar was a military populist, the leader of the mob against entrenched representatives of the constitutional order, and a tyrant. In this analysis, Cicero, a senator and consul, acted selflessly to try to preserve constitutional government against implacable forces of corruption and the abuse of military power. "During his childhood and youth," Everitt writes, "Cicero had watched with horror as Rome set about dismantling itself. If he had a mission as an adult, it was to recall the Republic to order."[3]

Everitt's Cicero reminds one of the remarkable career of Senator Robert Byrd, who first took the oath of office on January 7, 1959. While his state has profited from his powerful position in Washington—a great many public buildings in West Virginia are named "Byrd"—he has also tirelessly tried to educate his colleagues about the concept of a "republic" and why, when working properly, it is a bulwark of democracy.

In contrast, author Michael Parenti denigrates Cicero and other constitutionalists. Parenti portrays Caesar as a cross between Juan Perón and Franklin Delano Roosevelt—a ruthless populist. In his book *The Assassination of Julius Caesar: A People's History of Ancient Rome,* Parenti stresses the class warfare that dominated much of Roman life. His hero is Caesar, a man who came from a well-established family but nonetheless devoted himself to the common man and was murdered in the Senate by a conspiracy of blue bloods. "Caesar seems not to have comprehended that in the conflict between haves and have-nots, the haves are really have-it-alls," writes Parenti. "The Roman aristocrats lambasted the palest reforms as the worst kind of thievery, the beginning of a calamitous revolutionary leveling, necessitating extreme countermeasures. And they presented their violent retaliation not as an ugly class expediency but as an honorable act on behalf of republican liberty."[4] Parenti is repelled by what Cicero later wrote to Brutus, the leader of Caesar's killers on the Ides of March, 44 BC: "That memorable almost God-like deed of yours is proof against all criticisms; indeed it can never be adequately praised."[5]

Parenti's book is not just a paean to Caesar but also a polemic against establishmentarian history. "In the one-sided record that is called history," he contends, "it has been a long-standing practice to damn popular agitation as the work of riffraff and demagogues."[6] He is scandalized that in Gibbon, for example, there is "not a word . . . about an empire built upon sacked towns, shattered armies, slaughtered villagers, raped women, enslaved prisoners, plundered lands, burned crops, and mercilessly overtaxed populations."[7] Parenti accepts that "democracy, a wonderful invention by the people of history to defend themselves from the power of the wealthy, took tenuous root in ancient Rome," but he warns that "when their class interests were at stake, the senators had no trouble choosing political dictatorship over the most anemic traces of popular rule and egalitarian economic reform."[8]

Tom Holland, a leading BBC radio personality who has written highly acclaimed adaptations of Herodotus's *Histories* and Virgil's *Aeneid*, has produced *Rubicon: The Last Years of the Roman Republic*. Though he comments that "the comparison of Rome to the modern-day United States has become something of a cliché," he draws a picture of the late Republic that seems a model of the modern United States with its flamboyant excesses of wealth, bad taste, and arrogance, as well as its impulse toward militarism. His social history of republican decadence, highlighting a puerile Roman vision of politics and war, sounds very much like the second Bush administration and the shop-until-you-drop world of American consumerism.

"Celebrity chefs had long been regarded as a particularly pernicious symptom of decadence," Holland observes. Quoting from Livy's *History of*

Rome, Holland explains that "back in the virtuous, homespun days of the early Republic, so historians liked to claim, the cook 'had been the least valuable of slaves,' but no sooner had the Romans come into contact with the fleshpots of the East than 'he began to be highly prized, and what had been a mere function instead came to be regarded as high art.' In a city awash with new money and with no tradition of big spending, cookery had rapidly become an all-consuming craze. Not only cooks but ever more exotic ingredients had been brought into Rome on a ceaseless flood of gold. To those who upheld the traditional values of the Republic, this mania threatened a ruin that was as much moral as financial."[9] Sounds familiar, doesn't it?

On empire building, Holland notes, "The Romans killed to inspire terror, not in a savage frenzy but as the disciplined components of a fighting machine." After the worst Roman defeat of all time—the Carthaginian general Hannibal's adroit use of his cavalry to destroy eight legions at Cannae in 216 BC—they adopted the same strategy that the United States turned to after the collapse of the Soviet Union. Never again, the Romans swore, would they tolerate the rise of a Mediterranean power like Carthage, "capable of threatening their own survival. Rather than risk that, they felt themselves perfectly justified in launching a preemptive strike against any opponent who appeared to be growing too uppity."[10]

In 1992, when he was the Pentagon's undersecretary for policy, Paul Wolfowitz enunciated a similar strategy, which he and his colleagues began implementing in 2001 after Bush appointed him undersecretary of defense. According to Patrick E. Tyler, writing in the *New York Times,* "The Defense Department asserts that America's political and military mission in the post–Cold War era will be to ensure that no rival superpower is allowed to emerge in Western Europe, Asia, or the territory of the former Soviet Union. . . . The new [Wolfowitz] draft sketches a world in which there is one dominant military power whose leaders 'must maintain the mechanisms for deterring potential competitors from even aspiring to a larger regional or global role.'"[11] In 2002, this vision was officially embedded in the National Security Strategy of the United States, a key policy document. The goal of such megalomanic visions came to be called by the Romans a Pax Romana and by American pundits a Pax Americana.[12]

After the great Roman general Pompey's conquests in Asia Minor (66–62 BC), including his storming of Jerusalem in 63, "What had once been a toehold in the east was now to be a great tract of provinces. Beyond them was to stretch an even broader crescent of client states. All were to be docile and obedient, and all were to pay a regular tribute. This, hencefor-ward, was what the pax Romana was to mean."[13] Holland concludes that, ultimately, "Corruption in the Republic threatened to putrefy the world."[14] The American record has been comparable: the Bush administration waged preventive war against Iraq, "putrefied" that country through in-competence and massive corruption, and in the process produced global revulsion against the United States—similar to the "world of enemies" that eventually overwhelmed the Roman Empire.[15]

Even after two millennia there is little agreement on which of the mul-titude of comparisons Rome evokes are the most important, but perhaps the one most relevant to present-day America concerns how empire and its inescapable companion, militarism, subtly and insidiously erode the foundations of a republic. The United States took many of its key political principles from its ancient predecessor. Separation of powers, checks and balances, government in accordance with constitutional law, a toleration of slavery, fixed terms in office, the presidential "veto" (Latin for "I for-bid")—all of these ideas were influenced by Roman precedents. John Adams and his son John Quincy Adams often read Cicero and both spoke of him as a personal inspiration. The architects of the new American capi-tal were so taken with Rome that they even named the now filled-in creek that flowed where the Mall is today the "Tiber River."[16] Alexander Hamil-ton, James Madison, and John Jay, in writing the Federalist Papers to argue for the ratification of the Constitution, signed their articles with the pseu-donym "Publius Valerius Publicola"—who was the third consul of the Roman Republic and the first to personify its values. Yet, as Holland notes, "By the first century BC, there was only one free city left, and that was Rome herself. And then Caesar crossed the Rubicon, the Republic imploded, and none was left at all. . . . As a result, a thousand years of civic self-government were brought to an end, and not for another thousand, and more, would it become a living reality again."[17]

The Roman Republic failed to adjust to the unintended consequences of its imperialism, leading to drastic alterations in its form of government. The militarism that inescapably accompanied Rome's imperial projects slowly undermined its constitution as well as the very genuine political and human rights its citizens enjoyed. The American republic has, of course, not yet collapsed; it is just under great strain as its imperial presidency and its increasingly powerful military legions undermine Congress and the courts. However, the Roman outcome—turning over power to a dictator backed by military force welcomed by ordinary citizens because it seems to bring stability—suggests what might well happen sometime in the future as a result of George Bush's contempt for the separation of powers.

Obviously, there is nothing deterministic about such a progression, and many prominent Romans, notably Brutus and Cicero, paid with their lives trying to head it off. But there is something utterly logical about it. Republican checks and balances are simply incompatible with the maintenance of a large empire and a huge standing army. Democratic nations sometimes acquire empires, which they are reluctant to give up because they are a source of wealth and national pride, but their domestic liberties are thereby put at risk.

Many current aspects of our American government suggest a Roman-like fatigue with republican proprieties. As Holland puts it, "The Roman people, . . . in the end, grew tired of antique virtues, preferring the comforts of easy slavery and peace."[18] After Congress voted in October 2002 to give the president unrestricted power to use any means, including military force and nuclear weapons, in a preventive strike against Iraq whenever he—and he alone—deemed it "appropriate," it would be hard to argue that the governmental structure laid out in the Constitution of 1787 bears much relationship to the one that prevails today in Washington.

The Roman Republic is conventionally dated from 509 to 27 BC, even though Romulus's founding of the city is traditionally said to have occurred in 753 BC. All we know about its past, including those first two centuries, comes from the histories written by Livy and others and from the discoveries of modern archaeology. For the century preceding the republic, Rome was ruled by Etruscan kings from their nearby state of Etruria (modern Tuscany). In 510 BC, according to legend, Sextus, the son of King Tarquinius Superbus ("King Tarquin"), raped Lucretia, the daughter of a leading Roman family. A group of aristocrats backed by the Roman citizenry revolted against this outrage and expelled the Etruscans from Rome. The rebels were determined that never again would any single man be allowed to obtain supreme power in the city, and they created a system that for four centuries more or less succeeded in preventing that from happening. "This was the main principle," writes Everitt, "that underpinned constitutional arrangements which, by Cicero's time, were of a baffling complexity."[19]

At the heart of the unwritten Roman constitution was the Senate, which, by the early years of the first century BC, was composed of about three hundred members from whose ranks two chief executives, called consuls, were elected. The consuls took turns being in charge for a month, and neither could hold office for more than a year. Over time an amazing set of checks and balances evolved to ensure that the consuls and other executives whose offices conferred on them imperium—the right to command an army, to interpret and carry out the law, and to pass sentences of death—did not entertain visions of grandeur and overstay their welcome. At the heart of these restraints were the principles of collegiality and term limits. The first meant that for every office there were at least two incumbents, neither of whom had seniority or superiority over the other. Office holders were normally limited to one-year terms and could be re-elected to the same office only after waiting ten years. Senators had to serve two to three years in lower offices—as quaestors, tribunes, aediles, or praetors—before they were eligible for election to a higher office, including the consulship. All office holders could veto the acts of their equals, and higher officials could veto decisions of lower ones. The chief exception to these rules was the office of "dictator," appointed by the Senate in times of military emergency. There was always only one dictator and his decisions were immune to veto; according to the constitution, he could hold office for only six months or the duration of a crisis, whichever was shorter.

Once an official had ended his term as consul or praetor, the next post below consul, he was posted somewhere in Italy or abroad as governor of a province or colony and given the title of proconsul. For example, after serving as consul in 63 BC (the year of Octavian's birth), Cicero was sent to govern the colony of Cilicia in present-day southern Turkey, where his duties were both military and civilian. Apologists for the U.S. military today like to compare its regional commanders in chief for the Middle East (Centcom), Europe (Eucom), the Pacific (Pacom), Latin America (Southcom), and the United States itself (Northcom) to Roman proconsuls.[20] But the Roman officials were seasoned members of the Senate who had first held the highest executive post in the country, whereas American regional commanders are generals or admirals who have served their entire careers away from civilian concerns and have risen through the military ranks generally by managing to avoid egregious mistakes.

It is also important that during Rome's wars one or both consuls actually commanded the legions in the field. The American idea that the president acts as commander in chief of the armed forces probably derives from this precedent. But there was a difference: "The consuls may not have been always great, or even good, generals, but they were always soldiers of experience, because it was a requirement of a candidate for office in Rome during the Republic that he had to have a record of at least ten military campaigns."[21] During the administration of George W. Bush, neither the president, nor any appointive officer other than his first secretary of state, had any experience of war or barracks life.

Over time, Rome's complex system was made even more complex by the class struggle embedded in its society. During the first two centuries of the republic, what appeared to be a participatory democracy was in fact an oligarchy of aristocratic families who dominated the Senate. As Holland argues, "The central paradox of Roman society . . . [was] that savage divisions of class could coexist with an almost religious sense of community."[22] Parenti puts it this way: "In the second century BC, the senatorial nobles began to divide into two groups, the larger being the self-designated optimates ('best men'), who were devoted to upholding the politico-economic prerogatives of the well-born. . . . The smaller faction within the nobility, styled the populares or 'demagogues' by their opponents, were reformers who sided with the common people on various issues. Julius Caesar is considered the leading populuaris and the last in a line extending from 133 to 44 BC."[23] Everitt sees the problem in a broader perspective: "Since the fall of the monarchy in 510 BC, Roman domestic politics had been a long, inconclusive class struggle, suspended for long periods by foreign wars."[24]

After about 494 BC, when the plebs—that is, the ordinary, nonaristocratic citizens of Rome—had brought the city to a standstill by withholding their labor, a new institution came into being to defend their rights. These were the tribunes of the people, charged with protecting the lives and property of plebeians. Tribunes could veto any election, law, or decree of the Senate, of which they were ex officio members, as well as the acts of all other officials (except a dictator). They could also veto one another's vetoes. They did not have executive authority; their function was essentially negative. Controlling appointments to the office of tribune later became very important to generals like Julius Caesar, who based their power on the armies plus the support of the populares against the aristocrats.

The system worked well enough and afforded extraordinary freedoms to the citizens of Rome so long as all members of the Senate recognized that compromise and consensus were the only ways to get anything done. Everitt poses the issue in terms of the different perspectives of Cicero and Caesar; Cicero was the most intellectual defender of the Roman constitution whereas Caesar was Rome's, and perhaps history's, greatest general. Both were former consuls: "Cicero's weakness as a politician was that his principles rested on a mistaken analysis. He failed to understand the reasons for the crisis that tore apart the Roman Republic. Julius Caesar, with the pitiless insight of genius, understood that the constitution with its endless checks and balances prevented effective government, but like so many of his contemporaries Cicero regarded politics in personal rather than structural terms. For Caesar, the solution lay in a completely new system of government; for Cicero, it lay in finding better men to run the government—and better laws to keep them in order."[25]

Imperialism provoked the crisis that destroyed the Roman Republic. After slowly consolidating its power over all of Italy and conquering the Greek colonies on the island of Sicily, the republic extended its conquests to Carthage in North Africa, to Greece itself, and to what is today southern France, Spain, and Asia Minor. By the first century BC, Rome dominated all of Gaul, most of Iberia, the coast of North Africa, Macedonia (including Greece), the Balkans, and large parts of modern Turkey, Syria, and Lebanon. "The republic became enormously rich on the spoils of empire," Everitt writes, "so much so that from 167 BC Roman citizens in Italy no longer paid any personal taxes."[26] The republic also became increasingly self-important and arrogant, believing that its task was to bring civilization to lesser peoples and naming the Mediterranean Mare Nostrum (our sea), somewhat the way some Americans in the twentieth century came to refer to the Pacific Ocean as an "American lake."

The problem was that the Roman constitution made administration of so large and diverse an area increasingly difficult and subtly altered the norms and interests that underlay the need for compromise and consensus. Rome was the first case of what today we call imperial overstretch. There were several aspects to this crisis, but the most significant was the transformation of the Roman army into a professional military force and the growth of militarism. Well into the middle years of the republic, the Roman legions were a true citizen army, composed of conscripted small landowners. Unlike in the American republic, male citizens between the ages of seventeen and forty-six, except slaves and freedmen, were liable to be called for military service. One of the more admirable aspects of the Roman system was that only those citizens who possessed a specified amount of property (namely, a horse and some land) could serve, thereby making those who had profited most from the state also responsible for its defense. The Roman plebs, being nonlandowners, did their service as skirmishers for the army, or in the navy, which had far less honor attached to it. At the beginning of each term, the consuls appointed tribunes to raise two legions—a legion never much exceeded six thousand men—from the census roll of eligible citizens.

"Among the Romans," writes Holland, "it was received wisdom that 'men who have their roots in the land make the bravest and toughest soldiers.' . . . For centuries the all-conquering Roman infantry had consisted of yeoman farmers, their swords cleaned of chaff, their plows left behind, following their magistrates obediently to war. For as long as Rome's power had been confined to Italy, campaigns had been of manageably short duration. But with the expansion of the Republic's interests overseas, they had lengthened, often into years."[27]

Traditionally, when a campaign was over, the troops were promptly sent back to their farms, sometimes richer and flushed with military glory. Occasionally, the returning farmers got to march behind their general in a "triumph," the most splendid ceremony in the Roman calendar and a victory procession permitted only to the greatest of conquerors. The general himself, who paid for this parade, rode in a chariot, his face covered in red lead to represent Jupiter, king of the gods. A boy slave stood behind him holding a laurel wreath above his head while whispering in his ear, "Remember that you are mortal." In Pompey's great triumph of 61 BC, after he swept the seas of pirates and conquered Asia Minor, he actually wore a cloak that had belonged to Alexander the Great. Behind the conqueror came his prisoners in chains and finally the legionnaires, who by ancient tradition sang obscene songs satirizing their general.[28] Suetonius has recorded for history one of the ribald verses Caesar's soldiers sang during his Gallic Triumph, which is also evidence of Caesar's numerous affairs with women:

> *Home we bring our bald whoremonger;*
> *Romans, lock your wives away!*
> *All the bags of gold you lent him*
> *Went his Gallic tarts to pay.*[29]

By the end of the second century BC, in Everitt's words, "The responsibilities of empire meant that soldiers could no longer be demobilized at the end of each fighting season. Standing forces were required, with soldiers on long-term contracts."[30] The great general Caius Marius (c. 157–86 BC) undertook to reform the armed forces, replacing the old conscript armies with a professional body of career volunteers. Senator Robert Byrd explains: "Whereas the ownership of property had long been a requirement for entry into military service, Marius opened the door of recruitment to all, enrolling men who owned no property and were previously exempt. In accepting such troops, he remedied the long-standing manpower shortage and opened up a career for the employment of thousands of landless and jobless citizens. By this innovation, Marius created a new type of client army, bound to its commander as its patron. . . . Marius, in creating a professional army, had created a new base of power for ambitious men to exploit and use as an instrument of despotic authority."[31]

Members of this large standing army, equipped by the Roman state, signed up for twenty to twenty-five years. When their contracts expired, they expected their commanders, to whom they were personally loyal, to provide them with farms, which Marius had promised them. "From that moment on," writes Holland, "possession of a farm was no longer the qualification for military service but the reward."[32] Unfortunately, land in Italy was by then in short supply, much of it tied up in huge sheep and cattle ranches owned by rich, often aristocratic, families and run by slave labor. The landowners were the dominant conservative influence in the Senate, and they resisted all efforts at land reform. Members of the upper classes had become wealthy as a result of Rome's wars of conquest and bought more land as the only safe investment, driving small holders off

their properties. In 133 BC, the gentry arranged for the killing of the tribune Tiberius Gracchus (of plebeian origin) for advocating a new land-use
law. Rome's population thus continued to swell with landless veterans.
"Where would the land be found," asks Everitt, "for the superannuated
soldiers of Rome's next war?"[33]

Although the state owned a large amount of public property that theoretically could have been distributed to veterans, most of it had been illegally expropriated by aristocrats. Marius, who from the beginning allied
himself with the populares in the Senate, was willing to seize land for military purposes, but this inevitably meant a direct clash with the established order. "Cicero detested Roman militarism,"and Marius was exactly
the kind of leader he believed was leading Rome to ruin.[34] Utterly ruthless
and caring little for the Roman constitution, Marius served as consul an
unprecedented seven times, in clear violation of the requirement that
there be an interval of ten years between each re-election. Suzanne Cross,
an American scholar of classical antiquity, describes him as harsh and
vengeful.[35] Marius was the first Roman general to portray himself as "the
soldier's friend." Marius's nephew, Julius Caesar, built on this framework,
and Caesar's grandnephew, Octavian, who became Augustus Caesar, completed the transformation of the republic from a democracy into a military dictatorship.

During the final century before its fall, the republic was assailed by
many revolts of generals and their troops, leading to gross violations of
constitutional principles and on several occasions civil wars. Julius Caesar,
who became consul for the first time in 59 BC, enjoyed great popularity
with the ordinary people. After his year in office, he was rewarded by
being named governor of Gaul, a post he held between 58 and 49, during
which he both earned military glory and became immensely wealthy. In
49 he famously allowed his armies to cross the Rubicon, a small river in
northern Italy that served as a boundary against armies approaching the
capital, and plunged the country into civil war. Taking on his former ally
and now rival, Pompey, he won, after which, as Everitt observes, "No one
was left in the field for Caesar to fight. . . . His leading opponents were
dead. The republic was dead too: he had become the state."[36] Julius Caesar
exercised dictatorship from 48 to 44, and a month before the Ides of
March he arranged to have himself named "dictator for life." Instead, he
was stabbed to death in the Senate by a conspiracy of eight members, led

by Brutus and Cassius, both praetors, known to history as "principled tyrannicides."

Shakespeare's re-creation of the scenes that followed, based upon Sir Thomas North's 1579 translation of Plutarch from the French edition of 1559, has become as immortal as the deed itself. In Shakespeare's version of a speech to the plebeians in the Forum, Brutus famously defended his actions: "If there be any in this assembly, any dear friend of Caesar's, to him I say that Brutus' love to Caesar was no less than his. If then that friend demand why Brutus rose against Caesar, this is my answer: Not that I lov'd Caesar less, but that I loved Rome more. Had you rather Caesar were living, and all die slaves, than that Caesar were dead, to live all freemen?" However, Mark Antony, Caesar's chief lieutenant, speaking to the same audience, had the last word, and turned the populace against Brutus and Cassius. He sent the crowd racing forth to avenge Caesar's murder, as Shakespeare has him cynically say, "Cry 'Havoc!' and let slip the dogs of war."

Antony and Octavian, Caesar's eighteen-year-old grandnephew, formed an alliance to avenge the murder of Caesar. It would end with only one man standing, and that man, Caius Octavianus (Octavian), would decisively change Roman government by replacing the republic with an imperial dictatorship. Everitt characterizes Octavian as "a freebooting young privateer," who on August 19, 43 BC (just over a year after Caesar's death), became the youngest consul in Rome's history and set out, in violation of the constitution, to raise his own private army. Holland calls him an "adventurer and terrorist," while Parenti, quoting Gibbon, says he was a "subtle tyrant," who "crafted an absolute monarchy disguised by the forms of a commonwealth." Byrd laments, "There was absolute freedom of speech in the Roman Senate until the time of Augustus [Octavian]," who put limits on how far senators could go. "The boy," says Everitt, "would be a focus for the simmering resentments among the Roman masses, the disbanded veterans, and the standing legions."[37]

Cicero, who had devoted his life to trying to curb the kind of power represented by Octavian, now gave up on the rule of law in favor of realpolitik. He recognized that "for all his struggles the constitution was dead and power lay in the hands of soldiers and their leaders." In Cicero's view, the only hope was to try to co-opt Octavian, leading him toward a more constitutional position, while doing everything not to "irritate rank-and-file opinion, which was fundamentally Caesarian." Cicero would pay with his life for this last, desperate gamble. Octavian, still allied with Mark Antony, ordered at least 130 senators (perhaps as many as 300) executed and their property confiscated after charging them with having supported the conspiracy against Caesar. Mark Antony personally added Cicero's name to the list. When he met his death, the great scholar, orator, and Grecophile had with him a copy of Euripides' *Medea,* which he had been reading. His head and both hands were displayed in the Forum.[38]

A year after Cicero's death, following the battle of Philippi, where Brutus and Cassius were defeated and committed suicide, Octavian and Antony divided the known world between them. Octavian took the West and remained in Rome; Antony accepted the East and allied himself with Cleopatra, the queen of Egypt and Julius Caesar's former mistress. In 31 BC, Octavian set out to end this unstable arrangement, and at the sea battle of Actium in the Gulf of Ambracia on the western coast of Greece, he defeated Antony and Cleopatra's fleet. The following year in Alexandria, Mark Antony fell on his sword and Cleopatra took an asp to her breast. By then, both had been thoroughly discredited for claiming that Antony was a descendant of Caesar's and for seeking Roman citizenship rights for Cleopatra's children by Caesar. Octavian would rule the Roman world for the next forty-five years, until his death in 14 AD.

On January 13, 27 BC, Octavian appeared in the Senate, which had legitimized its own demise by ceding most of its powers to him and which now bestowed on him the new title of Augustus, first Roman emperor. The majority of the senators were his solid supporters, having been hand-picked by him. In 23 BC, Augustus was granted further authority by being designated a tribune for life, which gave him ultimate veto power over anything the Senate might do. But his real power ultimately rested on his total control of the armed forces.

His rise to power tainted by constitutional illegitimacy—not unlike that of our own putative Boy Emperor from Crawford, Texas—Augustus proceeded to emasculate the Roman system and its representative institutions. He never abolished the old republican offices but merely united them under one person—himself. Imperial appointment became a badge of prestige and social standing rather than of authority. The Senate was turned into a club of old aristocratic families, and its approval of the acts of the emperor was purely ceremonial. The Roman legions continued to march under the banner SPQR—*senatus populus que Romanus* (the Senate and the people of Rome)—but the authority of Augustus was absolute.

In response to the demands of empire, the army had grown so large as to be close to unmanageable. It constituted a state within a state, not unlike the Pentagon today. Augustus reduced the army's size, providing generous cash payments to those soldiers who had served more than twelve years. Of course, he made clear that this bounty came from him, not their military commanders. He also transferred all legions from Rome to the remote provinces and borders of the empire, to ensure that their leaders were not tempted to meddle in political affairs. Astutely, he created a Praetorian Guard, an elite force of nine thousand men whose task was to defend him personally and he stationed them in Rome. Their ranks were drawn from Italy, not from distant provinces, and they were paid more than soldiers in the regular legions. They began as Augustus's personal bodyguards, but in the decades after his death became decisive players in their own right in the selection of new emperors. It was one of the first illustrations of an old conundrum of authoritarian politics. If a bureaucracy, such as the Praetorian Guard, is created to control another bureaucracy, the regular army, before long the question will arise: *Quis custodiet ipsos custodes?* (Who will watch the watchers?)

Augustus is credited with forging the Roman Peace (Pax Romana), which historians like to say lasted more than two hundred years. It was, however, based on a military dictatorship and entirely dependent on the incumbent emperor. Therein lay the problem. Tiberius, who succeeded Augustus, reigning from 14–37 AD, retired to Capri with a covey of young boys who catered to his sexual tastes. His successor, Caligula, who held office from 37–41, was the darling of the army, but on January 24, 41 AD, the Praetorian Guard assassinated him and proceeded to loot the imperial palace. Modern archaeological evidence strongly suggests that Caligula was an eccentric maniac, just as history has always portrayed him.[39]

The fourth emperor, Claudius, who reigned from 41 to 54, was put in power by the Praetorian Guard in a de facto military coup. Despite the basically favorable portrayal of him by Robert Graves in his novel *I, Claudius* of 1934, and decades later adapted for TV (and played by Derek Jacobi), Claudius, who was Caligula's uncle, was addicted to gladiatorial games and fond of watching defeated opponents being put to death. As a child, Claudius limped, drooled, stuttered, and was constantly ill. He had

his first wife killed so he could marry Agrippina, daughter of Caligula's
sister, after having the law changed to allow uncles to marry their nieces.
On October 13, 54 AD, Claudius was killed with a poisoned mushroom,
probably fed to him by his wife, and at noon that same day, the sixteen-
year-old Nero, Agrippina's son by a former husband, was acclaimed
emperor in a carefully orchestrated piece of political theater. Nero, who
reigned from 54 to 68 AD, was probably insane as well as a tyrant. He set
fire to Rome in 64 and executed those famed early Christians Paul and
Peter, although his reputation has been somewhat rehabilitated in recent
years as a patron of the arts.[40]

After Augustus, not much recommends the Roman empire as an
example of enlightened government. The history of the Roman Republic
from the time of Julius Caesar suggests that imperialism and militarism—
poorly understood by all conservative political leaders at the time—
brought down the republic. The professionalization of a large standing
army in order to defend the empire created invincible new sources of
power within the Roman polity and prepared the way for the rise of populist generals who understood the grievances of their troops and veterans
as politicians could not.

Service in the armed forces of the United States has not been a universal male obligation of citizenship since 1973. Our military today is a professional corps of men and women who commonly join up to advance
themselves in the face of one or another cul-de-sac of American society.
They normally do not expect to be shot at, but they do expect all the benefits of state employment—steady pay, good housing, free medical benefits,
education, relief from racial discrimination, world travel, and gratitude
from the rest of society for their "service." They are well aware that the
alternatives on offer today in civilian life include difficult job searches,
little or no job security, regular pilfering of retirement funds by company
executives and their accountants, "privatized" medical care, bad public
elementary education, and insanely expensive higher education. They are
ripe not for the rhetoric of a politician who followed the Andover-Yale-
Harvard Business School route to riches and power but for a Julius Caesar,
Napoleon Bonaparte, or Juan Perón—a revolutionary, military populist
with little interest in republican niceties so long as some form of emperor-
ship lies at the end of his rocky path.

Regardless of who succeeds George W. Bush, the incumbent president will have to deal with an emboldened Pentagon, an engorged military-industrial complex, our empire of bases, and a fifty-year-old tradition of not revealing to the public what our military establishment costs or the kinds of devastation it can inflict. History teaches us that the capacity for things to get worse is limitless. Roman history suggests that the short, happy life of the American republic may be coming to its end—and that turning it into an openly military empire will not, to say the least, be the best solution to that problem.

One common response to this view is that ours is actually a "good empire" like the one from which we gained our independence in 1776. Whatever its faults and flaws, contemporary America, like England in the eighteenth and nineteenth centuries, is said to be a source of enlightenment for the rest of the world, a natural carrier of the seeds of "democracy" into benighted and oppressed regions, and the only possible military guarantor of "stability" on the planet. We are, therefore, the "cousins" and inheritors of the best traditions of the British Empire, which was, according to this highly ideological construct, a force for unalloyed good despite occasional unfortunate and unavoidable lapses.

The expatriate Scot and Harvard historian Niall Ferguson typically argues that the British Empire was motivated by "a sincere belief that spreading 'commerce, Christianity, and civilization' was as much in the interests of Britain's colonial subjects as in the interests of the imperial metropole itself."[41] He insists that "no organization [other than the British Empire] has done more to impose Western norms of law, order and governance around the world" and that "America is heir to the empire in both senses: offspring of the colonial era, successor today. Perhaps the most burning contemporary question of American politics is: Should the United States seek to shed or to shoulder the imperial load it has inherited?"[42] The *Los Angeles Times*'s right-wing columnist Max Boot thinks that "Afghanistan and other troubled lands today cry out for the sort of enlightened foreign administration once provided by self-confident Englishmen in jodhpurs and pith helmets."[43]

According to journalist Erik Tarloff, writing in the British newspaper *Financial Times*, "Claims that the British Raj redounded to the economic benefit of India as well as the mother country [are], I should think,

irrefutable."[44] Given that for two centuries—between 1757 and 1947—
there was no increase at all in India's per capita income, that in the second
half of Victoria's reign between thirty and fifty million Indians perished in
famines and plagues brought on by British misrule, and that from 1872 to
1921, the life expectancy of ordinary Indians fell by a staggering 20 percent, the idea that India benefited from British imperialism is at least open
to question.[45]

The rewriting of history to prettify the British Empire has long been
commonplace in England but it became politically significant in the
United States only after 9/11, when the thought—novel to most Americans—that their own country was actually an "empire" began to come out
of the closet. Beginning in late 2001, approval of American imperialism
became a prominent theme in the establishment and neoconservative
press. "It was time for America unabashedly and unilaterally, to assert its
supremacy and to maintain global order," writes Joshua Micah Marshall,
editor of an influential Washington Internet newsletter. "After September
11th, a left-wing accusation became a right-wing aspiration: conservatives
increasingly began to espouse a world view that was unapologetically
imperialist."[46]

Bernard Porter, a professor at the University of Newcastle upon Tyne
and a recognized specialist on Britain's imperial past, likes to argue that
his country acquired its empire unintentionally. Apologists for American
imperialism also contend that the United States acquired its continental
girth as well as its Caribbean and Pacific colonies in a fit of innocent
absentmindedness.[47] Despite his tendency to minimize the importance of
the British Empire, Porter is an acute observer of trends in the candor
with which this history has been approached. In the twentieth century,
he observes, "Imperialism—in the old, conventional sense—suddenly
became unfashionable. . . . [New books] took an entirely different line on
it from before: hugely downplaying the glorious military aspects of it;
almost giving the impression that most colonies had asked to join the
Empire; stressing Britain's supposed 'civilizing' mission; and presenting
the whole thing as simply a happy federation of countries at different
stages of 'development.' . . . A new word was coined for it, which was
thought to express this sort of thing better: 'Commonwealth.' A popular
metaphor was that of the 'family.' "[48]

In Porter's view, the ordinary Victorian Englishman was never much interested in the empire, which was always a plaything of the military classes and those who wanted (or had) to get out of the British Isles. But in America, the idea that the British Empire was really nice—totally unlike its French, German, Russian, and Japanese contemporaries—had long been well received by novel readers and latter-day fans of the long-running TV series *Masterpiece Theater.*

During the post-9/11 period of American enthusiasm for imperialism, one of its most influential proselytizers was Michael Ignatieff, a Harvard professor and self-appointed spokesman for "humanitarian imperialism," also known as "Empire Lite." As the demand for his cheerleading faded in light of the Iraq war, Ignatieff decided to return to his native Canada and became a politician. Back in Toronto, he acknowledged to a journalist that his many essays and op-eds had all been written as if he were an American, and he apologized for having used "we" and "us" some forty-three times throughout his essay entitled "Lesser Evils," which is a defense of official torture.[49]

In the *New York Times Magazine* of January 5, 2003, Ignatieff proudly asserts, "Ever since George Washington warned his countrymen against foreign entanglements, empire abroad has been seen as the republic's permanent temptation and its potential nemesis. Yet what word but 'empire' describes the awesome thing that America is becoming? It is the only nation that polices the world through five global military commands; maintains more than a million men and women at arms on four continents; deploys carrier battle groups on watch in every ocean; guarantees the survival of countries from Israel to South Korea; drives the wheels of global trade and commerce; and fills the hearts and minds of an entire planet with its dreams and desires."

In numerous one-liners, Ignatieff sings the praises of American imperialism: "Multilateral solutions to the world's problems are all very well, but they have no teeth unless America bares its fangs. . . . Regime change is an imperial task par excellence, since it assumes that the empire's interest has a right to trump the sovereignty of a state. . . . The question, then, is not whether America is too powerful but whether it is powerful enough. Does it have what it takes to be grandmaster of what Colin Powell has called the chessboard of the world's most inflammable region? . . . The case for empire is that it has become, in a place like Iraq, the last hope for democracy and stability alike."[50]

Ignatieff's warlike prose comes from an essay entitled "The Burden," an unmistakable reference to Rudyard Kipling's 1899 poem "The White Man's Burden," written while he was living in Vermont and addressed to Americans as they prepared to subjugate the Philippines:

> Take up the White Man's Burden
> And reap his old reward
> The blame of those ye better,
> The hate of those ye guard.

Michael Neumann, a professor of philosophy at Trent University in Ontario, compares Ignatieff's epistles to the Americans to "a sprig of cilantro on the nouveau-imperialist bucket of KFC [Kentucky Fried Chicken], transforming Bush's blunderings into a treat for liberal white folks the world over."[51]

Imperialism is, by definition, unpleasant for its victims. Even a supporter such as Niall Ferguson acknowledges that it is "the extension of one's civilization, usually by military force, to rule over other peoples."[52] Regimes created by imperialists are never polities ruled with the consent of the governed. Evelyn Baring (later known as Lord Cromer), who was the British consul general and de facto overlord of Egypt from 1883 to 1907—officially he was merely an "adviser" to the formally ruling khedive—once commented, "We need not always enquire too closely what these people . . . think is in their own interests. . . . It is essential that each special issue should be decided mainly with reference to what, by the light of Western knowledge and experience, . . . we conscientiously think is best for the subject race."[53] Lord Salisbury, Britain's conservative prime minister at the start of the twentieth century, put it more succinctly: "If our ancestors had cared for the rights of other people, the British empire would not have been made."[54]

Apologists for imperialism like Ferguson never consult the victims of the allegedly beneficent conquerors. As the American historian Kevin Baker points out, "The idea of Rome or the British empire as liberal institutions of any sort would have come as a surprise to, say, the Gauls or the Carthaginians, or the Jews of Masada; or, respectively, the Zulus or the

Boers or the North American Indians or the Maoris of New Zealand."[55] Eric Foner, the historian of American race relations, similarly reminds us that "the benevolence of benevolent imperialism lies in the eye of the beholder."[56] What can be said, however, is that the British were exceptionally susceptible to believing in the "goodness" of their empire and, in this, the United States has indeed proved a worthy imperial successor. In his analysis of Jane Austen's 1814 novel *Mansfield Park,* which depicted a wealthy English family whose comforts derived from a sugar plantation in Antigua built on slave labor, Edward Said observed, "European culture often, if not always, characterized itself in such a way as simultaneously to validate its own preferences while also advocating those preferences in conjunction with distant imperial rule."[57]

Actual, on-the-ground imperialists, as distinct from their political supporters and cheerleaders back home, know that they are hated; that is one of the reasons they traditionally detested imperial liberals, socialists, do-gooders, and other social critics remote from the killing fields, who criticized their methods or advocated the "reform" of some particular imperial project or other. Whether the imperial power is itself a democracy or a dictatorship makes a difference in the lives of the conquered, but only because that tends to determine how far the dominant country is willing to go in carrying out "administrative massacres," to use Arendt's potent term, when perpetuating its rule in the face of resistance.[58] A split between those who support imperialism and those who enforce it is characteristic of all imperialist republics. Both groups, however, normally share extensive rationales for their inherent superiority over "subject races" and the reasons why they should dominate and impose their "civilization" on others.

Those who supply such rationales of domination belong to what I call the "Jeane Kirkpatrick school of analysis." As Reagan's U.N. ambassador, Kirkpatrick once said, "Americans need to face the truth about themselves, no matter how pleasant it is."[59] Historians like Ferguson are of this persuasion, which particularly flourished in the first years after the attacks of September 11, 2001, in Anglo-American countries. That Britons and Americans have proven so comfortable with the idea of forcing thousands of people to be free by slaughtering them—with Maxim machine guns in the nineteenth century, with "precision-guided munitions" today—seems to reflect a deeply felt need as well as a striking inability to imagine the lives and viewpoints of others. While this, too, is typical of any imperial power, it has perhaps been heightened in the cases of Great Britain and the United States by the fact that neither has ever been defeated and occupied by a foreign military power.

On the other hand, even defeat in war did not cause the Japanese to give up their legends of racial, economic, and cultural superiority. Although the Japanese after World War II "embraced defeat," in the historian John Dower's memorable phrase, they never gave up their nationalist and racist convictions that in slaughtering over twenty million Chinese and enslaving the Koreans they were actually engaged in liberating East Asians from the grip of Western imperialism.[60] All empires, it seems, require myths of divine right, racial preeminence, manifest destiny, or a "civilizing mission" to cover their often barbarous behavior in other people's countries. As Foner points out, sixteenth-century Spaniards claimed to be "freeing" members of the Aztec, Mayan, and Incan civilizations from backwardness and superstition via Christian conversion, while Britons in the late nineteenth century liked to think that in massacring Africans they were actually helping to suppress the slave trade.[61]

There is, in fact, nothing new about such self-enhancing American military campaign names as "Operation Iraqi Freedom," "Infinite Justice" (as Centcom called the 2001 U.S. attack on Afghanistan until Muslim scholars and clerics objected that only God can dispense infinite justice), and "Just Cause" (Bush senior's vicious 1989 assault on Panama).[62] Such efforts reflect both justifications for imperialism and strategies for avoiding responsibility for its inevitable catastrophes. The first recourse in justification has long been racism—or at least a sense of superiority—in all of its forms, including the belief that victory over the "natives" (including their mass deaths due to diseases the imperialists introduce) is evidence that God or the gods have divinely sanctioned foreign conquest. As the American theologian Reinhold Niebuhr taught, "The tendency to claim God as an ally for our partisan values is the source of all religious fanaticism."[63] Then there has been the long list of what writer Sven Lindqvist, in his book *"Exterminate All the Brutes"*, which is a gloss on Joseph Conrad's *Heart of Darkness*, usefully terms pseudo-scientific "ideologies of extermination": eugenics, perversions of Darwinism, natural selection, survival of the fittest, Malthusian demography, and more.[64]

Racist defenses of imperialism have often been linked to the argument that the imperialists have bestowed some unquestioned benefits, often economic, on their conquered peoples even as they pauperize or enslave them. Examples from the last two centuries include the benefits of "free trade," globalization, the rule of (foreign) law, investor protection, "liberation" from other imperial powers or homegrown dictators, or "democracy." In supporting Bush's attack on Iraq, the Harvard historian Charles S. Maier notes approvingly, "Empires function by virtue of the prestige they radiate as well as by might, and indeed collapse if they rely on force alone. Artistic styles, the language of the rulers, and consumer preferences flow outward along with power and investment capital—sometimes diffused consciously by cultural diplomacy and student exchanges, sometimes just by popular tastes for the intriguing products of the metropole, whether Coca-Cola or Big Macs. As supporters of the imperial power rightly maintain, empires provide public goods that masses of people outside their borders really want to enjoy, including an end to endemic warfare and murderous ethnic or religious conflicts."[65]

Finally, in retrospect, there has been simple amnesia: the systematic omission of subjects that are impossible to square with the idea of "liberal imperialism." For example, both Ferguson and the *Cambridge Illustrated History of the British Empire* skip lightly over the fact that the empire operated the world's largest and most successful drug cartel. During the nineteenth century, Britain fought two wars of choice with China to force it to import opium. The opium grown in India and shipped to China first by the British East India Company and after 1857 by the government of India, helped Britain finance much of its military and colonial budgets in South and Southeast Asia. The Australian scholar Carl A. Trocki concludes that, given the huge profits from the sale of opium, "without the drug, there probably would have been no British empire."[66]

Other intellectual strategies have been concocted to avoid facing the reality of imperialist depredations. For example, the philosopher John Locke came up with the brilliant idea that the land in North America British colonists were stealing from the indigenous people was actually terra nullius, or "nobody's land." But let me expand briefly on just two of the rationalizations for imperialism: racism and economic benefits bestowed.

Racism has been the master imperialist rationale of modern times, one with which British imperialists are completely familiar. "Imperialism," Hannah Arendt wrote, "would have necessitated the invention of racism as the only possible 'explanation' and excuse for its deeds, even if no race-thinking had ever existed in the civilized world."[67] But what, exactly, needed to be explained by racism? Initially, it was the growing dominance by small groups of well-armed, ruthless Europeans over societies in South and East Asia that in the eighteenth century were infinitely richer and more sophisticated than anything then known in Europe. As the historian Mike Davis observes, "When the sans culottes stormed the Bastille [in 1789], the largest manufacturing districts in the world were still the Yangzi Delta [in China] and Bengal [in India], with Lingan (modern Guangdong and Guangxi) and coastal Madras not far behind."[68] In the early eighteenth century, India was a "vast and economically advanced subcontinent," producing close to a quarter of total planetary output of everything, compared with Britain's measly 3 percent.[69] As the British set about looting their captured subcontinent this reality proved an inconvenient one. It became indispensable for them to be able to describe the conquered populations as inferior in every way: incapable of self-government, lacking in the ability to reason, hopelessly caught up in "static" Oriental beliefs, overly fecund, and, in short, not members of the "fittest" races. In other words, their subjugation was not only their own fault but inevitable.

Joseph Conrad's closest friend and correspondent was the Scottish aristocrat and socialist R. B. Cunninghame Graham, who looked on his country's imperialism with a jaundiced eye. It seems likely that Graham's letters and published works inspired Conrad to write the most important book in English on imperialism—his 1899 novel *Heart of Darkness*. In 1897, in a story entitled "Bloody Niggers," Graham summed up the English imperial view of the world in the following fashion: "Far back in history, Assyrians, Babylonians, and Egyptians lived and thought, but God was aiming all the time at something different and better. He let Greeks and Romans appear out of the darkness of barbarity to prepare the way for the race that from the start was chosen to rule over mankind—namely, the British race."[70]

At its heart, British imperialist ideology revolved around the belief that history and human evolution—either divinely guided or as a result of natural selection—had led inexorably to the British Empire of the nineteenth century. As a result, the British extermination of the Tasmanians ("living fossils"); the slaughter of at least ten thousand Sudanese in a single battle at Omdurman on September 2, 1898; General Reginald "Rex" Dyer's use of Gurkha troops on April 13, 1919, at Amritsar to kill as many Punjabis as he could until his soldiers ran out of ammunition; the sanctioned use of explosive dumdum bullets (meant for big-game hunting) in colonial wars but prohibiting them in conflicts among "civilized" nations; and many similar events down to the sanguine, sadistic suppression of the Kikuyu people in Kenya in the 1950s were not morally indefensible crimes of imperialism but the workings of a preordained narrative of civilization.

What changed over time was the idea that a divine hand lay behind such work. As Lindqvist comments, "During the nineteenth century, religious explanations were replaced by biological ones. The exterminated peoples were colored, the exterminators white. It seemed obvious that some racial natural law was at work and that the extermination of non-Europeans was simply a stage in the natural development of the world. The fact that natives died proved that they belonged to a lower race. Let them die as the laws of progress demand."[71] On this, Ferguson concurs: "Influenced by, but distorting beyond recognition, the work of Darwin, nineteenth-century pseudo-scientists divided humanity into 'races' on the basis of external physical features, ranking them according to inherited differences not just in physique but also in character. Anglo-Saxons were self-evidently at the top, Africans at the bottom."[72] In this scheme of things, welfare measures and ameliorative reforms of harsh colonial practices should not be allowed to interfere with natural selection since this would only allow inferiors to survive and "propagate their unfitness."[73] These ideas were much admired by Adolf Hitler in *Mein Kampf,* where he wrote approvingly of Britain's "effective oppression of an inferior race," the Indians.[74]

Racist attitudes spread throughout the British Empire and retained a tenacious hold on English thought well into the twentieth century. As P. J. Marshall, editor of the *Cambridge Illustrated History of the British Empire,* observes, "The roots of South African apartheid, the most inflexible of all systems of racial segregation, can clearly be found in the period when Britain still had ultimate responsibility. The British were never inclined to condone racially mixed marriages, which were common in some other empires, and they rarely treated people of mixed race as in any way the equal of whites."[75] Niall Ferguson deserves credit for noting the sexual hysteria of the Victorians that contributed to these racist policies.[76] That theme, for instance, infuses several of the great novels of Indian life—E. M. Forster's *A Passage to India* (1924), Paul Scott's *The Jewel in the Crown* (1966), Ruth Prawer Jhabvala's *Heat and Dust* (1975), and Arundhati Roy's *The God of Small Things* (1997). It is ironic, then, that Edwina, Lady Mountbatten, wife of the last British viceroy in India, had a passionate love affair with independent India's first prime minister, Jawaharlal Nehru.[77]

"The overt racism of the British in India, which affected the institutions of government, contributed powerfully to the growth of nationalist sentiment," recalls Tapan Raychaudhuri, an emeritus fellow of St. Antony's College, Oxford. "All Indians, whatever their status, shared the experience of being treated as racial inferiors. . . . The life stories of Indian celebrities are full of episodes of racial insults."[78] For all its alleged liberalism and the capitalist institutions it forced on its captive peoples, the British Empire bred, inculcated, and propagated racism as its ultimate justification. Even though it was history's largest empire, its rulers seemed incapable of functioning without thoroughly deceiving themselves about why, for a relatively short period of time, they dominated the world. For this reason alone, the British Empire should not be held up as an institution deserving emulation, least of all by the first nation that broke free of it, the United States of America.

Racists though they may have been, Britons have long claimed that they bequeathed to the world the most advanced and effective economic institutions ever devised. "For many British people," as P. J. Marshall puts it, "it is axiomatic that their record in the establishment of colonies of settlement overseas and as rulers of non-European peoples was very much superior to that of any other power."[79] The popular Niall Ferguson, author of *Colossus*, an admiring if condescending book on America's emerging empire, is primarily an economic historian, and his influential glosses on the British Empire stress, above all, its contributions to what later came to be called "globalization." He is on the same wavelength with *New York Times* columnist Thomas Friedman, bestselling author of *The Lexus and the Olive Tree: Understanding Globalization* and *The World Is Flat*, who also thinks that the integration of capital markets and investor protection contribute mightily to the well-being of peoples under the sway of either the British or the American empires. Though the idea does not survive close scrutiny, it has proved a powerful ideological justification of imperialism.

It is not news that somewhere around 1 billion people today subsist on almost nothing. With rare exceptions, the countries that the various imperialisms of the nineteenth and twentieth centuries exploited and colonized remain poor, disease- and crime-ridden, and at the mercy of a rigged international trading system that Anglo-American propagandists assure us is rapidly "globalizing" to everyone's advantage. But, as the *New York Times* pointed out, "The very same representatives of the club of rich countries who go around the world hectoring the poor to open up their markets to free trade put up roadblocks when those countries ask the rich to dismantle their own barriers to free trade in agricultural products."[80] According to World Bank data, 390 million of India's 1.1 billion people— almost a third of them—live on less than one dollar a day.[81] Typically, the former U.S. colony of the Philippines, a resource-rich country with a large Sino-Malay population, remains the poorest nation in East Asia, the world's fastest-growing economic region—a direct result of U.S. imperialism. Similarly, impoverished Latin America still struggles to throw off the legacies of American "backyard" neocolonialism.[82] All this is among the best-known economic information in the world.

According to the apologists for the British Empire, however, such bad economic news cannot be true, because these problems were solved over 150 years ago. Ferguson maintains that "the nineteenth-century [British] empire undeniably pioneered free trade, free capital movements and, with the abolition of slavery, free labor."[83] After the Irish famine (1846–1850) and the Indian Mutiny (1857), the British "recast their empire as an economically liberal project, concerned as much with the integration of global markets as with the security of the British Isles, predicated on the idea that British rule was conferring genuine benefits in the form of free trade, the rule of law, the safeguarding of private property rights and non-corrupt administration, as well as government-guaranteed investments in infrastructure, public health, and (some) education."[84]

Unfortunately, this argument is an offshoot of the old nineteenth-century Marxist conception that politics are mere superstructural reflections of underlying economic relations, and that a single worldwide economic system is emerging that will usher in an era of unprecedented prosperity and peace for all. As the economic theorist John Gray observes, "It is an irony of history that a view of the world falsified by the Communist collapse should have been adopted, in some of its most misleading aspects, by the victors in the Cold War. Neoliberals, such as Friedman [and Ferguson], have reproduced the weakest features of Marx's thought—its consistent underestimation of nationalist and religious movements and its unidirectional view of history."[85]

The idea that the British Empire conferred economic benefits on any groups other than British capitalists is pure ideology, as impervious to challenge by empirical data as former Soviet prime minister Leonid Brezhnev's Marxism-Leninism or George Bush's belief that free markets mean the same thing as freedom. At the apex of those who profited from British-style "free trade" at the end of the nineteenth century was the Rothschild Bank, then by far the world's largest financial institution with total assets of around forty-one million pounds sterling. It profited enormously from the wars—some seventy-two of them—during Queen Victoria's reign, and financed such exploiters of Africa as Cecil Rhodes.

Ferguson, who wrote a history of the House of Rothschild, knows these things and does not deny them when he turns from imperial panegyrics to history. "In the age before steam power," he writes, "India had led the world in manual spinning, weaving, and dyeing. The British had first raised tariffs against their products; then demanded free trade when their alternative industrial mode of production had been perfected."[86] The result was poverty and dependence for India. As Oxford historian Tapan Raychaudhuri puts it, "Early in the nineteenth century India lost its export trade in manufactures and became a net importer of manufactured goods and a supplier of mainly agricultural products to Britain for the first time in its history. . . . In India the favorable terms granted to British exporters and the doctrine of laissez-faire meant that Indian industries received no protection and hardly any encouragement until the mid-1920s, and then only in response to persistent Indian pressure."[87] Precisely at the time that the British were preparing India for its poverty-stricken modern fate, two other nations were laying the foundations for their own contemporary status as the world's first and second most productive nations—the United States, protected from its inception to about 1940 by tariffs on manufactured imports that averaged 44 percent; and

Japan, which kept itself free of imperialist domination and copied the economic practices of Britain, the United States, and Germany rather than paying much attention to their economic treatises on free markets.[88]

What we are talking about here is, in Mike Davis's phrase, "the making of the third world," the poverty-stricken southern hemisphere that is still very much with us today. "The looms of India and China," Davis writes, "were defeated not so much by market competition as they were forcibly dismantled by war, invasion, opium, and a Lancashire-imposed system of one-way tariffs."[89] In a well-known formulation, the social theorist Karl Polanyi wrote in his seminal work *The Great Transformation* (1944): "The catastrophe of the native community is a direct result of the rapid and violent disruption of the basic institutions of the victim (whether force is used in the process or not does not seem altogether relevant). These institutions are disrupted by the very fact that a market economy is foisted upon an entirely differently organized community; labor and land are made into commodities, which, again, is only a short formula for the liquidation of every and any cultural institution in an organic society. . . . Indian masses in the second half of the nineteenth century did not die of hunger because they were exploited by Lancashire; they perished in large numbers because the Indian village community had been demolished."[90]

Ferguson agrees; it is just that he, like Marx, sees all this chaos as "creative destruction," the birth pangs of a new world order, Lenin's famous willingness to break eggs in order to make an omelet. ("But how many eggs must you break," one wag famously asked, "to make a two-egg omelet?") "No doubt it is true that, in theory, open international markets would have been preferable to imperialism," Ferguson argues, "but in practice global free trade was not and is not naturally occurring. The British empire enforced it."[91]

Thomas Friedman similarly acknowledges that contemporary American-sponsored globalization is not a naturally occurring process. American imperialism enforces it: "The most powerful agent pressuring other countries to open their markets for free trade and free investments is Uncle Sam, and America's global armed forces keep these markets and sea lanes open for this era of globalization, just as the British navy did for the era of globalization in the nineteenth century."[92] If Mexican corn farmers are driven out of business by heavily subsidized American growers and then the price of corn makes tortillas unaffordable, that is just the global market at work. But if poor and unemployed Mexicans then try to enter the United States to support their families, that is to be resisted by armed force.

After all their arguments have been deployed, how do analysts like Ferguson and Friedman explain the nineteenth-century poverty of India and China, the several dozen Holocaust-sized famines in both countries while food sat on the docks waiting to be exported, and their current status as "late developers"? Students of communism will not be surprised by the answer. In India, Ferguson argues, the British did not go far enough in enforcing their ideas. "If one leaves aside their fundamentally different resource endowments, the explanation for India's underperformance compared with, say, Canada lies not in British exploitation but rather in the insufficient scale of British interference in the Indian economy."[93]

When Mao Zedong introduced Soviet-style collective farms into China and did not get satisfactory results, he did not abandon them but turned instead to truly gigantic collectives called "communes." This Great Leap Forward of the late 1950s produced a famine that took some thirty million Chinese lives, a monument to communist extremism similar to the extremes of laissez-faire that the British dogmatically imposed on their conquered territories—and that Ferguson would have preferred to be yet more extreme.

The historical evidence suggests a strong correlation exists between being on the receiving end of imperialism and immiseration. The nations that avoided the fates of India, China, Mexico, and the Philippines did so by throwing off foreign rule early—as did the United States—or by modernizing militarily in order to hold off the imperialists (and ultimately join them)—as did Japan.

Even so, the United States is the heir to the British Empire in at least one sense: it is still peddling the same self-serving ideology that its London predecessors pioneered. In a typical speech from the White House, given on September 17, 2002, President George W. Bush said, "The United States will use this moment of opportunity to extend the benefits of freedom across the globe. We will actively work to bring the hope of democracy, development, free markets, and free trade to every corner of the world. . . . Free trade and free markets have proven their ability to lift whole societies out of poverty—so the United States will work with individual nations, entire regions, and the entire global trading community to build a world that trades in freedom and therefore grows in prosperity." This kind of rhetoric gives democracy a bad name.

Some who deplore the British Empire's racism and the fraudulent economic benefits it offered its imperial subjects are nonetheless willing to applaud its gentlemanly endgame, arguing that the way the empire dismantled itself after World War II was "authentically noble" and redeemed all that went before. Ferguson takes up this theme, too. "In the end, the British sacrificed her empire to stop the Germans, Japanese, and Italians from keeping theirs. Did not that sacrifice alone expunge all the empire's other sins?"[94] Much of this is Anglo-American claptrap, but at its core there is a theoretical distinction that is important. First, a look at the argument.

P. J. Marshall asserts categorically: "The British entered into partnerships with their nationalists and extricated themselves from empire with grace and goodwill. . . . The unwillingness of the British government after 1945 to be dragged into colonial wars is irrefutable, even if it is not easy to explain."[95] This idea, a staple of Anglophile romanticism, is simply untrue. When he was writing in 1996, Marshall was surely aware of the Malayan Emergency, a bloody colonial war to retain British possession of its main rubber-producing southeast Asian colonies that lasted from approximately 1948 to 1960. It was the British equivalent of the anti-French and anti-American wars that went on in nearby Indochina. Although the British claimed victory over the insurgents, much like the French did in Algeria, the long and deadly conflict led to independence for Britain's colonies and the emergence of the two successor states of Malaysia and Singapore.

The so-called Mau Mau Uprising in Kenya from 1952 to 1960—in the immediate wake of the global war against fascism—was one of the most vicious colonial wars Britain ever fought. No one knows precisely what "Mau Mau" means or even what language it comes from, but it was the Kikuyu, Kenya's largest ethnic group, some 1.5 million strong, who led the rebellion for freedom from British oppression. Kenya's white settler population was different from similar groups in other colonies. A great many came from Britain's upper classes, and they assumed privileges in their new East African enclave that had long since been abolished in their homeland. Caroline Elkins, an American historian who has reconstructed the revolt against these expatriates, writes, "Kenya's big men quickly established a leisurely life-style aspired to by all Europeans in the colony. On their estates or farms or in European neighborhoods in Nairobi, every white settler in the colony was a lord to some extent, particularly in relationship to the African population. . . . [T]hese privileged men and women lived an absolutely hedonistic life-style, filled with sex, drugs, and dance, followed by more of the same."[96]

When the Kenyans rebelled against ruthless land seizures by the settlers and their adamant refusal to share power in any way, the British retaliated—in the name of civilization—by detaining, torturing, and executing huge numbers of Africans. They imprisoned in concentration camps nearly the entire Kikuyu population, whom the British contended were not freedom fighters but savages of the lowest order. This colonial war may have slipped the mind of the editor of the *Cambridge History* because the British government did everything in its power to cover up the genocide it attempted there, including burning its colonial archives relating to Kenya on the eve of leaving the country in 1963.

"On the dreadful balance sheet of atrocities," Elkins explains, ". . . the murders perpetrated by Mau Mau adherents were quite small in number when compared to those committed by the forces of British colonial rule. Officially, fewer than one hundred Europeans, including settlers, were killed and some eighteen hundred loyalists [pro-British Kikuyu] died at the hands of Mau Mau. In contrast, the British reported that more than eleven thousand Mau Mau were killed in action, though the empirical and demographic evidence I unearthed calls into serious question the validity of this figure. I now believe there was in late colonial Kenya a murderous campaign to eliminate Kikuyu people, a campaign that left tens of thousands, perhaps hundreds of thousands, dead."[97] This was anything but an extrication from empire "with grace and goodwill."

Without doubt Niall Ferguson also knows about the way the British crushed the Mau Mau, since he and his family lived in Nairobi in the late 1960s, but he makes no mention of the rebellion in either of his books on the British Empire. Instead, he writes, "We had our bungalow, our maid, our smattering of Swahili—and our sense of unshakable security. It was a magical time, which indelibly impressed on my consciousness the sight of the hunting cheetah, the sound of Kikuyu women singing, the smell of the first rains and the taste of ripe mango."[98] The British seem to have no qualms about distorting the historical record in order to prettify their imperialism. Jan Christian Smuts, the Boer general who later defected to the British side and served twice in the early twentieth century as prime minister of the Union of South Africa, the British colony's successor state, called British indifference to their violations of international law during the Boer War "very characteristic of the nation which always plays the role of chosen judge over the actions and behavior of all other nations."[99]

There are still other post-1945 colonial wars that contradict any claim of an honorable British abdication of empire, for example, the joint Anglo-French-Israeli attack on Egypt in November 1956 in retaliation for Gamal Abdel Nasser's act of nationalizing the Suez Canal. Nothing came of it because the United States refused to join this exercise in gunboat diplomacy. Nonetheless, the incident revealed that some eighteen years after the British occupation of Egypt had supposedly ended, Britain still had eighty thousand troops based in the canal zone and did not want to leave.[100] And then there is the British military's 2003 return to what *Toronto Sun* columnist Eric Margolis calls "among the most disastrous and tragic creations of Britain's colonial policy"—namely, Iraq.[101] In 1920, following World War I, Britain violated every promise it had ever made to the diverse peoples of the Near East and created the hopelessly unstable country of Iraq from the Mesopotamian remnants of the Ottoman Empire. The new country combined mutually incompatible Kurds, Shia Muslims, and Sunni Muslims, whose struggles with each other were finally suppressed only by the brutal dictatorship of Saddam Hussein. In 1920, when the Iraqis revolted against the British, the Royal Air Force routinely bombed, strafed, and used poison gas against rebellious villages. It is remarkable that the British dared show their faces there again.

There are other problems with the thesis that the British Empire revealed its human greatness at its twilight. The bungled partition of India into India and Pakistan caused between two hundred thousand and a half million deaths and laid the foundation for the three wars to follow between the two countries and the ongoing conflict in Kashmir.[102] Raychaudhuri explains, "The British perception that Hindus and Muslims were two mutually antagonistic monoliths, a notion not rooted in facts, became an important basis for allocating power and resources. Hindu-Muslim rivalry and the eventual partition of India was the end result, and the British policy makers, when they did not actually add fuel to the conflict, were quite happy to take advantage of it."[103] In the partition, Lord Mountbatten, the last viceroy, openly sided with the Hindu-dominated Congress Party against the Muslim League.[104]

An empire such as Britain's that remains a democracy at home and a tyranny abroad always faces tensions between its people in the field and the home office. The on-the-spot imperialists usually exercise unmitigated power over their subordinated peoples whereas political leaders at home are responsible to parliaments and can be held accountable through elections. Writing about British imperialism, Hannah Arendt noted that "on the whole [it] was a failure because of the dichotomy between the nation-state's legal principles and the methods needed to oppress other people permanently. This failure was neither necessary nor due to ignorance or incompetence. British imperialists knew very well that 'administrative massacres' could keep India in bondage, but they also knew that public opinion at home would not stand for such measures. Imperialism could have been a success if the nation-state had been willing to pay the price, to commit suicide and transform itself into a tyranny. It is one of the glories of Europe, and especially of Great Britain, that she preferred to liquidate the empire."[105]

Even though I believe Arendt overstates the achievements of Britain, her point is the main one I have tried to illustrate in this chapter. Over any fairly lengthy period of time, successful imperialism requires that a domestic republic or a domestic democracy change into a domestic tyranny. That is what happened to the Roman Republic; that is what I fear is happening in the United States as the imperial presidency gathers strength at the expense of the constitutional balance of governmental powers and as militarism takes even deeper root in the society. It did not happen in Britain, although it was more likely and altogether less noble than either Arendt or contemporary apologists for British imperialism imply. Nonetheless, Britain escaped transformation into a tyranny largely because of a post–World War II resurgence of democracy and popular revulsion at the routine practices of imperialism.

The histories of Rome and Britain suggest that imperialism and militarism are the deadly enemies of democracy. This was something the founders of the United States tried to forestall with their creation of a republican structure of government and a system of checks and balances inspired by the Roman Republic. Imperialism and militarism will ultimately breach the separation of powers created to prevent tyranny and defend liberty. The United States today, like the Roman Republic in the first century BC, is threatened by an out-of-control military-industrial complex and a huge secret government controlled exclusively by the president. After the attacks of September 11, 2001, cynical and shortsighted political leaders in the United States began to enlarge the powers of the president at the expense of the elected representatives of the people and the courts. The public went along, accepting the excuse that a little tyranny was necessary to protect the population. But, as Benjamin Franklin wrote in 1759, "Those who would give up essential liberty to purchase a little temporary safety deserve neither liberty nor safety."

Rome and Britain are archetypes of the dilemma of combining democracy at home with an empire abroad. In the Roman case, they decided to hang on to the empire and lost their democracy. In the British case, they chose the opposite: in order to remain democratic they dumped their empire and military apparatus after World War II. For us, the choice is between the Roman and British precedents.

3

Central Intelligence Agency:
The President's Private Army

The enormous apparatus of government intelligence and spy operations, of subsidized think tanks and research institutes, and the entire discipline of "strategic studies" failed to prepare the ground for our understanding of what is arguably the most momentous political event of this century. In understanding the collapse of communism and the Soviet state, the supposed experts have been virtually irrelevant.

—RONALD STEEL,
Temptations of a Superpower (1995)

Let me tell you about these intelligence guys. When I was growing up in Texas, we had a cow named Bessie. I'd get her in the stanchion, seat myself, and squeeze out a pail of fresh milk. One day, I'd worked hard and gotten a full pail of milk, but I wasn't paying attention and old Bessie swung her shit-smeared tail through that bucket of milk. Now, you know, that's what these intelligence guys do. You work hard and get a good program or policy going, and they swing a shit-smeared tail through it.

—PRESIDENT LYNDON JOHNSON,
quoted by Robert M. Gates, *From the Shadows* (1996)

Two weeks after George Bush's re-election as president in November 2004, Porter J. Goss, the newly appointed director of central intelligence (DCI), wrote an internal memorandum to all employees that said in part, "[Our job is to] support the administration and its policies in our work. As agency employees, we do not identify with, support, or champion opposition to the administration or its policies."[1] Translated from bureaucratese, this directive essentially passes the following message to the CIA's employees: "You have always worked for the White House. I'm just reminding you of that fact. The intelligence you produce must first and foremost protect the president from being held accountable for anything he has done, ordered, or said concerning Iraq, Osama bin Laden, preventive war, torturing captives, the 'war on terror,' or any other subject on which critics might challenge him."

As it turns out, much of the information the Central Intelligence Agency had already produced on these subjects was false, misleading, or carefully circumscribed by administration needs and desires, as were key intelligence estimates derived from fabrications inspired by the president, the vice president, and the secretary of defense. Goss was merely trying to warn, and so head off, the increasing numbers of outraged, courageous CIA truth tellers who were leaking information harmful to the president before going down in flames. As Thomas Powers, an authority on the CIA, reminds us, "No one can understand, much less predict, the behavior of the CIA who does not understand that the agency works for the president. I know of no exceptions to this general rule. In practice it means that in the end the CIA will always bend to the wishes of the president. . . . The general rule applies both to intelligence and to operations: what the CIA says, as well as what it does, will shape itself over time to what the president wants."[2]

Since everything the CIA writes and does is secret, including its budget (regardless of article 1, section 9, of the Constitution, which says "a regular Statement and Account of the Receipts and Expenditures of all public Money shall be published from time to time"), accountability to the elected representatives of the people or even an accurate historical record of actions is today inconceivable. Congressional oversight of the agency— and many other, ever-expanding intelligence outfits in the U.S. government, including the Defense Intelligence Agency (DIA) and the National Security Agency (NSA)—is, at best, a theatrical performance designed to distract and mislead the few Americans left who are concerned about constitutional government. In fact, the president's untrammeled control of the CIA is probably the single most extraordinary power the imperial presidency possesses—totally beyond the balance of powers intended to protect the United States from the rise of a tyrant.

This situation is hardly new, although in late 2004, former CIA analyst Melvin A. Goodman declared that the Bush administration's record in relation to the CIA represented "the worst intelligence scandal in the nation's history."[3] Perhaps no comment caught the reality of the agency's

role better than James Schlesinger back in 1973. When the former chairman of the Atomic Energy Commission, who had briefly succeeded
Richard Helms as CIA director before becoming secretary of defense,
arrived at the agency's Virginia "campus," he immediately announced: "I
am here to see that you guys don't screw Richard Nixon."[4] Schlesinger
wanted to protect the Watergate-embattled president from revelations
that the CIA, on Nixon's orders, had tried to cover up the break-in of the
headquarters of the Democratic National Committee by his personal
agents as well as the agency's illegal infiltration of the anti–Vietnam War
movement within the United States. (At the time, the CIA was prohibited
from domestic spying operations.) Schlesinger underscored his point by
noting that he would be reporting directly to White House chief of staff
Bob Haldeman, not, as Helms had done, to National Security Adviser
Henry Kissinger.

In George W. Bush's White House, Goss did not need to bother going
directly to Karl Rove, Bush's political "brain," since the president's outgo-
ing and incoming national security advisers, Condoleezza Rice and
Stephen J. Hadley, spent the years 2001 to 2004 under Rove's tutelage
working to reelect the president.[5] Moreover, in April 2005, Goss's position
as director of central intelligence changed. He became merely the director
of the Central Intelligence Agency, not the director of Central Intelligence,
which has now become the purview of the newly appointed director of
National Intelligence, John Negroponte, who presides over the fifteen separate federal intelligence agencies in a post-9/11 attempt to bring some
coherence and coordination to them. As a result, Goss no longer briefed
the president every morning on the CIA's view of the world, and he
attended National Security Council meetings only at Negroponte's invitation. In May 2006, Bush fired Goss and replaced him with a four-star air
force general, Michael Hayden, former director of the nation's eavesdropping and cryptological intelligence unit, the National Security Agency.
Scott Ritter, author of *Iraq Confidential: The Untold Story of the Intelligence Conspiracy to Undermine the U.N. and Overthrow Saddam Hussein*,
commented that "Goss's tenure [as director of the CIA] will go down in
history as one of the worst ever (followed closely by that of George
Tenet)."[6] Whether anything has actually changed other than some titles
and bureaucrats is, however, an open question.

Whatever happens, the CIA will remain first and foremost the president's private army, officially accountable to no other branch of the government. How this could be so, why the CIA was created, what it actually does, and the ways presidents since 1947 have twisted it to their own ends remains a widely misunderstood set of topics, crucial to the waning of American democracy. In fact, the term "intelligence" has always rested uneasily in the name "Central Intelligence Agency." There is no question that the CIA was created in 1947 on the orders of President Truman for the sole purpose of acquiring, evaluating, and coordinating information collected both through espionage and from the public record, concerning the national security of the United States. Truman was determined to prevent another surprise attack on the United States like Pearl Harbor and to ensure that all information available to the government was compiled and presented to him in a timely and usable form.

The National Security Act of 1947 placed the CIA under the explicit direction of the National Security Council (NSC), the president's chief staff unit—composed of appointed members not subject to congressional approval—focused on making decisions about war and peace. The CIA was given five functions, four of them dealing with the collection, coordination, and dissemination of intelligence. It was the fifth—a vaguely worded passage that allowed the CIA to "perform such other functions and duties related to intelligence affecting the national security as the National Security Council may from time to time direct"—that turned the CIA into the personal, secret, unaccountable army of the president. At least since 1953, when it secretly overthrew the democratically elected government of Iran, the CIA has often been ordered into battle without Congress having declared war, as the Constitution requires.

Clandestine or covert operations, although nowhere actually mentioned in the CIA's enabling statutes, quickly became the agency's main activity. As Loch K. Johnson, one of the CIA's most impartial congressional analysts and former chief assistant to Senator Frank Church, chairman of the post-Watergate Senate Select Committee to Study Governmental Operations with Respect to Intelligence Activities, observed, "The covert action shop had become a place for rapid promotion within the agency."[7] The Directorate of Operations (DO) soon absorbed two-thirds of the CIA's budget and personnel, while the Directorate of Intelligence limped along, regularly producing bland documents known as National Intelligence Estimates (NIEs)—summaries of intelligence gathered by all the various intelligence agencies, including those in the Department of Defense. I personally read a good many of these when I served, from 1967 to 1973, as an outside consultant to what was then known as the CIA's Office of National Estimates. This consulting function was abolished by Kissinger and Schlesinger during Nixon's second term precisely because they did not want outsiders interfering with their ability to tell the president what to think.[8]

Meanwhile, CIA covert operations were mobilized in support of various criminal, dictatorial, or militarist organizations around the world so long as they were (or pretended to be) anticommunist. CIA operatives also planted false information in foreign newspapers and covertly fed large amounts of money to members of the Christian Democratic Party in Italy and the Liberal Democratic Party in Japan, to King Hussein of Jordan, and to clients in Greece, West Germany, Egypt, Sudan, Suriname, Mauritius, the Philippines, Iran, Ecuador, and Chile. Clandestine agents devoted themselves to such tasks as depressing the global prices of agricultural products in order to damage uncooperative Third World countries, attempting to assassinate foreign leaders, and sponsoring guerrilla wars or insurgencies in places as diverse as the Ukraine, Poland, Albania, Hungary, Indonesia, China, Tibet, Oman, Malaysia, Iraq, the Dominican Republic, Venezuela, North Korea, Bolivia, Laos, Cambodia, Vietnam, Thailand, Haiti, Guatemala, Cuba, Greece, Turkey, Vietnam, Afghanistan, Angola, and Nicaragua, to name only a few of those on the public record.[9]

All this was justified by the Cold War and no one beyond a very small group inside the executive branch was supposed to know anything about most of these activities, although over the years much information about them became public. The Central Intelligence Act of 1949 modified the National Security Act of 1947 with a series of revisions that, in the words of the pioneer scholar of the CIA Harry Howe Ransom, were meant "to permit [the CIA] a secrecy so absolute that accountability might be impossible."[10] No congressional oversight of the agency in any form existed until 1974, when, in the wake of Watergate, the Church Committee exposed the CIA's illegal domestic surveillance, its assassinations of overseas leaders, and its lying to Congress. The committee's report led Congress to create intelligence committees in both houses, but even that modest attempt at instituting oversight procedures has been thwarted by excessive secrecy—which the CIA has managed to impose on the work of

Congress meant to bring a little sunlight to the agency. Since the mid-1970s, governmental secrecy has expanded exponentially, and Vice President Dick Cheney has made it his personal crusade to try to reverse the Church Committee's reforms.[11]

The irony is that Congress created the "central" intelligence agency in 1947 to concentrate vital information in one place and ensure that it went to the president and all other officials with a need-to-know. Instead the intelligence "community" has become a hotbed of competition, turf wars, and confusion. Failure to get intelligence into the right hands had clearly been one of the reasons for the catastrophic surprise of December 7, 1941, and—despite the multibillions that went into the CIA and other intelligence units and the spread of a culture of secrecy—it would be again on September 11, 2001. Overclassification and the use of secrecy to protect political and bureaucratic careers and departmental jurisdictions have rendered the entire intelligence apparatus unable to focus on much of anything.[12] To further enhance secrecy and add to the confusion, the president and the CIA have increasingly turned to completely "off-the-books" operations. The unsuccessful attempt to rig the Iraqi election of January 30, 2005, in favor of the White House's preferred candidate, former CIA operative Iyad Allawi, by using "retired" agents, funds not appropriated by Congress, and other means is but one contemporary example of this phenomenon.[13] The public learns about these operations, if it ever does, only as a result of leaks by insiders. The CIA belongs as much to the president as the Praetorian Guard once belonged to the Roman emperors.

Regardless of what it spends most of its time doing, the CIA is still tasked with providing accurate information to the president to enable him to avoid a surprise attack and protect the nation's security. In the foyer of the CIA's headquarters at Langley, Virginia, is inscribed a biblical quotation: "And ye shall know the truth and the truth shall make you free" (John 8:32). Loch Johnson suggests that Allen Dulles, former director of the CIA under Presidents Dwight Eisenhower and John F. Kennedy, probably thought it meant, "And ye shall know the truth—if ye be me, or the president."[14] Richard Helms, former DCI under Presidents Lyndon Johnson and Richard Nixon, once maintained to the *Washington Post*'s Bob Woodward that the early-warning function of the CIA "is everything, and underline everything."[15] But the CIA's mandate to provide such often unrequested (and sometimes unwelcome) information to a president constitutes a potential restraint on the president's freedom of action. It may, as in the case of the Bush administration and warnings about 9/11, threaten to totally derail his policies, particularly since such intelligence is very rarely certain or unambiguous. If anything, over the years, the powers of the director of the CIA to compel a president to read and attend to an unwanted intelligence estimate have been systematically diluted.

When information supposedly supplied to the president about a possible attack or any other matter under the CIA's purview is leaked to the public, both the agency and the intelligence in question tend to become politically radioactive. Such revelations have usually taken one of two forms. In the first instance, the president turns out to have been shielded from or refused to read or respond to accurate intelligence. In the second instance, the president secretly orders the suppression of the intelligence or has intelligence fabricated about a nonexistent danger to support his preferred policies. President Bush has engaged in both types of behavior, but he is certainly not the first president to do so.

In 1961, at the time of the Bay of Pigs invasion of Cuba, Richard Bissell, then head of the Directorate of Operations, gained the ear of President John F. Kennedy and assured him that elated Cubans would welcome American-supported insurgents, strew rose petals in their path, and help U.S.-based Cuban exiles overthrow the Castro government. Bissell simply did not show Kennedy estimates, also in his possession, that indicated the depth of Cuban leader Fidel Castro's popularity, suggesting that no popular uprising would occur and that the invasion would surely fail dismally.

Similarly, in May 1970, in the midst of the Vietnam War, as President Richard Nixon and Henry Kissinger plotted their "incursion" into Cambodia, the CIA's Board of National Estimates (BNE) concluded that "an American invasion of Cambodia would fail to deter North Vietnamese continuation of the war."[16] DCI Helms did not even bother to deliver this estimate to the White House, knowing what the BNE did not—that the decision to invade had already been made and was unstoppable. Robert M. Gates, former DCI under Presidents George H. W. Bush and Bill Clinton, puts it this way: "It has been my experience over the years that the usual response of a policymaker to intelligence with which he disagrees or which he finds unpalatable is to ignore it."[17]

Examples of the outright distortion or fabrication of intelligence are rarer, but they have occurred. During the Vietnam War, General William

Westmoreland, U.S. military commander from 1964 to 1968, omitted from his estimate of enemy forces all communist guerrillas and informal local defense forces—perhaps as many as 120,000–150,000 fighters—which another military estimate indicated had been responsible for up to 40 percent of American losses. His apparent intent was to make victory in Vietnam look more plausible. On March 14, 1967, DCI Helms included Westmoreland's figures in an NIE going to the White House even though he "knew that the figures on enemy troop strength in Vietnam provided by military intelligence were wrong—or, at any rate, quite different from CIA figures. Yet he signed the estimate without dissent. The apparent reason, according to his biographer, was that 'he did not want a fight with the military, supported by [National Security Adviser Walt] Rostow at the White House.'"[18]

Another example of the suppression or distortion of intelligence occurred in 1969–70 over the issue of whether or not the Soviet SS-9 ICBM (intercontinental ballistic missile) could carry three warheads and whether those warheads could be fired at separate and distinct targets—that is, whether or not the SS-9 carried MIRVs (multiple independently targetable reentry vehicles). If true, this would perhaps have given the Soviet Union a first-strike capability against the United States. The SS-9 came in four models, the first of which had its initial flight test on September 23, 1963, and began to be deployed in the summer of 1967. All Western intelligence agencies agreed that models one through three carried a single warhead, some with huge yields (in the range of eighteen megatons). Disagreement arose over model four, which seemed to carry three warheads that might—or might not—have been independently targetable.

National Security Adviser Henry Kissinger and Secretary of Defense Melvin Laird argued that the fourth version of the SS-9 was a MIRVed weapon; the CIA in its NIE on the subject claimed that it was not. At first the CIA rejected the pressure coming from the policy makers and, in fact, strengthened its evidence against MIRVs. Ultimately, however, DCI Helms removed the paragraph arguing against Soviet preparations for a first strike after "an assistant to [Secretary of Defense Laird] informed Helms that the statement contradicted the public position of the Secretary."[19] As it turned out, the CIA was right. The SS-9s were armed with MRVs (multiple reentry vehicles), not MIRVs—that is, they could produce only a cluster of explosions in a single area. The Soviet Union did not deploy MIRVs until 1976, six years after the United States had done so.[20] So it was we, not they, who accelerated the nuclear arms race—and we did so on the basis of fabricated intelligence.

When it comes to ignoring accurate CIA intelligence, the preeminent example in the Bush administration was National Security Adviser Condoleezza Rice's indifference to al-Qaeda—she also rejected warnings on the subject from officials of the departing Clinton administration—and her failure to ensure that the president read and understood the explicit warnings of an imminent surprise attack that the agency delivered to her. On August 6, 2001, in a blunt one-page analysis headlined, "Bin Laden Determined to Strike in U.S.," the CIA presented its President's Daily Brief to Bush at his Crawford, Texas, ranch. According to Steve Coll of the *Washington Post,* "The report included the possibility that bin Laden operatives would seek to hijack airplanes. The hijacking threat, mentioned twice, was one of several possibilities outlined. There was no specific information about when or where such an attack might occur."[21]

After the extent of its failure became known, and under extreme pressure from the public and families of the victims of 9/11, the Bush administration reluctantly authorized the creation of a National Commission on Terrorist Attacks upon the United States (also known as the 9/11 Commission) and permitted National Security Adviser Rice to testify before it in public. But the fix was in: the commission was constrained to concentrate on "intelligence failures" instead of the failure of policy makers to heed the intelligence that came their way, and on the need to "reform" the CIA—but not to such an extent as to damage the president's ability to blame it for his mistakes and use it in future operations of his choice.

After the 9/11 attacks and the Bush administration's decision to go to war with Iraq, the focus shifted from ignoring unwanted intelligence to actively creating false intelligence that would support its regime-change war of choice. The critical item in the administration's rush to war was the NIE of October 1, 2002, entitled "Iraq's Continuing Program for Weapons of Mass Destruction," which became known inside the agency as the "whore of Babylon."[22] It explicitly endorsed Vice President Cheney's contention of August 26, 2002—"We know that Saddam has resumed his efforts to acquire nuclear weapons"—and was signed by DCI George Tenet with "high confidence." "The intelligence process," wrote CIA veteran analyst Ray McGovern, "was not the only thing undermined. So was the Constitution. Various drafts of the NIE, reinforced with heavy doses of 'mushroom-cloud' rhetoric, were used to deceive congressmen and senators into ceding to the executive their prerogative to declare war—the all-important prerogative that the framers of the Constitution took great care to reserve exclusively to our elected representatives in Congress."

In succeeding months, numerous review commissions revealed that the October NIE was only one of numerous failures by the government's supposed truth tellers to do what the people of the United States pay them to do. The Senate Intelligence Committee, the 9/11 Commission, and the CIA's Iraq Survey Group, under Charles Duelfer, all reported that the CIA's intelligence on Iraqi WMD was largely fictitious. Even more dangerous for the White House, these reports suggested that much of this intelligence had been manufactured by neoconservative officials in the Pentagon long eager to invade Iraq.

In particular, the third-highest-ranking civilian defense official in the Pentagon, Douglas Feith, had set up the Office of Special Plans, devoted to going through all the raw intelligence available to the various spy agencies and ferreting out items that offered possible evidence of (or hints of evidence of) links between Saddam Hussein and Osama bin Laden.

It was this effort to get around both the CIA and the Defense Intelligence Agency, neither of whose analysts had found any links or ties between Iraq and the 9/11 attacks, that eventually led some officials to break ranks and charge publicly that the war against Iraq was in fact undercutting the "war on terrorism." The most prominent of these whistle-blowers were Richard A. Clarke, the White House's coordinator for counterterrorism in both the Clinton and Bush administrations, who published a tell-all book, *Against All Enemies,* and the CIA's Michael Scheuer, who, in his book *Imperial Hubris* and in a letter to the House and Senate Intelligence Committees entitled "How Not to Catch a Terrorist," charged: "In the CIA's core, U.S.-based Bin Laden operational unit today there are fewer Directorate of Operations officers with substantive expertise on al-Qaeda than there were on 11 September 2001."[23]

But there were others. In July 2003, after over twenty years of service, Lieutenant Colonel Karen Kwiatkowski resigned her air force commission and left the Pentagon's Near East and South Asia department to reveal how Feith's Iraq-war-planning unit had manufactured scare stories about Iraq's weapons and its ties to terrorists.[24] Former ambassador Joseph C. Wilson, with experience in several African countries and on the National Security Council, was asked by the CIA to go to the Saharan nation of Niger to investigate allegations that it had secretly sold uranium to Saddam Hussein's Iraq, charges that President Bush had endorsed with his famous "sixteen words" in his January 28, 2003, State of the Union address. When the Bush administration continued to retail intelligence on the subject of Niger "yellowcake" that it knew to be forged and false, Wilson went public with an op-ed in the *New York Times* in which, among other things, he wrote, "Based on my experience with the administration in the months leading up to the war, I have little choice but to conclude that some of the intelligence related to Iraq's nuclear weapons program was twisted to exaggerate the Iraqi threat."[25] In retaliation, top administration officials conspired to "out" his wife, an undercover CIA agent working on nuclear proliferation and weapons of mass destruction. This was clearly meant to be a warning to any other officials or former officials who might care to leak or come forward with information damaging to the administration.

Gary C. Schroen, CIA station chief in Islamabad, Pakistan, from 1996 to 1999, has provided secret details about the way the agency paid off Afghanistan's Northern Alliance warlords in the autumn of 2001 to reopen the civil war against the Taliban in Afghanistan and on the bungling of U.S. Special Forces in the subsequent campaign.[26] Melissa Boyle Mahle, a former CIA clandestine services officer fluent in Arabic, denounced former director George Tenet for his "total denial of failure" after September 11, 2001.[27] Although not an American whistle-blower, the late British foreign secretary Robin Cook also deserves mention as the only cabinet-rank statesman in any country to resign over the war in Iraq—he stepped down as leader of the House of Commons in 2003 to protest the invasion—and then to denounce official lies that were being told about the threat posed by Saddam Hussein. "Instead of using intelligence as evidence on which to base a decision about policy," he charged, "we used intelligence as the basis on which to justify a policy on which we had already settled."[28]

After George Tenet resigned as George Bush's DCI in July 2004 and went on the lecture circuit at $35,000 an appearance—he had earned well over a half million dollars by November 2004—Bush appointed Porter Goss to stanch the leaks at Langley.[29] The Senate confirmed him by a vote of 77 to 17 (six senators did not vote), suggesting the increasing worthlessness of Senate oversight of the executive branch. The new head of the CIA quickly got rid of as many messengers like Scheuer as he could identify. Goss had clearly been ordered to make it appear that the agency misled the president (rather than the other way around, as was actually the case). He was then supposed to shake up what he called a "dysfunctional" organization.

Before representing the Fourteenth District of Florida in the House for some sixteen years, Goss worked in the CIA's Directorate of Operations (DO). During that time he was stationed primarily in Latin America, and rumors persist that he left the agency under a cloud. In 1995, he was appointed to the House Intelligence Committee and, in 1997, the ex-agent became its chairman. There is no evidence that he ever did anything useful in this position, like investigating the intelligence lapses that preceded 9/11 or the failure of the CIA to place a single spy anywhere in Saddam Hussein's regime. During the 2004 election campaign he actually gave speeches attacking candidate John Kerry for "slashing intelligence funding" without mentioning that, in 1995, he himself had cosponsored a measure calling for the firing of 20 percent of all CIA personnel over five years.

Goss brought with him to the agency a group of Republican activist staff members from the House Intelligence Committee and set them up in prominent executive positions. They helped unleash a witch hunt against any and all intelligence officers who sought to put accuracy and integrity ahead of service to George W. Bush. Goss began his shake-up of the CIA by forcing out the director and deputy director of operations, even though this is not the primary place where the failures of the CIA in recent years have occurred. (This, in turn, led to speculation that it was a way to keep his own service record in the DO under wraps.) Shortly thereafter, Goss fired Jami A. Miscik, deputy director for intelligence, who had worked in the agency since 1983 and was a close associate of George Tenet. She had led the Directorate of Intelligence since May 2002, a period in which much of the false reporting on Iraq occurred. It might have seemed logical that Miscik would be held responsible for the politicized intelligence produced on her watch; but under the circumstances it seems clear that she was actually a scapegoat for President Bush and Vice President Cheney, who ordered up the false intelligence in the first place.[30] As Spencer

Ackerman of the *New Republic* has written, "If Goss thought the CIA was dysfunctional before, he has guaranteed that it is now."[31]

At the same time, President Bush ordered that the number of clandestine service officers within the agency be doubled, placing a much greater emphasis on covert operations.[32] The CIA remains the main executive-branch department in charge of overthrowing foreign governments, promoting regimes of state terrorism, kidnapping people of interest to the administration and sending them to friendly foreign countries to be tortured and/or killed, assassination and the torture of prisoners in violation of international and domestic law, and numerous other "wet" exercises that both the president and the country in which they are executed want to be able to deny.

CIA covert operations are distinguished from military assaults carried out by the Department of Defense (which is also rapidly expanding its covert operations) chiefly by the requirement that the president must be able plausibly to deny that he ordered them or that he even knew about them. Covert operations are therefore protected by the most rigorous secrecy. As Loch Johnson observes, this sort of secrecy also destroys the last shreds of agency accountability. "Under a system of plausible denial it often becomes uncertain who really does know about, and has approved of, any given covert action. The lines of accountability wash away like markings in the sand."[33]

From the creation of the CIA in 1947 down to the Hughes-Ryan Act of 1974 (formally entitled Section 602(a) of the Foreign Assistance Act of 1974), there were virtually no officials of government who actually supervised or gave approval for covert acts or knew in detail about them or what they were supposed to accomplish. "The foreign policy establishment in Washington trusted the CIA," Thomas Powers wrote in 1979, "and still trusts it, for that matter, but beyond governing circles the political foundation of the CIA rested on nothing more substantial than a popular fascination with espionage and a conviction that we are the good guys."[34] The Church Committee estimated that the National Security Council itself knew about and approved of no more than about 14 percent of all covert actions from 1961 to 1975.[35]

For example, when it came to investigating the CIA's several attempts to assassinate President Fidel Castro of Cuba (and a few other heads of state), the Church Committee had to throw in the towel. Numerous cabinet officials, including Secretary of Defense Robert McNamara, testified under oath that it was unthinkable that either Presidents Eisenhower or Kennedy had authorized such a mission. As Powers writes, "The committee was forced to confess in the end that while it had no evidence that the CIA had been a rogue elephant rampaging out of control, it also had no evidence that Eisenhower or Kennedy or anyone speaking in one of their names had ordered the CIA to kill Castro. The only indisputable fact was that the CIA did, in fact, try to do so."[36] Plausible denial, extreme secrecy, the power of the presidency, and a culture of loyalty to the agency rather than to the Constitution cause this kind of endemic confusion—exceedingly useful to those in power—about who is responsible for what the CIA does, a problem that still haunts the government today.

The 1974 Hughes-Ryan Act, named after its authors, Senator Harold E. Hughes (Democrat from Iowa) and Representative Leo J. Ryan (Democrat from California), for the first time tried to enforce the CIA's accountability to the elected representatives of the people. It states that "No funds . . . may be expended by or on behalf of the Central Intelligence Agency for operations in foreign countries . . . unless and until the President finds that each such operation is important to the national security of the United States." The verb "finds" is the origin of the odd term "finding," which is governmental argot for the document that the president now signs approving and setting into motion a covert operation. The law also stipulates that the president must give the appropriate committees of Congress "in a timely fashion" a description of each operation and its scope.

This law has not worked well. In the middle of the Reagan administration, members of Congress first read in the newspapers that, on orders of the president's national security adviser, Vice Admiral John M. Poindexter, CIA operatives were covertly and illegally selling arms to the revolutionary government of Iran and using the funds thus obtained to finance a congressionally forbidden insurgency against the elected government of Nicaragua. This disaster led to much stronger demands for intelligence oversight, but the president and his secret army found numerous ways to get around such pressures. For example, in lieu of a specific finding, "worldwide findings" have given the CIA blanket authority to conduct

certain types of unspecified covert operations—say, those against terrorists. Operations have also been "privatized" by getting foreign governments and U.S. corporations to pay for them, or kept totally hidden via
"off the books" personnel and funds. To illustrate what the CIA does best,
let us look briefly at its record in Chile, in Afghanistan, and in carrying out
so-called extraordinary renditions.

CIA activities in Chile, ranging from the early 1960s to 1990, occurred
in both the pre- and postaccountability eras. Before 1974, they were
intended to overthrow the oldest and most stable democracy in Latin
America, dating from the country's independence in 1818, and replace it
with "the vilest of Latin American dictators in recent history."[37] Having to
report to Congress had little effect on CIA operations in Chile. If findings
were ever signed and passed to Capitol Hill, we have no record of them.
What we do have is a vast archive of thousands of highly classified reports
and cables from the Oval Office, the CIA, the National Security Council, the State Department, the American embassy in Santiago, and the FBI
that the U.S. government was forced to declassify because of the blowback
that the operations themselves generated, including lawsuits by Chilean
torture victims and demands for the arrest and trial of former secretary of
state Henry Kissinger.[38]

Chile was certainly not the first instance in which the United States
government used its clandestine services to manipulate, undermine, or
overthrow a fellow democracy. It had done so in many other places,
including Italy in 1947–48, Iran in 1953, Guatemala in 1954, Indonesia in
1957–58, Brazil from 1961 to 1964, Greece from 1964 to 1974, South
Korea from 1961 to 1987, and the Philippines in every year since it gained
its independence from the United States in 1946. But Chile provides us
with the first written record of a U.S. president ordering the overthrow of
a democratically elected government—namely, the handwritten notes of
CIA director Richard Helms reflecting the orders given to him by President Richard Nixon in the White House on September 15, 1970.[39] Even
the heavily censored CIA documents released to the Church Committee
in 1975 led Senator Church to produce his own definition of "covert
action." It is a "semantic disguise for murder, coercion, blackmail, bribery,
the spreading of lies, and consorting with known torturers and international terrorists."[40]

From the moment the Kennedy administration came to power in 1961 until the overthrow and death of Chile's president Salvador Allende on September 11, 1973, the CIA spent some $12 million on a massive "black" propaganda campaign to support Allende's primary political opponent, Eduardo Frei, the candidate of the Christian Democratic Party, and to denigrate Allende as a stooge of the Soviet Union. In addition, the International Telephone and Telegraph Corporation (which owned the Chilean telephone system) and other American-owned businesses in Chile gave the CIA an extra $1.5 million to help discredit Allende. ITT properties in Chile, including two Sheraton Hotels, were worth at least $153 million. In July 1970, two months before Allende was elected president, John McCone, director of central intelligence from 1961 to 1965 and in 1970 a member of the board of directors of ITT, set up an appointment with then DCI Richard Helms. He offered money and cooperation from ITT "for the purpose of assisting any [U.S.] government plan . . . to stop Allende." ITT presented a plan "aimed at inducing economic collapse" in Chile.[41]

In the 1964 election, the CIA directly underwrote more than half of Frei's campaign expenses. It spent more than $2.6 million in support of the election of the Christian Democratic candidate. More sinister was the agency's disinformation campaign, which it later held up as a model of how to do it. The Church Committee reported, "Extensive use was made of the press, radio, films, pamphlets, posters, leaflets, direct mailings, paper streamers, and wall painting. It was a 'scare campaign,' which relied heavily on images of Soviet tanks and Cuban firing squads and was directed especially to women."[42] The CIA placed radio spots that featured the sound of a machine gun, followed by a woman's cry: "They have killed my child—the communists." One poster, printed in the thousands, showed children with a hammer and sickle stamped on their foreheads. Juanita Castro, Fidel's anticommunist sister, said on the radio, "If the Reds win in Chile, no type of religious activity will be possible. . . . Chilean mothers, I know you will not allow your children to be taken from you and sent to the Communist bloc, as in the case of Cuba."[43]

The CIA boasted that it produced and planted in various media around the world some 726 stories against an Allende presidency. Most of these appeared first in Latin American newspapers and were later reprinted in Chilean ones; some appeared in the CIA's own secret outlets, which included *Der Monat* in Germany, *Encounter* in Britain, the *Daily American* of Rome, and the *South Pacific Mail* of Santiago. Some seeped into the *New York Times* and the *Washington Post*, including the idea that Allende was a paid agent of the USSR.[44] In 1964, these "dirty tricks" produced the desired results. Frei received 56 percent of the vote to Allende's 39 percent, an unprecedented and almost statistically impossible outcome, given Chile's multiparty electoral system. The targeted scare tactics worked well. While Chilean men voted for Allende by a plurality of more than 67,000, women gave Frei 469,000 more votes than Allende.[45] As a reward and an insurance policy, the U.S. government promptly began to pay off Frei. Under the U.S.'s Alliance for Progress, a scheme to prevent the spread of leftist views in Latin America, "Chile received more American aid per capita than just about any other country in the world—Vietnam excepted."[46]

The next presidential election was scheduled for September 4, 1970. Even though the CIA kept up its blistering disinformation campaign, Chilean voters had become warier of the increasingly preposterous American propaganda and its "false flag" agents who tried to convince Chilean business and military elites that "an Allende victory means violence and Stalinist repression." As a matter of fact, there was no issue of potential Soviet influence in Chile. Allende was not a communist and, in any case, after he came to power in 1970 the Soviet Union wisely urged him to "put his relations with the United States in order."[47] In August 1970, Henry Kissinger had ordered a special national intelligence estimate to answer the question "What would happen in the event of an Allende victory?" It concluded: "An Allende election carried no military, strategic, or regional threat to U.S. interests in security and stability."[48]

In the September 4 election, Allende finally won a plurality, but not a majority, of the vote. However, he confidently expected that on October 24 the Chilean Congress would choose him to be president—normal parliamentary practice.

In an attempt to prevent this, the Nixon White House and the CIA sprang into action. On October 16, 1970, CIA headquarters dispatched a secret "eyes only" cable to Henry Hecksher, the CIA Santiago station chief. The actual sender, presumably DCI Helms, is blacked out in the text. "It is firm and continuous policy that Allende be overthrown by a coup. It would be much preferable to have this transpire prior to 24 October, but efforts in this regard will continue vigorously beyond this date. We are to continue to generate maximum pressure toward this end utilizing every appropriate resource. It is imperative that these actions be implemented clandestinely and securely so that the USG [United States government] and American hand be well hidden."[49]

For months, the CIA had been sounding out senior Chilean military officers on the issue of a coup, promising extensive help to any who agreed to participate. The agency's operatives soon discovered that the main obstacle was the commander in chief of the army, General René Schneider, who represented what the CIA called "the apolitical, constitution-oriented inertia of the Chilean military."[50] Therefore, the CIA set out to find and arm dissident Chilean forces who would assassinate him. One group it approached asked for submachine guns, ammunition, and $50,000 to do the job, and the agency obliged, shipping the weapons from Washington to Santiago in the regular diplomatic pouch.[51] Local CIA agents then delivered them to the plotters at 2 a.m. on October 22, 1970; at 8 a.m. the assassins surrounded General Schneider's chauffeur-driven car, knocked out the rear window, and fatally wounded him. He died in a hospital three days later.

The CIA went to great lengths to cover its tracks, including paying hush money to the conspirators and driving to a general's home to retrieve the guns they had given him. Colonel Paul Wimert, the military attaché in the U.S. embassy in Santiago, had to pistol-whip the general to force him to comply.[52] The agency then dumped the machine guns in the ocean to ensure that they could not be traced back to the U.S. government.

But Washington and the CIA had overplayed their hands. "Far from fostering a coup climate," Peter Kornbluh, the chief Chilean specialist at the National Security Archive in Washington, D.C., writes, "the Schneider shooting produced an overwhelming public and political repudiation of violence and a clear reaffirmation of Chile's civil, constitutional tradition."[53] The Chilean Congress voted 153 to 57 to ratify Allende as president, with all seventy-four senators and congressmen from the Christian Democratic Party voting with Allende's own party. This result did not, however, even begin to slow down Washington's venomous campaign. For the next three years, the Nixon administration tried in every way to undermine Allende by producing economic chaos in Chile, and the CIA worked tirelessly to find a suitable general to put in power. They finally identified a likely candidate in the summer of 1971—the cruel, ruthless, and corrupt General Augusto Pinochet.

The Chilean military under Pinochet finally moved against Allende on "the other 9/11"—September 11, 1973. During the attack on La Moneda, the presidential palace, Pinochet's forces offered Allende an airplane to fly him and his family into exile. (Pinochet was taped giving radio instructions to his troops, in which he says, "That plane will never land."[54]) Allende apparently took his own life rather than agreeing to any offer or allowing himself to be captured. He was found dead of gunshot wounds in his office around 2 p.m. on September 11.

Thus began Pinochet's seventeen-year dictatorship and reign of terror—sponsored and paid for by the U.S. government. During this period, the Chilean military was responsible for the murder, disappearance, or death by torture of some 3,197 citizens, according to the postdictatorship *Report of the Chilean National Commission on Truth and Reconciliation*, released in 1991. In November 2004, the National Commission on Political Imprisonment and Torture, chaired by Monsignor Sergio Valech, published a twelve-hundred-page report that documented more than 27,000 confirmed cases of political imprisonment and "the most grotesque forms of torture."[55]

Pinochet's major instrument of oppression was the army's Directorate of National Intelligence (DINA), headed by Colonel Manuel Contreras. In addition to carrying out fierce repression within Chile, Contreras was the creator of Operation Condor, which a top-secret CIA report describes laconically as "a cooperative effort by the intelligence/security services of several South American countries to combat terrorism and subversion."[56] It was, in fact, a conspiracy among the intelligence services of Chile, Argentina, Paraguay, Uruguay, and Bolivia, subsequently joined by Brazil, and backed by the Nixon administration, to hunt down and assassinate leftists within these countries and, in particular, those living abroad in exile. Kornbluh describes Condor as "the most sinister state-sponsored terrorist network in the Western hemisphere, if not in the world."[57] John Dinges, a Columbia University professor and author of *The Condor Years*, estimates that Condor agents killed at least 13,000 people in the six participating countries.[58]

Among its trademark atrocities were the car-bomb killings of the exiled general Carlos Prats and his wife—Prats had been General Schneider's successor—in Buenos Aires on September 30, 1974, and of Orlando Letelier, Allende's ambassador to Washington and later foreign minister, and his twenty-six-year-old American colleague, Ronni Karpen Moffitt, on a street in Washington, D.C., on September 21, 1976. Both assassinations were carried out by the most famous member of DINA's foreign branch, Michael Vernon Townley, an American born in Waterloo, Iowa. The killing of Letelier and an American citizen in the nation's capital was one of the most flagrant acts of international terrorism carried out in the United States prior to September 11, 2001. It set off a furious FBI investigation that ultimately led Chile to turn over Townley, who confessed to his role in the crime. During this period, the CIA was notoriously passive, lacking all signs of interest in the Letelier case—even though on August 25, 1975, the agency had hosted a luncheon for Colonel Contreras in Washington and that same year put him on its payroll, making a personal payment to him of $5,000.[59] The CIA has, to date, never been directly connected to the Letelier murder, but many of the most critical documents about the case remain secret and many questions remain about the full scope of the agency's role in Chilean politics.

In reaction to the Letelier case, the Carter administration imposed sanctions on Chile, but these were quickly lifted when Ronald Reagan came to power. Pinochet's regime was a particular favorite of both Reagan and British prime minister Margaret Thatcher. The end of the military dictatorship came only when the passive resistance of the people of Chile forced Pinochet to hold a plebiscite. On October 5, 1988, with 98 percent of eligible Chileans turning out, 54.7 percent voted to end the dictatorship. Pinochet left office and electoral politics were hesitantly restored, but the military thoroughly protected itself through various amnesty laws and other measures.

Pinochet was ultimately discredited by two events. On October 16, 1998, while he was visiting London for medical treatments, a British judge signed a warrant for his arrest after a Spanish judge sought his extradition to face trial for the torture of Spanish citizens in Chile. Held under house arrest near London for 503 days, he was finally returned to Chile, where the international controversy over the arrest of a former head of state for human rights violations made it increasingly impossible for the Chilean courts to continue to honor the immunity he had essentially granted himself.[60] Public opinion in Chile finally turned decisively against him when a

U.S. Senate committee, investigating money laundering by the Riggs Bank of Washington, D.C., revealed that between 1974 and 1997 various countries around the world had paid Pinochet some $12.3 million. In 1976, the U.S. government alone contributed some $3 million. Pinochet and his wife had siphoned off between $4 million and $8 million of these funds and hired the Riggs Bank to hide the money for them in secret, frequently moved accounts. On December 24, 2004, a Chilean special investigation into Pinochet's wealth determined that between 1985 and 2002, he had actually hidden $16 million—twice the previously reported amount—at Riggs. The revelation that, with so much money stashed away, he was still receiving a monthly pension of $2,000 utterly destroyed his claim that he had done everything "for the good of Chile."[61]

As in Chile, so in Afghanistan, the CIA record was filled with payoffs, murders, corrupt public officials in Washington, and support for local villains. The Afghan operation, according to several CIA partisans, was "the biggest, meanest, and far and away most successful CIA campaign in history."[62] That was the short-term view. As a matter of fact, the CIA's covert operations in Afghanistan from 1979 to the victory of the Taliban in 1996 produced the worst instance of blowback among all of America's secret wars—namely, al-Qaeda's attack on New York and Washington on September 11, 2001. Neither the United States nor the world can stand many more "victories" of that sort.

The Carter administration deliberately provoked the Soviet invasion of Afghanistan, which occurred on Christmas Eve 1979. In his 1996 memoir, former CIA director Robert Gates acknowledges that the American intelligence services began to aid the anti-Soviet mujahideen guerrillas not after the Russian invasion but six months before it.[63] On July 3, 1979, President Carter signed a finding authorizing secret aid to the opponents of the pro-Soviet regime then ruling in Kabul. His purpose—and that of his national security adviser, Zbigniew Brzezinski—was to provoke a full-scale Soviet military intervention. Carter wanted to tie down the USSR and so prevent its leaders from exploiting the 1979 anti-American revolution in Iran. In addition, as Brzezinski put it, "We now have the opportunity of giving to the USSR its Vietnam War."[64]

Before it was over, the CIA and the USSR between them turned Afghanistan, which had been a functioning state with a healthy middle class, into a warring collection of tribes, Islamic sects, and heroin-producing warlords. In human terms, the effort cost 1.8 million Afghan casualties and sent 2.6 million fleeing as refugees, while ten million unexploded land mines were left strewn around the country. It also took the lives of about 15,000 Soviet soldiers and contributed to the dissolution of the USSR.

The destruction of Afghanistan actually began in 1973. In that year, General Sardar Mohammed Daoud, the cousin and brother-in-law of King Zahir Shah, overthrew the king, declared Afghanistan a republic, and instituted a program of modernization. Zahir Shah went into exile in Rome. These developments made possible the rise of the People's Democratic Party of Afghanistan, a pro-Soviet communist party, which, in early 1978, with extensive help from the USSR, overthrew then president Daoud.

The communists' policies of secularization in turn provoked a violent response from devout Islamists. The anticommunist revolt that began in western Afghanistan in March 1979 was initially a response to a government initiative to teach girls to read, something that devout Sunnis opposed. A triumvirate of anticommunist nations—the United States, Pakistan, and Saudi Arabia—came to the aid of the rebels. Each had diverse, even contradictory motives for doing so, but the United States did not take these differences seriously until it was too late. By the time the Americans woke up, at the end of the 1990s, the radical Islamist Taliban had established a fundamentalist government of the most extreme sort in Kabul. Recognized only by Pakistan, Saudi Arabia, and the United Arab Emirates, it granted Osama bin Laden freedom of action and offered him protection from American efforts to capture or kill him.

During the 1980s, the Cold War shaped the perspectives of the Reagan White House and of the CIA. Both wanted to see as many Soviet soldiers as possible killed, the "Evil Empire" drained, and an aura of rugged machismo as well as credibility restored to the United States that they feared had been lost when the Shah of Iran was overthrown. As it turned out, other than pinning down Soviet troops beyond the borders of the USSR, the CIA had no coherent strategy for its Afghan war and seemed almost entirely innocent of the history, culture, religion, and aspirations of the country or its own allies. Howard Hart, the CIA representative in the Pakistani capital, said that the agency told him, in effect, "You're a young man; here's your bag of money, go raise hell. Don't fuck it up, just go out there and kill Soviets."[65]

Hart's marching orders came from a most peculiar American, one of the few CIA directors who was genuinely close to his president. Educated by Jesuits, William Casey, Reagan's DCI from January 1981 to January 1987, was a Catholic Knight of Malta. The *Washington Post*'s Steve Coll in his book *Ghost Wars* describes Casey's religiosity this way: "Statues of the Virgin Mary filled his mansion, 'Maryknoll,' on Long Island. He attended mass daily and urged Christianity on anyone who asked his advice. Once settled at the CIA, he began to funnel covert action funds through the Catholic Church to anticommunists in Poland and Central America, sometimes in violation of American law. He believed fervently that by increasing the Catholic Church's reach and power he could contain communism's advance, or reverse it."[66] From Casey's convictions grew the most important U.S. foreign policies of the 1980s—support for a clandestine anti-Soviet crusade in Afghanistan and sponsorship of an Operation Condor–like campaign of state terrorism in Nicaragua, El Salvador, and Guatemala.

Casey knew next to nothing about Islam or the grievances of Middle Eastern nations against Western imperialism. He saw political Islam and the Catholic Church as natural allies in covert actions against Soviet imperialism. He believed that the USSR was trying to strike at the United States in Central America and in the oil-producing states of the Middle East. He supported Islam as an answer to the Soviet Union's atheism and he sometimes even confused lay Catholic organizations such as the right-wing Opus Dei with the Muslim Brotherhood, the Egyptian extremist organization in which Ayman al-Zawahiri, Osama bin Laden's chief lieutenant, became a passionate member. The Muslim Brotherhood's branch in Pakistan, the Jamaat-e-Islami, was strongly backed by the Pakistani army, and Casey, more than any other American, was responsible for creating an alliance of the CIA, Saudi intelligence, and the intelligence forces of General Mohammed Zia-ul-Haq, Pakistan's military dictator from 1977 to 1988. On the suggestion of the Pakistani Inter-Services Intelligence (ISI) organization, Casey went so far as to print thousands of copies of the Koran, which he shipped to the Afghan frontier for distribution in Afghanistan and Soviet Uzbekistan. Without presidential authority, he also fomented Muslim attacks inside the USSR and always maintained that the CIA's clandestine officers were too timid. He preferred the type represented by his friend Oliver North, the marine lieutenant colonel at the heart of the Iran-Contra scandal, who, as a top Reagan administration official, organized the clandestine selling of weapons to Iran (for use against Iraq) in order to generate funds for the Nicaraguan Contra rebel group in violation of U.S. law.[67]

Over time, Casey's position hardened into CIA dogma that its agents, protected by secrecy from ever having their ignorance exposed, enforced in every way they could. The agency resolutely refused to help choose winners and losers among the Afghan jihad's guerrilla leaders. The result was that, as Coll puts it, "Zia-ul-Haq's political and religious agenda in Afghanistan gradually became the CIA's own."[68] In the era after Casey, some scholars, journalists, and members of Congress questioned the agency's lavish support of the murderous Pakistan-backed Islamist Afghan general Gulbuddin Hekmatyar, especially after he refused to shake hands with Ronald Reagan because he was an "infidel." But Milton Bearden, the Islamabad station chief from 1986 to 1989, and Frank Anderson, chief of the Afghan task force at Langley, vehemently defended Hekmatyar on the grounds that "he fielded the most effective anti-Soviet fighters."[69]

Perhaps the most remarkable aspect of the CIA's operations in Afghanistan was the roles played in them by two wholly out-of-control Americans, one a member of the Appropriations Committee of Congress and the other an exceptionally ruthless CIA clandestine services officer who, once he had teamed up with the congressman, operated more or less independent of any agency supervision. Nothing more readily illustrates the dangers of secrecy in the United States government than the ways an ignoramus of a congressman and a high-ranking CIA thug managed to hijack American foreign policy. Under the covert guidance of Representative Charlie Wilson and CIA operative Gust Avrakotos, the agency flooded Afghanistan with an incredible array of extremely dangerous weapons and "unapologetically mov[ed] to equip and train cadres of high tech holy warriors in the art of waging a war of urban terror against a modern superpower"—initially, the USSR.[70]

From 1973 to 1996, Charlie Wilson represented the Second District of Texas in the House of Representatives. He had graduated from the Naval Academy in 1956, eighth from the bottom of his class and with more demerits than any other cadet in Annapolis's history. After serving in the Texas state legislature, he arrived in Washington in 1973 and quickly became known as "Good Time Charlie, the biggest playboy in Congress."

He hired only good-looking women for his staff because, as he told visitors in his booming voice, "You can teach 'em to type but you can't teach 'em to grow tits," and was known for escorting "a parade of beauty queens . . . to White House parties."[71] His biographer describes him as "a seemingly corrupt, cocaine snorting, scandal prone womanizer who the CIA was convinced could only get the agency into terrible trouble if it permitted him to become involved in any way in its operations."[72] Nonetheless, he managed to do so thanks to lax congressional oversight and corruption.

Wilson's partner in influencing CIA policy toward Afghanistan was Gust Avrakotos, the son of working-class Greek immigrants from the steel workers' town of Aliquippa, Pennsylvania. Only in 1960 had the CIA begun to recruit officers for the Directorate of Operations from among what it called "new Americans," meaning ethnics, such as Chinese-, Japanese-, Hispanic-, and Greek-Americans. Up until then, it had followed the British model, taking only Ivy League sons of the Eastern establishment. Avrakotos joined the CIA in 1961 and came to nurture a hatred for the blue bloods, or "cake eaters," as he called them, who looked down on him. After spook school at Camp Peary, next door to Jamestown, Virginia, he was posted to Athens because he was fluent in Greek, and he remained there right through the CIA-sponsored reign of terror of the Greek colonels. He left the country in 1978 but could not get another decent assignment—he tried for Helsinki—because the head of the European Division regarded him as too uncouth to send to any European capital. He sat around Langley for a long period without any work until he was recruited by John McGaffin, head of the Afghan program. "If it's really true that you have nothing to do," McGaffin said, "why not come upstairs? We're killing Russians."[73]

If Charlie Wilson was the moneybags and spark plug of this pair, Avrakotos was the street fighter who relished arming the tribesmen in Afghanistan with Kalashnikovs and Stinger surface-to-air shoulder-fired missiles. In 1976, Wilson became a member of the House Appropriations Committee at a time when its chairman used to have a sign mounted over his desk: "Them that has the gold make the rules." Wilson acted on this principle and advanced rapidly on this most powerful of all congressional committees. He was first appointed to the Foreign Operations Subcommittee, which doles out foreign aid. He then did a big favor for Speaker

Tip O'Neill and, in return, O'Neill assigned Wilson to the Defense Appropriations Subcommittee.

Wilson soon discovered that all of the CIA's budget and 40 percent of the Pentagon's budget is "black"—that is, totally hidden from the public and all but a privileged few congressmen. As a member of the Defense Appropriations Subcommittee, he could add virtually any amount of money to whatever black project he supported. In short, he had stumbled upon the world of "earmarks," a euphemism that refers to the power of members of Congress to insert into appropriations bills funds for special projects that the executive branch has not asked for and that are often not in the nation's best interest.

The practice of earmarking continues in widespread use at the present time. In 1998, the 2,000 earmarks slipped into all thirteen appropriations bills had an overall value of $10.6 billion. By 2004, the numbers had grown to 15,584 earmarks worth $32.7 billion. In a 2005 interview, Wilson, by then a lobbyist for Pakistan, said, "We would never have won the [anti-Soviet Afghan] war if it hadn't been for earmarking because the [CIA] would have never spent the money the way we wanted it to."[74] So long as Wilson did favors for other members on the subcommittee by supporting defense projects in their districts, they never objected to his private obsessions. In 1986, Wilson was finally able to join the House's Intelligence Committee, which only added to his ability to earmark, doubling and tripling the secret funds he could direct to Afghan operations.

Like several influential Americans with right-wing political orientations, Wilson came under the influence of the charismatic head of Pakistan's army, General Mohammed Zia-ul-Haq. In July 1977, Zia had seized power, declared martial law, and in 1979 hanged the president who had promoted him, Zulfikar Ali Bhutto. In retaliation, President Jimmy Carter cut off all U.S. aid to Pakistan. However, in 1980, Congressman Wilson visited Pakistan at the urging of a conservative lady friend from Houston and came under the spell of the general. He also learned for the first time about the heroic anticommunist mujahideen who were fighting against the Soviet Union across the border in Afghanistan, and became a convert to their cause. Using earmarked funds, he restored Zia's aid money and added several million dollars to the CIA's efforts to arm the Afghan guerrillas, each dollar of which the Saudi government secretly matched. Pakistan provided the fighters with sanctuary, training, arms, and even sent its own officers into Afghanistan as advisers on military operations. Saudi Arabia served as the fighters' banker, providing hundreds of millions with no strings attached. Several governments, including Egypt, China, and Israel, secretly supplied arms.

However, Pakistan's motives in Afghanistan were very different from those of the United States. Zia was a devout Muslim and a passionate supporter of Islamist groups in his own country, Afghanistan, and throughout the world, but he was not a fanatic and had some quite practical reasons for supporting Afghanistan's jihadists.

Zia feared above all that Pakistan would be squeezed between a Soviet-dominated Afghanistan and a hostile India. He also had to guard against an independence movement among the Pashtuns, the largest tribal group in Afghanistan and one of the largest in Pakistan, that, if successful, might cause the breakup of Pakistan. In other words, while he backed the Islamic militants in Afghanistan and Pakistan on religious grounds, he was quite prepared to use them strategically. From the beginning, Zia demanded that all weapons and aid for the Afghans from whatever source first pass through the hands of Pakistan's military intelligence, the ISI. The CIA was delighted to agree. In doing so, the agency helped lay the foundation not just for the decimation of Afghanistan and the rise of the Taliban but for Pakistan's anti-Indian insurgency in Kashmir in the 1990s.

Congressman Wilson's greatest preoccupation in cooperating with Zia was to supply the Afghans with weaponry that would be effective against the Soviets' most feared weapon—the Mi-24 Hind helicopter gunship. The Red Army used it to slaughter innumerable mujahideen as well as—in Vietnam War fashion—to shoot up Afghan villages. Wilson actually favored giving the Afghans the Oerlikon antiaircraft gun made in Switzerland. (It was later charged that he was on the take from the Zurich-based manufacturer of the weapon.)[75] His CIA sidekick Avrakotos considered it too heavy for guerrillas to move easily but could not openly stand in Wilson's way. After months of controversy, the Joint Chiefs of Staff finally dropped their objections to supplying the Afghans with the far lighter American-made Stinger shoulder-fired missile, which had never before been used in combat. It proved to be murderous against the relatively slow-moving Hinds, and Soviet premier Mikhail Gorbachev decided to cut his losses by getting out altogether. In Wilson's post-Soviet-withdrawal tour of Afghanistan, mujahideen fighters triumphantly fired their Stingers just for his benefit. They also presented him with a souvenir—part of the launcher of the first Stinger to bring down a Hind gunship—which he still proudly displays today in his Washington office.

Zia died in a mysterious plane crash on August 17, 1988, four months after a set of Geneva Accords ratified the formal terms of Soviet withdrawal from Afghanistan. As the Soviet troops departed, the warlord Hekmatyar embarked on a clandestine plan to eliminate his rivals and establish his Islamic party, dominated by the Muslim Brotherhood, as the most powerful national force in Afghanistan.

Meanwhile, with the fall of the Berlin Wall in 1989, followed by the implosion of the USSR in 1991, the United States lost virtually all interest in Afghanistan. The pro-Soviet government in Kabul did not fall immediately. Hekmatyar was never ultimately as good as the CIA imagined him to be. His only real accomplishment was to plunge the country into a murderous civil war. In 1994, both Pakistan and Saudi Arabia transferred their secret support to the newly created Taliban, who proved to be the most militarily effective of the warring groups. On September 26, 1996, the Taliban conquered Kabul, now practically a city of rubble. The next day they killed the formerly Soviet-backed President Najibullah, expelled eight thousand female undergraduate students from Kabul University, and fired a similar number of women schoolteachers. As the Taliban closed in on his palace, Najibullah told reporters: "If fundamentalism comes to Afghanistan, war will continue for many years. Afghanistan will turn into a center of world smuggling for narcotic drugs. Afghanistan will be turned into a center for terrorism."[76] His predictions would prove all too accurate.

Saudi Arabian motives differed from those of both the United States and Pakistan. Saudi Arabia is, after all, the only modern nation-state created by jihad. The Saudi royal family, which came to power at the head of a movement of Wahhabi religious extremists, espoused Islamic radicalism elsewhere as a way to keep it under control in their kingdom. "Middle-class, pious Saudis flush with oil wealth," Steve Coll writes, "embraced the Afghan cause as American churchgoers might respond to an African famine or a Turkish earthquake. . . . The money flowing from the kingdom arrived at the Afghan frontier in all shapes and sizes: gold jewelry dropped on offering plates by merchants' wives in Jedda mosques; bags of cash delivered by businessmen to Riyadh charities as *zakat,* an annual

Islamic tithe; fat checks written from semi-official government accounts by minor Saudi princes; bountiful proceeds raised in annual telethons led by Prince Salman, the governor of Riyadh; and richest of all were the annual transfers from the Saudi General Intelligence Department, or Istakhbarat, to the CIA's Swiss bank accounts."[77]

From the moment agency money and weapons started to flow to the mujahideen in 1980, Saudi Arabia matched U.S. payments dollar for dollar. The Saudis also bypassed Pakistan's ISI and supplied funds directly to groups in Afghanistan they favored, particularly the one led by their own pious young millionaire Osama bin Laden. According to the CIA's Milton Bearden, private Saudi and Arab funding of up to $25 million a month flowed to Afghan Islamist armies. Equally important, starting in 1986, Pakistan trained between 16,000 and 18,000 fresh Muslim recruits on the Afghan frontier every year, and another 6,500 or so were instructed by Afghans inside the country beyond ISI control. Most of these eventually joined bin Laden's fundamentalist army of 35,000 "Arab Afghans."[78]

Even after the Soviet Union withdrew from Afghanistan in 1988, the CIA continued to follow Pakistani initiatives, such as aiding Hekmatyar's successor, the one-eyed Mullah Omar, leader of the Taliban, and watched Afghanistan descend into one of the more horrific civil wars of the twentieth century. The CIA did not fully awaken to its naive and ill-informed reading of Afghan politics (which was a typical Cold War superpower's blindness to the distinctiveness of contested local areas) until after bin Laden bombed the U.S. embassies in Nairobi and Dar es Salaam on August 7, 1998. Even then, the agency defined the Islamist threat almost exclusively in terms of Osama bin Laden's leadership of al-Qaeda and failed to take in the larger context, including the policies of Pakistani military intelligence, or the funds flowing to the Taliban and al-Qaeda from Saudi Arabia and the United Arab Emirates. Instead, it devoted itself solely to trying to capture or kill bin Laden himself.

On February 23, 1998, bin Laden had summoned newspaper and TV reporters to the camp at Khost, in the eastern part of Afghanistan, that the CIA had built for him at the height of the anti-Soviet jihad. There he announced the creation of a new organization—the International Islamic Front for Jihad Against Jews and Crusaders—and issued a manifesto saying that "to kill and fight Americans and their allies, whether civilian or military, is an obligation for every Muslim who is able to do so in any country." Just over five months later, he and his associates put this manifesto into effect with their devastating embassy truck bombings in Africa.

By then the CIA had identified bin Laden's family compound in the open desert near Kandahar Airport, a collection of buildings called Tarnak Farm. It is possible that more satellite footage has been taken of this site than of any other place on Earth; one famous picture seems to show bin Laden standing outside the home of one of his wives. The CIA conceived an elaborate plot to kidnap bin Laden from Tarnak Farm with the help of Afghan operatives and spirit him out of the country, but CIA director George Tenet canceled the project because of the high risk of civilian casualties (for which the operations wing of the agency would later scorn him). Meanwhile, the Clinton White House ordered submarines to be stationed in the northern Arabian Sea with the map coordinates of Tarnak Farm preloaded into their missile-guidance systems. They were waiting for hard evidence from the CIA that bin Laden was in residence.[79]

Within days of the East Africa bombings, President Clinton signed a top secret finding authorizing the CIA to use lethal force against bin Laden. On August 20, 1998, he ordered seventy-five cruise missiles, costing $750,000 each, to be fired at the Zawhar Kili camp (about seven miles south of Khost), reportedly the site of a major al-Qaeda meeting. The attack killed twenty-one Pakistanis but bin Laden had been forewarned, perhaps by Saudi intelligence. Two of the missiles fell into Pakistan, causing Islamabad to denounce the U.S. action. At the same time, the United States fired thirteen cruise missiles into a chemical plant in Khartoum that the CIA claimed was partly owned by bin Laden and secretly manufacturing nerve gas. (It was actually a pharmaceutical factory.)

The American public and many critics around the world were skeptical about both the claims and the motivation for the attacks because three days earlier Clinton had publicly confessed to his sexual liaison with Monica Lewinsky. The film *Wag the Dog* had also just been released. In it a president in the middle of an election campaign is charged with molesting a "Girl Guide" and manufactures a fake war against an Eastern European country in order to distract public attention. As a result, Clinton became more cautious, while he and his aides began to question the quality of the CIA's intelligence they were being offered. The May 1999 bombing of the Chinese embassy in Belgrade by an American B-2 stealth bomber, thanks to faulty intelligence, further discredited the agency during Clinton's air assault against Serbia. (A year later, DCI Tenet would fire an intelligence officer and reprimand six managers, including a senior official, for their bungling of that incident.)[80] The Clinton administration made two more unsuccessful attempts to capture or kill bin Laden. He was, of course, still around as the second Bush administration began, and he ordered the infamous strikes against the United States itself. He then survived the American invasion of Afghanistan to fight another day (and release endless videotaped analyses and exhortations to his followers for years to come).

In the end, the CIA's covert operations in Afghanistan were detrimental to any American foreign policy goals. They usually became entangled in hopeless webs of secrecy and ignorance, invariably laying the foundations for devastating future blowback operations. Former presidential terrorism adviser Richard Clarke argues that "the CIA used its classification rules not only to protect its agents but also to deflect outside scrutiny of its covert operations," and Peter Tomsen, the American liaison with the Afghan anti-Soviet resistance during the late 1980s, concluded that "America's failed policies in Afghanistan flowed in part from the compartmented, top secret isolation in which the CIA always sought to work."[81]

A more recent example of CIA folly overlaid by baroque attempts at secrecy, all on orders from the president, is the carrying out of extraordinary renditions—a bit of official jargon intended to hide one of the more morally depraved practices of the executive branch of the U.S. government. "Extraordinary renditions" simply mean the CIA kidnappings of terror suspects off the streets of foreign cities, flying them either to countries with no record of human rights protections or else to secret CIA prisons outside the U.S., and there having them tortured. The practice seems today to have become an integral part of the imperial presidency, protected by the argument developed by administration lawyers that in time of war (even when that war has been unilaterally declared by the president and deemed a generational struggle) the president as commander in chief is essentially beyond the law.

Secret police and state terrorist agencies normally try to disguise what they are doing by hiding behind bland euphemisms for their most odious operations. As long ago as the eighteenth century, Voltaire observed, "Those who can make you believe absurdities can make you commit atrocities." On sanitizing language, the Stanford University psychologist Albert Bandura writes, "By camouflaging pernicious activities in innocent or sanitizing parlance, the activities lose much of their repugnancy. Bombing missions are described as 'servicing the target,' in the likeness of a public utility. The attacks become 'clean, surgical strikes,' arousing imagery of curative activities. The civilians whom the bomb kills are linguistically converted to 'collateral damage.' . . . In the vocabulary of the lawbreakers in Nixon's administration, criminal conspiracy became a 'game plan,' and the conspirators were 'team players,' like the best of sportsmen."[82]

Typifying this deliberate whitewashing, the Nazi Party's SS had its "transportations," meaning the shipping of trainloads of prisoners to death camps; the British had their "civilizing mission" in Kenya, meaning the rounding up of members of the indigenous population and sodomizing, castrating, and killing thousands of them; the Japanese had their "comfort women," meaning girls and women they kidnapped in occupied countries and forced at gunpoint to work as frontline prostitutes; and the CIA has its "renditions." This is an unusual locution. In most dictionaries, a "rendition" is a performance or an interpretation of a piece of music or a role in a play, as in: "That was a nice rendition of Duke Ellington's 'Jubilee Stomp.'" But the CIA uses it as a transitive verb—to render (as in "render unto Caesar the things that are Caesar's"), to hand over, to surrender.

There is no evidence that such illegal kidnappings have ever contributed anything to the security of the United States, but according to retired FBI agent Dan Coleman, who blew the whistle on the CIA's torturing of prisoners at Guantánamo Bay, "The CIA liked rendition from the start. They loved that these guys would just disappear off the books, and never be heard of again. They were proud of it."[83] The CIA added the term "extraordinary" to indicate that this was not just the capture of a fugitive abroad and the rendering of him or her to U.S. authorities to stand trial but that the target would disappear into the netherworld of some foreign prison, probably an idea learned from colleagues in Chile and Argentina when these countries were military dictatorships and from its work with Central American death squads during the Reagan administration.[84]

As far as is publicly known, the first CIA rendition was a sting operation carried out jointly with the FBI in September 1987. Code-named "Operation Goldenrod," it occurred in the wake of a series of airplane hijackings between 1984 and 1986. Congress had passed laws making air piracy and attacks on Americans abroad federal crimes, and in 1986 President Reagan signed a finding authorizing the CIA to kidnap foreigners wanted for terrorism and return them for trial in the United States. On June 11, 1985, Fawaz Yunis and four other heavily armed Lebanese took control of Royal Jordanian Airlines Flight 402 in Beirut. They ordered it flown out over the Mediterranean as far as Tunis, beat the Jordanian sky marshals on board, and returned to Beirut where they released the hostages, blew up the plane, and escaped. American hostages had been on board but were not harmed. Two years later, the CIA and FBI lured Yunis to a yacht in international waters off Cyprus with the promise that he would be part of a big drug-smuggling deal. Instead, he was taken into U.S. custody and transported to Washington. On March 14, 1989, he was convicted in federal court of aircraft piracy, hostage-taking, and conspiracy. On March 28, 2005, after sixteen years in an American prison, he was released and deported to Lebanon. There have been various legal challenges to the precedent set by this case, but it is generally regarded as a well-conducted law-enforcement operation.[85]

The Clinton-Bush version of extraordinary rendition is far more sinister. Michael Scheuer, the former CIA official who criticized the agency and the Bush administration for their alleged timidity in pursuing terrorists, takes credit for creating the program. In an interview with the *New Yorker*'s Jane Mayer, he claimed: "In 1995, American agents proposed the rendition program to Egypt, making clear that [the CIA] had the resources to track, capture, and transport terrorist suspects globally— including access to a small fleet of aircraft."[86] At the time, Scheuer was in charge of the Bin Laden Unit in the CIA's Counterterrorism Center and was extremely frustrated by his inability to move against al-Qaeda operatives whom the agency had identified and located.

On the basis of the new agreement with Egypt, between 1995 and 1998 the CIA carried out a series of renditions aimed particularly at Islamic freedom fighters working in the Balkans, many of them originally from Egypt. Virtually all the people the CIA kidnapped in these operations were killed after being delivered into Egyptian hands. Predictably enough, these kidnappings generated blowback, although ordinary Americans did not perceive it as such because the actions that provoked the retaliation were, of course, kept totally secret. On August 5, 1998, the International Islamic Front for Jihad, in a letter to an Arab-language newspaper in London, promised a reprisal for recent U.S. renditions from Albania. Two days later, al-Qaeda blew up the U.S. embassies in Kenya and

Tanzania with a loss of 224 lives.[87] The U.S. renditions continued with the CIA and FBI carrying out some two dozen of them in 1999 and 2000.[88] These, in turn, helped provoke the attacks on the navy destroyer USS *Cole* in the Yemeni port of Aden on October 12, 2000. Former CIA director George Tenet testified before the 9/11 Commission that there were more than seventy renditions leading up to 9/11.

Within days of the September 11, 2001, attacks, President Bush expanded the original finding Bill Clinton had signed, giving the CIA authority to act without case-by-case approval from Washington.[89] No one knows the exact number of renditions after that date, but the *New York Times* quotes "former government officials" as saying, "Since the September 11 attacks, the CIA has flown 100 to 150 suspected terrorists from one foreign country to another."[90] These numbers are probably a significant underestimate. Using methods I shall describe below, the *London Times,* CBS News's *60 Minutes,* and other sources were able to identify at least 600 flights of CIA airplanes to forty different countries, including 30 trips to Jordan, 19 to Afghanistan, 17 to Morocco, 16 to Iraq, with stops in Egypt, Libya, and Guantánamo.[91] Aircraft known to be involved in CIA rendition operations have landed at British airports at least 210 times since 9/11.[92]

In April 2006, investigations ordered by the European Parliament upped the number of such flights significantly beyond what had been previously imagined by anyone. According to Dan Bilefsky of the *New York Times,* "data gathered from air safety regulators and others found that the Central Intelligence Agency had flown 1,000 undeclared flights over European territory since 2001." After this disclosure, the Council of Europe ordered its own investigation based mostly on flight logs provided by the European Union's air traffic agency, Eurocontrol. Its sixty-seven-page report concluded that fourteen European nations, including Britain, Germany, Italy, Sweden, Romania, and Poland, had colluded with the CIA to seize and hold terror suspects without filing charges against them, fly them to secret detention centers, and establish prisons for them in Europe and elsewhere. The report concluded that the United States and its collaborators had violated international human rights law, including the European Convention on Human Rights.[93]

We have a few hints from official statements about the possible size of the rendition program. In his 2003 State of the Union address, President

Bush said that some terrorism suspects who were not caught and brought to trial had been "otherwise dealt with," and he then observed that "more than 3,000 suspected terrorists have been arrested in many countries, and many others have met a different fate. Let's put it this way: they are no longer a problem to the United States and our friends and allies." In April 2003, Cofer Black, who from 1999 to 2002 had been head of the CIA's Counterterrorism Center, added: "A large number of terrorist suspects were not able to launch an attack last year because they are in prison. More than 3,000 of them are al-Qaeda terrorists and they were arrested in over 100 countries."[94]

According to Dana Priest and Joe Stephens of the *Washington Post,* "Much larger than the group of prisoners held by the CIA are those who have been captured and transported around the world by the CIA and other agencies of the U.S. government for interrogation by foreign intelligence services."[95] If this statement is true, the number of post-9/11 renditions could be quite large. Human Rights Watch has identified at least twenty-four secret detention and interrogation centers worldwide operated by the CIA. These include: al-Jafr prison in the southern desert of Jordan; Kohat prison in Pakistan; holding sites in Afghanistan including in Kabul and Kandahar, at Bagram Air Base and Camp Salerno, near Khost; at least three locations in Iraq, including CIA-controlled parts of Abu Ghraib prison; at Guantánamo Bay, Cuba, the Camp Echo complex, and the new Camp 6; a secret location at Al-Udeid Air Base, Qatar; prisons in Egypt, Thailand, and in brigs on U.S. ships at sea; at least two CIA prisons in the old Soviet satellites in Eastern Europe, probably in Poland and Romania; in Morocco at secret police headquarters in Temara, near the capital, Rabat, and at a new CIA torture center under construction at Ain Aouda, south of Rabat's diplomatic district; and possibly at the U.S. naval base on the British island of Diego Garcia in the Indian Ocean.[96]

The people held in this U.S. version of the gulag are known as "ghost detainees," completely off-the-books. No charges are ever filed against them, and they are hidden away even from the inspectors of the International Committee of the Red Cross. In an unusual typology of rendition sites, Robert Baer, a former CIA operative in the Middle East and the author of *Sleeping with the Devil: How Washington Sold Our Soul for Saudi Crude,* has commented, "We pick up a suspect or we arrange for one of our partner countries to do it. Then the suspect is placed on a civilian transport to a third country where, let's make no bones about it, they use torture. If you want a good interrogation, you send someone to Jordan. If you want them to be killed, you send them to Egypt or Syria. Either way, the U.S. cannot be blamed as it is not doing the heavy work."[97]

Despite a near fanatical desire for secrecy, the CIA's rendition capers began to be exposed to public scrutiny less than six weeks after 9/11. This was almost inevitable, although completely unanticipated by the agency, when it chose to conduct abductions via the world of civil aviation. The CIA's operatives seemed not to understand that international airports are simply loaded with knowledgeable people at all hours of the day and night—aircrews, flight controllers, ticket clerks, baggage handlers, refuelers, airplane cleaners, police and customs officers, and passengers—many of whom are alert to everything going on around them.

The agency also appears to have been totally ignorant of the world of hobbyist airplane spotters or the fact that the Federal Aviation Administration's registry of all airplanes licensed to American owners is Internet accessible, as is its archive of airplane logs and flight plans, or the degree to which the CIA's criminal activities over several decades have mobilized a large cadre of amateur intelligence analysts. According to Mark Hosenball of *Newsweek*, "U.S. intel sources complain that 'plane spotters'—hobbyists who photograph airplanes landing or departing local airports and post the pix on the Internet—made it possible for CIA critics to assemble details of a clandestine transport system the agency set up to secretly move cargo and people—including terrorist suspects— around the world."[98]

On October 26, 2001, a Pakistani journalist named Masood Anwar broke a story in an Islamabad newspaper. Pakistani intelligence officers, he reported, had handed over to U.S. authorities a Yemeni microbiologist named Jamil Qasim Saeed Mohammed. He was allegedly wanted in connection with the bombing of the USS *Cole*. The handover occurred early in the morning of October 23 in a remote area of Karachi Airport, where airport staff nonetheless observed and reported to Anwar that the captive was hustled aboard a white, twin-engined, turboprop Gulfstream V executive jet with the registration number N379P—and this is crucially important—painted on its tail. It took off at 2:40 a.m. for an unknown destination. As the *Washington Post* later reported, at 19:54:04 on October 26, Anwar's story was posted on the FreeRepublic.com Web site. Thirteen minutes later a blogger provided the aircraft's registered owner—namely, Premier Executive Transport Services, Inc., 339 Washington Street, Dedham, Massachusetts. Shortly after, another reader posted a message saying, "Sounds like a generic name. Kind of like Air America" (the CIA's secret airline, not shut down until 1976, which had flown weapons and supplies into, and heroin out of, Laos during the Vietnam War).[99]

I happen to know something about airplane spotting because from 1947 until the early 1960s, I was a passionate participant in this activity. In 1956, I was one of three cofounders of the American Aviation Historical Society, the leading organization of airplane spotters and photographers in the United States, which in 2005 published the fiftieth volume of its journal.[100] Dana Priest describes airplane spotters as hobbyists "standing at the end of runways with high-powered binoculars and cameras to record the flights of military and private aircraft."[101] This is accurate enough as far as it goes, but there is more to airplane spotting than just collecting raw information. Watching airplanes closely and recording the squadron markings and serial numbers on them goes back to the last days of the London Blitz during World War II.

On January 2, 1941, with official support, Temple Press Ltd. published the first issue of the *Aeroplane Spotter,* a twelve-page newspaper intended to improve the quality of aircraft recognition among British civilian air defense volunteers. It ceased publication on July 10, 1948, after 217 issues. This legendary periodical included photos and silhouettes of the major aircraft types, both friend and foe, and was the first publication to pay attention to military serial numbers, changes in the registry of civilian aircraft, camouflage schemes, squadron markings, and unusual personal insignia. Such markings are important because, once a data base has been compiled, an analyst can use it to infer the number of a particular aircraft or its variant in service, to deduce the size and composition of squadrons, and to keep track of sales, modifications, and losses. The *Aeroplane Spotter* remains to this day an invaluable historical reference on the aircraft of the Luftwaffe, the Royal Air Force, and the U.S. Army Air Corps during World War II. Its legacy lives on in the activities of today's airplane spotters, including their Web sites that publish not just photos and data but also search engines that can trace virtually any aircraft through its serial or registration number.[102]

Based on the work of spotters, journalists, and airport workers around the world, many crucial details about the CIA's rendition fleet have been made public. As of late September 2005, the CIA had leased a fleet of perhaps thirty-three aircraft that it has used for various purposes but particularly for extraordinary renditions.[103] Most of these planes have been identified and their "N" numbers recorded. (*N* is the international civil aviation code letter assigned to American airplanes, just as *G* stands for British planes, *F* for French, *D* for German, and *J* for Japanese.) The CIA acquired its fleet through classified contracts issued by an obscure military agency called the Navy Engineering Logistics Office (NELO) located in Arlington, Virginia. (NELO is not even listed in the *U.S. Government Manual*, the official compilation of federal departments, agencies, and offices.)[104] The registered owners of the planes are some ten fake aviation companies with untraceable executives, many of whose addresses are post office boxes in northern Virginia (near CIA headquarters in Langley). The listed officers of the companies have social security numbers all issued when they were over fifty years old, strong evidence of the creation of a new or fake identity.

When the press identifies one of these aircraft and tries to contact the company that allegedly owns it, the aircraft is usually quickly "sold" to another shell company and the registration number changed. Thus, for example, the Gulfstream V, N379P, spotted at Karachi Airport in October 2001, was manufactured in 1999 (constructor's number 581, the only identification on an aircraft that never changes and is always listed on registers) and initially licensed as N581GA. After the CIA acquired it, the number was changed to N379P and its phantom owner became Premier Executive Transport Services of Dedham, Massachusetts. It was engaged in several important renditions from 2001 to 2003. In December 2003, the Shannon Peace Campers, an antiwar group of airplane spotters at Shannon International Airport in Ireland, outed it on the Internet as the "Guantánamo Bay Express." The same month N379P became N8068V, still owned by Premier Executive Transport. The Shannon spotters saw it three more times during 2004 in its new livery; then, on December 1, 2004, the plane was "sold" to Bayard Foreign Marketing, LLC, 921 S.W. Washington Street, Portland, Oregon, another CIA front company, and relicensed as N44982.[105]

The CIA's known fleet consists of two Gulfstreams, a small Cessna, three Lockheed Hercules cargo aircraft, a Gulfstream 1159a, a Learjet 35A, an old DC-3, two Boeing 737s, and a fifty-three-passenger De Havilland DH8. The De Havilland was photographed by plane spotters in Afghanistan.[106] The agency's second Gulfstream was registered N829MG when it was used on October 8, 2002, to fly the Canadian citizen Maher Arar from John F. Kennedy Airport, New York, to Jordan and on to Syria, where he was held in a coffin-sized cell and tortured for ten months before being told that his arrest had been a mistake. After the exposure of this disgraceful incident, the Gulfstream's registration was changed to N259SK.[107]

The main base for these aircraft is a remote corner of Johnson County Airport in Smithfield, North Carolina, where they are serviced by Aero Contractors Ltd., a company founded in 1979 by Jim Rhyne, a legendary CIA officer and the former chief pilot for Air America.[108] The airport is convenient to nearby Fort Bragg, headquarters of the Special Forces, and has no control tower that would allow unauthorized persons to see into the enclave. The fact that Aero's aircraft have permission to land at any U.S. military base worldwide is a dead giveaway to their provenance, since, according to the *Chicago Tribune*'s John Crewdson, "Only nine companies [including Premier Executive Transport Services] . . . have Pentagon permission to land aircraft at military bases worldwide."[109]

The CIA's transfer of two Egyptian refugees from Bromma Airport, Stockholm, to Cairo on December 18, 2001, using Gulfstream N379P, is one of the best-documented renditions on record. On May 17, 2004, Stockholm's TV4 program *Kalla Fakta* (*Cold Facts*) aired a more or less complete exposé of what happened. The broadcasters obtained on-camera statements from many of the participants, including Sven Linder, former Swedish ambassador to Egypt; Arne Andersson, the Swedish Security Police (SÄPO) officer in charge; Mary Ellen McGuiness, spokesperson for Premier Executive Transport Services; Hans Dahlgren, Swedish vice foreign minister; and above all Paul Forell, a police inspector with twenty-five years' experience who was on duty at Bromma Airport that day. Many others spoke to TV4 on an anonymous basis.[110]

The Swedish case is of major political importance because it revealed that Swedish authorities collaborated with the CIA. It is now clear that in a number of European countries, some of the local intelligence people were in on these renditions to one degree or another and that throughout

Europe several governments pretended ignorance and simply looked the other way. Given the one thousand CIA flights to European destinations, it is hard to imagine that local governments could have been completely ignorant of their purposes. Whether all Western European governments were involved; whether some of their intelligence services were functionally working for the CIA rather than their own governments; or whether deniability had been built into their arrangements with the CIA, we do not know. But obviously more was going on than merely bad Americans and good but ignorant Europeans.

No evidence has ever been offered that the two men the CIA kidnapped from Sweden and then delivered to the tender mercies of the Egyptians had participated in terrorist activities. In September 2000, after many years as a fugitive from the Egyptian dictatorship, Ahmed Agiza, age thirty-nine, with his wife and four children, arrived in Sweden (his fifth child was born after they were admitted). Muhammed al-Zery, age thirty-three, fled Egypt illegally in 1991, having been tortured by the authorities. He entered Sweden in August 1999. The Swedish Migration Board judged in both cases that the men, who were acquainted with each other but did not live in the same Swedish city, needed protection and should be granted asylum.

At about 5:00 p.m. on December 18, 2001, the Swedish secret police picked up Agiza on a street on his way home from a Swedish-language class in Karlstad; minutes later they nabbed al-Zery in a shop in Stockholm. Kjell Jönsson, al-Zery's attorney, testified that he received a call from his client that afternoon, only to be interrupted when someone said, "Put the receiver down." He promptly called the officials in charge of al-Zery's case at the Foreign Office but got only busy signals; the rest of the ministry was at a Christmas party. The police transported the two Egyptians to the Stockholm city airport, Bromma, an hour before it was scheduled to close. The police cars were quickly admitted and drove to the office of Police Inspector Paul Forell, who was on duty. There, obviously by prior agreement, they were met by eight balaclava-wearing Americans in business suits who had landed a few minutes earlier in N379P. The Americans used scissors to cut the clothes off Agiza and al-Zery, who were still in handcuffs and ankle chains. They then inserted suppositories presumably containing tranquilizers into their anuses, dressed them in diapers and jumpsuits, and took them out to the Gulfstream. At 21:49, the Egyptians, Americans, and two SÄPO officers took off for Cairo.

The decision to expel the two Egyptians had been made at noon that same day by Prime Minister Göran Persson and his government, although there is some reason to believe that they thought they were merely extraditing the two at Egypt's request and had no knowledge of the American involvement. The Swedish government received formal assurances from the Egyptians that the two men would be treated fairly and would not be harmed. TV4 claimed that the Americans had supplied evidence that the two Egyptians were terrorists. The TV journalists concluded, "A few months after the attack on the World Trade Center, Sweden accepted to become a pawn in the United States' worldwide manhunt." They traced the Gulfstream back to Premier Executive Transport Services in Massachusetts and, when they inquired about chartering the plane itself, were told: "It only flies for the U.S. government." Arne Andersson of SÄPO refused to supply details about the operation, saying to TV4 only, "This could disturb our relations with another service, and it could also affect the foreign relations of Sweden. As a nation."

As details of what had happened began to leak out, embarrassing the Swedish government, its ambassador in Cairo was ordered to look into the matter. He discovered that after some two years of intermittent torture of both men, the Egyptian authorities decided that al-Zery was innocent and sent him back to his native village, ordering him not to leave it without official permission. They sentenced Agiza to twenty-five years in Masra Tora Prison for membership in a radical organization, presumably the Muslim Brotherhood. Visits to the prison by the Swedish ambassador produced only meetings with the warden and no interviews with Agiza, whose wife and five children remain in Sweden but are faced with the continual threat of deportation.

In the weeks immediately after 9/11, it seems that the CIA conducted a global vacuuming operation seeking to "disappear" suspicious young Islamic men from various countries, including our own. In the course of these activities the agency acquired the names of Agiza and al-Zery, then pressured the SÄPO to arrest them and turn them over to a rendition team. At least some Swedish authorities involved knew that transferring any prisoner to a country where he might be tortured was a violation of Swedish law as well as of article 3 of the 1984 U.N. Convention Against Torture, which Sweden had signed and ratified. This case damaged Sweden's reputation as a champion of the international protection of human rights.

In the spring of 2004, a Swedish parliamentary investigation concluded that CIA agents had indeed broken the country's laws by subjecting the two Egyptians to "inhumane treatment." The Swedish security police chief Klas Bergenstrand assured the press that his agency would never again allow foreign agents to interfere in Swedish affairs. In August 2005, the neighboring Danish government announced that it was prohibiting CIA flights of any sort through its airspace. The CIA has never said anything about this case.[111]

The Swedish affair accomplished nothing other than ruining the lives of two men, a wife, and children, for no reason other than showing off the hubris of the CIA. By contrast, the CIA caper that began in Milan, Italy, on February 17, 2003, would be a farce—but one that severely worsened U.S. relations with a long-standing ally, interrupted an ongoing Italian intelligence operation, led to the disappearance and possible death of an Islamic imam, and politically weakened the then Italian prime minister, Silvio Berlusconi. The bunglers who thought up and executed this escapade have aptly been termed "the spies who came in from the hot tub."[112]

On June 24, 2005, an Italian judge signed a 213-page criminal arrest warrant for thirteen CIA operatives, including the former Milan station chief Robert Seldon Lady, charging them with kidnapping an Egyptian in Milan who held political refugee status in Italy. The victim was also under Italian police surveillance as a possible recruiter of mujahideen for service in Afghanistan and Iraq, although recruiting fighters for foreign battles is not illegal in Italy. The warrants for the thirteen CIA men and women, together with their photos, were forwarded to the European police authority, which authorized their arrest anywhere on the continent. It is the first time that a fellow NATO member has ever filed criminal complaints against employees of the United States government acting in an official capacity. In late July, another Italian court issued arrest warrants for six more CIA operatives, bringing the total number to nineteen (thirteen men and six women). Ultimately, the Italians issued extradition requests to the United States for twenty-two CIA operatives based on a 477-page police analysis of what they had done.[113] All of them except for Station Chief Lady were working under assumed names and had left Italy.

The abductee in this case is (or was) a forty-two-year-old Islamic cleric, Hassan Mustafa Osama Nasr, known as "Abu Omar." In 1991, if not earlier, Omar fled Egypt for Albania because he belonged to the outlawed Muslim organization Jamaat al-Islamiyya and the police were after him. In Tirana, the Albanian capital, he worked for four years for various Islamic charities, but did not himself participate in any illegal activities. After 9/11, the Bush administration labeled the charities he worked for as supporters of terrorists. While in Tirana he married an Albanian woman, Marsela Glina, and they had a daughter and a son.

In 1995, at the urging of the CIA, the Albanian National Intelligence Service recruited Omar as an informer. He readily agreed to cooperate. The Albanians did not pay him, but they did help smooth out a dispute he had with the landlady of the bakery he had opened, and they fixed his residence permit after his marriage. Abu Omar was the first Arab willing to betray his colleagues to the Albanians, and the information the Albanians supplied to the CIA, thanks to him, greatly elevated the CIA's respect for their service. However, after a few weeks for unknown reasons—perhaps his fellow Islamic exiles got wind of his cooperation with the police—he and his family fled the country. The CIA later informed the Albanians that he was living in Germany. In 1997, he surfaced in Rome where he was granted political refugee status. Shortly thereafter, he moved to Milan, the center of radical Islamist activities in Italy, and began preaching at a mosque that had a reputation as a gathering place for religious and political extremists. The Italian counterterrorism police placed a tap on his telephone, while hiding microphones in his apartment and at another mosque where he preached. Although the police believed they had enough evidence to arrest him for "associating with terrorists," they held off because the information they were gathering via the wiretaps was proving valuable and they were sharing it with the CIA.[114]

On Monday, February 17, 2003, shortly after noon, Abu Omar was walking down the Via Guerzoni toward a mosque to attend daily prayers when he was stopped by an officer of Italy's paramilitary carabinieri police force. According to the Milan prosecutor, Armando Spataro, the Italian carabiniere had been hired by the CIA to approach Abu Omar and conduct a routine documents check. The participation of the Italian police officer, code-named "Ludwig," has raised suspicions that the Sismi, the Italian intelligence service, was cooperating with the Americans. Former prime minister Berlusconi's office has repeatedly denied any role, but the Milanese prosecutors are doubtful and are continuing their investigation.[115]

According to a passerby's account, two men speaking "bad" Italian then emerged from a parked white van, sprayed a chemical in Abu Omar's face, and hustled him into the van, which drove away at high speed followed by at least one and possibly two other cars. Between 2 and 5 p.m., the van drove northeast to the NATO air base at Aviano where it was met by a U.S. Air Force officer, Lieutenant Colonel Joseph Romano, who escorted it to the flight line. Abu Omar was put aboard a civilian Learjet and flown to Ramstein Air Base in Germany. There, he was transferred to a civilian Gulfstream, which departed at 8:30 that night for Cairo. When Omar's plane arrived in Cairo early on the morning of February 18, Egyptian authorities took him into custody. Accompanying Omar to Egypt in the Gulfstream was CIA Milan station chief Robert Lady.[116]

Although Italian political leaders have steadfastly maintained that they did not collaborate in any way with this kidnapping, it is obvious that police authorities knew a great deal about it. The nineteen-person CIA abduction team of commandos, drivers, and lookouts left an astonishing trail of evidence that suggests they were utterly indifferent to the possibility that they were being observed. The first operative arrived in Milan on December 7, 2002, and stayed at the Milan Westin Palace, according to court documents. The others started arriving in early January and by February 1, 2003, virtually all of them were there. They did not hide in safe houses or private homes but checked into four-star palaces like the Milan Hilton ($340 a night) and the Star Hotel ($325 a night). Seven of the Americans stayed at the Principe di Savoia—billed as "one of the world's most luxuriously appointed hotels"—for between three days and three weeks at nightly rates of $450. Eating lavishly at gourmet restaurants, they ran up bills of at least $144,984, which they paid for with Diners Club cards that matched their fake passports. At each hotel, the staff photocopied their passports, which is how the police obtained their photos if not their real names.[117] After the delivery of Abu Omar to Aviano, four of the Americans checked into luxury hotels in Venice and others took vacations along the picturesque Mediterranean coast north of Tuscany, all still on the government tab.

Most embarrassingly, the U.S. embassy in Rome had supplied the CIA agents with a large number of Italian cell phones, on which they communicated with each other while planning the abduction, during the actual operation, and en route to Aviano. All their transmissions were recorded by the Italian police. No one can explain this lapse in tradecraft. Unless its power is completely off and its antenna retracted, a European mobile phone remains in constant contact with the nearest cell-base station even when not in use. Since a phone is served by several base stations at any given time, investigators can easily triangulate its location. In cities like Milan, where the network of base stations is dense and overlapping, such tracking can be done with a margin of error of just a few yards.[118] Thus, the Italian police were able to follow everything that the nineteen agents did both prior to and on the actual day of the rendition.

After Abu Omar's disappearance, the Italian police opened a missing person's investigation but did not pursue it very vigorously. That changed radically in April and May 2004, when Omar unexpectedly telephoned his wife from Cairo and explained that he had been kidnapped and taken to U.S. air bases in Italy and Germany, flown to Cairo, and tortured by the Egyptian police. The Italian authorities recorded these calls, having kept the wiretap on Omar's apartment in place. He informed his wife that he had been let out of prison but remained under house arrest. There is speculation that, as a result of reports on these conversations in Italian newspapers, the Egyptian police rearrested him. In any case, as far as is known, he remains in Egyptian custody, not charged with any crime but allowed occasional visits by his mother.

There is still no explanation for the CIA's sloppy work in Milan—except that some of its operatives seemed to have wanted a nice holiday at the taxpayers' expense and believed they could operate with complete impunity in Silvio Berlusconi's Italy. The Milan case goes into the record books as one more foolish and counterproductive felony committed by the CIA on the orders of the president. Ironically, the Milan CIA station chief had bought a house in Asti, near Turin, and planned to retire there. As the police bore down on him, he and his wife hurriedly fled their home, and a comfortable old age in Italy ceased to be an option for them.

Unfortunately, carrying out extraordinary renditions such as the ones in Sweden and Italy, torturing captives in secret prisons, shipping weapons to Islamic jihadists without checking their backgrounds or motives, and undermining democratically elected governments that are not fully on our political wavelength are the daily work of the Central Intelligence Agency. That was not always the case nor was it the intent of its founders or the expectations of its officials during its earliest years. As conceived in the National Security Act of 1947, the CIA's main function was to compile and analyze raw intelligence to make it useful to the president. Its job was to help him see the big picture, put the latest crisis in historical and economic perspective, give early warning on the likely crises of the future, and evaluate whether political instability in one country or another was of any importance or interest to the United States. It was a civilian, nonpartisan organization, without vested interests such as those of the military-industrial complex, and staffed by seasoned, occasionally wise analysts with broad comparative knowledge of the world and our place in it. As the *New York Times*'s Tim Weiner notes, "Once upon a time in the Cold War, the CIA could produce strategic intelligence. It countered the Pentagon's wildly overstated estimates of Soviet military power. It cautioned that the war in Vietnam could not be won by military force. It helped keep the Cold War cold."[119]

One of the CIA's best-known historians, Thomas Powers, laments, "The resignation of Porter Goss after 18 months of trying to run the Central Intelligence Agency and the nomination [subsequently confirmed] of General Michael Hayden to take his place make unmistakable something that actually occurred a year ago: the CIA, as it existed for 50 years, is gone."[120] I think it was actually gone long before. My own view is that President Bush's manipulation of intelligence to deceive the country into going to war and then blaming his failure on the CIA's "false intelligence" delivered only the final coup de grâce to the CIA's strategic-intelligence function. Henceforth, the CIA will no longer have even a vestigial role in trying to discern the forces influencing our foreign policies. That work will now be done, if it is done at all, by the new director of national intelligence. The downgraded CIA will attend to such things as assassinations, dirty tricks, renditions, and engineering foreign coups. In the intelligence field it will be restricted to informing our presidents and generals about current affairs—the "Wikipedia of Washington," as John McLaughlin, deputy director and acting director of central intelligence from October 2000 to September 2004, calls it.[121]

Thomas Powers is unquestionably correct when he writes, "Historically the CIA had a customer base of one—the president." But equally historically, it was not understood at the beginning that the CIA would become the president's private army as well as his private adviser. Over the years, presidents shaped what the CIA would become. They increasingly believed that its strategic intelligence was a nuisance while its covert side greatly enhanced their freedom of action. Perhaps the idea of supplying leaders with strategic perspectives from an independent, nonpolitical source was always unrealistic. It seemed that the CIA only worked more or less as it was intended when the secretary of state and the director of central intelligence were brothers—as John Foster and Allen Dulles were under President Eisenhower. The reality was and is that presidents like having a private army and do not like to be contradicted by officials not fully under their control. Thus the clandestine service long ago began to surpass the intelligence side of the agency in terms of promotions, finances, and prestige. In May 2006, Bush merely put strategic analysis to sleep once and for all and turned over truth-telling to a brand-new bureaucracy of personal loyalists and the vested interests of the Pentagon.

This means that we are now blinder than usual in understanding what is going on in the world. But, equally important, our liberties are also seriously at risk. The CIA's strategic intelligence did not enhance the power of the president except insofar as it allowed him to do his job more effectively. It was, in fact, a modest restraint on a rogue president trying to assume the prerogatives of a king. The CIA's bag of dirty tricks, on the other hand, is a defining characteristic of the imperial presidency. It is a source of unchecked power that can gravely threaten the nation—as George W. Bush's misuse of power in starting the war in Iraq demonstrated. The so-called reforms of the CIA in 2006 have probably further shortened the life of the American republic.

4

U.S. Military Bases in Other People's Countries

The basing posture of the United States, particularly its overseas basing, is the skeleton of national security upon which flesh and muscle will be molded to enable us to protect our national interests and the interests of our allies, not just today, but for decades to come.

—COMMISSION ON REVIEW OF OVERSEAS MILITARY FACILITY STRUCTURE,
Report to the President and Congress, May 9, 2005

9/11 has taught us that terrorism against American interests "over there" should be regarded just as we regard terrorism against America "over here." In this same sense, the American homeland is the planet.

—*THE 9/11 COMMISSION REPORT,*
Authorized Edition (2004)

Wherever there's evil, we want to go there and fight it.

—GENERAL CHARLES WALD, deputy commander
of the U.S.'s European Command, June 2003

If you dream that everyone might be your enemy, one day they may become just that.

—NICK COHEN,
Observer, April 7, 2002

Five times since 1988, the Pentagon has maddened numerous communities in the American body politic over an issue that vividly reveals the grip of militarism in our democracy—domestic base closings. When the high command publishes its lists of military installations that it no longer needs or wants, the announcement invariably sets off panic-stricken lamentations among politicians of both parties, local government leaders, television pundits, preachers, and the business and labor communities of the places where military facilities are to be shut down. All of them plead "save our base." In imperial America, garrison closings are the political equivalents of earthquakes, volcanic eruptions, or category five hurricanes.[1]

The military, financial, and strategic logic of closing redundant military facilities is inarguable, particularly when some of them date back to the Civil War and others are devoted to weapons systems such as Trident-missile-armed nuclear submarines that are useless in the post–Cold War world. At least in theory, there is a way that this local dependence on "military Keynesianism"—the artificial stimulation of economic demand through military expenditures—could be mitigated. The United States might begin to cut back its global imperium of military bases and relocate them in the home country.

After all, foreign military bases are designed for offense, whereas a domestically based military establishment would be intended for defense.[2] The fact that the Department of Defense regularly goes through the elaborate procedures to close domestic bases but continues to expand its network of overseas ones reveals how little interested the military is in actually protecting the country and how devoted to what it calls "full spectrum dominance" over the planet.

Once upon a time, you could trace the spread of imperialism by counting up colonies. America's version of the colony is the military base; and by following the changing politics of global basing, one can learn much about our ever more all-encompassing imperial "footprint" and the militarism that grows with it. It is not easy, however, to assess the size or exact value of our empire of bases. Official records available to the public on these subjects are misleading, although instructive. According to the Defense Department's annual inventories from 2002 to 2005 of real property it owns around the world, the *Base Structure Report,* there has been an immense churning in the numbers of installations. The total of America's military bases in other people's countries in 2005, according to official sources, was 737. Reflecting massive deployments to Iraq and the pursuit of President Bush's strategy of preemptive war, the trend line for numbers of overseas bases continues to go up (see table 1).

Interestingly enough, the thirty-eight large and medium-sized American facilities spread around the globe in 2005—mostly air and naval bases for our bombers and fleets—almost exactly equals Britain's thirty-six naval bases and army garrisons at its imperial zenith in 1898. The Roman

TABLE 1

NUMBERS OF AMERICAN MILITARY BASES IN
FOREIGN COUNTRIES BY SIZE AND MILITARY SERVICE

a. By Size*

	2002	2003	2004	2005
Large	17	15	15	16
Medium	18	19	19	22
Small**	690	668	826	699
Total	725	702	860	737

b. By Military Service

	2002	2003	2004	2005
Army	394	381	373	368
Navy	46	44	195	83
Air Force	283	275	269	266
Marine Corps	2	2	23	20
Total	725	702	860	737

* Large bases are those with a total plant replacement value (PRV) as calculated by the Pentagon of $1.584 billion; medium are those with PRVs of less than $1.584 billion and greater than $845 million; small are those with PRVs of less than $845 million.

** The large fluctuations in small bases between 2003 and 2005 probably reflect deployments for the invasion of Iraq.

SOURCE: Department of Defense, Office of the Deputy Undersecretary of Defense (Installations and Environment), *Base Structure Report*, fiscal years 2002 (data as of September 30, 2001), 2003 (data as of September 30, 2002), 2004 (data as of September 30, 2003), and 2005 (data as of September 30, 2004).

Empire at its height in 117 AD required thirty-seven major bases to police its realm from Britannia to Egypt, from Hispania to Armenia.[3] Perhaps the optimum number of major citadels and fortresses for an imperialist aspiring to dominate the world is somewhere between thirty-five and forty.

Using data from fiscal year 2005, the Pentagon bureaucrats calculated that its overseas bases were worth at least $127 billion—surely far too low a figure but still larger than the gross domestic products of most countries—and an estimated $658.1 billion for all of them, foreign and domestic (a base's "worth" is based on a Department of Defense estimate of what it would cost to replace it). During fiscal 2005, the military high command deployed to our overseas bases some 196,975 uniformed personnel as well as an equal number of dependents and Department of Defense civilian officials, and employed an additional 81,425 locally hired foreigners. The worldwide total of U.S. military personnel in 2005, including those based domestically, was 1,840,062 supported by an additional 473,306 Defense Department civil service employees and 203,328 local hires. Its overseas bases, according to the Pentagon, contained 32,327 barracks, hangars, hospitals, and other buildings, which it owns, and 16,527 more that it leased. The size of these holdings was recorded in the inventory as covering 687,347 acres overseas and 29,819,492 acres worldwide, making the Pentagon easily one of the world's largest landlords.[4]

These numbers, although staggeringly big, do not begin to cover all the actual bases we occupy globally. The 2005 *Base Structure Report* fails, for instance, to mention any garrisons in Kosovo (or Serbia, of which Kosovo is still officially a province)—even though it is the site of the huge Camp Bondsteel built in 1999 and maintained ever since by the KBR corporation (formerly known as Kellogg Brown & Root), a subsidiary of the Halliburton Corporation of Houston. The report similarly omits bases in Afghanistan, Iraq (106 garrisons as of May 2005), Israel, Kyrgyzstan, Qatar, and Uzbekistan, even though the U.S. military has established colossal base structures in the Persian Gulf and Central Asian areas since 9/11. By way of excuse, a note in the preface says that "facilities provided by other nations at foreign locations" are not included, although this is not strictly true. The report does include twenty sites in Turkey, all owned by the Turkish government and used jointly with the Americans.[5] The Pentagon continues to omit from its accounts most of the $5 billion worth of military and espionage installations in Britain, which have long been conveniently disguised as Royal Air Force bases. If there were an honest count, the actual size of our military empire would probably top 1,000 different bases overseas, but no one—possibly not even the Pentagon—knows the exact number for sure.

In some cases, foreign countries themselves have tried to keep their U.S. bases secret, fearing embarrassment if their collusion with American imperialism were revealed. In other instances, the Pentagon seems to want to play down the building of facilities aimed at dominating energy sources, or, in a related situation, retaining a network of bases that would keep Iraq under our hegemony regardless of the wishes of any future Iraqi government. The U.S. government tries not to divulge any information about the bases we use to eavesdrop on global communications, or our nuclear deployments, which, as William Arkin, an authority on the subject, writes, "[have] violated its treaty obligations. The U.S. was lying to many of its closest allies, even in NATO, about its nuclear designs. Tens of thousands of nuclear weapons, hundreds of bases, and dozens of ships and submarines existed in a special secret world of their own with no rational military or even 'deterrence' justification."[6]

In Jordan, to take but one example, we have secretly deployed up to five thousand troops in bases on the Iraqi and Syrian borders. (Jordan has also cooperated with the CIA in torturing prisoners we deliver to them for "interrogation.") Nonetheless, Jordan continues to stress that it has no special arrangements with the United States, no bases, and no American military presence.[7] The country is formally sovereign but actually a satellite of the United States and has been so for at least the past ten years. Similarly, before our withdrawal from Saudi Arabia in 2003, we habitually denied that we maintained a fleet of enormous and easily observed B-52 bombers in Jeddah because that was what the Saudi government demanded. So long as military bureaucrats can continue to enforce a culture of secrecy to protect themselves, no one will know the true size of our baseworld, least of all the elected representatives of the American people.

In 2005, deployments at home and abroad were in a state of considerable flux. This was said to be caused both by a long overdue change in the strategy for maintaining our global dominance and by the closing of surplus bases at home. In reality, many of the changes seemed to be determined largely by the Bush administration's urge to punish nations and domestic states that had not supported its efforts in Iraq and to reward those that had. Thus, within the United States, bases were being relocated to the South, to states with cultures, as the *Christian Science Monitor* put it, "more tied to martial traditions" than the Northeast, the northern Middle West, or the Pacific Coast. According to a North Carolina businessman gloating over his new customers, "The military is going where it is wanted and valued most."[8]

In part, the realignment revolved around the Pentagon's decision to bring home by 2007 or 2008 two army divisions from Germany—the First Armored Division and the First Infantry Division—and one brigade

(3,500 men) of the Second Infantry Division from South Korea (which, in 2005, was officially rehoused at Fort Carson, Colorado). So long as the Iraq insurgency continues, the forces involved are mostly overseas and the facilities at home are not ready for them (nor is there enough money budgeted to get them ready). Nonetheless, sooner or later, up to 70,000 troops and 100,000 family members will have to be accommodated within the United States. The attendant 2005 "base closings" in the United States are actually a base consolidation and enlargement program with tremendous infusions of money and customers going to a few selected hub areas. At the same time, what sounds like a retrenchment in the empire abroad is really proving to be an exponential growth in new types of bases—without dependents and the amenities they would require—in very remote areas where the U.S. military has never been before.

After the collapse of the Soviet Union in 1991, it was obvious to anyone who thought about it that the huge concentrations of American military might in Germany, Italy, Japan, and South Korea were no longer needed to meet possible military threats. There were not going to be future wars with the Soviet Union or any country connected to any of those places. In 1991, the first Bush administration should have begun decommissioning or redeploying redundant forces; and, in fact, the Clinton administration did close some bases in Germany, such as those protecting the Fulda Gap, once envisioned as the likeliest route for a Soviet invasion of Western Europe. But nothing was really done in those years to plan for the strategic repositioning of the American military outside the United States.

By the end of the 1990s, the neoconservatives were developing their grandiose theories to promote overt imperialism by the "lone superpower"—including preventive and preemptive unilateral military action, spreading democracy abroad at the point of a gun, obstructing the rise of any "near-peer" country or bloc of countries that might challenge U.S. military supremacy, and a vision of a "democratic" Middle East that would supply us with all the oil we wanted. A component of their grand design was a redeployment and streamlining of the military. The initial rationale was for a program of transformation that would turn the armed forces into a lighter, more agile, more high-tech military, which, it was imagined, would free up funds that could be invested in imperial policing.

What came to be known as "defense transformation" first began to be publicly bandied about during the 2000 presidential election campaign.

Then 9/11 and the wars in Afghanistan and Iraq intervened. In August 2002, when the whole neocon program began to be put into action, it centered above all on a quick, easy war to incorporate Iraq into the empire. By this time, civilian leaders in the Pentagon had become dangerously overconfident because of what they perceived as America's military brilliance and invincibility as demonstrated in its 2001 campaign against the Taliban and al-Qaeda—a strategy that involved reigniting the Afghan civil war through huge payoffs to Afghanistan's Northern Alliance warlords and the massive use of American airpower to support their advance on Kabul.

In August 2002, Secretary of Defense Donald Rumsfeld unveiled his "1-4-2-1 defense strategy" to replace the Clinton era's plan for having a military capable of fighting two wars—in the Middle East and Northeast Asia—simultaneously. Now, war planners were to prepare to defend the United States while building and assembling forces capable of "deterring aggression and coercion" in four "critical regions": Europe, Northeast Asia (South Korea and Japan), East Asia (the Taiwan Strait), and the Middle East, be able to defeat aggression in two of these regions simultaneously, and "win decisively" (in the sense of "regime change" and occupation) in one of those conflicts "at a time and place of our choosing." As the military analyst William M. Arkin commented, "[With] American military forces . . . already stretched to the limit, the new strategy goes far beyond preparing for reactive contingencies and reads more like a plan for picking fights in new parts of the world."[9]

A seemingly easy three-week victory over Saddam Hussein's forces in the spring of 2003 only reconfirmed these plans. The U.S. military was now thought to be so magnificent that it could accomplish any task assigned to it. The collapse of the Baathist regime in Baghdad also emboldened Secretary of Defense Rumsfeld to use "transformation" to penalize nations that had been, at best, lukewarm about America's unilateralism—Germany, Saudi Arabia, South Korea, and Turkey—and to reward those whose leaders had welcomed Operation Iraqi Freedom, including such old allies as Japan and Italy but also former communist countries such as Poland, Romania, and Bulgaria. The result was the Department of Defense's Integrated Global Presence and Basing Strategy, known informally as the "Global Posture Review."[10] President Bush first mentioned it in a statement on November 21, 2003, in which he pledged to "realign the global posture" of the United States. He reiterated the phrase and elaborated on it on August 16, 2004, in a speech to the annual convention of the Veterans of Foreign Wars in Cincinnati.

Because Bush's Cincinnati address was part of the 2004 presidential election campaign, his comments were not taken very seriously at the time. While he did say that the United States would reduce its troop strength in Europe and Asia by 60,000 to 70,000, he assured his listeners that this would take a decade to accomplish—well beyond his term in office—and made a series of promises that sounded more like a reenlistment pitch than a statement of strategy. "Over the coming decade, we'll deploy a more agile and more flexible force, which means that more of our troops will be stationed and deployed from here at home. We'll move some of our troops and capabilities to new locations, so they can surge quickly to deal with unexpected threats. . . . It will reduce the stress on our troops and our military families. . . . See, our service members will have more time on the home front, and more predictability and fewer moves over a career. Our military spouses will have fewer job changes, greater stability, more time for their kids and to spend with their families at home."[11]

On September 23, 2004, however, Secretary Rumsfeld disclosed the first concrete details of the plan to the Senate Armed Services Committee.[12] With characteristic grandiosity, he described it as "the biggest re-structuring of America's global forces since 1945." Quoting then undersecretary Douglas Feith, he added, "During the Cold War we had a strong sense that we knew where the major risks and fights were going to be, so we could deploy people right there. We're operating now [with] an entirely different concept. We need to be able to do [the] whole range of military operations, from combat to peacekeeping, anywhere in the world pretty quickly."[13]

Though this may sound plausible enough, in basing terms it opens up a vast landscape of diplomatic and bureaucratic minefields that Rumsfeld's militarists surely underestimated. In order to expand into new areas, the Departments of State and Defense must negotiate with the host countries such things as Status of Forces Agreements, or SOFAs, which are discussed in detail in the next chapter. In addition, they must conclude many other required protocols, such as access rights for our aircraft and ships into foreign territory and airspace, and Article 98 Agreements. The latter refer to article 98 of the International Criminal Court's Rome Statute, which allows countries to exempt U.S. citizens on their territory from the ICC's jurisdiction. Such immunity agreements were congressionally mandated by the American Service-Members' Protection Act of 2002, even though the European Union holds that they are illegal. Still other necessary accords are acquisitions and cross-servicing agreements or ACSAs, which concern the supply and storage of jet fuel, ammunition, and so forth; terms of leases on real property; levels of bilateral political and economic aid to the United States (so-called host-nation support); training and exercise arrangements (Are night landings allowed? Live firing drills?); and environmental pollution liabilities. When the United States is not present in a country as its conqueror or military savior, as it was in Germany, Japan, and Italy after World War II and in South Korea after the 1953 Korean War armistice, it is much more difficult to secure the kinds of agreements that allow the Pentagon to do anything it wants and that cause a host nation to pick up a large part of the costs of doing so. When not based on conquest, the structure of the American empire of bases comes to look exceedingly fragile.

In its Global Posture Review, the Pentagon now divides its military installations into three types. First are Main Operating Bases (MOBs), which have permanently stationed combat forces, extensive infrastructure (barracks, runways, hangars, port facilities, ammunition dumps), command and control headquarters, and accommodations for families (housing, schools, hospitals, and recreational conveniences). Examples include Ramstein Air Base in Germany (with a 2005 plant replacement value of $3.4 billion and 10,744 uniformed troops and Department of Defense civilians in residence); Kadena Air Base in Okinawa, Japan (with a PRV of $4.7 billion and 9,693 personnel); Aviano Air Base in Italy (with a PRV of $807.5 million and 4,786 personnel); and the Yongsan Garrison, in Seoul, South Korea (with a PRV of $1.3 billion and 12,178 personnel), soon to be replaced by Camp Humphreys, located farther south in Korea and so out of missile range of North Korea (with a PRV of $954.3 million and 5,622 personnel).

These bases are often known colloquially as "little Americas," but the culture they replicate is not that of mainstream America but rather places like South Dakota, Gulf Coast Mississippi, and Las Vegas. For example, even though more than one hundred thousand women live on our overseas bases, including women in the services, spouses, and relatives of military personnel, obtaining an abortion—a constitutionally protected right of American citizens—is prohibited in military hospitals. Since some fourteen thousand sexual assaults or attempted sexual assaults are reported in the military each year, women who become pregnant overseas and want an abortion have no choice but to try the local services, which cannot be either easy or pleasant in parts of our empire these days. Sometimes they must fly home at their own expense.[14]

Another difference between the bases abroad and those at home is the presence of military-owned slot machines in officers' clubs, bowling alleys, and activities centers at overseas facilities. The military takes in more than $120 million per year on a total slot machine cash flow of about $2 billion. According to Diana B. Henriques of the *New York Times,* "Slot machines have been a fixture of military life for decades. They were banned from domestic military bases in 1951, after a series of scandals. They were removed from Army and Air Force bases in 1972, after more than a dozen people were court martialed for skimming cash from slot machines in Southeast Asia during the Vietnam War. . . . Today, there are approximately 4,150 modern video slot machines at military bases in nine countries."[15] For example, the enlisted club at Ramstein Air Base is loaded with them. The result has been a serious rise in compulsive gambling and family bankruptcies among our forces deployed abroad.

The second type of overseas bases are called Forward Operation Sites (FOSs). These are major military installations whose importance the Pentagon goes out of its way to play down. Knowing full well that many foreigners see American military facilities as permanent imperialist enclaves, Rumsfeld has said, "We're trying to find the right phraseology. We know the word 'base' is not right for what we do."[16] Essentially FOSs are smaller MOBs, except that families are not allowed and the troops are supposed to be rotated in and out on six-month, not three-year, tours as at the larger installations.

Examples are the Sembawang port facility in Singapore for our visiting aircraft carriers (with a PRV of $115.9 million and 173 personnel) and Soto Cano Air Base in Honduras, unlisted in the 2005 *Base Structure*

Report but one of the U.S. Southern Command's main operational centers for exercising hegemony over Latin America. Other examples are the British-owned Diego Garcia naval and air base in the Indian Ocean where B-2 bombers are stationed (with a PRV of $2.3 billion and 521 personnel); the thirty-seven-acre Manas Air Base near Bishkek, Kyrgyzstan's capital, with facilities for 3,000 troops and a 13,800-foot runway originally built for Soviet bombers; and the former French Foreign Legion base in Djibouti at the southern entrance to the Red Sea, known as Camp Lemonier, housing 1,800 mostly Special Forces troops. (In 1962, I visited Djibouti when it was still a Foreign Legion base. It was a hellhole then and, according to American GIs, still is. Today, it contains a "Sensitized Compartmentalized Information Facility"—a billion-dollar civil-military eavesdropping and intelligence center.)[17] In the past, these kinds of bases have usually ended up as permanent enclaves of the United States regardless of what the Defense Department calls them.

The third type of overseas base is the smallest and most austere. The Pentagon has termed these Cooperative Security Locations (CSLs), failing to specify in what sense they are "cooperative" or to whose security they contribute. In Defense Department jargon these are the new "lily pads" that we are trying to establish all over the globe's "arc of instability," which is said to run from the Andean region of South America through North Africa and then sweep across the Middle East to the Philippines and Indonesia. In a May 2005 report, the Overseas Basing Commission defines this arc as containing "more than its fair share of ethnic strife, religious and ideological fanaticism, failed governments, and—above all—antipathy and hatred toward the West in general and the United States in particular."[18] Why this would make it an ideal place to expand our military presence, other than the fact that it is congruent with many of the oil-producing states of the world, is not made clear.

These "lily pad" facilities contain prepositioned weapons and munitions (running the risk of theft or appropriation for other purposes) to which U.S. access has already been negotiated, but they are to have little or no permanent U.S. presence, except in times of emergency. These are places to which our troops could jump like so many well-armed frogs from the homeland or our major bases elsewhere. Lily pad facilities now exist in Dakar, Senegal, for example, where the air force has negotiated contingency landing rights, logistics, and fuel-contracting arrangements. In 2003, it served as a staging area for our small-scale intervention in the Liberian civil war.

Other lily pads are located in Ghana, Gabon, Chad, Niger, Equatorial Guinea, São Tomé and Príncipe in the oil-rich Gulf of Guinea, Mauritania, Mali, and at Entebbe International Airport in Uganda as well as on the islands of Aruba and Curaçao in the Netherlands Antilles near Venezuela.[19] Lily pads are under construction in Pakistan (where we already have four larger bases), India, Thailand, the Philippines, and Australia; and in North Africa, in Morocco, Tunisia, and especially Algeria (scene of the slaughter of some one hundred thousand civilians since 1992, when the military took over, backed by our country and France, to quash an election). Six are planned for Poland.[20]

The models for all these new installations, according to Pentagon sources, are the string of bases we have built around the Persian Gulf in the last two decades in such antidemocratic autocracies as Bahrain, Kuwait, Qatar, Oman, and the United Arab Emirates, even though most of these are actually too large to be thought of as "lily pads."[21] Mark Sappenfield of the *Christian Science Monitor* has observed, "The goal . . . is to cement as many agreements as possible across the world, so that if one country changes course and denies the United States access, the Pentagon will have other options near at hand. But the new course will call on Pentagon leaders to be statesmen as well as military strategists."[22]

Thomas Donnelly and Vance Serchuk of the American Enterprise Institute (AEI), the unofficial Washington headquarters for the neocons, explain how the new structure of MOBs, FOSs, and CSLs is supposed to function. Invoking American Wild West imagery, they cheerfully assert, "Transformation involves a world's worth of new missions for the U.S. military, which is fast becoming the 'global cavalry' of the twenty-first century. Among the many components in this transformation is the radical overhaul of America's overseas force structure, which seeks to create a worldwide network of frontier forts. . . . The preeminent mission of the U.S. military is no longer the containment of the Soviet Union, but the preemption of terrorism. . . . Like the cavalry of the old west, [the armed forces'] job is one part warrior and one part policeman—both of which are entirely within the tradition of the American military. . . . The realignment of our network of overseas bases into a system of frontier stockades

is necessary to win a long-term struggle against an amorphous enemy across the arc of instability."[23]

Aware that Germans are growing increasingly dissatisfied with the way the U.S. military is damaging the environment around its bases and its refusal to clean up its messes, the AEI recommends building more "frontier stockades" in the poorer countries that Donald Rumsfeld so famously termed "the New Europe"—Bulgaria, Poland, and Romania, in particular—because of their "more permissive environmental regulations." The Pentagon always imposes on countries in which it deploys our troops Status of Forces Agreements, which usually exempt the United States from cleaning up or paying for the environmental damage it causes. Part of this attitude, however, simply reflects the desire of the Pentagon to put itself beyond any of the restraints that govern civilian life anywhere, an arrogance increasingly at play in the "homeland" as well. For example, the 2004 defense authorization bill exempts the military from abiding by the Endangered Species Act and the Marine Mammal Protection Act, even though both already contain possible exemptions for genuine national security needs.

The Pentagon's grand scheme has many critics, some of whom it did not anticipate because it has become so accustomed to having its own way with the budget and with Congress. In the Department of Defense's report to Congress, *Strengthening U.S. Global Defense Posture,* Undersecretary Feith started a small homeland firestorm by explicitly writing, "Global defense posture changes will have direct implications for the forthcoming [2005] round of Base Realignment and Closure (BRAC): some personnel and assets will return to the United States; others will move to forward U.S. locations or to host nations. Both efforts—global posture changes and BRAC—are critical components of President Bush's defense transformation agenda." This was something he might well have left unsaid, since nothing more quickly catches the eye of politicians than closing domestic military bases and so putting their constituents out of work.

In a preemptive strike to protect bases in their respective states, the two mother hens of the Senate's Military Construction Appropriations Subcommittee—Chairperson Kay Bailey Hutchison (Republican from Texas) and ranking minority member Dianne Feinstein (Democrat from California)—promptly demanded that the Pentagon close overseas bases

first, bringing the troops stationed there home to domestic bases, which could then remain open. Hutchison and Feinstein also included in the Military Construction Appropriations Act of 2004 money for an independent commission to investigate and report on overseas bases that were no longer needed.[24] Secretary Rumsfeld opposed this provision but it passed anyway and was signed into law by the president on November 22, 2003. The commission did its work quite thoroughly and revealed itself as rather more expert and realistic on overseas bases than the undersecretary of defense for policy. Its May 2005 report on the overseas basing structure is harshly critical of sloppy work at the Pentagon, particularly with regard to base construction and accounting for the funds it spends, something unusual in our "imperial presidential" system.

Most Americans do not know that some "host nations" for our military bases abroad pay large sums to the United States to support our presence in their countries. Somewhat like the Romans of old, who taxed their colonies mercilessly, the Americans have added a modern basing twist to military imperialism. They have convinced sovereign nations in which our bases are located that they have an obligation to help pay for them in order to deter our common enemies. This is called "burden sharing." Japan spends by far the largest amount of any nation—$4.4 billion in 2002—and every year tries to get its share cut. Perhaps whenever Japan finally succeeds in lowering its "host nation support," the Pentagon will start moving our troops and airmen out of the numerous unneeded locations there. Until then, however, Japan's American outposts are too lucrative and comfortable for the Pentagon to contemplate relocating them. On a per capita basis, the small but rich emirates of the Persian Gulf are the biggest spenders on this form of protection money. Bahrain pays a total of $53.4 million, Kuwait $252.98 million, Qatar $81.3 million, and the United Arab Emirates $217.4 million.[25]

The Overseas Basing Commission noted that Germany paid $1.6 billion in 2002 dollars for its U.S. bases, Spain $127.6 million, Turkey $116.8 million, and the Republic of Korea $842.8 million. Yet these are the key nations the Pentagon wants to punish for their lack of cooperation on Iraq. If the United States actually brings its troops home, the host-nation support will have to come from the U.S. taxpayer. The commission also notes laconically that the "extent to which host-nation funding would be

available to support new basing requirements in any countries not currently hosting U.S. forces remains to be seen."[26] In addition, it concluded that the Pentagon was wildly unrealistic in estimating the costs of reshuffling our empire. "The secretary of defense has stated that no extra funds will be asked for in the budget process to pay for the implementation of the Global Posture Review. . . . DoD [Department of Defense] has estimated the implementation of the Global Posture strategy to be between $9 billion and $12 billion with only about $4 billion currently budgeted from fiscal years 2006 through 2011."[27] As a result of its tours of overseas bases and a careful recalculation of construction costs, the commission estimated that Rumsfeld's repositioning plan would actually cost closer to $20 billion.[28]

Other criticisms of the Global Posture Review center on the intangible relationships that form the bedrock of the American military empire and the distinct possibility that the Pentagon will irretrievably damage them. The international relations commentator William Pfaff predicted, "For every foreign intrusion into a country, particularly one so dramatic as establishing a military base, a nationalist reaction can be expected. . . . Expanding the base system encourages Washington's tendency to apply irrelevant military remedies to terrorism, as well as to political problems."[29]

Exactly what Pfaff feared happened in Uzbekistan in the summer of 2005. In 2001, the Uzbek government had granted the United States use of the Karshi-Khanabad base, an old Soviet airfield close to the Afghan border in southeastern Uzbekistan (known to the Pentagon officially as "Camp Stronghold Freedom" and unofficially as "K-2").[30] Uzbekistan was the first of the former Soviet republics in Central Asia to agree to help the United States after 9/11. Heavy use was then made of the facility to support Special Forces operations in Afghanistan and to fly intelligence and reconnaissance missions over that country. About 800 U.S. military personnel were deployed at K-2, which was a typical American "foreign operating site." In 2004, the United States spent $4.6 billion on military equipment for Uzbekistan and more than $90 million on so-called International Military Education and Training for Uzbek forces. The other main American base in Central Asia, at Manas in Kyrgyzstan, was not as useful as Karshi-Khanabad for ongoing military operations because Kyrgyzstan does not have a common border with Afghanistan. The only alternative, building a base in adjoining Tajikistan, where the United States has permission for emergency landings and occasional refueling, is less attractive due to the lack of good roads into Afghanistan.[31]

Since the breakup of the USSR in 1991, however, Uzbekistan's president, Islam Karimov, has presided over one of the harshest dictatorships in the world. The Bush administration made use of this reality for a while. The capital Tashkent became a regular delivery point for CIA renditions, thanks to the well-established reputation Karimov's regime has for torturing prisoners. In 2003, Britain recalled its ambassador Craig Murray after he publicly denounced Uzbekistan's abysmal human rights record. Murray disclosed that the Uzbek government's specialty for prisoners kidnapped by the CIA was boiling them alive. The ambassador's deputy, sent to talk to the CIA's Tashkent station chief about this, was told, "The CIA doesn't see this as a problem." The Pentagon took the view that "Uzbekistan has been a good partner in the war on terror." In 2002, the State Department quietly removed Uzbekistan from its annual list of countries where freedom of religion is under threat, despite Karimov's repression of Islamic fundamentalists.[32]

By 2005, this official American endorsement was being offset, in Karimov's eyes, by the activities of some nongovernmental organizations (NGOs) paid for by the U.S. government's National Democratic Institute in Washington. He was alarmed and suspicious, probably accurately, that one wing of the Bush administration was secretly financing opposition movements in his country, hoping to bring to power an even more malleable government. Such efforts had already helped overthrow governments in Georgia in 2003 (the Rose Revolution), in the Ukraine in 2004 (the Orange Revolution), and in nearby Kyrgyzstan in March 2005 (the Tulip Revolution).[33] In particular, the protests that drove President Askar Akayev of Kyrgyzstan into exile alarmed all of the ex-Soviet republics in Central Asia, since they were, if anything, more vulnerable to charges of ignoring human rights and being indifferent to popular aspirations for democracy than he was.

In Uzbekistan, demonstrators broke into the city jail of Andijan on May 12, 2005, and freed a group of local businessmen the government had charged with Islamic extremism. Fearing another bloodless revolution, this time in his own country, President Karimov promptly used his U.S.-equipped and trained troops to massacre at least five hundred unarmed demonstrators and bystanders. Relations with Washington rapidly soured. On July 29, the Uzbek government delivered a written request to the U.S. embassy to withdraw from the Karshi-Khanabad base by January 25, 2006. In late September 2005, after discussions with President Karimov in Tashkent, Assistant Secretary of State Daniel Fried said that the United States would comply "without further discussion." On November 21, 2005, the last U.S. airmen formally returned control to the Uzbek government and flew out of K-2.[34]

What had happened in Tashkent set off reverberations throughout Central Asia, particularly in Bishkek, the capital of neighboring Kyrgyzstan, which is the home of our sole remaining air base in the area. In light of Uzbekistan's expulsion of the Americans, Kyrgyz president Kurmanbek Bakiyev decided to impose a hundred-fold increase in the rent he charges the United States for the use of Manas Air Base (called by the air force "Chief Peter J. Ganci Air Base" after the highest-ranking officer of the New York Fire Department to perish in the collapse of the World Trade Center towers). The annual fee went from $2.7 million per year to $200 million. Bakiyev said that there would be "no room for haggling" and that he would evict the Americans if they did not come through. As of July 14, 2006, the U.S. government had agreed to pay as much as $150 million in total compensation over the next year for use of the base, but no agreement had been reached.[35] Given the number of uncoordinated U.S. military-politico activities around the world, many more requests for us to get out or pay up will likely be forthcoming.

More serious than the closing of any FOSs or CSLs would be our expulsion from one or more MOBs. That might spell the beginning of the unraveling of America's military empire. Germany has long been one of the more hospitable nations toward the huge American military presence. However, because of the Bush administration's irritation with former chancellor Gerhard Schröder's public stance on Iraq, the United States began making plans to close thirteen army bases in Germany.[36] Current designs are to reduce air force personnel in Europe from 29,100 to 27,500, navy personnel from 13,800 to 11,000, and army personnel from 62,000 to 24,000.[37] This will have serious economic consequences for the city of Würzburg and its suburbs (home of the First Infantry Division, which is to return to the United States in mid-2006) and for Wiesbaden (home of the First Armored Division, which will depart the following year). If some

Germans see these withdrawals, and the accompanying German job losses, as payback for Berlin's opposition to the unilateral attack on Iraq, other Germans are pleased to see our troops leave. In 2005, Oskar Lafontaine, former chairman of the Social Democratic Party and one of Germany's most charismatic politicians, said, "We are not a sovereign country; as long as the U.S. can operate from here, we are a participant in the Iraq War."[38]

In contrast, the United States chose not to close any of its bases in Italy, in a period when then prime minister Silvio Berlusconi was one of President Bush's most loyal allies. In fact, the Global Posture Review calls for moving U.S. Naval Headquarters in Europe from London to Naples, rather than to Spain as originally planned, because the new socialist government of Prime Minister José Luis Rodríguez Zapatero decided in 2004 to withdraw all 1,400 of his country's troops from Iraq.[39]

There have, in fact, been many more public and official protests in Italy about the American presence than in either Germany or Spain. These include demands by the regional president of Sardinia that the navy remove its 2,500 military personnel from La Maddalena island at the northern tip of Sardinia, a base since 1972. Despite being a well-known resort area and a national park, La Maddalena plays host to American nuclear submarines that are anything but a tourist attraction, particularly after one of them, the USS *Hartford,* ran aground there in October 2003. Apparently in an unsuccessful attempt to help Berlusconi get re-elected and as an acknowledgment that there was virtually no continuing post–Cold War need for nuclear submarines, on November 23, 2005, Defense Secretary Donald Rumsfeld announced that the United States would close La Maddalena as part of its Global Posture Review.[40]

Mainland Italians have been made nervous by reports published in the national daily *Corriere della Sera* that Camp Darby, occupying a thousand hectares of pine woods on the Tuscan coast between Pisa and Livorno, is the "biggest American ammunition dump outside the United States." It regularly stockpiles twenty thousand tons of artillery and aerial munitions, eight thousand tons of high explosives, and nearly four thousand antipersonnel cluster bombs. Built in 1951, Darby has begun seriously to deteriorate, and the army's Corps of Engineers has had to clear some bunkers because of the threat that there might be an explosion. The

Corriere della Sera's report called it "a small miracle that nothing had gone wrong."[41] Here, however, there is no movement toward closure.

U.S. planners claim they want to move the bases in Germany to forward operating sites (FOSs) and cooperative security locations (CSLs) in Poland, Romania, and Bulgaria because they are closer to potential areas of conflict. In December 2005, Secretary of State Condoleezza Rice signed an access agreement with Romania to set up U.S. military bases there.[42] However, in its planning, the Pentagon does not seem to take into account just how many buildings, hangars, airfields, and warehouses we occupy in Germany and how expensive it would be to build even slightly comparable facilities in former communist countries such as Romania, one of Europe's poorest places. Lieutenant Colonel Amy Ehmann, a military spokesperson in Hanau, Germany, pointed out to the press in 2003, "There's no place to put these people" in Romania and Bulgaria. According to many press reports, the Bush administration had a special interest in Mihail Kogalniceanu Air Base in Romania not for defense but as a secret CIA prison for the interrogation and torture of terrorism suspects.[43] This may come closer to the real uses to which bases in such poor countries of Eastern Europe may be put. One thing is certain: American commanders have no intention of living in a backwater like Constanta, Romania, and plan to hang on to their military headquarters in Stuttgart and Heidelberg, convenient as they are to so many nearby military golf courses and the armed forces ski center at Garmisch in the Bavarian Alps.

According to the Global Posture Review, the United States intends to retain three facilities in Germany no matter what: Ramstein Air Base, nearby Spangdahlem Air Base, and the huge Grafenwöhr training area and firing ranges near Nuremberg in Bavaria. The United States has grown used to thinking of these as virtually American territory. Ramstein Air Base, in particular, represents the largest community of Americans— over forty thousand—and the most immense military installation outside of the United States. Its military hospital is the biggest such facility overseas. The Ramstein complex is located in a rural and relatively underdeveloped part of southwestern Germany, adjacent to the small town of Kaiserslautern, known to linguistically challenged GIs as "K-town."[44] The Natural Resources Defense Council, a New York–based research organization, contends that the United States still has 480 nuclear warheads in

Europe, 130 of them deployed at Ramstein. Three of Germany's center-left parties deeply oppose this.[45] The air base also houses important espionage facilities, including part of the global Echelon eavesdropping system, and the Twenty-sixth Intelligence Group, a unit of the Air Intelligence Agency affiliated with the National Security Agency.[46] In addition to all the usual schools, housing estates, and supermarkets, Ramstein maintains one of the finest eighteen-hole golf courses in Europe.

Today, Ramstein has also become a logistics base for the U.S. fleet of 180 C-17 Globemasters. It took over this function from Frankfurt's Rhein-Main Air Base, which the United States was forced to give up in October 2005. Rhein-Main was the main staging area for the Berlin Airlift of 1948–49, whereas Ramstein was not built until 1953. During 2004, some 624,000 American soldiers and their families passed through Rhein-Main, most of the troops en route to or from Iraq. The air base shared runways with Frankfurt International Airport, Europe's second busiest. The German government finally bought out the U.S. interest in the property so that it could build a third passenger terminal in preparation for the Airbus A380, the world's largest passenger jet, when it goes into service in 2006. Although Rhein-Main was long a symbol of postwar German-American friendship and cooperation, according to the *New York Times,* "Germans are generally dry-eyed about the decline in American visibility."[47]

The question is: How long will Germany accept the current base structure when the United States seems interested in having bases in Europe's most powerful country only to serve narrow American interests? The same question could be asked of the Spanish government's toleration of the air force's Morón air base and our naval station at Rota, on the Atlantic coast halfway between Gibraltar and the border of Portugal. The Turkish government may not continue to feel comfortable about our joint use of the air base at Incirlik, and the South Korean government's forbearance may in future years wane when it comes to the huge array of American bases in its country since the United States refuses to give it any say in when or how they will be used.

The Global Posture Review is a purely military analysis of where the United States might like to have military bases in light of possible future wars, including those we might start. It contains almost no political understanding of the foundations of the American empire or of the way Bush administration policies have threatened its cornerstone bases, not to speak of the global loathing these have generated.[48] The longevity of the U.S. empire depends less on hypertechnical military and strategic calculations than on whether its junior partners trust the good sense of the U.S. government, factors to which the Bush administration seems to be totally blind.

Peter Katzenstein, a political economist at Cornell University, has argued that the jewels in the crown of the American empire are Germany and Japan and the regions they dominate—Europe and Northeast Asia. Japan is the world's second- or third-largest economy, depending on how one evaluates China, and Germany is the fifth. They bear much the same relationship to the American empire that the so-called white dominions—Canada, Australia, New Zealand, and South Africa—had with the British Empire. "Germany's and Japan's unconditional surrender and occupation by the United States," Katzenstein has written, "created two client states that eventually rose to become core regional powers. . . . It is not American dictates to the world that are its most important and enduring source of power. It is the American capacity to generate and tolerate diversity in a loose but shared sense of moral order. . . . Total defeat in war was the precondition for Japan's and Germany's belated conversion to the American way of informal liberal rule."[49]

After the implosion of the Soviet Union in 1991 and the unification of Germany, these mutually profitable relationships seemed destined to have a very long life. But the coming to power and influence in the United States of men and women with only a superficial knowledge of history and international affairs has greatly diminished "the consent and cooperation that remain indispensable to America's imperium."[50] It is no longer inconceivable that our satellites might one day kick us out—and get away with it, just as the East Europeans did with the Soviet Union in 1989.

The huge arrays of bases in Germany and Japan and their semipermanent quality are the forms of empire preferred by U.S. government planners. It is clear today that the Bush administration intended, upon Saddam Hussein's certain defeat, to create military bases in Iraq similar to those we built or took over in Germany and Japan after World War II. The covert purpose of our 2003 invasion was empire building—to move the main focus of our military installations in the Middle East from Saudi Arabia to Iraq, gain control over Iraq's oil resources, and make that country a permanent Pentagon outpost for the control of much of the rest of the "arc of instability."

In response to the question, "What were the real reasons for our invasion of Iraq?" retired air force lieutenant colonel Karen Kwiatkowski, a former strategist inside the Near East Division of the Office of the Secretary of Defense, suggested: "One reason has to do with enhancing our military-basing posture in the region. We had been very dissatisfied with our relations with Saudi Arabia, particularly the restrictions on our basing. . . . So we were looking for alternate strategic locations beyond Kuwait, beyond Qatar, to secure something we had been searching for since the days of Carter—to secure the energy lines of communication in the region. Bases in Iraq, then, were very important."[51] In the spring of 2005, Kwiatkowski further noted, Pentagon leaders regarded Iraqi bases as vital for protecting Israel and as potential launching pads for preventive wars in Syria and Iran, part of the administration's strategic vision of reorganizing the entire region as part of an American sphere of influence. So it seems likely we intend to stay there whether the Iraqis want us or not.[52]

Our publicly stated policy, as the Overseas Basing Commission puts it, has continued to be: "Decisions on temporary, permanent, or 'enduring' U.S. bases in Iraq have yet to be made. . . . U.S. presence in Iraq is a subject for discussions with the Iraqi government once it is formed."[53] On February 17, 2005, for instance, Secretary Rumsfeld testified to the Senate Armed Services Committee, "I can assure you that we have no intention at the present time of putting permanent bases in Iraq." The actual policy being implemented on the ground, however, is to build a number of stable, hardened facilities (the military avoids the term "permanent") that, according to Lieutenant General Walter E. Buchanan III, chief of air operations in the U.S.'s Central Command, "will remain available for U.S. use for at least another decade or two."[54]

One can infer from numerous unofficial comments by American military officials in Iraq that, even if a future Iraqi government should attempt to kick us out, the Pentagon nonetheless plans to retain at least four crucially located and heavily fortified bases. In February 2005, Larry Diamond of the Hoover Institution, who was an adviser on democratization to our chief envoy in Iraq, L. Paul Bremer, summed up the basing situation this way: "[W]e could declare . . . that we have no permanent designs on Iraq and we will not seek permanent military bases in Iraq. This one statement would do an enormous amount to undermine the suspicion that we have permanent imperial intentions in Iraq. We aren't going to do that. And the reason we're not going to do that is because we are building permanent military bases in Iraq."[55]

These permanent bases are the successors to the formerly permanent bases we hoped to hang on to in Saudi Arabia. However, on August 26, 2003, in a small ceremony at Prince Sultan Air Base, near Riyadh, the Saudi capital, the United States ended its thirteen-year presence in the kingdom. By then it had relocated its Persian Gulf headquarters to Al-Udeid Air Base in the small neighboring emirate of Qatar and launched a $1.2 billion program to upgrade the sixteen major airfields we already occupied elsewhere in the Middle East. In an interview with the *New York Times*, Lieutenant General Buchanan claimed that there were only two "enduring" bases for American operations in the Middle East outside Iraq: al-Udeid in Qatar and al-Dhafra air base in the United Arab Emirates.[56] The problem with this statement is that it depends entirely on what the air force means by "enduring." There are quite substantial bases in Kuwait, Bahrain, the United Arab Emirates, and Oman that Lieutenant General Buchanan overlooks. In any case, the U.S. Army's Corps of Engineers and the KBR Corporation of Houston were making major improvements to both of the bases Buchanan cited, largely financed by the host governments.

In Iraq, using funds appropriated for military operations, the U.S. military has hired KBR and other companies to build or rebuild around a dozen semipermanent, reinforced bases. According to Joshua Hammer, the Jerusalem bureau chief for *Newsweek*, since the original contracts of potentially $7 billion awarded to KBR in 2003, "it has received another $8.5 billion for work associated with Operation Iraqi Freedom. By far the largest sum—at least $4.5 billion—has gone to construction and maintenance of U.S. bases."[57] These funds were contained in an $82 billion supplementary war-spending bill approved by Congress in May 2005.[58]

According to Christine Spolar of the *Chicago Tribune*, we began our occupation of Iraq in the spring of 2003 with some 120 "forward operating bases."[59] Two years later we had returned 14 to the Iraqis and still occupied 106, plus four prisons holding more than eleven thousand prisoners and several logistics centers for servicing truck convoys from

Kuwait. Bradley Graham of the *Washington Post* quoted an unnamed general as saying, "If we're going to withdraw, we need a base plan."[60] This planning process led to the crash program to build permanent structures made of mortar-resistant concrete at some fourteen of the bigger bases and to concentrate on four airfields away from urban areas that we intend to keep as long as possible.

Any visitor to Iraq, according to *Newsweek*'s Hammer, could not fail to note "[t]he omnipresence of the giant defense contractor KBR, . . . the shipments of concrete and other construction materials, and the transformation of decrepit Iraqi military bases into fortified American enclaves." In its report of May 2005, the Overseas Basing Commission "observed the immense amount of military construction to support U.S. operations that has taken place and is currently being planned within USCENTCOM."[61] Since the secretary of defense has not explicitly authorized this construction, although he undoubtedly knows about it, there is no straightforward list of these "enduring" bases in Iraq. The Department of Defense maintains a pervasive silence on the subject, and members of Congress of both parties routinely say it is not part of their "agenda."[62] The following compilation of facilities that the United States would like to keep has therefore been pieced together from various fragmentary accounts. By far the most important compilation is by the Global Security Organization of Alexandria, Virginia.[63]

Three of the bases are in or around Baghdad itself. First is the Green Zone, the four-square-mile enclave in the middle of the city encircled by fifteen-foot concrete walls and rings of concertina wire. Its buildings include Saddam Hussein's former presidential palace, which is headquarters for the current Iraqi government, the U.S. embassy, and offices for numerous military and civilian functionaries.[64]

The new U.S. embassy is as permanent a base as they come. Located in a 104-acre compound, it will be the biggest embassy in the world—ten times the size of a typical American embassy, six times larger than the U.N., as big as Vatican city, and costing $592 million to build. It will be defended by blast walls and ground-to-air missiles. A workforce of nine hundred mostly Asian workers who live on the site has been imported to do the actual construction. They work around the clock (at a time when most Iraqis are enduring blackouts of up to twenty-two hours a day, the embassy site is floodlit by night). This diplomatic "facility" will have its own apartment buildings (six of them) for a staff of perhaps 5,500 (many of them troops for guard duty), its own electricity, well-water, and waste-treatment facilities, plus the de rigueur "swimming pool, gym, commissary, food court, and American Club, all housed in a recreation building." The London *Times*'s Daniel McGrory reports that Baghdad residents are properly cynical watching what they call, in mock-honor of Saddam Hussein's famously self-glorifying building projects, "George W's palace," as it rises on the banks of the Tigris River while their lives crumble around them. It goes without saying that, like the former American embassy in Saigon, the Baghdad embassy will have one or more helipads on the roofs.[65]

The other two bases in the Baghdad vicinity are Camp Victory North, adjacent to the international airport, and al-Rashid Military Camp, the capital's former military airport. At Victory North, KBR has built an encampment for 14,000 troops housed in air-conditioned barracks with access to the largest post exchange in Iraq. (Other sources assert that the biggest PX is at Camp Taji north of Baghdad.) Camp Victory North includes Qasr al-Fao, one of Saddam Hussein's ornate palaces, which sits in the middle of a man-made lake stocked with carp and catfish. The palace is now occupied by senior military commanders. At first, there was some concern about American generals occupying such ostentatious buildings associated with the Saddam era, but the high command decided it was too expensive to build replacement facilities.[66] So they continue to occupy at least fifteen former presidential palaces spread around the country. Camp Victory North, it should be noted, is twice the size of Camp Bondsteel in Kosovo, constructed by KBR in 1999 and until the Iraq war the largest overseas base built since the Vietnam War.[67]

Some seventeen miles north of Baghdad is Taji Air Base, renamed Camp Cooke by the Americans after a First Armored Division sergeant killed in Baghdad in December 2003 and then in September 2004 changed back to Camp Taji.[68] Taji was a former Republican Guard "military city." According to the description of the base by the Global Security Organization, "The quality of life at Camp Taji gets better every day. The Camp now has . . . a Subway, Burger King, and Pizza Hut. They also have a newly built dining facility, which is three times larger [than the old one] and the food selection is unbelievable. There are several gyms and MWR facilities [Morale, Welfare, and Recreation] where soldiers can exercise, watch movies or sporting events, and play games. Soldiers live in air-conditioned and heated trailers, have hot showers, and can eat four meals a day in the new dining facility."

Thirteen miles north of Camp Taji is the fifteen-square-mile Balad Air Base, the largest American base in the country, and its associated army facility, Camp Anaconda, so gigantic it requires nine internal bus routes for soldiers and civilian contractors to get around inside the earthen berms and concertina wire. During 2004, Anaconda was headquarters of the Third Brigade, Fourth Infantry Division, whose job it was to police some 1,500 square miles of Iraq north of Baghdad, from Samarra to Taji. Despite extensive security precautions, the base has frequently come under mortar attack, notably on the Fourth of July 2003, just as Arnold Schwarzenegger was chatting up our wounded at the local field hospital. During 2005, the military spent $228.7 million to upgrade ramps, runway lights, and parking facilities for some 138 army helicopters at Balad. Military flights that once flew into Baghdad International Airport now use Balad to allow for the resumption of commercial flights at Baghdad. Its air traffic is second only in the world to London's Heathrow.[69] Balad houses over 250 aircraft.

In the far north, next door to Mosul Airport, is Camp Marez, where on December 21, 2004, a suicide bomber blew himself up in a tent dining room, killing at least thirteen U.S. soldiers and four KBR employees. Al-Asad Air Base in the western province of Anbar is another major military airport and garrison that the United States is urgently rebuilding as one of its enduring sites. It is the second-largest air base in Iraq, with two main runways measuring fourteen thousand and thirteen thousand feet. Al-Asad is the most important base near the Syrian frontier. The Americans have one other major air base in Anbar province, al Taqaddum, near Ramadi, where Seabees have been upgrading runways and facilities. Then there is the huge complex in the south clustered around Tallil Air Base adjacent to the ancient ziggurat of Ur. Still another is Camp Renegade, a former Iraqi fighter base with facilities for at least two squadrons, located just outside the oil-rich city of Kirkuk, near the Kirkuk refinery and petrochemical plant.

Camp Qayyarah ("Q-West" to American soldiers), a former military air base about thirty miles south of Mosul, was occupied in 2003 by units of the 101st Airborne Division. It is considered a hardship post but is located in a strategically important area. Al Sahra airfield is a sprawling former Iraqi air force base just south of Tikrit. Its army base is named

Camp Speicher after navy lieutenant commander Michael Speicher, who was shot down over Iraq on January 17, 1991, the opening night of the first Persian Gulf war. It contains the largest structure the U.S. military has built in Iraq so far, a $6.7 million divisional headquarters that will replace the current headquarters, located in a monumental pink marble palace built by Saddam Hussein in his hometown. The United States gave the palace back to the Iraqis in November 2005.[70]

Undoubtedly there are also some bases in Basra, currently occupied by British forces, that the United States will try to retain. But if push comes to shove, according to information gathered by Bradley Graham of the *Washington Post,* the United States has chosen four Iraqi bases that it will try to hang on to come what may: Tallil Air Base in the south, al-Asad Air Base in the west, Balad Air Base in the center, and either Camp Qayyarah or an unnamed airfield near Irbil in the north.[71] Whether the United States retains any of these facilities and for how long is an open question. For now, however, the Americans have built a much more powerful imperial presence in Iraq than they ever enjoyed in Saudi Arabia and many billions of dollars have been spent in the process.

Turning to other parts of the world where the United States is widely detested and there is suspicion of everything it does, Paraguay illustrates a somewhat different approach to how the U.S. military goes about penetrating an area. The U.S. Southern Command's efforts there are aimed at keeping control over Latin America, where the United States is probably more unwelcome than at any time since the open imperialism of the Spanish-American War of 1898.

Most citizens of Latin American countries know about our armed interventions to overthrow popularly supported governments in Guatemala (1954), Cuba (1961), Dominican Republic (1965), Chile (1973), Grenada (1983), and Nicaragua (1984–90). Many know about Fort Benning's School of the Americas, the U.S. Army's infamous military academy that specializes in training Latin American officers in state terrorism and repression. (It was renamed the Western Hemisphere Institute for Security Cooperation in 2000 to try to disguise its past.) Some are aware of the 1997 creation of the Center for Hemispheric Defense Studies within the National Defense University in Washington to indoctrinate Latin American civilian defense officials, as well as the Pentagon's endless efforts to create close "military-to-military" relations by sending U.S. Special Forces to train and arm Latin American armies. Finally, there is the steadfast advocacy of radical free-market capitalism that, when implemented by the International Monetary Fund, the World Bank, and the World Trade Organization, have invariably left Latin American countries more indebted and poverty stricken than they were before.

As a result of these and other accumulated grievances, by late 2005 regimes openly cool to the United States had come to power in Brazil, Uruguay, Argentina, and Venezuela. On December 18, 2005, Bolivia followed suit by electing Evo Morales, leader of the country's indigenous population and its first Indian president, who quickly nationalized Bolivia's extensive gas resources and was planning to legalize the growing of coca. In Ecuador, which has in the last decade alone toppled three presidents before their terms expired, a deep hostility to American-sponsored neoliberal economic policies prevails. In Mexico, the government of Vicente Fox became the hundredth nation to ratify the International Criminal Court treaty, making it unlikely that the United States will ever try to station troops there.

Other than Colombia and Honduras, about the only place left where the American military is welcome is El Salvador, scene of numerous American-sponsored war crimes during the 1980s and the only Latin American country still to have a truly symbolic contingent of troops in Iraq. In order to push back against these anti-American trends, the Southern Command has fallen back on old tricks: it tries to merge its antidrug efforts with the war on terrorism (drug trafficking is now called "narcoterrorism"), discredits genuinely democratic outcomes by labeling them "radical populism," and revives the old specter of "Castro Communism" in the form of a newly discovered villain, President Hugo Chávez of Venezuela.[72]

The Southern Command is also trying in a highly stealthy manner to build Forward Operating Sites and Cooperative Security Locations in places that are so small and weak they do not have the resources even to think of resisting. As of mid-2005, the Southern Command's older facilities in the Americas included the huge base and prisons at Guantánamo Bay, Cuba, and an FOS at Soto Cano Air Base, near Palmerola, Honduras. Soto Cano houses 448 military personnel and 102 civilians and dependents. During the Reagan-era counterrevolutionary war of the Contras against the leftist Sandinista government in Nicaragua, Honduras was the main support facility and, at the time, the largest CIA base on Earth. Soto Cano was acquired during that period.

Southern Command also includes four CSLs, two located on the islands of Aruba and Curaçao, both Dutch colonies in the Caribbean near Venezuela.[73] Another, operated by the navy, is Comalapa, El Salvador; and the most important is Eloy Alfaro Air Base, on the Ecuadorian coast at Manta. Aruba and Curaçao have about 450 military personnel between them and Comalapa about 100. The United States also possesses at least seventeen radar sites, mostly in Peru and Colombia, each typically staffed by about 35 people. There is also a Peruvian-owned base at Iquitos from which the CIA directs local military pilots to shoot down airplanes it believes are smuggling narcotics. In April 2001, planes from the base happened to shoot down a small airplane carrying an American missionary family. In Colombia, about 800 U.S. troops, Special Forces, and mercenaries are training and advising local troops trying to defeat a long-standing drug-financed guerrilla war against the Colombian establishment and incidentally protect an oil pipeline owned by the Occidental Petroleum Company.[74]

The Manta base in Ecuador, which is the model for the CSL being built in Paraguay, is a perfect illustration of "mission creep." In 1999, the Ecuadorian government agreed to let the United States refurbish an old airfield for counternarcotics surveillance flights. The American government promised that the base would be used only for daytime missions and would not permanently house U.S. military personnel.[75] The United States began in a classically deceptive manner by distributing used clothing and school supplies to local day-care centers "to help the poor children . . . and to reach out to the community." According to the investigative journalist Michael Flynn, writing in the *Bulletin of the Atomic Scientists* and quoting local activists, many Ecuadorians saw through this. A typical comment was: "Remember how Columbus gave glass beads to the Indians."[76] The United States has spent some $80 million upgrading the airfield and farmed out its maintenance to DynCorp, a well-known "private military company."[77]

Southcom soon expanded Manta's missions to include stopping, and in some cases sinking, ships that it suspects of carrying illegal immigrants to the United States, coordinating a failed 2002 coup against President Hugo Chávez of Venezuela, and providing military protection for American petroleum interests in the Andean region. Shortly after they arrived, American officials signed a ten-year lease agreement for the base with President Jamil Mahuad. The president, however, failed to submit the agreement to Ecuador's Congress for approval as required by its constitution, and in 2000 Mahuad was overthrown in a military coup. Nonetheless, Manta soon acquired a contingent of 475 U.S. military personnel and a constant stream of navy warships calling at its harbor.[78] The Pentagon has also not hesitated to build a Sensitive Compartmentalized Information Facility on the base, the same kind of supersecret civil-military eavesdropping and intelligence post it has at Djibouti in the Horn of Africa. It would appear that the United States has settled down in Manta unannounced on a more or less permanent basis.

Planners in the Pentagon believed that they needed at least one more CSL in the cone of South America to monitor developments in Bolivia, the poorest country in South America. They want to be ready to intervene against the new Evo Morales government, now that it has nationalized the second-largest natural gas field on the continent, should propitious circumstances develop. Paraguay seemed ideal for these purposes. A small, extremely poor, landlocked country bordering on Bolivia, Paraguay's chief economic activities are subsistence agriculture, the illicit production and export of cannabis, and small-scale trading operations that serve primarily the interests of its two large and powerful neighbors, Argentina and Brazil. Its population as of July 2005 was a mere 6.3 million.

One unusual feature of the country is that about 15,000 Lebanese immigrants live in the small, run-down town of Ciudad del Este where the borders of Paraguay, Argentina, and Brazil converge. Many of these Lebanese arrived about twenty years ago and like their brethren in many other big Latin American cities such as São Paulo, Brazil, engage primarily in small retailing and textile manufacturing. Syrians and Lebanese began immigrating to Brazil more than 120 years ago, and an estimated 9 million or 5 percent of Brazil's 186 million inhabitants have their ancestral roots in the Middle East. In fact, Brazil has more citizens of Lebanese origin than there are in Lebanon.[79] Across the Paraná River from Ciudad del

Este is the richer and better-policed Brazilian town of Foz do Iguaçu, near the most spectacular waterfalls in the Western Hemisphere. This is where most of the successful Lebanese traders actually live. The two cities together have a population of around two hundred thousand.

This so-called triborder area has a reputation as an "unruly region," in the words of the CIA's unclassified *World Factbook,* a place where marijuana and cigarette smuggling into the Brazilian and Argentine markets has led to money laundering and arms and narcotics trafficking, much like any town on the U.S.-Mexican border.[80] No one gave the place any thought until President Bush launched his global war on terror, at which time the presence of Muslims provided a pretext for future penetration. All of a sudden a spate of feverish articles appeared in American magazines typically describing the triborder area "as one of the most lawless places in the world."[81] A leader of this campaign in Washington was then deputy secretary of state Richard Armitage. The veteran *New Yorker* journalist Jeffrey Goldberg declared, "This Muslim community has in its midst a hard core of terrorists," and Jessica Stern of Harvard's John F. Kennedy School of Government and the author of *Terror in the Name of God: Why Religious Militants Kill* warned in *Foreign Affairs* that the triborder region is "a place where terrorists with widely disparate ideologies . . . meet to swap tradecraft."[82]

The problem is that there is no evidence for the presence of terrorists, or even of fund-raising activities for extremist groups such as Hamas and Hezbollah, in the triborder area. The former U.S. ambassador to Brazil said as much and the commander of Southcom, General James Hill, agreed with her. As the head of the Brazilian Federal Police in Foz remarked, "We have a marijuana problem and cigarette smuggling, but we don't have any concrete evidence that this is a terrorist region."[83] The Brazilian ambassador to the United States wrote to *Foreign Affairs* complaining about "Jessica Stern's groundless assertions."[84] According to the State Department's annual report on "Patterns of Terrorism," between 1961 and 2003 only 1.2 percent of worldwide terrorist activity took place in Argentina, Brazil, Paraguay, Uruguay, and Chile combined.[85] Nonetheless, the Pentagon insisted that the Paraguayan government badly needed American help in fighting terrorism, narcotics trafficking, and corruption, and that, if Asunción would accept an American military mission, we would also throw in some "medical assistance." Thus the penetration of Paraguay began.

After some hard-sell negotiations and a little bribery, on May 26, 2005, the Pentagon got what it wanted. The Paraguay Senate approved an agreement with the United States allowing four hundred Special Forces troops to enter the country on July 1 and conduct some thirteen joint military exercises lasting until December 31, 2005. Washington offered a funding package of approximately $45,000 per exercise.[86] According to the Inter Press News Service journalist Alejandro Sciscioli, the Paraguay Senate approved the agreement "with no debate and without any information on it being published in the press."[87]

The U.S. embassy in Paraguay explained that the exercises in question would involve humanitarian and medical assistance to poor communities "as well as military training," but the deputy speaker of the parliament, Alejandro Ugarte, let slip that only two of the thirteen exercises "are of a civilian nature."[88] In September 2005, Reuters carried photos of members of an army medical team performing checkups on small children in the Paraguayan city of Pilar on the Paraná River.[89] Some Paraguayans commented that the sight of men in uniform frightened the children—this being a part of the world where uniforms have long been associated with dictatorial power and violence—and that such work would better be entrusted to a civilian organization such as Médecins Sans Frontières.

In order to soften up Paraguay, the Bush administration put on the sort of display of hospitality usually reserved for leaders of its closest satellites. On September 26, 2003, Paraguay's newly elected president, Nicanor Duarte Frutos, was received in the Oval Office, the first Paraguayan head of state to be so honored. In June 2005, Duarte's vice president, Luis Castiglioni, on a visit to Washington met with vice president Dick Cheney, former assistant secretary of state for Western Hemisphere Affairs Roger Noriega, and Secretary of Defense Rumsfeld. The Paraguayan journalist Alfredo Bocca Paz noted dryly, "That's a big fuss to make over a vice president of Paraguay."[90] In mid-August 2005, Rumsfeld flew to Asunción for an on-the-spot inspection. While there he promised that he would send experts from the Center for Hemispheric Defense Studies to work on a joint "planning seminar on systems for national security."[91] The FBI announced that it would open an office in Asunción in 2006.

When the first American troops arrived in Paraguay in the summer of

2005, they did not, in fact, go anywhere near the unruly triborder area, as one might have expected, but instead established their base at an old airport some 434 miles away in the Chaco region of northern Paraguay, not far from the Bolivian border. This was enough to convince many Paraguayans and most of their neighbors that the United States was building a new base in the heart of South America.

Back in 1982, the United States had helped General Alfredo Stroessner, Paraguay's dictator from 1954 until 1989, to build a massive military airfield near the town of Mariscal Estigarribia, which now has a population of about two thousand, of whom three hundred are Paraguayan soldiers. The airfield has runways long and strong enough to take B-52 bombers and C-5 Galaxy transports, plus a fully equipped radar system, large hangars, and an air traffic control tower. It is actually bigger than the international airport in the capital, Asunción. The only thing of note that ever happened at Estigarribia before the American troops arrived was Pope John Paul II's landing there, in May 1988. In the summer of 2005, the Americans immediately set about refurbishing and further enlarging the base.

American troops are free to do almost anything they want in Paraguay. In the May 26, 2005, agreement, the Bush administration extracted a provision exempting its officials and military from the jurisdiction of both the local judicial system and the International Criminal Court. The Special Forces are not subject to customs duties and are free to transport weapons and medical supplies anywhere in Paraguayan territory.[92] This is important for various reasons. Under the terms of Mercosur, the agreement among Argentina, Brazil, Uruguay, and Paraguay creating a southern-cone trading bloc, all parties pledge to inform each other about international developments and to coordinate their foreign policies. Like virtually all other nations in Latin America, Argentina, Brazil, and Uruguay have rejected Bush administration demands for Article 98 Agreements protecting Americans from being turned over to the International Criminal Court. The United States has cut off all forms of aid to the three as a result. In 2004, despite the presence of the Manta base, Ecuador, too, forfeited $15.7 million in U.S. aid, much of it for military equipment, rather than go along with America's pressure tactics.[93] By giving the United States carte blanche in its country, Paraguay is breaking ranks with its neighbors, which has led to speculation that the United States wants to destroy Mercosur.

The asymmetries in size and power between small nations like Paraguay and Ecuador and the United States inevitably make our relations with them imperialist in nature when we act in a high-handed way. Paraguay has no need for an American military base, nor for U.S training of its armed forces. Paraguay is not likely to go to war with its powerful neighbors, particularly given the nineteenth-century War of the Triple Alliance (1865–70) in which it was badly defeated and lost a large part of its territory. But the United States is always ready to use its overwhelming might to force small nations to bend to its will.

It is impossible to foresee in detail the future use to which the American empire of bases may be put, but there is at least a growing understanding of and sophistication about U.S. basing policies among peoples on the receiving end. The Argentine pacifist and antiwar activist Adolfo Pérez Esquivel, winner of the 1980 Nobel Peace Prize, commented on the developments in Paraguay, "Once the United States arrives, it takes a long time to leave."

5

How American Imperialism Actually Works:
The SOFA in Japan

Okinawans have learned the built-in weaknesses of Japan . . . through endless failed or ignored petitions to the Japanese government for the reduction and eventual closure of the U.S. military bases in Okinawa. The stock answer of the Japanese leaders is: "We will let America know of Okinawa's wishes." . . . Okinawa's wishes are only gossip topics, never a part of Japan's national policy issues deserving of serious negotiation with the U.S. . . . The Marines believe that they are above the law and can do anything with impunity.

—KOJI TAIRA, editor,
Ryukyuanist, Summer 2004

In seeking permission to build or use one or more military bases in a foreign country, the United States first negotiates a fundamental contract—one that commonly creates an "alliance" with the other state. These basic agreements are usually short, straightforward treaties that express "common objectives" related to "national security" and "international threats to the peace." Examples include the 1949 charter setting up the North Atlantic Treaty Organization, the Convention on the Presence of Foreign Forces in the Federal Republic of Germany (October 1954), and the renegotiated Japan-U.S. Security Treaty (January 1960).

Once the United States has concluded this basic document, it then negotiates a Status of Forces Agreement (SOFA), intended above all to put any U.S. forces stationed in the host country as far beyond its domestic laws as possible. The legal systems of some of these "hosts" are every bit as sophisticated as our own, ones in which Americans would be unlikely to find themselves seriously disadvantaged by local law enforcement. What SOFAs do, however, is give American soldiers, contractors, Department of

Defense civilians, and their dependents a whole range of special privileges that are not available to ordinary citizens of the country or to non-American visitors. In the great tradition of "extraterritoriality" that began in the world of nineteenth-century Western colonialism, they are almost never reciprocal—that is, the SOFAs bestow on Americans privileges that are not available to citizens of the host nation if they should visit or be assigned to the United States. The major exception is the SOFA governing NATO, which is reciprocal. Military forces of a NATO nation working in the United States are supposed to receive the same rights and benefits given to American troops in Europe.

Most empires, ancient or modern, have not felt the need to establish a legal basis for their activities in subordinate countries. Might makes right, and imperialists normally do as they please. In wartime, this is called the "law of the flag." From 1945 on, the presence of the occupying Soviet armed forces in the former German Democratic Republic (East Germany), for example, was never subject to any treaty. But in this area, American administrations have proved legalistic sticklers, crossing the *t*'s and dotting the *i*'s of the largely one-sided agreements they make to garrison the planet.

SOFAs are not in themselves basing or access agreements. For example, article 6 of the Japan-U.S. Security Treaty simply says, "For the purpose of contributing to the security of Japan and the maintenance of international peace and security in the Far East, the United States of America is granted the use by its land, air, and naval forces of facilities and areas of Japan. The use of these facilities and areas as well as the status of the United States armed forces in Japan shall be governed by a separate agreement."[1] SOFAs implement these more basic agreements and spell out what the host nation has actually obligated itself to allow the United States to do.

SOFAs create many local problems for host nations. For instance, American military bases and the activities they engender regularly do damage to the environment. Article 6 of both the Japan and the South Korea SOFAs stipulates: "The United States is not obliged, when it returns facilities and areas . . . on the expiration of this Agreement or at an earlier date, to restore the facilities and areas to the condition in which they were at the time they became available to the United States armed forces, or to compensate Japan [or the Republic of Korea] in lieu of such restoration."[2]

This is a typical and often deeply resented aspect of U.S. SOFAs and an invitation to the U.S. military to pollute in any way it wants without fear of accountability. For example, the Fukuchi Dam provides most of the water supply to the 1.3 million residents of the island of Okinawa, but the U.S. armed forces use the dam's reservoir for river-crossing exercises. Significant amounts of discarded munitions have been discovered in the surrounding watershed area. The South Korean government so resents this provision of the SOFA, which was imposed on South Korea in the wake of the devastation of the Korean War, that in 2006 it rejected the U.S. military's attempt to return twenty-five closed military camps until it at least removed underground fuel tanks and undertook remediation of the water tables at each of them. In a classic of militarist hypocrisy, General B. B. Bell, commander of U.S. Forces Korea, responded, "It is fair to say that we loved this land and its people enough to die for it. To state now that we have been irresponsible stewards of Korean land, while standing side by side with you, is a charge that hurts my heart."[3]

A subtler form of pollution—also much resented by those who live near U.S. bases—is noise. The sounds of warplanes and helicopters become a perpetual backdrop to daily life. The citizens of the large urban prefecture of Kanagawa have protested for years that U.S. Navy planes from Atsugi air base practicing night landings keep them awake. Cities located near large American airfields have even successfully sued for damages. In February 2005, a district court awarded the communities around Okinawa's Kadena Air Base 2.8 billion yen ($24,472,000) in compensation for noise pollution. However, even though the citizens who brought this suit won in court, they are unlikely ever to receive any compensation from the U.S. government. Article 18 (5) (3) of Japan's SOFA stipulates, "Where the United States alone is responsible [in a civil claims case], the amount awarded or adjudged shall be distributed in the proportion of 25 percent chargeable to Japan and 75 percent chargeable to the United States." The Japanese Ministry of Foreign Affairs has been trying unsuccessfully since 1994 to get the United States to pay its share of earlier noise judgments. U.S. administrations have regularly professed to find it "strange" that the American military should have to pay damages for practicing warfare to protect Japan. The U.S. government demands that Japan abide by what it has signed but is indifferent about its own obligations under the SOFA.[4]

The NATO SOFA and the agreements with individual European countries do not contain exemptions from responsibility for environmental
and noise pollution, which is undoubtedly one reason Secretary of Defense Rumsfeld wants to move American bases from Germany to the "new
Europe," those ex-communist satellites of Eastern Europe that are poor
and desperate enough to be willing—at least for now—to let the Americans pollute as they wish, cost free, in order to get what economic benefits
they can.

SOFAs actually take the question of American entrances and exits out
of the hands of host countries—which, of course, gives the very term
"host" a curious, new meaning. Article 9(2) of Japan's SOFA is typical.
"Members of the United States armed forces," it says, "shall be exempt
from Japanese passport and visa laws and regulations." This means that
American servicemen accused of crimes in Japan have sometimes been
spirited out of the country without facing legal obstacles, and the Japanese
can do nothing about it.

Or take, for example, the simple matter of driving skills in countries
like Japan where the direction of road traffic is the reverse of that in the
United States. Article 10(1) of the Japanese SOFA states: "Japan shall
accept as valid, without a driving test or fee, the driving permit or license
or military driving permit issued by the United States to a member of the
United States armed forces, the civilian component, and their dependents." Citizens of Okinawa have paid a high price for this clause in head-
on crashes and hit-and-run accidents since 1972, when the island was
restored to Japanese sovereignty and driving on the left-hand side of the
road once again became the law of the land—except for confused GIs.
Article 13(1) only aggravates article 10: "The United States armed forces
shall not be subject to taxes or similar charges on property held, used or
transferred by such forces in Japan." The governor of Okinawa, Keiichi
Inamine, contends that U.S. military personnel now pay less than one-
fifth of what Japanese citizens pay for the public services they receive and
that if their vehicles were taxed as those of ordinary citizens are, Okinawa's
income would increase by 780 million yen ($6.8 million).[5]

There are a legion of other complex problems associated with SOFAs,
including the large tracts of otherwise valuable land in land-poor countries like Japan that the United States "leases" for free; the host-nation
employees who work on our military bases without the protection of

either their own or U.S. labor laws; and the fact that host-nation customs officers are denied access to U.S. military cargos.

However, easily the most contentious issues between the United States and nations on the receiving end of our empire of bases involve problems of civil and criminal jurisdiction. For civil matters, such as damage caused by off-duty American personnel driving their cars, SOFAs often stipulate how the injury is to be determined and compensated—including the possibility of requiring our forces to carry personal property damage insurance. For criminal cases, all SOFAs differ, but most award primary jurisdiction to the United States if the crime was committed by one soldier against another or if a crime was committed while a service member was engaged in his or her official duties. In other types of crimes, the host nation usually retains jurisdiction.

This seemingly straightforward distinction has unfortunately been anything but. What if a crime, committed by a service member on duty, was unrelated to those duties? Who then gets to decide jurisdiction in such instances? The most famous Japanese-American SOFA case went all the way to the U.S. Supreme Court (*Wilson v. Girard*, 354 US 524 [1957]). It concerned an incident in which the United States and Japan agreed on the facts, but the Americans claimed that their soldier was performing his duties while the Japanese insisted he was acting well beyond them. In January 1957, a twenty-one-year-old army specialist third class, William S. Girard, was guarding a machine gun on a practice range. A Japanese woman—a mother of six who earned her living by selling scrap metal—intruded onto the range to scavenge for expended shell casings. Girard, using a grenade launcher, fired an empty shell casing at her, killing her.

According to testimony, Girard lured the woman closer by tossing empty shell casings toward her and then shot her as a "joke."[6] The United States at first claimed primary jurisdiction under the SOFA in effect at the time, but then agreed to turn over Girard to Japan because of the public furor the incident generated. Girard sued the secretary of defense, Charles E. Wilson, claiming that, according to law, he should be tried by a U.S. court-martial, not by a Japanese court. The U.S. District Court for the District of Columbia agreed with Girard, but the Supreme Court then reversed this decision. A Japanese court gave Girard a three-year suspended sentence and he soon returned to the United States accompanied by his Japanese wife.[7]

It remains a major issue of constitutional law in the United States whether the Pentagon can, by ordering a soldier to serve in a particular foreign country, force him or her to give up the guarantees provided under the Bill of Rights.[8] Much of the American press at the time of the Girard case was outraged by the Supreme Court's decision. "The basic rights of the American soldier have been violated," trumpeted Hearst's *New York Journal-American.* But Tokyo's *Asahi Evening News* expressed pleasure that Japan was granted this minimal display of sovereignty. "At no time since the signing of the San Francisco peace treaty have Japanese thought so kindly of the U.S. and the American sense of justice and fair-play."[9] Unfortunately, since the Girard case, it has been all downhill.

Between 1998 and 2004, U.S. military personnel in Japan have been involved in 2,024 reported crimes or accidents while on duty. Only one led to a court-martial. Commanders ordered "administrative discipline" in 318 instances; the remaining 1,706 presumably went unpunished.[10]

SOFAs invariably infringe on the sovereignty of the host nation. In the Girard case, the U.S. Supreme Court paraphrased Chief Justice John Marshall, fourth chief justice of the United States, defining a sovereign nation as one that "has exclusive jurisdiction to punish offenses against its laws committed within its borders unless it expressly or impliedly consents to surrender its jurisdiction." SOFAs quite explicitly take away sovereign rights, which is why they are more easily imposed on defeated or occupied nations like Germany and Japan after World War II and South Korea after the Korean War, or extremely weak and dependent nations like Ecuador and Honduras. But while they attempt to regularize the largely one-sided relationships of the American military empire and are often willingly enforced by allied, satellite, or dependent governments, they also introduce notions that can grow into long-term discontent and popular opposition to empire itself. SOFAs cannot help but give rise to explosive political disputes when American laws and the expectations of its troops create a climate of impunity in the host nation. Outrage is then often sparked by simple differences in legal cultures. For example, in South Korea, murder is defined simply as causing the death of a Korean citizen, regardless of the presence of intent, negligence, or even motive. American troops are thus fearful of being tried in Korean courts, even though, ironically enough, they have often been dealt with more leniently in Korean courts than they would be in American ones. At the same time, Koreans are understandably outraged by U.S. military courts that define killings as "unavoidable accidents" and acquit servicemembers who seem self-evidently guilty by Korean standards.[11]

In 1957, according to *Time* magazine, there were "more than" forty SOFAs "designed to legalize the status of 700,000 U.S. servicemen in friendly countries."[12] In April 1996, the State Department said that we had SOFAs with fifty-three countries.[13] By 9/11, the United States had publicly acknowledged SOFAs with ninety-three countries, although some SOFAs are so embarrassing to the host nation, particularly in the Islamic world, that they are kept secret.[14] While the U.S. empire of bases has been expanding at a rapid rate since the mid-1990s, the true number of existing SOFAs remains publicly unknown.

The range of problems SOFAs breed could be illustrated by looking at almost any of our large complexes in almost any (non–Western European) nation, but the network of bases on the Japanese island of Okinawa catches the world of the SOFA especially sharply, suggesting some of the ways in which any Status of Forces Agreement engenders, even among America's closest allies, a sense of being occupied, of inequality, of injustice, and of anti-Americanism in the local political system. Reaching a Status of Forces Agreement, which theoretically nails down certain long-term rights for the United States, often is like planting dangerous seeds in local soil that may, in the end, curtail or terminate those very imperial rights. A SOFA almost invariably creates resentment, turning local communities where Americans are based (but are beyond the reach of local law and authorities, beyond, that is, accountability) into potential flash points in which any set of criminal acts, impositions, or slights may stir opposition. Many of the problems created by a SOFA—and the bases that are its concrete manifestation—may seem minor and distinctly parochial to an outsider, but these are the material from which long-term changes may arise. Even as the present Japanese government moves ever closer to the needs and desires of the Bush administration, the soil in which another kind of Japan may be growing is being prepared.

Okinawa is Japan's most southerly prefecture and its poorest. As of 2005, it was host to thirty-seven of the eighty-eight American military bases in Japan. These Okinawan bases cover a total area of 233 square kilometers, representing 75 percent of the territory occupied by U.S. military facilities in Japan, even though Okinawa itself has only .6 percent of

Japan's total land area.[15] Since 2001, Okinawa has been the scene of a particularly fierce confrontation over the Japanese-American SOFA.

Japan, like Germany, has been a post–World War II keystone of the American military empire. If it should ever defect from our embrace, the rest of our imperial structure in East Asia would likely unravel. The Bush administration has already alienated Germany through its unilateralist diplomacy and its war with Iraq. Despite a far more obsequious government in Tokyo, Washington may sooner or later be in danger of doing the same with Japan, thanks to the way our SOFA agreement emphasizes American ignorance of and insensitivity to the fissures our military presence has opened in that country. While the United States mechanically relies on the SOFA to shield military felons from the application of Japanese law, Defense Secretary Donald Rumsfeld schemes to reform our global base structure in part by enlisting Japan to become a much more active imperial partner with us, to become an "East Asian Britain," as the Pentagon phrases it. Japan never agreed in the Japan-U.S. Security Treaty to help the United States garrison Asia or the Persian Gulf, and much of its population is deeply opposed. The various, never-ending local disputes in Okinawa, where U.S. Marines and Japanese citizens live cheek by jowl, over how the SOFA dilutes Japanese sovereignty is the place where the wounds fester and threaten to spread.

As of November 2004, according to Pentagon statistics, the United States had stationed some 36,365 uniformed military personnel in Japan, not counting 11,887 sailors attached to the Seventh Fleet at its bases at Yokosuka (Kanagawa prefecture) and Sasebo (Nagasaki prefecture), some of whom are intermittently at sea. In addition there were 45,140 American dependents, 27,019 civilian employees of the Department of Defense, and approximately 20,000 Japanese citizens working for the U.S. forces in jobs ranging from maintaining golf courses and waiting on tables in the numerous officers' clubs to translating Japanese newspapers for the Central Intelligence Agency and the Defense Intelligence Agency.[16]

Okinawa is host to more than 50,000 of these American troops, military-related civilians, and dependents. According to Japanese researchers, the largest group of U.S. forces in Okinawa consists of 16,015 uniformed marines, 733 Department of Defense civilians, and 8,809 marine family members, adding up to a marine cohort of 25,557. The air force contributes 7,100 pilots and maintenance crews at the island's huge Kadena

Air Base, the largest U.S. base in East Asia, joined by 622 civilians and 12,333 family members for a total of 20,055 affiliated with the air force. The army contingent (2,233) and the navy contingent (5,081) of troops and camp followers are much smaller.[17] Even without these foreign guests, Okinawa is a seriously overcrowded island.

By far the greatest SOFA-related popular outrage in Japan concerns article 17, which covers criminal justice. This article is over two pages long and contains twelve complex subclauses. It is further modified by three pages of "agreed minutes" consented to during the negotiations over the Security Treaty and which are not normally included in the publicly available, authoritative texts of the SOFA.[18] Opinion in Okinawa is virtually universal that article 17 should, at the very least, be rewritten, whereas the U.S. military clings intransigently to its every stipulation—in 2003, even rescinding a slight concession it made in 1996.

The locally detested words in article 17(3)(c) are: "The custody of an accused member of the United States armed forces or the civilian component over whom Japan is to exercise jurisdiction shall, if he is in the hands of the United States, remain with the United States until he is charged." This means that Japanese authorities investigating a crime cannot have exclusive access to a suspect until Japanese prosecutors have actually indicted him in court; that the Japanese police are hobbled in carrying out an investigation in which an American serviceman is involved; and that prosecutors may be reluctant to bring charges against an American serviceman because of their inability to gather sufficient evidence.

These long-standing grievances burst into the open in the wake of the most serious incident to influence Japanese-American relations since the Security Treaty was signed in 1960. On September 4, 1995, two marines and a sailor from Camp Hansen, a huge marine base in central Okinawa, abducted a twelve-year-old girl they picked out at random, beat and raped her, and left her on a beach while they returned to their base in a rented car. The Okinawan press reported that the three military suspects were lolling around the pool eating hamburgers and had the run of the base while the child victim was in the hospital badly injured. This attack, combined with the refusal of the U.S. high command on the island to turn over the suspects to the Japanese police in accordance with article 17(3)(c), led to some of the largest anti-American demonstrations in postwar history. On October 21, 1995, 85,000 Okinawans gathered in a park in the city of Ginowan to demand that the American and Japanese governments pay some attention to their grievances.

Comments by American military leaders contributed to the popular outrage. The then commander of U.S. Forces Japan, Lieutenant General Richard Myers, who would become President George W. Bush's chairman of the Joint Chiefs of Staff, remarked that this was a singular tragedy caused by "three bad apples" even though he knew that sexually violent crimes committed by U.S. soldiers against Okinawans were running at the rate of two per month. Even worse, Myers's superior, Admiral Richard C. Macke, commander of all U.S. forces in the Pacific, said to the press, "I think that [the rape] was absolutely stupid. For the price they paid to rent the car [with which to abduct their victim], they could have had a girl." The American military in Japan has never been allowed to forget these disgraceful acts and the spin put on them by very high ranking officers.[19]

All servicemen in Okinawa know that if, after committing a rape, robbery, or assault, they can make it back to base, they will remain in American custody until indicted even if the Japanese execute a warrant for their capture. By contrast, Japanese criminal law gives the police twenty-three days during which they can hold and question a suspect without charging or releasing him. During this period, a suspect meets alone with police investigators who attempt to elicit a confession, the "king of evidence" (*shoko no o*) in the minds of all Japanese prosecutors and most citizens. The Japanese believe that a lengthy process of reasoning with a suspect will cause him to see the error of his ways and that acknowledging publicly what he has done will restore the "harmony" (*wa*) of society. Japanese judges treat guilt established in this way much more leniently than American criminal proceedings would. (It is perhaps closest to the American practice of plea bargaining, itself uncommon in Japan.) On the other hand, a suspect in a Japanese courtroom who pulls an "O.J. defense," refusing to cooperate or continuing to assert his innocence in the face of strong material evidence and witnesses, is likely to receive a harsh sentence. During the period of interrogation, a criminal suspect is not permitted to consult an attorney, be released on bail, or seek the equivalent of a habeas corpus hearing. In Japan, a criminal suspect who is arrested and charged is much more likely to be found guilty than in the United States, but the Japanese police and courts are much less likely to arrest or convict an innocent suspect.[20]

The American military contends that these procedures, a long-standing part of Japanese culture, could lead American soldiers to make false confessions and so constitute political violations of their "human rights." This argument does not carry much weight in Okinawa (or anywhere else for that matter, given the Bush administration's record of protecting human rights at Guantánamo, Abu Ghraib, and in its other secret prisons around the world). Every time there is a sexually violent crime in which the prime suspect is an American soldier, the victim Okinawan, and the military refuses to turn him over until a Japanese court has issued an indictment, there are calls from the governor, unanimous votes in the prefectural assembly, and street demonstrations demanding a total rewriting of the SOFA.

Until the rape of September 4, 1995, the United States had never turned over a military criminal suspect to Japanese authorities prior to his being indicted. (In the Girard case, the Japanese authorities had already charged him with homicide.) Pressure, however, mounted on the United States to become more flexible if it hoped to keep its troops in Okinawa. In February 1996, President Clinton and Prime Minister Hashimoto met at an emergency summit in Santa Monica, California, to think of ways to defuse Okinawan anger. Finally, the United States made a concession. In a meeting of a joint committee authorized by article 2(1)(a) of the SOFA, the United States agreed in future cases to give "sympathetic consideration" (*koiteki koryo*) to Japanese requests that a military culprit be handed over to Japanese authorities before indictment if suspected of "especially heinous crimes"—a category left undefined but generally taken to mean murder or rape. Despite this "flexible application" of the SOFA, the United States rejected all but one subsequent request for early hand-over until the sensational incidents considered below.[21]

Governor Inamine's predecessor as chief executive of Okinawa prefecture was Masahide Ota, a retired university professor, prolific writer on the history of the Ryukyu Islands (of which Okinawa is the largest), and a devoted antibase activist. After leaving office in 1998, Ota became a socialist member of the upper house of the Diet, or national parliament. By contrast, Inamine, a conservative businessman, was president of Ryukyu Petroleum before taking office. He ran against Ota's record of base protest, claiming that he could broker the return of friendly relations with the ruling Liberal Democratic Party in Tokyo and the U.S. military. In the seven years since he was elected, however, Inamine has drawn ever closer to Ota's positions.

In talking about excessive crime rates among American servicemen in Okinawa, Inamine likes to refer to the different perspectives of the U.S. military and Okinawans. The American high command, he says, treats each rape or murder as an exceptional "tragic occurrence" committed by a one-in-a-million "bad apple," for which the American ambassador and commanding general now invariably apologize profusely. According to Inamine, Okinawans see not discrete crimes but rather a sixty-year-long record of sexual assaults, bar brawls, muggings, drug violations, drunken driving accidents, and arson cases committed by privileged young men who claim they are in Okinawa to protect Okinawans from the dangers of political "instability" elsewhere in East Asia. During a visit to the island in November 2003, Secretary of Defense Rumsfeld said to the governor, "This region has been at peace during the existence of our bilateral security treaty [which has] greatly benefited our two nations."[22] Rumsfeld's remark infuriated Okinawans, ignoring as it did the Korean and Vietnamese wars during both of which Okinawa played a central role as a staging area for the U.S. military.

Inamine invited the Japanese and foreign press to sit in on his November 16 meeting with Rumsfeld, the only open one Rumsfeld held during his trip to Japan, and the governor conspicuously delivered a seven-point petition outlining Okinawa's grievances, including a demand for a fundamental review of the SOFA. Inamine later acknowledged that he had been deliberately discourteous and that Rumsfeld was "visibly angered," but, as he explained, both the American and Japanese governments take Okinawa completely for granted, which left him little choice but to use this "rare occasion" to make the people's case.[23]

The transformation of Governor Inamine into a resolute advocate of rewriting the SOFA began several years after he came into office, when three further sexual assaults occurred (on June 29, 2001, November 2, 2002, and May 25, 2003). The first of these began around 2:30 a.m. in a parking lot within the American Village entertainment and shopping plaza in the town of Chatan, just outside the main gate of Kadena Air Force Base. Several off-duty servicemen observed twenty-four-year-old air force staff sergeant Timothy Woodland of the 353rd Operations Support Squadron at Kadena with his pants down to his knees having sex with a twenty-year-old Okinawan woman on the hood of a car. Several of them later testified that they heard the woman yell, "No! Stop!" Marine lance corporal Jermaine Oliphant later testified in court that he saw Woodland rape the woman as she struggled to get away. The defense contended that Oliphant regarded the air force sergeant as his rival. Woodland fled the scene in a car with a military license plate.[24] On July 2, following a complaint by the woman, the Japanese police issued a warrant for his arrest on suspicion of rape and sodomy. After vacillating for four days, on July 6, the American authorities reluctantly turned him over to the Japanese—before prosecutors had obtained an indictment.

Japanese reaction, local and national, to this incident was overwhelming. In Tokyo, the Foreign Affairs Committee of the House of Representatives, irritated over the four-day delay in turning over Woodland, voted unanimously for a revision of the SOFA. The crime and the U.S. military's response "gave great concern and shock to the people of Okinawa, and the people of Japan are feeling indignation." Chief Cabinet Secretary Yasuo Fukuda—the second-most influential official in the government and perhaps a future prime minister—announced that Japan would not seek a revision of the SOFA but would ask for a faster, less contentious application of the existing agreement.[25] (The American embassy had already informed Fukuda that the United States was adamantly opposed to a wholesale revision of the SOFA.)

Secretary of Defense Rumsfeld publicly asserted his fear of setting a precedent. "One Pentagon official said the United States was concerned that if Sergeant Woodland were transferred to the local authorities before being indicted, he would have no guarantee of having a lawyer or even an interpreter with him during questioning, and that the authorities could conduct their questioning in any manner and for any length of time."[26]

In fact, the police did interrogate Woodland for thirty hours—without eliciting a confession. He contended that the sex on the morning of June 29, 2001, was "consensual" and pleaded not guilty to the charges. Most Okinawans thought it highly unlikely that consensual sex would have taken place on the hood of a car with several other men looking on. American soldiers disagreed. Several of them argued in print that the victim was merely an "Amejo" (an American groupie) or a "night owl," and one went so far as to say, "Every Japanese girl I have dated or known as a friend has stated that she is intrigued by having sex in public." Another soldier referred to the victim as "a miniskirt-wearing little 'yellow cab' who couldn't remember what her name was. . . . Most of these trashy tramps can't think far enough ahead to order fries with their Big Mac." Even the Japanese (and female) foreign minister Makiko Tanaka tried to blame the victim by saying that she should not have been out so late, drinking in a bar frequented by American servicemen.[27]

Presiding judge Soichi Hayashida was having none of this. On March 28, 2002, he found Woodland guilty, declaring that the "testimony offered by the victim is highly trustworthy," and sentenced Woodland to two years and eight months in a Japanese prison.[28] Okinawan residents welcomed the verdict (though they generally found the sentence too light). The Okinawan Prefectural Assembly adopted a resolution seeking revision of the SOFA. There the dispute rested until seven months later, when another serious rape occurred, and this time the Americans refused to turn over the suspect.

In 2002, Major Michael J. Brown was forty-one years old, an eighteen-year veteran, attached to the headquarters of the Third Marine Expeditionary Force at Camp Courtney, a large deployment of several thousand marines in central Okinawa. It was his second tour of duty in the Ryukyu Islands. Within the Corps, Brown was a "mustang," that is, an officer who came up from within the ranks. At the time, Brown was living off base in the nearby community of Gushikawa with his American wife, Lisa, and two young children.

No one could remember another time when an officer was in trouble with the Okinawan police. On that November day, upon completion of his day's work, Brown went to the Camp Courtney officers' club. It was karaoke night, and he spent the evening with fellow officers and their wives (not including his own), drinking, playing pool, and crooning into a microphone to recorded accompaniment. When the club closed at midnight, he decided to walk to his home two miles away via an auxiliary rear gate to the base, which proved to be locked. So he walked back to the main gate. He had also forgotten his coat at the club and was getting cold. He admits he was intoxicated.

According to his own account, as he was walking back to Camp Courtney's main gate around 1:00 a.m., he was offered a ride home by Victoria Nakamine, a forty-year-old Filipina barmaid and cashier at the officers' club. She is married to an Okinawan. Brown says that once they left Camp

Courtney in her car they stopped on a quiet road and had a heated argument about the proper route to take. Both agree that he grabbed Nakamine's cell phone, apparently in order to prevent her from calling for help, and threw it into the nearby Tengen River.

According to Brown, Nakamine, now infuriated, drove back to the main gate alone, where she told the military police that he had twice tried to rape her. The MPs replied that since the incident occurred off base, they would have to call the Okinawan prefectural police. Gushikawa policemen came to the scene and took her complaint. She said she had fought Brown off and left the car, and when she returned to see if he had calmed down, he seized her phone and again tried to assault her. She claimed she fought ferociously to fend off his attacks.

Brown was ambiguous: in some accounts he said they just had a loud, unpleasant argument; in others, he claimed that Nakamine made sexual advances to him. He repeatedly said he "was seduced by the woman and when I would not go along with the seduction, she got angry and filed the complaint."[29]

Proceeding cautiously, the police delayed acting for a month on Nakamine's complaint. Finally, on December 3, the Naha (Okinawa) District Court issued a warrant for Brown's arrest on a charge of attempted rape and destroying private property (the cell phone).[30] The Ministry of Foreign Affairs in Tokyo asked the Marine Corps to turn him over. After delaying for two days, the U.S. embassy curtly announced that it had decided to retain custody of Major Brown, declaring, "The government of the United States has concluded that the circumstances of this case as presented by the government of Japan do not warrant departure from the standard practice as agreed between the United States and Japan."[31] The Okinawan press speculated that the Americans did not consider a failed rape a "heinous crime." U.S. intransigence did not go down well with anyone, except perhaps members of the Marine Corps.

On December 6, a large number of Okinawan police raided Brown's off-base home and carried off anything that looked promising, in the process frightening his wife and children.[32] Prime Minister Junichiro Koizumi said that the United States' refusal to turn over Major Brown was acceptable, but his foreign minister, Yoriko Kawaguchi, proved less accommodating. She asserted that Japan would need a clarification of what was included under the 1996 "sympathetic consideration" agreement.[33]

Governor Inamine declared, "It is a heinous crime infringing upon the human rights of a woman, and it is unforgivable in that it was committed by a serviceman who is required to act as a leader. It . . . causes me to feel strong indignation." Most significantly, a newly formed liaison group of all fourteen governors of prefectures in which American bases are located urged the Liberal Democratic Party "to secure a true Japan-U.S. partnership through a revised Status of Forces Agreement."[34]

Finally, on December 19, Naha prosecutors indicted Brown and, in strict accordance with the SOFA, the United States handed him over the same day.[35] From that point on, Brown, with the help of his family, waged a campaign of legal maneuvers and publicity, charging, among other things, that the Japanese criminal justice system was unfair and that American officials were willing to see him railroaded in order to keep their bases in Japan and obtain Japan's cooperation for George W. Bush's pending invasion of Iraq.

One of Brown's first acts was to obtain an American lawyer, Victor Kelley of the National Military Justice Group, who, on March 7, 2003, filed a petition in U.S. federal court in Washington, D.C., for an emergency writ of habeas corpus. Kelley argued that, in turning over Brown to the Japanese, the U.S. government had violated his constitutional rights as an American citizen "to be free from compulsory incrimination, the right to the effective assistance of counsel, and the right to a reasonable bail." He added, "[In Japan,] due process has no meaning. The Japanese 'conviction' rate is nearly 100 percent. To be indicted is to be convicted. The presumption of innocence is a mockery of justice. Almost without exception, all are convicted; no one goes free." Needless to say, the Washington court did not grant the writ.[36]

Brown also sought to apply political pressure. He obtained the support of Senator Kay Bailey Hutchison (Republican from Texas) and of his Republican representative in Texas's Twenty-first District, Congressman Lamar Smith. Both of them informed the secretary of defense of their deep concern that Brown was not being treated fairly. Brown urged his friends and fellow marines to write to their elected representatives, suggesting that they say, "It is way past time for President Bush to intervene and no longer allow the Japanese government to persecute this innocent Marine."

Brown's family in the United States create,
Brown" Web site, and the commentaries posted o.
uted to marines on Okinawa. As time wore on, b.
began to lash out at everyone they could think of, fr\
legal officers to ordinary Okinawans—"I would love to see
get their land and their island back and I would love to see
vicemen leaving that island and spending their money elsewhe.   .east
then, the slimy Okinawan officials couldn't get their hands on our guys
anymore. This solution would make us all happy, right? The Okinawans
obviously don't want us there. They don't want our soldiers funding their
local economy. They don't want the jobs our bases provide. They don't like
the exorbitant fees we pay them to rent their lands. They don't want us as a
deterrent for their enemies. And, they don't want us as neighbors."[37]

From Brown's point of view, the big break in his case came May 13,
2003, when, in open court, Victoria Nakamine testified, "I want . . . to
withdraw my complaint. I cannot speak Japanese very well. I signed my
written statement, but I didn't understand what was written." This was a
serious development. Hiroyuki Kawakami, deputy chief prosecutor at the
Naha District Public Prosecutors Office, commented, "This is an offense
subject to prosecution only on complaint from the victim, so it's unlikely
that a criminal case can be established in defiance of the victim's intent."[38]
In response, the court released Major Brown on 10-million-yen ($87,000)
bail but with the provisos that his passport be taken from him, he be confined to Camp Courtney, and he not try to leave Okinawa. This action was
unusual as Japanese courts accept defendants' requests for bail in only
14.6 percent of cases.[39]

Japanese criminal trials are normally adjudicated by a panel of three
judges, not by juries, and these judges regard themselves—and are
regarded by the public—as highly experienced experts on whether or not
someone is telling the truth. They are not subject to rules of evidence, and
they want to hear anything and everything about a case, including hearsay
evidence, gossip, and rumor. One admirable element of Japanese law is the
presumption by judges that the testimony of a woman who claims to be a
victim of a sex crime should be given more weight than that of the suspected offender. In the Brown case, presiding judge Nobuyuki Yokota
found Nakamine's original statement to the police believable, inferring

had probably withdrawn it under pressure from her employer the society in which she lived. He therefore ordered Brown's trial to proceed.

Brown erupted. In a letter to American ambassador Howard Baker, Brown charged that there had been "collusion between the court and prosecutor" and that he had been framed by the Gushikawa police. He instructed his attorney to appeal to the Okinawa branch of the Fukuoka High Court and then to the Japanese Supreme Court, asking that the three judges in his case be dismissed for prejudice. Neither appeal succeeded, but they kept Brown's case in the newspapers and heightened the growing worries of the American embassy that the cultural conflicts embedded in the SOFA were an insoluble problem.[40]

By the summer of 2003, Brown's Web site had received more than sixty-eight thousand hits, and inquiries from congressional staff assistants about the fairness of Japanese justice were becoming routine at the State Department. Moreover, the war in Iraq was influencing attitudes. Given the rising casualty rate among American troops, the Pentagon increasingly felt that the protection of the "human rights" of military personnel was a morale matter. The *Asahi Shimbun* quoted a U.S. official as saying, "American soldiers are in Okinawa to defend Japan. They're even prepared to die if necessary. And yet, when something happens, they [the Okinawans] will treat U.S. military personnel as criminals right away."[41]

On July 8, 2004, at the Naha District Court, Judge Yokota finally delivered the verdict. He dismissed the attempted rape charge against Brown but found him guilty of indecent assault and destroying Nakamine's property (her cell phone). He sentenced Brown to a one-year prison sentence suspended for three years and fined him about $1,400. Judge Yokota said it was clear to the court that a degree of consensual contact had occurred, but marks on Nakamine's neck showed that Brown had also used force in an attempt to compel her to perform an "indecent act."

The most sensational revelation in the verdict was that, on the day before Nakamine changed her story in court, an unknown person or group had deposited $13,500 into her bank account. The court did not know who had done this—Brown, his family, Filipino friends of Nakamine's, fellow workers at Camp Courtney's officers club, or the U.S. government—but concluded that the money probably caused her to change her story. Brown received a suspended sentence because he had no prior criminal record.[42]

As it turned out, there was a sad sequel to the Major Brown case. In August 2005, he left Okinawa and reported for duty at the Marine Corps base in Quantico, Virginia. His wife and children had already moved back to Texas. Brown was actually living at his brother's house in Laurel, Maryland, and commuting to Quantico. On October 4, 2005, a Maryland SWAT team arrested him in Laurel and charged that, on October 2, he had kidnapped an eighteen-year-old Chinese high school student, Lu Jin, at a flea market in Milton, West Virginia. Extradited to West Virginia, on October 20, he was indicted on a felony kidnapping charge, released on $75,000 bond, and ordered to keep out of West Virginia until his trial. If convicted, he could face life in prison.[43]

Meanwhile, in May 2003 in Okinawa, while Major Brown's case was still pending, yet another brutal rape and beating further inflamed popular sentiment. Kin is a small, central Okinawan village with many once-unspoiled beaches. The huge expanse of Camp Hansen dominates the village. The Marine Corps uses Kin's beaches to practice amphibious landings as well as for recreation by the troops and their families. In 1995, Kin had been the scene of the abduction, beating, and rape of the twelve-year-old schoolgirl that launched the Okinawan mass movement to get rid of the American bases.

At around 3:15 a.m. on Sunday morning, May 25, 2003, a twenty-one-year-old Camp Hansen marine, Lance Corporal José Torres, left a Kin village bar with a local nineteen-year-old woman, had sex with her in a nearby alley, and hit her in the face, breaking her nose. A female friend of hers went to the Camp Hansen main gate and reported Torres, whom the MPs at once took into custody. On June 12, the local police opened an investigation and, on June 16, obtained a warrant for Torres's arrest for rape and battery.

The same day, the Japanese government in Tokyo asked the U.S. embassy to hand him over. The newly arrived U.S. ambassador, Howard Baker, promptly apologized for the incident and urged Lieutenant General Wallace C. Gregson, commander of all marine forces in Okinawa, to comply rapidly. Gregson vacillated but did call on Governor Inamine to express "regret." Inamine replied, "I expect that [the United States] will hand over the suspect to Japan as soon as possible, without wasting a minute or even a second."[44] In Phnom Penh, while attending a meeting of the ASEAN (Association of Southeast Asian Nations) Regional Forum, then secretary of state Colin Powell also apologized to Foreign Minister Yoriko Kawaguchi.

The Bush administration now sensed that it had to turn over the suspect quickly, but it also decided that the time had come to force Japan to modify its criminal procedures. This decision produced a Japanese-American deadlock. On June 18, two days after the arrest warrant was issued, the marines turned Torres over to the Japanese authorities. At first he claimed that the sex was "consensual"—that the victim was a prostitute he had hired—but on July 8, after prosecutors had indicted him, Torres confessed to charges of raping and beating the woman. On September 12, the Naha District Court sentenced Torres to three and a half years in prison for his crime.[45]

This case, as banal and routine as it was in the context of the vast array of military sex crimes in Okinawa, was nonetheless the last straw for both the Japanese and American governments and led them to harden their positions. On the Japanese side, the issue of the SOFA and Japan's sovereignty was already in the public eye. Major Brown's trial was continuing; in March 2003, a drunken Defense Department employee from Camp Hansen had driven his car head-on into another car, killing its Okinawan driver; on May 7, a marine was arrested for mugging a store clerk as he was walking home; the wife of a marine assigned to Camp Foster punched and tried to strangle an Okinawan woman in the restroom of an Okinawa City bar; and on May 31—the day after they were paid—five drunken marines were arrested between 1:00 and 3:00 a.m. for failing to pay a 4,800-yen ($42) cab fare, trespassing on the premises of a private home, and damaging the glass entrance to the civic hall in Okinawa City. Okinawa City, which lies directly outside Kadena Air Base, had changed its name from Koza in 1972, after the Ryukyus reverted to Japanese administration, because Koza had become synonymous with incessant bar brawls and race riots among American servicemen.[46]

During June 2003, Governor Inamine and his deputy governor set out on a "pilgrimage" to the thirteen other Japanese prefectures that host U.S. military facilities and asked each governor to cooperate in a campaign to force the central government to revise the SOFA. All the governors agreed, including Tokyo's governor, Shintaro Ishihara, a popular right-wing politician with a long record of hostility to the American bases. Ishihara commented, "America's international strategy cannot be implemented without the bases in Japan. We are doing them a big favor here. . . . A half century has passed since the end of World War II, but Japan remains in an inferior position. It is strange to anyone who looks at it."[47] This remark from the politically powerful governor of one of the world's largest cities put further pressure on the national government to end its timidity toward the Americans.

However, just as the Japanese side was fortifying its position, the Americans also decided to toughen their stance. In turning over Torres to the Japanese police, the American embassy stated that it wanted immediate negotiations to ensure that American servicemen "will be treated in a fair and humanitarian manner while in the local police's custody."[48] The United States now claimed that, when it agreed in 1996 to give "sympathetic consideration" to requests for preindictment turnovers, it had asked for a quid pro quo—that Japan give U.S. servicemen special treatment to compensate for the differences between the legal systems of the two countries. The Bush administration now demanded that Japan quit stalling on new rules governing implementation of the SOFA—and that it do so within forty-five days.

The *Asahi Shimbun* noted the refusal of the United States to join the new International Criminal Court, which had just gone into operation in The Hague, calling it a sign that the Bush administration was determined to set new rules for the world, not just for Japan. It also noted the administration's refusal to abide by many international laws that the United States had once helped enact, its invasion of Iraq without legal sanction, and its belief that America possessed such power that it could act more or less as it pleased in international affairs. Professor Masaaki Gabe of the University of the Ryukyus, probably Japan's best-informed commentator on base problems, has observed, "Deputy Secretary of Defense Wolfowitz and other U.S. officials in the present administration believe that American justice will pass muster anywhere in the world, and they do not necessarily give priority to the bilateral relationship with Japan." According to Gabe, difficult military operations in Iraq and Afghanistan caused such officials to put a higher priority on maintaining the morale of troops stationed abroad than on the endless cases of military misbehavior in Okinawa.[49]

The Japanese soon agreed to the United States's request for negotiations, and talks convened on July 2, 2003, in Tokyo. The United States asked that one of its officials and an American-selected interpreter, for which it was willing to pay, be assigned to every military suspect turned over to the Japanese to ensure that he or she understood the questioning and was not tricked into confessing. The Ministry of Justice and the National Police Agency said that this request would be inconceivable interference in Japan's settled ways of investigating crimes. The United States responded that in most of its SOFAs with other countries it turns over military suspects only after they have been indicted and that it was already giving Japan "preferential treatment." After two days, the talks deadlocked.

When the talks resumed in Washington at the Pentagon on July 11, they proved no more productive than those in Tokyo. The main issue clearly centered not on the interpreter, since the Japanese already supply foreigner detainees with interpreters, but on the presence of that American official, possibly an attorney, at all interrogation sessions. "In our country," Japanese officials argued, "a lawyer is not allowed to attend investigations under normal circumstances and nothing in the SOFA says that Japan has an obligation to let persons connected with the U.S. government attend investigations by Japanese authorities."[50] Japan's negotiators also pointed out that measures taken by American authorities to maintain discipline and prevent sex crimes in Okinawa had been manifestly insufficient. The United States responded that without progress in the consultations, it would not in the future agree to turn over U.S. military suspects before indictment.

The two sides could agree only upon the scheduling of a third meeting on July 24 at U.S. Pacific Fleet headquarters in Honolulu, where the American delegation would be headed by Richard P. Lawless, deputy assistant secretary of defense for Asian and Pacific affairs, who was a former National Security Council staff member in the Reagan administration and before that a CIA operational agent. He is said to speak some Korean. The Japanese Ministry of Foreign Affairs made clear that, while it was prepared to accept the American requests, the Justice Ministry and Police Agency were dead set against it. The talks ended in failure, with negotiators on both sides saying that the issue would have to be referred to a higher political level.

Sometime between July 25 and 29 (to the great consternation of Japan's Ministry of Foreign Affairs), President Bush telephoned Prime Minister Koizumi and talked over the matter. The result was that Deputy

Chief Cabinet Secretary Teijiro Furukawa ordered senior officials in the Foreign and Justice Ministries to produce a compromise. At a fourth round of talks in Washington on July 31, Japan agreed to allow a U.S. government representative to be present during interrogations of military suspects, but only in cases of "heinous crimes." Such a U.S. governmental presence would be authorized in the name of Japanese-American "investigative cooperation," not "human rights," and the Japanese investigators could, at their discretion, ask the U.S. official briefly to leave the room at critical points in the interrogation. The Bush administration rejected this compromise, insisting that it would not tolerate any conditions being placed on U.S. officials, who had to be present for all charges, not just heinous crimes. With the failure of negotiations, the 1996 agreement on "sympathetic consideration" was a dead letter. A Pentagon source argued that the military had no choice in the matter since its forces would be demoralized if their human rights abroad could not be ensured.[51]

From August, when the SOFA discussions collapsed, until early November, when Secretary of Defense Rumsfeld toured Japan, Okinawa, and South Korea, the Americans and the Japanese had nothing important to say to each other on the subject. On his tour, Rumsfeld merely noted that the presence of thousands of U.S. troops on Japanese soil was a source of friction and "[p]erhaps the toughest of those tensions is the question of whether to extend fuller legal protections to U.S. service members accused of crimes," leaving the issue unresolved.[52] While in Okinawa—the first secretary of defense to visit since President George H. W. Bush's secretary Dick Cheney did so thirteen years earlier—Rumsfeld took a flight over Marine Corps Air Station Futenma, which is completely surrounded by the city of Ginowan. Looking out the window, he reportedly commented, "It is amazing that an accident has not occurred."[53]

Futenma has been an American military base since the battle of Okinawa in 1945. In 1958, the marines began to build permanent hangars and barracks; in 1960, the airfield was commissioned as a "Marine Corps Air Facility." With some 3,259 servicemen in 2005, Futenma provides air support for the Third Marine Expeditionary Force, also garrisoned in Okinawa. The airfield covers some 1,187 acres and is a major obstacle to improving the urban infrastructure of Ginowan (Manhattan's Central Park, by contrast, is only 843 acres). Roads, sewers, and water mains have to be awkwardly and expensively rerouted around the marine base. The functions of Futenma could easily have been moved years ago to the huge Kadena Air Base a short distance to the north, but interservice rivalries regularly make any rational use of land by the U.S. military in Okinawa inconceivable.

It is a scandal of American military administration that civilian leadership in the Pentagon took so long to discover the time bomb that was ticking away at Futenma. And then did nothing about it. To understand what happened when the time bomb finally exploded in the summer of 2004, however, a brief historical note is required. Nine years earlier, the widely reported abduction and rape of a twelve-year-old schoolgirl by American servicemen had led to huge anti-American demonstrations. In an emergency meeting convened in February 1996, President Clinton asked Prime Minister Hashimoto what it would take to defuse the situation. According to press reports, Hashimoto replied with one word: "Futenma." Clinton had no idea what Hashimoto meant, but when he was told that the prime minister wanted a Marine Corps airfield in Okinawa closed because it was a serious safety hazard, he agreed. At the time, this accord was hailed as a breakthrough in Japanese-American relations. Weeks later, it was disclosed that the U.S. embassy and the Marine Corps had quietly added a qualifier to the president's offer. The Americans were unwilling simply to shut down the old base and the Japanese did not want it moved anywhere on their main islands. It was therefore agreed that Futenma could be closed only by relocating the airfield to some undetermined place elsewhere within Okinawa.

In December 1996, the two governments announced that an alternative air base would be built in northern Okinawa. The Okinawans regarded this as a betrayal. They wanted Futenma permanently removed from their island. More demonstrations ensued, as well as years of futile negotiations with various recalcitrant Okinawan localities that Tokyo tried to bribe with the promise of huge public-works expenditures. Only in July 2002 did the two governments announce that they had settled on a site—the Henoko subdivision of the Okinawan city of Nago, home of the old Marine Corps base of Camp Schwab. A new, sea-based facility would be constructed, including a 2,500-meter runway built on a coral reef more than a mile offshore.

The Americans liked the idea of an airfield surrounded by water, which would eliminate protests from nearby residents over accidents and noise; and the politically powerful Japanese construction industry liked the exceedingly expensive, unconventional plans for constructing it. (Japan had agreed to pay for the new airfield.) Even though the proposed location was directly in the Pacific Ocean's "typhoon alley" and nothing like it had ever been built before, the United States enthusiastically endorsed the proposal. The Okinawan government, however, accepted the relocation only on two conditions: that the airport would be for joint civil-military use and that the American military presence would end after fifteen years. The United States went along with the planning while stonewalling on the conditions. What neither the Tokyo government nor the Americans had factored in was the reaction of local Okinawans, who deeply resented the potential destruction of one of the few coral reefs still surrounding their semitropical island.

Environmentalists further pointed out that the airport would ruin the habitat of an endangered, protected, and iconic sea mammal, the dugong. In 2004, when the Japanese government began to construct seabed drilling platforms over the reef, some thirty thousand Okinawans joined by supporters from other prefectures and overseas sympathizers (including representatives of the environmental group Greenpeace) began a sit-in that brought the work to a halt. The protesters occupied the drilling rigs and went to sea in small boats and canoes to chase away the surveyors. Tokyo had planned to drill in some sixty-three locations, but by mid-2004 no work had begun.[54]

Then, on Friday, August 13, the accident that Secretary Rumsfeld had predicted occurred. A thirty-year-old Marine Corps CH-53D Sea Stallion helicopter took off from Futenma—widely described in the Okinawan press as "the most dangerous base on earth"—and crashed into the main administration building of nearby Okinawa International University. It was the forty-first military helicopter crash in Okinawa since Japan regained sovereignty in 1972, and it transformed the 2004 situation.[55] In an unexpected way, the crash again raised the issue of the SOFA, set off massive Okinawan protests, forced the Pentagon to make closing Futenma a priority in its global force transformation schemes, and caused the Japanese government finally to try to break the domestic standoff over where Futenma's replacement should go.

The three-man crew of the helicopter that crashed survived without life-threatening injuries and, miraculously, no one on the ground was killed. The rear vertical stabilizer and rotor of the helicopter broke off in flight, falling to the street, but the university itself was closed for summer vacation. This accident raised at once the issue of slipshod maintenance. And what happened immediately afterward turned it into a major political incident.

Within minutes of the crash, a woman in the neighborhood called the fire department, which promptly dispatched four fire engines. Simultaneously, some twenty marines from Futenma showed up and began assisting the Ginowan firemen in rescuing the crew and bringing the fire under control. However, the moment the local firemen withdrew, the marines surrounded the crash site with yellow tape carrying the English words, "No Entry." They barred everyone, including firefighters, from returning to the crash scene, ran through the university administration building and ordered everyone out, halted all traffic on an adjacent street, and tried to stop TV cameramen from photographing the wreck. By then, several hundred people had gathered nearby and on the university grounds, shouting, "What kind of authority do they have? Whose country is this? The occupation isn't over."

Yoichi Iha, the mayor of Ginowan, was also barred from the site. It was "too dangerous," he was told, even though relaxed American troops could be seen lounging about and pizza-delivery motorbikes were allowed into the crash scene.[56] The following morning a large delegation of Ginowan police officers visited the scene armed with a court order to investigate possible violations of aviation safety laws, but they, too, were prevented from entering and informed that they could do so only with the permission of U.S. military authorities. The marines, they were assured, would investigate the crash and let the Japanese government know their findings.

That morning, Shogo Arai, a Liberal Democratic member of the Diet and parliamentary vice minister of foreign affairs, flew in from Tokyo to view the scene. Afterward, he called a press conference to announce: "I myself was not allowed onto the crash site. Japan is not Iraq. To claim American sovereignty in this situation is ridiculous."[57] The police formally asked Lieutenant General Robert L. Blackman, the marine commanding general in Okinawa, for authorization to investigate the cause of the crash. He vacillated for several days and then denied the request. Without getting permission from the university, the marines used chain saws to cut down over thirty trees on the campus, hauled away the helicopter's burned fuselage, and scraped off the topsoil where the helicopter had come down. When the Japanese were finally allowed in, there was nothing left to inspect.

It soon became clear that the marines were relying on a section of the so-called Agreed Minutes to the SOFA. These additional rules included article 17, paragraph 10(b): "The Japanese authorities will normally not exercise the right to search, seizure, or inspection with respect to any person or property within facilities and areas in use by and guarded under the authority of the United States or with respect to property of the United States armed forces wherever situated, except in cases where the competent authorities of the United States armed forces consent to such search, seizure, or inspection by the Japanese authorities of such persons or property."[58]

This provision of the SOFA had been unknown to the Japanese public. Okinawa and virtually all other Japanese prefectures housing U.S. bases demanded an instant revision of the SOFA. It was pointed out that both Germany and Italy have the right to investigate military accidents occurring on their territories, while Okinawan authorities were unable even to interview the helicopter pilots or gather other valuable evidence. The nationwide newspaper *Asahi Shimbun* asked rhetorically, "Is Japan Still Under U.S. Occupation?"[59] The widespread outrage reflected a new popular understanding of just how unequal and colonial Japan's relations with the United States really were.

Okinawans suspected that there might have been secret technology involved in the crash, explaining why the Americans were so eager to keep them away, but the CH-53D is actually so old that everything connected with it is public knowledge. It was possible that the helicopter might have been transporting depleted-uranium ammunition, in violation of American agreements with Japan, which would explain why some marines were spotted carrying Geiger counters around the site and why all the topsoil was removed. But the most persuasive reason the Japanese press could come up with for the incident was simply to maintain the "almighty SOFA," the forty-five-year-old license governing America's imperial presence in their country.[60]

The next year, on July 29, 2005, the association of governors of prefectures housing U.S. bases submitted to the Japanese Defense Agency and Foreign Ministry a list of seventy-one changes to the SOFA that it said were desperately needed.[61] The governors argued that Tokyo was far too obsequious toward the Pentagon and indifferent to the hardships the bases inflicted on ordinary Japanese. Their view was bolstered by the fact that, at the time of the crash, Prime Minister Koizumi was spending a two-week vacation in an upscale Tokyo hotel room watching the summer Olympics and refused even to meet with Governor Inamine until he returned to work nor did he ever visit the crash site in Ginowan.[62] Many commentators observed that had the crash occurred on the campus of Keio University in Tokyo—the Princeton of Japan—vacation or no, he would have been there in a flash.

The official American accident report was not released to the public, but a few leaked details confirmed American negligence. The CH-53D that crashed was one of several being prepared for shipment to Iraq on board the amphibious assault ship USS *Essex*. Maintenance crews were working night and day to get the helicopters ready. One mechanic testified that after three consecutive days of seventeen-hour shifts, he was so exhausted he had to be relieved. He had reattached the main bolt holding the rear rotor but had not yet installed the cotter pin, which prevents a bolt from becoming unscrewed due to vibration in flight, when he went back to his quarters. He failed to tell his day-shift replacement to do so. The bolt subsequently came off, sending the helicopter out of control.[63]

The helicopter accident and arguments over the Japanese SOFA were the context in which President Bush and Defense Secretary Rumsfeld introduced their grand plans for redesigning the United States's military empire. The issues of local crime and criminal jurisdiction in Okinawa did not go away, but they were upstaged by the strategic implications of China's explosive economic growth, which is soon likely to challenge the United States's status as "the world's only superpower." It has long been an article of neocon faith that the United States must do everything in its power to prevent the development of rival power centers, whether friendly or hostile, which meant that after the collapse of the Soviet Union they turned their attention to China as one of our probable next enemies. In 2001, having come to power along with George W. Bush, the neocon-servatives had shifted much of our nuclear targeting from Russia to China. They also began regular high-level military talks with Taiwan, China's breakaway province, over defense of the island; ordered a shift of army personnel and supplies to the Asia-Pacific region; and worked strenuously to promote the remilitarization of Japan.

On April 25, 2001, during an interview on national television, President Bush was asked whether he would ever use "the full force of the American military" against China for the sake of Taiwan. He responded, "Whatever it takes to help Taiwan defend herself."[64] This was American policy until 9/11, when China enthusiastically joined the "war on terrorism" and the president and his advisers became preoccupied with their "axis of evil" and making war on Iraq. At the time, the United States and China were also enjoying extremely close economic relations, which the big-business wing of the Republican Party did not want to jeopardize. The Middle East thus trumped the neocons' Asia policy.

While the Americans were distracted, China went about its economic business for almost four years, emerging as a powerhouse of Asia and the center of gravity for all Asian economies, including Japan's. Rapidly industrializing China also developed a voracious appetite for petroleum and other raw materials, which brought it into direct competition with the world's largest importers, the United States and Japan. By the summer of 2004, Bush's strategists again became alarmed over China's growing power and its potential to challenge American hegemony in East Asia. The Republican Party platform, unveiled at its convention in New York in August 2004, proclaimed that "America will help Taiwan defend itself."

Toward that end, the United States has repeatedly pressured Japan to revise article 9 of its constitution (renouncing the use of force except as a matter of self-defense) and become what American officials call a "normal nation." On August 13, 2004, in Tokyo, Secretary of State Colin Powell stated baldly that if Japan ever hoped to become a permanent member of the U.N. Security Council it would first have to get rid of its pacifist constitution. Bush administration officials would like to turn Japan into what they call the "Britain of the Far East"—and then use it as a proxy in checkmating North Korea and balancing China. Another major goal of the Americans is to gain Japan's active participation in their massively expensive missile defense program. The Bush administration is seeking, among other things, an end to Japan's ban on the export of military technology, since it wants Japanese engineers to help solve some of the technical problems of its so far failing Star Wars system. The Koizumi cabinet has not

resisted this American pressure since it complements a renewed nationalism and xenophobia among Japanese voters—attitudes that the Koizumi
government has fostered—and a fear that a burgeoning capitalist China
threatens Japan's established position as the leading economic power in
East Asia.

What the Bush strategists and the Pentagon do not seem to understand
is that China has real grievances against Japan and that American policy
is exacerbating them. During World War II, the Japanese killed approximately twenty-three million Chinese throughout East Asia—higher casualties than the staggering ones suffered by Russia at the hands of the
Nazis—and yet Japan refuses to atone for or even acknowledge its historical war crimes. Quite the opposite, it continues to rewrite history, portray-
ing itself as the liberator of Asia and a victim of European and American
imperialism.[65] In what for the Chinese is a painful act of symbolism,
Junichiro Koizumi made his first official visit to Yasukuni Shrine in Tokyo
after becoming Japanese prime minister in 2001, a practice he has
repeated every year since. Koizumi likes to say that he is merely honoring
Japan's war dead, but Yasukuni is anything but a military cemetery or a
war memorial. It was established in 1869 by Emperor Meiji as a Shinto
shrine (though with its torii archways made of steel rather than the traditional red-painted wood) to commemorate the lives lost in domestic military campaigns aimed at returning direct imperial rule to Japan. During
World War II, Japanese militarists took over the shrine and used it to promote patriotic and nationalistic sentiments. Today Yasukuni is said to be
dedicated to the spirits of approximately 2.4 million Japanese who have
died in the country's wars, both civil and foreign, since 1853.

In 1978, for reasons that have never been made clear, General Hideki
Tojo and six other wartime leaders who had been hanged by the Allied
Powers as war criminals were collectively enshrined at Yasukuni. The current chief priest of the shrine denies that they were war criminals, saying
only, "The winner passed judgment on the loser."[66] In a museum on the
shrine's grounds, there is a fully restored Mitsubishi Zero Type 52 fighter
aircraft that, according to a placard, made its 1940 combat debut over
Chongqing, then the wartime capital of the Republic of China. It was
undoubtedly no accident that, during the 2004 Asian Cup soccer finals in
Chongqing, Chinese spectators booed the playing of the Japanese national
anthem.[67]

Yasukuni's priests have always claimed close ties to the Japanese imperial household, but the late emperor Hirohito last visited the shrine in 1975 and Emperor Akihito has never been there. In July 2006, the Tokyo press reported on recently discovered diaries kept by a former high-ranking aide to Emperor Hirohito. They revealed that the wartime emperor objected to the 1978 decision of the Yasukuni priests to add the names of fourteen World War II leaders who had been convicted of crimes against humanity to the list of those honored at the shrine. According to the diarist, who died in 2003, Hirohito said to him, "That is why I have not visited the shrine since." Hirohito died in 1989.

The Chinese regard Koizumi's visits to Yasukuni as insulting and somewhat comparable to President Reagan's ill-considered 1985 visit to Bitburg cemetery in Germany, where SS soldiers are buried. The Chinese thus are not inclined to see the reorganization of American bases in Japan as a response to the Okinawans' outrage over the SOFA or any other technical issue. Instead, Beijing regards the new deployments as part of a provocative policy of American imperialism to shore up its hegemony in East Asia.

On November 27, 2003, President Bush issued an official statement: "Beginning today, the United States will intensify . . . our ongoing review of our overseas force posture."[68] The administration indicated that nations such as Germany, South Korea, and even Japan could see significant redeployments of military forces as the Pentagon focused more on the "war on terror." China was not mentioned directly, but it was certainly on the minds of Bush's advisers. If, in the cases of Germany and South Korea, the United States was retaliating—for German hostility to the invasion of Iraq and South Korea's openly expressed feeling that including North Korea in the president's "axis of evil" was a strategic blunder—Japan was still being touted as the "keystone" to America's position in East Asia.

Nonetheless, the Bush administration had clearly not given much thought to how to sell its plans for "global force repositioning" to Japan. In their monthly meetings with Japanese defense officials, Pentagon subordinates began by talking about making Japan into a "frontline base" or an "East Asian Britain." These trial balloons so alarmed the Japanese that they asked for further discussions to be delayed until after the July 2004 elections for the upper house of the Diet. While the United States complied, the Japanese press reported that "the Pentagon is irritated by Japan's unenthusiastic response to U.S. plans."[69]

From July 15 to 17, 2004, the two sides met in San Francisco, where American negotiators introduced some of their concrete proposals. The United States would replace the air force lieutenant general who normally commanded U.S. Forces Japan (USFJ) with an army four-star general, and move USFJ headquarters from Yokota Air Force Base to Camp Zama, the elegant old army base south of Tokyo (and site of the prewar Japanese military academy). All army, navy, air force, and marine troops stationed in Japan would be placed under the general, who would also replace the army commander in Korea—his headquarters would be abolished—giving the new commander authority to direct all American military operations in the Pacific and Indian Oceans. His only superior officer would be the PACOM commander in Hawaii. The Thirteenth Air Force headquarters in Guam would be merged with that of the U.S. Fifth Air Force at Yokota, near Tokyo, while the headquarters of the army's First Corps, stationed at Fort Lewis, Washington, would be moved to Zama, closer to possible imperial policing duties. The idea behind these changes was to have American troops "forward based" but not in potential areas of conflict, as in Korea.[70]

The Pentagon has many other plans for Japan, including replacing the forty-five-year-old aircraft carrier USS *Kitty Hawk,* currently homeported at the old Japanese naval base of Yokosuka, with the USS *George Washington,* a nuclear-powered aircraft carrier, despite Japan's well-known "nuclear allergy."[71] The United States, in short, is planning to turn Japan into the "control tower" of U.S.-enforced security in Asia.[72]

For the Japanese, such changes are intensely controversial, unleashing powerful grassroots protests not just in Okinawa but in many Japanese prefectures, particularly Kanagawa, which includes Prime Minister Koizumi's own electoral district. From the autumn of 2004 through 2005, the United States and Japan engaged in acrimonious negotiations, while Richard Lawless, the chief American negotiator, berated the Japanese for their "false kabuki"—a reference to the allegedly slow pace of traditional Japanese theater.[73] The most important issue at stake, however, is not base realignment but the Japan-U.S. Security Treaty itself.

When the treaty was first drawn up in the aftermath of World War II, the intent on both sides was not just to protect Japan in case of international conflict but to keep Japan, then seen as the scourge of Asia, disarmed. As a result the treaty is deeply one-sided. In return for bases in Japan, the United States pledges to defend the country; Japan, however, does not assume any comparable responsibilities toward the defense of the United States. Moreover, according to the treaty, the bases in Japan are to be used for "the security of Japan and the maintenance of international peace and security in the Far East," not to shore up and police the U.S. global empire. Article 9 of Japan's American-drafted constitution explicitly states that Japan will not maintain any offensive military capability or resort to war in its international relations. In fact, however, other than nuclear arms, virtually all of Japan's postwar pacifism is, some fifty-plus years after Article 9 was written, a fiction. According to one source, Japan, with 139 warships, now has the second most powerful navy on the planet.[74] Its army, navy, and air force has a total of 239,000 officers and men, deploys 452 combat aircraft, and is financed by a budget roughly equal to China's military expenditures. Despite its low profile, Japan is a growing military powerhouse and its conservative leaders have increasingly wanted to stretch the country's martial legs and the boundaries of Article 9. Deployment of a fairly large contingent of soldiers to Iraq gave Prime Minister Koizumi the chance to overcome the old constraints and precedents on Japanese "offensive" operations. When the Bush administration "persuaded" him to send troops to Iraq, Koizumi finessed the constitutionality of his action by insisting that the troops would only be engaged in peaceful reconstruction and not take part in warfare.

Large sections of the Japanese public remain devoted to Article 9, even if only as a statement of an ideal. They do not want to be dragged into America's "preventive wars" as a result of the Security Treaty.[75] The political left in Japan, although in decline, argues that the military realignments in Japan are changing the nature of the treaty from defense to war.[76] Some influential politicians on the right, which is dominant, see the basing changes the Pentagon now favors as challenges to Japan's sovereignty.

The U.S. at first tried to argue that since Japan depends on oil from the Middle East, its security should not technically be restricted to the "Far East" and that support for the broader American mission in Iraq and elsewhere under the rubric of the war on terror is therefore not in conflict with the Security Treaty. This formulation convinced no one, particularly since many Japanese believe that U.S. policy in the Middle East actually threatens their fuel supply. To finesse this issue, the United States decided to call Zama a "forward operational headquarters" and pledged that it will not do "global control" from there, although it certainly will. This linguistic hairsplitting temporarily resolved the legal difficulties, but the population around Camp Zama—an upscale residential area—remains adamantly opposed to enlarging the base. The Japanese government ultimately agreed to an upgraded military command at Camp Zama, but before that came about, the acrimonious dispute concerning the relocation of Futenma Air Base within Okinawa had to be resolved.[77]

In 2005, after protesters had stopped even survey work for the airfield on the coral reef, the Japanese government proposed building it on land within the little-used Camp Schwab.[78] The United States rejected this recommendation. Japan then proposed building half of the airport in Camp Schwab and half on pilings extending into the ocean. The United States rejected this as well, suggesting among other things that it would be too noisy for the troops barracked at the base. At this point, the talks broke down.[79]

The two sides never seriously discussed the most obvious solution—simply closing Futenma and moving what few functions it still performs into existing locations elsewhere in Japan or to Guam or Hawaii. Lawless rejected this out of hand on grounds that the United States has to maintain a "deterrent capability" in Okinawa, particularly to restrain China, and his view was seconded by the U.S. consul general in Okinawa.[80] The idea that China might be "deterred" by an understrength American marine division on a distant island is, of course, absurd, not to mention that during 2004 and 2005 significant numbers of the marines based in Okinawa were actually in Iraq.

After intense negotiations, on October 29, 2005, Defense Secretary Rumsfeld, Secretary of State Condoleezza Rice, the Japanese Defense Agency chief, and the minister of foreign affairs finally signed an "Interim Agreement."[81] It included setting up the army's command headquarters at Camp Zama and moving Futenma to the ecologically delicate coastal area of Henoko within Camp Schwab. (There was no agreement on joint civil-military use nor on the fifteen-year limit demanded by the Okinawans.) The United States promised that if everything goes as agreed, it would transfer several thousand marines, mostly headquarters and staff personnel, from Okinawa to Guam over a six-year period. Until the new airport is completed—an estimated decade in the future—Futenma remains open and a threat to surrounding communities.

Rumsfeld seems not to have understood a fundamental feature of Japanese politics. The Japanese people are riven about their defense relationship with the United States. They like being protected by the United States against possible threats from China and North Korea, but they do not like having foreign troops living anywhere near them. Over the past half century of alliance, the Japanese government has cynically dealt with this problem by using Okinawa as the dumping ground for the overwhelming majority of U.S. forces based in Japan. From the perspective of the Liberal Democratic Party, which has ruled Japan since 1955, Okinawan anger is a small price to pay so long as the troops are physically removed from daily contact with the politically more influential population on the main islands.

By deciding to shift bases around Japan like so many chess pieces, Rumsfeld disturbed this Japanese political arrangement for living with the American military. While the defense secretary has gotten the Koizumi government to agree to his proposals, his actions may sooner or later turn the endemic antibase protests of Okinawa into a feature of mainstream Japanese life. Many of the affected communities in the base repositioning scheme are, for the first time, expressing their solidarity with Okinawa. The officials say they will take their cue from whatever the Okinawan prefectural government espouses; Okinawa's initial reaction was to reject the Interim Agreement in favor of moving Futenma Air Base entirely out of Japan.[82] On these developments, Masaaki Gabe wrote, "Historians in the future may note that the bilateral alliance between Japan and the United States gradually declined after it peaked in November 2005. In the ongoing talks between the Japanese and U.S. governments over the realignment of U.S. forces in Japan, the Japanese government neglected to seek public support. An alliance that is not supported by the people is fragile. . . . The interim report has encountered a deep-seated backlash from Okinawa and Kanagawa prefectures. . . . If the U.S. troops do not have the support of the local base-hosting communities, the troops will probably have to withdraw from their bases."[83]

To resolve this impasse, at least for the time being, the Japanese government resorted to the old tried-and-true practice of bribery. It offered huge amounts of central government money to Okinawa and other affected communities if they would go along with what the U.S. and Japanese governments had already agreed to do. Prime Minister Koizumi made clear that acceptance of the planned reorganization of American forces—even if it amounted to a de facto rewriting of the Japan-U.S. Security Treaty—was settled national policy and could not be further modified. In view of this stance, most of the localities, despite some ambiguous responses, caved in. On May 30, 2006, the cabinet formally approved the planned realignment of U.S. forces in Japan.

The terms of the May 30 decision are extraordinary. They include an agreement by the United States to remove some 8,000 marines from Okinawa and relocate them to new facilities to be built on the American island of Guam. Secretary Rumsfeld estimates that this transfer will cost some $10.3 billion and take at least six years to accomplish. Astonishingly enough, the Japanese government agreed to pay $6.1 billion—a highly unusual decision in that the funds will be used to build quarters for American forces and their families on American territory. In addition, Japan will construct a new seaside airport within Camp Schwab in northern Okinawa for the troops and aircraft now based at Futenma. Japan will also accept a new army command center to be located at Camp Zama and a nuclear aircraft carrier to replace the conventional one homeported at Yokosuka.

Article 4 of the cabinet decision says, "[These accords] are among the government's most critical policy measures to ensure bilateral security arrangements in order for Japan to maintain its peace and security. . . . The government will consider the wishes of local public entities to be additionally burdened in implementing the realignment-related steps. In return for their great contributions to Japan's peace and national security, the government will implement economic stimulus packages, including measures for the development of local communities."[84]

This may work. It has in the past. But the complex negotiations failed even to address the Japanese-American disagreements over the SOFA and Japan's criminal justice procedures. Meanwhile, American servicemen continue to make sensational headlines in the Japanese press. In early July 2005, a drunken air force staff sergeant molested a ten-year-old Okinawan girl on her way to Sunday school. He at first claimed to be innocent, but then the police found a photo of the girl's nude torso on his cell phone. In November, a Japanese court sentenced him to eighteen months in prison, suspended for four years. On November 2, 2005, six marines from Okinawa who had been dispatched to the Philippines to "train" Filipino soldiers in antiterrorist tactics allegedly raped a Filipina student outside the former U.S. naval base at Subic Bay. The mayor of Okinawa City commented, "No matter how many times we ask the U.S. military to strengthen discipline, such incidents are repeated." In June 2006, a court in Kanagawa prefecture sentenced a twenty-two-year-old crew member of the USS *Kitty Hawk* to life in prison for robbing and beating to death a fifty-six-year-old woman outside the railroad station in Yokosuka.[85]

The Koizumi government and its right-wing supporters, eager to come out of the military closet and into the world as a rearmed major power, acceded to various unpalatable U.S. basing decisions despite popular opposition. They did so because their perceptions of the security situation and their desire not to be marginalized by China overrode any difficulties that living with American military forces pose for citizens of their country. They ignored the facts that they themselves were responsible for much of the deterioration in their relations with China and that America's doctrine of preemptive war threatened to draw them into conflicts not of their choosing. Far from bringing stability to international relations in East Asia, the United States and Japan are contributing to heightened tensions with China and North Korea. How long this increasingly fragile situation can be perpetuated is an open question.

6

Space: The Ultimate Imperialist Project

Our vision calls for prompt global strike space systems with the capability to directly apply force from or through space against terrestrial targets.

—AIR FORCE SPACE COMMAND,
Strategic Master Plan, Federal Year 2004 and Beyond

Space offers attractive options not only for missile defense but for a broad range of interrelated civil and military missions. It truly is the ultimate high ground. We are exploring concepts and technologies for space-based intercepts.

—PAUL WOLFOWITZ,
deputy secretary of defense, October 2002

Whoever has the capability to control space will likewise possess the capability to exert control of the surface of the Earth.

—GENERAL THOMAS D. WHITE,
air force chief of staff, November 29, 1957

On March 23, 1983, in a speech promoting greater defense spending against the Soviet Union, President Ronald Reagan challenged the "scientific community"—"those who gave us nuclear weapons"—and Americans in general to launch a huge research and development (R&D) effort to create an impermeable antimissile shield in space. He would call this endeavor the Strategic Defense Initiative, or SDI, and, in his vision, it would employ new high-concept technologies such as chemical lasers in space and on Earth to make nuclear weapons forever "impotent and obsolete."[1]

The proposal was meant in part to deflect a large-scale antinuclear movement that had developed in the United States and that had, the previous June, put almost a million protesters on the streets of New York. It was promptly attacked by these same critics and derisively labeled "Star Wars" (after director George Lucas's space opera). However, Reagan proved why he was known as the "Teflon president." He promptly appropriated the term. ("If you'll pardon my stealing a film line—the Force is with us.") And so a vast military-industrial undertaking to conquer and militarize space began into which billions of dollars have since been poured.[2]

As it happened, Reagan's impenetrable shield in space was a mere fantasy and, over the years, all that remains in practicable terms is a fabulously expensive, ground-based, minimalist antiballistic missile system. A series of futuristic conceptions, still in various stages of research and, in some cases, actual development, is aimed not at protecting the American people from a nuclear attack by another country but at the future control of the planet from space and the militarization of the heavens. These new devices included not only antisatellite satellites but weaponry in space that could be fired at Earth.

On the air force's developmental drawing boards, for instance, are ideas that would once have been found only in science fiction novels, including the aptly nicknamed "Rods from God," officially known as "Hypervelocity Rod Bundles." These are meant, according to reporter Tim Weiner of the *New York Times,* "to hurl cylinders of tungsten, titanium, or uranium from the edge of space to destroy targets on the ground, striking at speeds of about 7,200 miles an hour with the force of a small nuclear weapon."[3] Another futuristic weapons program, according to Weiner, "would bounce laser beams off mirrors hung from space satellites or huge high-altitude blimps, redirecting the lethal rays down to targets around the world."

Far closer to actual deployment is the CAV, or Common Aero Vehicle. According to Walter Pincus of the *Washington Post,* it will be "an unmanned maneuverable spacecraft that would travel at five times the speed of sound and could carry 1,000 pounds of munitions, intelligence sensors, or other payloads."[4] Part of Donald Rumsfeld's planned "Global Strike Force," it theoretically could hit any target on Earth with a massive dose of conventional munitions on a half hour's notice and the first generation of such weapons is now scheduled to be ready in 2010.

Although, as far as we know, the Bush administration has not officially issued a presidential directive that would allow the deployment of U.S.

weaponry in space, Weiner reports that the air force has been pushing hard for such a directive. Whether made official or not, the militarization of space has clearly been on the secret agenda for some time. Somewhere between boondoggle and imperial venture, the program to conquer the "high frontier" is also essentially a program for creating the equivalent of bases in space where, once the issue of militarization is settled, no SOFAs would be necessary. There would be no foreign governments to negotiate with, pay off, or placate; no issues of crime and justice to sort out. Best of all, the weaponizing of space enables us to project power anywhere in the world from secure bases of operation. It is, by definition, the global high ground.

Nonetheless, of all the high-frontier weapons into which R&D money has been poured since President Reagan's speech, only one—the distinctly Earth-bound "defensive shield"—has come into even partial being. That is the modest antiballistic missile (ABM) defense system being installed at Fort Greely, Alaska, and Vandenberg Air Force Base, California. It is no longer—as Reagan envisioned—focused on defending against a massive nuclear strike by a major enemy but on a tiny strike or even an errant missile from a "rogue state" like North Korea.

How this came to pass, after the Soviet Union disappeared and the threat of a missile attack receded, is a tale about the military-industrial complex at its most persistent. As the Pentagon commentator Alexander Zaitchik has observed, "The line connecting missile defense and space weapons is direct, thick, and no secret."[5] In the 1990s, neoconservative lobbyists joined with big arms manufacturers and ambitious military officers, none of whom actually cared whether a national missile-defense system could stop a nuclear attack. Their interest was in the staggering sums such a project would require. By manipulating a Republican Congress and creating a missile defense lobby in both houses, they achieved all their goals, although actual missile defense remained as distant as ever. General Eugene Habiger, head of the U.S. Strategic Command in the mid-1990s, said, "A system is being deployed that doesn't have any credible capability." Philip Coyle, former assistant secretary of defense for test and evaluation in the Clinton administration, concluded that the United States had squandered over $100 billion dollars of taxpayers' money on a "high-tech scarecrow."[6]

The neoconservative mind-set that brought this project to fruition also had its origins in the Reagan years, when many young strategists, usually with neither military service nor war experience on their résumés, became impatient with the influence of internationalists and realists—the people who had dominated U.S. foreign policy making since World War II. They were also convinced that the collapse of the Soviet Union had been significantly due to U.S. technological prowess and that pouring more money into advanced technology was a sure way to achieve perpetual domination of the world. The only real debate among them was over whether American hegemony "would be welcomed as the cutting edge of human progress," or overwhelming American power—"shock and awe"—would be enough to terrify others into submission.[7] They were committed to ending all arms control treaties that constrained U.S. power, to a vast expansion of spending on armaments as well as futuristic armaments research, and to a belief that the planet could easily be mastered from the high frontier of outer space. A typical member of this group was Frank Gaffney Jr., founder of the Center for Security Policy (CSP), creator of the congressional missile defense lobby, and behind-the-scenes player in the policy shifts of the 1990s that would lead to the near-weaponization of space.

Gaffney's views are close to those of the neocon polemicist Richard Perle, with whom he worked in the late 1970s in the office of the Democratic senator Henry M. "Scoop" Jackson, from Washington State, home of the Boeing Corporation. Jackson influenced both men through his passionate anticommunism and his easy acceptance of the title "senator from Boeing." Gaffney went on to become a staff member of the Senate Armed Services Committee from February 1981 to August 1983. President Reagan then appointed him deputy assistant secretary of defense for Nuclear Forces and Arms Control Policy, under his mentor Richard Perle. Rather like John Bolton in the second Bush administration, Gaffney distinguished himself at the Pentagon by his hostility to all arms control agreements. In 1987, the new secretary of defense, Frank Carlucci, let both Perle and Gaffney go, and Gaffney set out on his new career as a promoter of space weaponry.

When Gaffney returned to civilian life, he created the CSP, which set out to challenge the government's intelligence on the dangers of future nuclear missile threats from "rogue nations" and to promote the defense of our space assets. The CSP is funded primarily by the major weapons manufacturers in the missile defense field—Lockheed Martin, Boeing, Northrop Grumman, Raytheon, Science Applications International Corporation (SAIC), and others—and by conservative donors such as the Coors family, Richard Mellon Scaife, and the Colorado heiress Helen Krieble.[8] CSP has received well over $3 million in corporate donations since its founding in 1988.

The first major success of Gaffney's special-interest-funded think tank came in 1994, when Republican representatives Newt Gingrich and Dick Armey released their "Contract with America"—a political platform with which the Republican Party hoped to regain control of Congress. It contained a plank that called for "renewing America's commitment to an effective national missile defense system by requiring the Defense Department to deploy anti-ballistic missile systems."[9] An American ABM was the only weapons program included in the contract, and Gaffney took credit for having persuaded Gingrich and Armey to include it.

After the Republicans became the majority party in Congress in 1994, their leaders discovered that they still could not move decisively on missile defense because many of the members were suffering from "sticker shock." The Congressional Budget Office estimated that a basic ground-based system against only a minimally armed "rogue state" would cost up to $60 billion. Republican representative Curt Weldon, an advisory board member of CSP, decided that the best and most time-honored way to rouse the American people and their representatives to action would be to scare them to death. As a result, he obtained passage of a resolution calling for the creation of a special commission to assess the rogue-nation ballistic-missile threat to the United States. This commission, chaired by Donald Rumsfeld, issued its report in July 1998. Crucially, it disputed the CIA's estimate that any nation without a large and advanced industrial base would need at least ten years to fifteen years to build a ballistic missile, claiming instead that a mere five years would be sufficient.

In an incisive analysis, Michelle Ciarrocca and William D. Hartung, weapons experts at the World Policy Institute, pointed out that the congressionally mandated commission was anything but impartial on such matters. Most of its members were affiliated with the CSP and were eager to opt for a worst-case scenario by systematically ignoring the difficulties involved both in missile development and in the miniaturization of the nuclear warhead to be fitted to it. "The five year estimate was based in significant part on briefings from missile engineers at major U.S. defense contractors, including Lockheed Martin and Boeing—hardly unbiased sources, given the billions their firms stand to gain from building a missile defense system to thwart the alleged threat posed by Third World ICBMs."[10]

The Rumsfeld report, unbalanced and deceptive though it was, achieved what the high-frontier congressmen, militarists, and industrialists behind it wanted. In mid-March 1999, both houses of Congress overwhelmingly passed the National Missile Defense Act, which declared: "It is the policy of the United States to deploy a national missile defense." Just before the House voted, Donald Rumsfeld, then a civilian who had served as secretary of defense over twenty years earlier, gave a ninety-minute briefing to some 250 of its members.[11] In recognition of his services, Gaffney's Center for Security Policy later bestowed its Keeper of the Flame Award on him at a gala fund-raising dinner.

There was still one major obstacle—the president himself. Bill Clinton was by then adept at capitulating to right-wing pressures from both parties as part of a strategy of co-opting Republican positions and then not implementing them. He had already allowed several billion dollars to be spent on national missile defense, but on September 1, 2000, he decided not to deploy the ABM system. "I simply cannot conclude with the information I have today that we have enough confidence in the technology, and the operational effectiveness of the entire NMD [national missile defense] system, to move forward to deployment." He would, he declared, leave to his successor the decision whether or not to build it.[12] Unfortunately for the country and the world, five months later George W. Bush became president and Donald Rumsfeld returned to the Pentagon.

In addition to the missile defense commission's report of 1998, Rumsfeld brought with him a second report that urged the secretary of defense to prepare for possible warfare in space. He had chaired the group that wrote this inflammatory report just as he had the first missile-defense commission. The Commission to Assess United States National Security Space Management and Organization delivered its final report to Congress on January 11, 2001, a few days before Bush was sworn in and Rumsfeld took over the Department of Defense. The report was the brainchild of the congressional missile defense lobby, which got it through Congress as part of the National Defense Authorization Act for fiscal year 2000 and stacked the commission with seven—out of thirteen—members from aerospace companies that would benefit directly from any expanded space weapons programs. Many of them were former admirals and generals who had retired into highly compensated positions as executives or board members of munitions companies. The 2001 report they produced famously warned that the United States "is an attractive candidate for a 'space Pearl Harbor,'" and went on to state:

> The United States must develop, deploy, and maintain the means to deter attack on and to defend vulnerable space capabilities. Explicit national security guidance and defense policy is needed to direct development of doctrine, concepts of operations, and capabilities for space, including weapons systems that operate in space and that can defend assets in orbit and augment air, land, and sea forces. This requires a deterrence strategy for space, which in turn must be supported by a broader range of space capabilities.[13]

Statements of congressional commissions usually go unread and have little lasting influence. But the two Rumsfeld documents—the one from 1998 on missile defense and the 2001 report on protecting space assets—have assumed the status of holy writ even though both are biased and partisan in the extreme. As Michael Dobbs reported in the *Washington Post*, "Since the beginning of the Bush administration . . . and Rumsfeld's reappointment as Defense Secretary, the conclusions of the Rumsfeld Commission have been elevated to quasi-doctrinal status within the government, according to several officials. 'Nobody dares say a word against Rumsfeld, at least in public,' said one government nonproliferation expert."[14] The country was thus finally committed to building and deploying a system to destroy nuclear weapons delivered by missiles and ultimately to place weapons in outer space.

It is important to stress that at present no country has antisatellite weapons in space, that the only country talking about a possible space war is the United States, and that the only threat ever uncovered to U.S. space assets was six handheld Global Positioning System ground-jammers that Saddam Hussein's regime possessed. Nonetheless, air force spokesmen have used the 2001 report to insinuate that a space war is both inevitable and now a settled part of military doctrine.[15] They have enthusiastically manufactured threats that serve their own institutional interests, not the security of the United States.

The head of the Air Force Space Command, General Lance Lord, has led the charge. "Space superiority is not our birthright, but it is our destiny," he told an air force conference in September 2004. "Space superiority is our day-to-day mission. Space supremacy is our vision for the future." "Simply put," he said to Congress, "it's the American way of fighting." We must have "freedom to attack as well as freedom from attack" in space.[16] The former secretary of the air force and director of the National Reconnaissance Office Peter B. Teets, once the president and chief operating officer of the nation's biggest arms manufacturer, Lockheed Martin, assured the Air Force Association in a January 2003 speech, "If America doesn't weaponize space, an enemy will."[17] Keith Hall, Clinton's assistant secretary of the air force for space, whom the George W. Bush administration retained, commented, "With regard to space dominance, we have it, we like it, and we're going to keep it."[18]

On August 2, 2004, the air force for the first time issued a new statement of official doctrine on what it calls "counterspace operations." According to General John Jumper, air force chief of staff, "Counterspace operations are critical to success in modern warfare. . . . Counterspace operations have defensive and offensive elements. . . . These operations may be utilized throughout the spectrum of conflict and may achieve a variety of effects from temporary denial to complete destruction of the adversary's space capabilities."[19]

None of these military officers shows any interest in the arms race in space that their policies are guaranteed to elicit. Yet, it is inconceivable, observes Theresa Hitchens, an authority on weapons in space and vice president of the independent Washington research organization Center for Defense Information, "that either Russia or China would allow the United States to become the sole nation with space-based weapons." She quotes a 1998 article in *Airpower Journal,* by Lieutenant Colonel Bruce M. DeBlois, "Once a nation embarks down the road to gain a huge asymmetric advantage, the natural tendency of others is to close that gap. An arms race tends to develop an inertia of its own."[20] The air force, however, has an answer to such thinking. Everett Dolman, a neoconservative and a professor in the School of Advanced Air and Space Studies, the air force's graduate school for airpower and space power strategists at Maxwell Air Force Base, Alabama, argues, "The time to weaponize and administer space for the good of global commerce is now, when the United States could do so without fear of an arms race there. The short answer is, if you want an arms race in space, do nothing now."[21] Dolman thinks it is our destiny to "seize military control of low Earth orbit. Only the United States can be trusted to regulate space for the benefit of all."[22]

Virtually all of the air force's rhetoric about a future space war is ideological posturing, similar to the propaganda it put out at the end of the Eisenhower administration and the beginning of the Kennedy years about a "missile gap" with the Soviet Union. The purpose then was to beef up the air force's budget and carve out turf justifying its continued growth as an organization. There was no missile gap, as the leaders of the American government knew from U-2 flights over the USSR and photographs from the first Corona spy satellites.[23] Similarly today, there can be no rationale for a space war because one unintended but unavoidable consequence would be to destroy our own preeminent position in space. A major but little-noticed reason for this is because a conflict in space using antisatellite weapons of any kind would vastly increase the amount of orbiting garbage, which would threaten our whole network of military and commercial spacecraft. That, in turn, would threaten the whole American— even planetary—way of life. Yet space debris is a subject that the air force's "counterspace doctrine" never so much as mentions.[24]

Space, particularly in low Earth orbits (LEO), is anything but empty. The space age is hardly forty-five years old and we have already filled its most critical zones with thousands of pieces of lethal junk. The radars of the air force's Space Surveillance Network can see objects as small as ten centimeters—the size of a baseball—in low Earth orbit and to about one meter in higher geosynchronous orbits, where most of the world's communications and broadcast satellites reside. The air force is currently tracking some 13,400 man-made objects in space, of which only a few hundred are active satellites. It acknowledges that there are more than 100,000 pieces of smaller, untrackable debris, each about the size of a marble (one centimeter) and millions of still smaller fragments. NASA officials have estimated that there may be about four million pounds of space junk in LEO alone.[25] This debris includes dead or dying satellites, pieces of spent rocket boosters, all manner of metal shrouds and fairings, tools, nuts, bolts, and clamps of every size and description, lens caps, and even frozen sewage. In LEO they are traveling at the same speed as the space shuttle—17,500 miles per hour—or they would fall into the Earth's atmosphere and be burned up.

Astronaut Sally Ride, the first woman in space aboard the Challenger space shuttle in 1983 and 1984, a member of the presidential commission that investigated the Challenger's explosion in 1986, and a professor of physics at the University of California, San Diego, has been adamant that the use of antisatellite weapons would be "disastrous" because of the debris they would be likely to create. On her inaugural mission in June 1983, an incident fixed her opinion on this subject: "About halfway through the flight there was a small pit in the window of the space shuttle and we didn't know what it was. An awful lot of analysis was done while we were in orbit to make sure that the strength of the window would sustain reentry. It did. We were all fine. But the analysis afterward showed that our window had been hit by an orbiting fleck of paint, and the relative velocities were enough that the paint actually made a small but visible gouge in the window. Well, a fleck of paint is not the same as a small piece of metal travelling at that same speed. So, as soon as you start increasing the amount of junk in a low Earth orbit, you have an unintended by-product that starts putting some of your own quite valuable satellites at possible risk."[26]

Joel Primack, a professor of physics at the University of California, Santa Cruz, agrees: "Weaponization of space would make the debris problem much worse, and even one war in space could encase the entire planet in a shell of whizzing debris that would thereafter make space near the Earth highly hazardous for peaceful as well as military purposes. . . . Every person who cares about the human future in space should also realize that weaponizing space will jeopardize the possibility of space exploration."[27] Primack observes that the density of debris is already so great at the 900- to 1,000-kilometer altitude (563 to 625 miles) and at the 1,500- to 1,700-kilometer altitude (938 to 1,063 miles) that pieces of junk colliding with each other could set off a chain reaction or cascade of collisions—the Kessler Effect, predicted mathematically in the 1970s by the NASA scientist Donald Kessler—that would make the zones useless.[28] The Council on Foreign Relations Study Group on Space Weapons defines space debris as "unguided, hyper-velocity kinetic-energy weapon[s]" and concludes, "Because the United States owns a significant majority of the world's satellites, it would suffer disproportionately from any increase in the amount of space debris." Its overall conclusion is that "space weapons are not suited to the threats currently facing the United States in space or are outpaced by terrestrial alternatives."[29] All forms of space weapons, it noted, cost much more than terrestrial weapons systems, which of course do not have to be boosted into orbit, a cost that commercial operators put at between $300 million to $350 million per satellite.[30] Earth-based weapons such as unmanned aerial vehicles (UAVs), cruise missiles, ICBMs, or submarine-launched intermediate-range ballistic missiles can do anything space-based weapons can, and a Tomahawk cruise missile costs a mere $600,000.

The air force has been conspicuously reluctant to discuss these issues. On September 15, 2004, the Pentagon's Missile Defense Agency (MDA) said in a public statement that it was contemplating putting space-based missile interceptors in orbit by 2012 but acknowledged that such "kinetic kill vehicles," in Pentagon jargon—weapons that destroy their targets simply by colliding with them at very high speeds—would create a great deal of space debris. It noted that a chunk of debris ten centimeters in diameter is likely to be as damaging to an orbiting spacecraft as twenty-five sticks of dynamite.[31] Nonetheless, it planned to proceed with its antisatellite interceptors.

Some air force officers take the view, despite ample evidence to the contrary, that debris in low Earth orbit does not last long and quickly falls back into the atmosphere where it is burned up. The MDA report states, for instance, that in most cases debris that might be created by a missile-defense intercept would re-enter the atmosphere before completing a full orbit, and therefore would put satellites at risk only briefly. It advocates that vulnerable spacecraft such as the International Space Station and the Hubble Telescope be maneuvered out of the way to avoid collisions with debris. There is some evidence that debris resulting from missiles fired from the Earth might indeed quickly fall back into the atmosphere, but this would not be true of debris from space-based kinetic vehicles.[32] Debris from satellites placed in the higher geosynchronous orbits will, of course, never descend into the atmosphere but go on spinning around the Earth forever. That is why much greater attention should be paid to moving spent communications satellites into "graveyard orbits," reserved for space junk and off-limits to voyagers and satellites.

Meanwhile, the *Orbital Debris Quarterly News,* published by NASA's Johnson Space Center in Houston, continues to monitor and report on what the space garbage is actually doing. The *News* was first published in August 1996 and is now in its tenth volume. On January 17, 2005, according to the April 2005 issue, the remains of a U.S. Thor 2A upper stage rocket that had been used back in 1974 to put a satellite in orbit rear-ended a large fragment of the third stage of a Chinese CZ-4 launch vehicle that had exploded in March 2000. The collision altered the orbits of both pieces of debris and three more chunks—large enough to be detected and catalogued—were knocked off the old American rocket. *Orbital Debris Quarterly News* concluded, "As the number of objects in Earth orbit increases, the likelihood of accidental collisions will also increase. Currently, hundreds of close approaches . . . between catalogued objects occur on a daily basis. If future spacecraft and rocket bodies are not removed from LEO within a moderate amount of time after the end of [a] mission, e.g., within 25 years, the rate of accidental collisions will increase markedly later in the century."[33]

Despite air force propaganda, there is no way to protect our satellites by putting weapons in space. The only rational active defense would involve building redundancy into our space systems so that the loss of a particular spacecraft would not cripple us; the maintenance of replacement satellites ready to be launched into orbit whenever they are needed; the hardening of electronic components on particularly important satellites against microwave, laser, or other directed-energy attacks; and finally learning how better to disguise the laser, radar, visible, and infrared signatures of satellites, making them much harder to target in orbit.

Thirty years ago, during the period of Japan's high-speed economic growth, I was in Tokyo talking with an official from that country's trade ministry. Japan was then, as today, totally dependent on imported petroleum from the Middle East. I pointed out that Japan's supertankers were highly vulnerable. What, I asked, would Japan do if a hostile power sank one of its tankers in the narrow straits around Singapore? His answer was straightforward: call Lloyd's Insurance Company. It would be much cheaper to construct a new tanker than to defend the sea-lanes from Japan to the Persian Gulf by building a navy. There is a lesson in this for the

United States. We cannot afford our air force's plans to protect our space assets militarily, and the air force does not know how to do so in any case.

The missile-defense program is easily the most important place to examine the air force's failures. There are potentially three ways to bring down an ICBM: first, in its boost phase, when the warhead and the rocket are still joined and both are heading up through the atmosphere to outer space; second, after the warhead has separated from the booster and is speeding through space toward its target; and finally, in its terminal phase, the extremely short period (measured in seconds) when the warhead reenters the atmosphere and plunges toward the Earth. The Clinton administration worked only on a midcourse interception by ground-based "kill vehicles." The Bush administration took over this project and accelerated it but added brand-new and very expensive research objectives: downing a missile shortly after liftoff and during its final descent. Dubbed the "multi-tiered missile defense," it aimed at giving the United States as many opportunities as possible to stop an incoming missile.

More than five years after George W. Bush committed himself to an initial deployment by election day 2004, elaborate plans had been laid and huge amounts of money spent but nothing had been completed that actually worked. Shortly after June 13, 2002, when President Bush's withdrawal of the United States from the 1972 Anti-Ballistic Missile Treaty became final, Arizona senator Jon Kyl declared that the United States was now dedicated to "peace through strength, not peace through paper."[34] In fact, the ABM Treaty had restrained the only country truly capable of launching an attack on the United States with intercontinental ballistic missiles, namely, Russia, and replaced it with—paper.

Unsurprisingly, the Clinton-era Ground-based Midcourse Defense system, or GMD, as it is known within the Pentagon and the missile industry, remains by far the most advanced and important part of the whole multi-tiered system, as revealed in budget priorities. In the fiscal year 2002 budget, for example, $3,762.3 million was devoted to GMD whereas boost-segment research got $599.8 million and terminal-segment research $200.1 million.[35] (Actually, that terminal-phase figure should be increased by $898.7 million, that year's funding for the Patriot PAC-3 missile, reported separately in the defense budget and the current favorite when it comes to trying to hit a warhead just before impact.)

Meanwhile, the GMD system as it is being conceived and built will, at best, be capable of hitting a single long-range missile or a very few of them launched by a technologically unsophisticated Third World nation like North Korea. Russia has already deployed ICBMs that can defeat any antiballistic-missile system we could conceivably produce, and China will no doubt do so soon. On March 7, 2006, the commander of American forces in South Korea, General Burwell B. Bell, told the Senate Armed Services Committee, "In the years since the late nineties, the last six years, seven years, we have seen very little activity by the North Koreans to actively continue to develop and test long-range missile systems."[36] Nonetheless, three months later, the U.S. military announced that North Korea had a Taepodong-2, its longest-range rocket, sitting on a launching pad fueled and ready for flight. It consists of a set of old Russian Scuds bolted together. The U.S. military claimed that it had a range of up to 9,300 miles, more than enough to reach the U.S. mainland, and that the United States had only a limited ability to shoot down such a missile should North Korea launch it.[37] On July 4, 2006, North Korea test-fired this and other shorter-range missiles. The Taepodong-2 crashed after forty-two seconds of flight.

The Ground-based Midcourse Defense system that we have been building against North Korea consists of three separate elements: an array of interceptor missiles housed in silos in the ground that are at least theoretically linked to spy satellites in orbit as well as enormous, terrestrially based X-band radars meant to detect and track missile launches ("X-band" is merely a reference to its wavelength, 2.5–4 cm, which is small and therefore more sensitive; most airliners, for example, are equipped with X-band radars to detect turbulence). All of this equipment is then connected to a battle-management command-and-control center with massive computers for superspeed-processing of data, final determination that a launched missile is hostile, and the ability to transmit commands to launch the interceptors. There are problems with every phase of this, so many in fact that charges of faked tests of parts of it have been commonplace. Some people, myself included, suspect that the GMD is simply a cover for long-term research and development plans aimed not at defense on Earth but at the domination of space.[38]

It is important to remember that the three approaches to interception—boost phase, midcourse, and terminal—are utterly different and each has its own constraints. Any boost-phase interception, no matter how technologically sophisticated, has to originate fairly close to the launch site of the enemy missile to have any chance of success. Our current missile defense sites, for example, are nowhere near close enough to have a hope of intercepting a Chinese launch from its Central Asian province of Xinjiang. Such a Chinese attack could be intercepted only in the midcourse or terminal phases.[39] The terminal phase usually lasts only a minute or two and is currently beyond the data-processing capabilities of our computers. That is why the GMD remains the most important option since it offers the greatest chance of success, problematic as even that may be.

Boeing is the GMD's prime contractor. As of December 17, 2005, the company had built eight interceptors that were placed in silos at Fort Greely, Alaska, and two more at Vandenberg Air Force Base, California. These make up the entirety of the known missile defense system deployed by the United States to date. The Missile Defense Agency has announced that it will not release any further information about future emplacements, even though Fort Greely is scheduled ultimately to house forty interceptors. Victoria Samson of the Center for Defense Information believes that this "unwillingness to give specifics about the program is a sure indicator that things are going poorly."[40] She may well be right.

The problems of the GMD itself are legion. The interceptor—technically known as an "exoatmospheric kill vehicle" (EKV)—consists of a two-stage booster, followed by a liquid-fuel rocket that steers it on the last leg of its journey. Its speed should be about 13,400 miles per hour at impact. The interceptors are supposed to carry infrared sensors that will help them determine whether a target is a warhead or a decoy, although so far there is no evidence that these work. Other on-board sensors take over from ground guidance at close range, making the rocket, which does not carry a heavy explosive warhead, somewhat maneuverable. It is designed to destroy the target simply by colliding with it.[41]

Test failures have revealed numerous problems with the interceptor. On December 15, 2004, a simulated warhead was fired from Kodiak Island, Alaska, south over the Pacific, but its intended interceptor, launched from the Ronald Reagan Ballistic Missile Defense Test Site at the Kwajalein Missile Range in the Marshall Islands, never left its silo. On February 14, 2005, the Missile Defense Agency tried again. This time the interceptor shut down due to a "software error." These are peculiar failures since the

United States has had decades of experience in missile launches.[42] Keep in mind that the interceptor has yet to be tested with the much more powerful booster rocket designed for it and intended to give it the necessary speed to intercept a real missile. The surrogate rocket used in the Pacific tests does not produce the vibration and stress that will accompany real-world conditions, which threaten to damage the on-board computer, thrusters, antennas for receiving data, optics for navigating, sensors, and a refrigeration unit for cooling the sensors, which are extremely sensitive to heat.[43]

The most notorious problem with the tests is that, when the interceptors have actually lifted off, they have been artificially guided to their targets by Global Positioning System homing devices and electronic beacons because our new spy satellite and radar systems for detecting and tracking missiles have not yet been built. We do not yet have the means to detect a hostile ballistic missile coming at us, which means that the interceptors sitting in the ground in Alaska are functionally blind. Defense Department veteran Philip Coyle says that for the GMD system to work in its present condition, North Korea would have to give us advance notice of its intention to launch an ICBM and supply the relevant target information. "To be credible," Coyle writes, "the GBI [ground-based interceptor] must eventually show that it can hit a target with no targeting aids on-board the target re-entry vehicle."[44] It has yet to do so.

There are major delays and cost overruns in other vital parts of the GMD system, particularly the not-yet-built new-and-improved surveillance satellites and a huge X-band radar mounted on a seagoing, oil-drilling rig, which is supposed to be moored at Adak, Alaska.[45] The probably insurmountable problem that faces the whole GMD system, however, is its inability to distinguish between warheads and decoys in flight. Increasingly, it seems that, in the foreseeable future, no amount of science will be able to overcome this difficulty. Any nation or terrorist group capable of building an intercontinental ballistic missile would have no difficulty in adding a few appropriately painted balloon decoys to its payload. If our interceptor missiles cannot tell one from another, the entire effort is a waste of time and money, a point that serious strategists have long understood. In 1986, the renowned Russian physicist and winner of the 1975 Nobel Peace Prize, Andrei Sakharov, advised the Soviet government that Reagan's strategic defense initiative could easily be fooled and/or overwhelmed simply by firing decoys along with Soviet missiles and increasing the number of missiles in any assault. There was no reason, he said, to waste money trying to match an American ABM system.[46] Twenty years later, nothing has happened that would alter his conclusion in any way.

In the weightlessness of outer space, a decoy cannot be detected simply because of its lighter weight. Some experts believe that the new X-band radars and the sensors mounted on our interceptors will sooner or later be able to detect an infrared signature that would distinguish a warhead from a decoy, but there is no test evidence to support this belief.

Professor Theodore C. Postol of MIT, one of our country's leading authorities on ballistic missile defenses, has been warning about the problem of decoys for many years. In a now famous June 15, 2002, letter to the *Boston Globe,* Postol wrote: "The current National Missile Defense interceptor tries to identify warheads and decoys by 'looking at them' with infrared eyes. Because the missile defense is essentially using vision to tell which objects are decoys and which are bombs, this technique is no more effective than trying to find suitcase bombs at an airport by studying the shape and color of each suitcase." He concluded: "The [Missile Defense] agency has no technical program for solving this fundamental problem. It has also been unable to provide any credible scientific evidence or analysis to show that it can ever solve this problem. So what it proposes to do is to classify the fact that the targets it is flying [in tests] have been preconstructed in ways that will allow it to tell one from another. This misuse of the classification system to hide the fact that the National Missile Defense System has no credible scientific chance of working is a serious abuse of our security system."

The decoy problem is one of the reasons why the Pentagon has begun to invest heavily in a boost-phase intercept. This form of attack—while the incoming rocket and its warhead are still coupled and moving relatively slowly into space—would destroy any decoys before they could separate from the missile, thereby solving that problem. There are at least fifty different proposals for developing boost-phase interceptors, but all of them suffer from a fundamental inability to tell whether a missile just after liftoff is carrying a warhead or is merely launching a satellite. In addition, most forms of boost-phase attack, particularly lasers, would not be able to fully disable the warhead, which will surely be heavily shielded and thermally insulated in order to be able to withstand re-entry into the Earth's atmosphere. The danger is that an attack on an ascending rocket will merely knock it off course, causing it to fall back into a neighboring, possibly friendly, country. For example, a missile launched from Iran against Washington, D.C., and attacked in its boost phase would threaten several Middle Eastern countries as well as Turkey and possibly even Europe.[47] Air force officers and members of the Center for Security Policy do not allow such considerations to worry them, arguing that "collateral damage" may be unavoidable to protect the United States.

There has been a great deal of writing about a space-based boost-phase antimissile laser, but it is at present little more than a concept and would almost surely be too heavy ever to put into orbit. The main research focus for a boost-phase weapon is an airborne laser (ABL). Mounted in the nose of a modified Boeing 747-400F commercial airplane, the ABL's high-energy laser is expected to be in the megawatt range—more than a million watts. When working properly, the laser would fire a beam of directed energy at the speed of light toward the body of an ascending rocket that might be hundreds of miles from the aircraft, heating its shell until it failed structurally. Whether such a laser would actually produce enough energy is still an open question. The chosen source of directed energy is a chemical oxygen iodine laser that produces energy through the reaction of hydrogen peroxide with chlorine gas. According to Miranda Priebe, a physicist and a research assistant at the Center for Defense Information, "The ABL beam will be generated by several laser modules. When light from these modules is amplified with a resonator (a set of mirrors that must be able to withstand the intense energy of the laser beam), the combined output is a single, powerful beam."[48]

On December 3, 2004, the prototype ABL aircraft had its first two-hour flight aborted by Missile Defense Agency officials after twenty-two minutes because of a false warning from on-board instruments of an air-pressure problem. Boeing, Northrop Grumman, and Lockheed Martin share the work with the agency. The ABL's price is now in the range of $5.1 billion for one fully equipped airplane, twice the original estimate. On March 9, 2005, Lieutenant General Henry Obering, director of the Missile Defense Agency, told the press that the ABL "is not out of the woods yet. I can't declare that [it is] a totally risk free program."[49] His remark was a major understatement.

Leaving aside the fact that putting a high-energy laser aboard an aircraft involves fitting an incredible array of sensors, computers, chemicals, and mirrors into a constricted, dusty, vibrating space, a major problem is weight. The original plan called for fourteen SUV-sized modules working in tandem to generate laser light that would be projected through a telescope mounted in the 747's nose. However, that idea proved to be impossible, so the number was cut to six modules. Even the six-module system weighs about 180,000 pounds—5,000 pounds more than the original design weight for the fourteen-module scheme—and still puts pressure on the airframe. The Boeing 747-400 freighter, the largest commercial cargo transport in service, can carry a maximum of 248,000 pounds, but this weight has to be distributed throughout the aircraft. The laser consists of six large machines lashed together on the main deck plus chemicals and crew to monitor the laser resonators. In addition, it was discovered on the 2004 test flight that the laser beam ignites dust particles in its path. These produce flickers of visible light called "fireflies," which weaken the beam's overall energy. The Missile Defense Agency has decided that the ABL cannot be used at lower altitudes where dust is plentiful, which of course radically reduces the time available for an interception. Similarly, the first flight revealed problems of airframe vibration and atmospheric turbulence that generate what is called "jitter," which also impedes the laser beam and produces wear and tear on the delicate equipment.

Finally, the heavily laden Boeing 747 lumbers through the sky at a slow speed and is incapable of defending itself. It would thus require fighter aircraft protection in a combat situation, which in turn would necessitate the presence of aerial refueling tankers. It seems likely that any organization adept enough to build an ICBM carrying a weapon of mass destruction could also field a surface-to-air missile, such as the one that, on May 1, 1960, shot down Francis Gary Powers's U-2 spy plane over Sverdlovsk, Russia, at 70,500 feet.[50] It is hard to imagine how an ABL lurking within the necessary hundreds of miles of a launch site with a boost-phase interception in mind could be effectively protected, something that will not be lost on an ABL 747's aircrew.

Terminal-phase interception is not much more promising than the ABL, but at least it is not so esoteric. The chief problem is not detecting the warhead as it re-enters the atmosphere, which is comparatively easy, but designing a missile fast enough to catch it and collide with it in the one or two minutes available. The main weapon the United States proposes to use for this purpose is the Patriot PAC-3 (Patriot Advanced Capability), manufactured by Lockheed Martin Missiles and Fire Control of Dallas, Texas. The PAC-3 is an improved version of the Patriot missiles used during the first war against Iraq in 1991 with such dismal results. (They failed to bring down any Scuds Iraq fired at General Schwarzkopf's forces or at Israel.) The new one is, however, much faster and without the heavy explosive warhead of its ancestor. PAC-3, however, was never designed for defense against an ICBM warhead but rather for downing shorter-range tactical and cruise missiles. Using a solid propellant rocket motor, the PAC-3 flies at great speed to an intercept point specified by its ground-based fire-solution computer and destroys the target by colliding with it.

According to former assistant secretary of defense Philip Coyle, "Although [the PAC-3] appeared to be doing well in development tests—hitting ten out of eleven targets—those early tests involved the usual artificialities of preplanned intercepts. In more realistic operational tests conducted [in 2002], the PAC-3 hit only three targets out of seven tries, or less than 45 percent."[51] The main problem with terminal defense is that it can, by definition, protect only a limited area, such as a city. To be effective we would have to deploy innumerable terminal-defense systems all over the country. The deliberate destruction of an atomic weapon over a city or other site might also produce massive nuclear fallout, which could be extremely damaging to the defending country.

By the end of 2004, Defense Secretary Rumsfeld acknowledged that while any planned defense against missile attack would be inadequate, the United States would nonetheless soon have a "modest capacity."[52] Two devastating investigations into procurement and testing practices—one by the Missile Defense Agency itself and one conducted by the Government Accountability Office—concluded that the Pentagon had actually sacrificed rigorous testing and quality control in order to meet President Bush's pledge of a 2004 deployment, and both called for much greater accountability and an end to flagrant cost overruns.[53] In October 2005, the Senate Appropriations Committee quietly disclosed that the Pentagon was giving up on trying to make further improvements in its GMD interceptors and that the first generation of ground-based exoatmospheric kill vehicles would also be the last.[54] Lisbeth Gronlund of the Union of Concerned Scientists reported on the results of this internal criticism: "There is no evidence the GMD system would have any military utility, which is why it has not been declared operational. It is a little-known fact that the Pacific and Strategic military commands, which perform their own assessments separate from those of the MDA, have refused to make it operational."[55]

In fact, the whole Pentagon effort has been devoted to meeting a non-credible threat from rogue-nation ballistic missiles while ignoring a genuine challenge to the very concept of missile defense—that of Russia and its Topol-M ICBM. As Scott Ritter, a former weapons inspector in the Soviet Union (1988–90) and later in Iraq (1991–98), has observed, "On Christmas Eve 2004, the Russian Strategic Missile Force fired an advanced SS-27 Topol-M road-mobile intercontinental ballistic missile (ICBM). This test probably invalidated the entire premise and technology used in the National Missile Defense (NMD) system currently being developed and deployed by the Bush administration."[56]

The Topol-M was Russia's original answer to President Reagan's Star Wars fantasies. It was designed during the late 1980s, but Russia did not produce it immediately because of the collapse of the USSR and because it discovered that Star Wars itself could be rather easily defeated by decoys and large numbers of conventional ICBMs. However, on June 13, 2004, the very day that George W. Bush succeeded in killing off the Anti-ballistic Missile Treaty of 1972, Aleksei Arbatov, one of Russia's leading experts on military affairs, advocated in parliament that Russia respond by speeding development of the Topol-M. A year and a half later, on December 24, 2005, Colonel General Nikolai Solovtsov, chief of the Strategic Missile Forces, attended a ceremony at the Tatishchevo missile base in the Volga River's Saratov region. He was commissioning a new set of Topol-Ms, which he declared to be "capable of penetrating any missile defense system." The Topol-M was first put into service in December 1998 but was deployed only in silos. An off-road mobile version entered combat service in 2006.[57] It is a truly formidable weapon.

Among its features are high-speed solid-fuel rockets that rapidly lift the missile into the atmosphere and make boost-phase interception inconceivable unless a defense system were located practically next door to the launcher; hardening and reflecting coatings to protect it against laser weapons; up to three independently targetable warheads and four sophisticated decoys; an ability to maneuver to avoid midcourse or terminal-phase missile attacks; and a range of over 6,250 miles. There is no known defense against such a weapon. Diplomacy and deterrence are the only means to ensure that it will never be used, and the Bush administration has repeatedly rejected diplomacy as a useful tool of American foreign policy. The conclusion is unavoidable: Washington has given us at best the illusion of protection against a nuclear attack without reducing the odds of such an attack.[58]

There are so many things wrong with the missile defense program that it is difficult to think of it as merely an ambitious scientific effort having start-up problems. From space debris to the inability to identify clearly a hostile launch or sort out the decoys, its failures suggest that if Congress had even a slightly prudent commitment to fiscal integrity, it might well have scuttled the project long ago. That its members did not even discuss the possibility raises disturbing questions. Did the Bush administration and its Republican associates in Congress actually intend to build a missile defense system or were they only interested in a plausible public relations cover for using the defense budget to funnel huge amounts of money to the military-industrial aerospace corporations? As a cash cow, missile defense goes on enriching its sponsors precisely when it is not working and they have to go back to their drawing boards.

America's imperial project to dominate the space surrounding our planet has provided a nearly perfect setting for official corruption. The air force and the military-industrial complex interests meshing with power-ful congressional lobbies that want to bring space-oriented industries to their districts and perpetuate their own safe seats in Congress, as well as unimaginable sums of money protected from public scrutiny by "black budgets," "special access programs," and other forms of secrecy, all add up to a prescription for legal thievery on an unprecedented scale. Norman Ornstein, a specialist on Congress at the American Enterprise Institute, has observed that when individual members of Congress have the ability to earmark—that is, privately attach—federal funds for pet projects and slip them unopposed into the Pentagon's budget, "You are creating the most fertile environment for corruption imaginable."[59]

During the first years of the new century, an array of experienced Pentagon and congressional budget officers began sounding the alarm that the purchase of weapons systems is now totally beyond public control—or often even public visibility. Of all the weapons systems, the most expensive and most prone to misuse and abuse has been the whole project to create an intercontinental-ballistic-missile defense system. At $8.8 billion, it was, after all, the largest single weapons request in the fiscal year 2006 defense budget. The Center for Strategic and Budgetary Assessments in Washington estimated that "black budget" requests for fiscal year 2007 amounted to $30.1 billion, the highest level since 1988 during the Cold War, 75 percent of them going to the air force mostly for space programs and new satellites. William D. Hartung, Frida Berrigan, Michelle Ciarrocca, and Jonathan Wingo of the World Policy Institute have summed up our military ventures in space and space defense as "Pork barrel in the sky."[60]

The raw monetary figures have been literally astronomic. From Reagan's 1983 "Star Wars" speech to 2006, depending on which expert you listen to, the United States has spent between $92.5 billion and $130 billion on the basic problem of shooting down an ICBM in flight—and that's without even once having succeeded in doing so.[61] One comprehensive analysis of the ultimate cost of the entire ballistic missile defense system by its distinctly theoretical date of completion in 2015—and excluding its most expensive and problematic component, a space-based laser—is $1.2 trillion.[62]

There can be no question that the whole system is surrounded by an environment of corruption that has been much aided and abetted by the way Defense Secretary Rumsfeld vastly increased the Clinton administration's missile defense spending, moved virtually all missile defense projects into the classified budget, and ended normal reports to Congress concerning failures to meet delivery dates, cost increases, and the actual performance of equipment. He also cut some two thousand auditors from the Defense Contract Audit Agency.[63] "The Pentagon's new approach to missile defense testing is a contractor's dream and a taxpayer's nightmare," writes the World Policy Institute's Ciarrocca. "Pumping in more money while reducing outside scrutiny is an invitation to corruption and cost-overruns."[64]

In December 2003, Franklin C. "Chuck" Spinney, a former air force officer and for thirty years a budget analyst in the Pentagon, spoke to journalist Bill Moyers about what he called the "moral sewer on the Potomac."[65] Perhaps Spinney's most important insight is that the primary emotion driving this system is not patriotism, greed, or need, but fear. The attacks of 9/11 unquestionably generated real fear, but continuous air force hyperbole in favor of ultra-high-tech projects, presidential statements tying 9/11 to missile defense, and alarmist claims that our dependence on orbiting satellites leaves us no choice but to defend them militarily all capitalize on prevailing fears and undermine a realistic defense.

President Bush is, in this sense, the fear-monger-in-chief. In a speech to the cadets of The Citadel on December 11, 2001, exactly three months after 9/11, the president said, "The attacks on our nation made it even more clear that we need to build limited and effective defenses against missile attack. (Applause) . . . Suppose the Taliban and the terrorists had been able to strike America or important allies with a ballistic missile. Our coalition would have become fragile, the stakes in our war much, much higher. We must protect Americans and our friends against all forms of terror, including the terror that could arrive on a missile." But neither the Taliban nor the 9/11 terrorists had missiles or the knowledge or industrial base to build one. And there are other, far cheaper, more accessible, and more effective ways to deliver a weapon of mass destruction than by missile. For example, one could be secretly imported in a cargo container on a transport ship, or fired from an offshore vessel using a short-range cruise missile, or constructed domestically as did the bombers of the Oklahoma City Murrah Federal Building in 1995, or sent as a priority package via FedEx.

But what if some terrorists really had access to an intercontinental missile? Given that we have in continuous orbit the world's most effective intelligence satellites devoted to tracking missile launches, as soon as we had determined that such a launch was not an error, we would retaliate instantly and catastrophically against whatever nation had allowed a missile to be fired against us. The government's own experts agree that a long-range ballistic missile is the least likely way a hostile state or terrorist group would choose to deliver a weapon of mass destruction against a U.S. target.

Why then did the Bush administration increase spending on missile defense in fiscal year 2002 by 43 percent? The answer lies in a complex amalgam of neoconservative ideology, the influence of right-wing think tanks, air force desires to protect what it sees as its "turf" while expanding its share of the DoD budget, powerful congressmen devoted to enriching their districts, lobbies of arms manufacturers who supply virtually unlimited funds to re-elect their friends, and the interests of places like Huntsville, Alabama, which has lived off missiles ever since rocket scientist and former Nazi SS major Wernher von Braun arrived there after World War II to lead the U.S. Army's rocket development team.[66]

Missile defense has almost nothing to do with defense and nothing whatsoever to do with the war on terrorism. ABM weapons may actually prove to be useless against incoming ICBMs, but they might be highly effective offensive weapons against other nations' satellites, and this is why almost nothing said officially by the administration, the Pentagon, or the Congress on the subject of missile defense can be taken at face value. These dual-use weapons are less likely to be employed for missile defense than as a stealthy way to introduce weapons in outer space with the intent of dominating the globe.

On December 14, 2004, General Lance Lord, head of Air Force Space Command at Peterson Air Force Base in Colorado, repeated to the press what has become an air force mantra: "The war in space began during Operation Iraqi Freedom."[67] This overstatement is based on the claim that, at the outset of our invasion of Iraq in 2003, Saddam Hussein attempted to jam the reception of radio signals from U.S. Global Positioning System (GPS) satellites. His men allegedly used six commercially available jammers based on Russian designs and available for purchase on the Internet to try to interfere with our "precision-guided" bombs.[68] The U.S. military has many uses for the GPS, a system of satellites capable of precisely locating any object or spot on Earth. It is ideal for guiding so-called smart bombs to their targets. Iraq's handheld jammers turned out to have no influence on the GPS satellites or ground stations and were quickly taken out using GPS-guided munitions. (Jamming instantly reveals the location of the jammer, painting a bull's-eye on him.) Even if jamming had been successful, the U.S.'s munitions have backup systems, which deliver the bombs only slightly less efficiently to their targets.

"To get big-bucks Congressional funding for space-control schemes," comments Mike Moore, former editor of the *Bulletin of the Atomic Scientists,* "a threat to U.S. space assets must be manufactured, and Hussein's pathetic attempts to jam GPS signals seem to be the best (and only) evidence space warriors can produce to 'prove' that space war is already underway. . . . [General Lord's assertions are] part of a sophisticated public relations campaign waged by the Air Force and Defense Department to persuade the public that space war is here."[69]

It is certainly true that the Global Positioning System highlights the U.S. military's remarkable dependence on an array of satellites that orbit the planet, held aloft by the tension between their own speed and Earth's gravitational pull. They provide our armed forces with intelligence, communications systems of all sorts, computer displays of battlefields in real time, guidance for unmanned aerial vehicles (UAVs) such as the Predator and the Global Hawk and for extremely high altitude manned spy planes such as the U-2. They also provide navigational aids, accurate weather forecasts, and numerous nonmilitary functions. The reliance American forces place on such spy and communications satellites may already constitute a militarization of space but not yet a weaponization of space. Satellites are, in a sense, the opposite of weapons—extremely vulnerable "sitting ducks" following fixed paths around the Earth and an immense boon to all mankind. Their military applications are probably among their least significant uses.

The Global Positioning System (known in the U.S. military as the Navstar GPS) is probably the greatest advance in navigation since the discovery of the compass and the invention of the sextant. It is the general term for at least twenty-four satellites, each circling the Earth twice a day, that are positioned in a "medium Earth orbit" (12,600 to 14,760 miles above the planet). A GPS receiver on a ship, automobile, aircraft, bomb, or a hiker's handheld navigational device decodes a time signal from four of these satellites, which carry extremely accurate atomic clocks, and then calculates a position based on the different times and distances to the various satellites. As of 2005, the GPS could determine your position at any moment within about sixteen feet (five meters), a steady improvement over the previous fifteen years.[70] Although created for military use, the GPS is today available to any and all users worldwide, providing strikingly accurate information on position and time in all weather conditions. The GPS has spawned a multibillion-dollar industry in applications, including handheld guidance devices for the blind.

The U.S. military operates over 500,000 GPS receivers, most of them on cruise missiles, precision-guided bombs, and other munitions.[71] It invented the system and launched its first GPS satellite into orbit in February 1978. The cost of maintaining the system is approximately

$400 million per year, including replacements for aging satellites. The air force keeps twenty-eight satellites in orbit at all times, four as backups to ones that might fail. Satellites cannot be repaired, have a limited life span, and a failure rate of about two per year. Management of the entire system is in the hands of the Second Space Operations Squadron at Schriever Air Force Base, Colorado.

The air force has not always been a good steward of the GPS, which has evolved over time into a global public utility, not just a guidance system for bombs. Until August 31, 1983, GPS was exclusively a U.S. military system. On that date, Soviet fighters shot down a Korean Air Lines Boeing 747 that had drifted off its flight plan into Soviet airspace. American authorities realized that if the airliner been equipped with a GPS receiver, it could have avoided its catastrophic navigation error. So the air force slowly began making GPS available for civilian use. Today, many commercial airlines integrate GPS tracking into their TV entertainment systems so that passengers can follow the course of their flight on-screen.

From the beginning, U.S. officials knew that they could not prevent other nations or private users from tuning in to its satellites' signals, and they feared that sophisticated technicians might be able to adapt the GPS to provide guidance for their own cruise or ballistic missiles. The United States therefore required that commercial GPS receivers have limits on the velocities and altitudes at which GPS would supply positions. Moreover, the air force has never thought of itself as a supplier of public goods but rather as an overlord of the globe. Insisting on making civilian and foreign users of GPS dependent on the United States, it implemented something that it called "selective availability," which degraded GPS's accuracy by adding signal errors for civilian users—normally about ten meters horizontally and thirty meters vertically. Only the U.S. military and selected allies received the unadulterated data. The air force also retained the ability to switch off GPS on a regional basis and to jam receivers in a war zone. Needless to say, this dependency on the "goodwill" of the United States irritated a lot of people, who began to devise ways to get around selective availability.

One rather expensive solution came to be known as "differential GPS," useful primarily for geographic imaging, weather forecasting, mining, agriculture, and high-altitude surveying. Differential GPS involves setting up one GPS receiver—the base station—at a precisely known location.

The base station then calculates its position based on GPS satellite signals and compares this location to its known location. The difference is applied to GPS data recorded by roving GPS receivers, thereby correcting the selective availability errors.[72] But the more definitive answer to selective availability was, of course, a GPS system not run as a U.S. Air Force monopoly.

The Russians already had a primitive version of GPS called Glonas (global navigation system), which as of 2004 had only twelve active satellites and was uncompetitive. On May 1, 2000, the United States unilaterally ended selective availability, magnanimously declaring it to be an American humanitarian gesture: "As part of his ongoing effort to bring the benefits of government investments in science and technology to the civilian and commercial sectors, President Clinton ordered that the intentional degrading of the civilian Global Positioning System (GPS) be discontinued at midnight tonight."[73] Nonetheless, the air force retained all its capabilities to limit service, to turn off GPS regionally, and to jam receivers. Slowly and fitfully, the European Union decided to build an alternative, which it named "Galileo." This satellite navigation system, when operational, will be more accurate and not subject to shutdown for military purposes. When completed it will be available to all world users, civilian and military, and at its full capacity will require only a Galileo receiver. As René Oosterlinck, head of the European Space Agency's Navigation Department, summed matters up, "Europe cannot accept reliance on a military system which has the possibility of being cut off."[74]

European nations at first were reluctant to put up the money for Galileo and, after the attacks of September 11, 2001, the project almost died. The United States has always recognized that Galileo was intended to break its stranglehold on the use of satellites for navigational purposes, but it did not know what to do about it. The terrorism of 9/11 gave it an opportunity to act. The Bush administration wrote directly to the European Union arguing that Galileo, by ending America's ability to shut down GPS in times of military operations, would threaten the success of the war on terror. This ploy backfired badly. By mid-2002, virtually all European Union states were on board and had overfunded the project.

Galileo will be a system of thirty spacecraft in orbit—twenty-seven active and three spares—14,514 miles above the Earth. Each satellite has a projected lifetime of twelve years. The system aims at an accuracy of less

than a meter, with greater penetration into urban centers, inside buildings, and under trees, a faster fix, and atomic clocks that are ten times
better than those on board the GPS satellites. The European Space Agency
plans to launch the required thirty satellites between 2006 and 2010,
and the system is planned to be up and running under civilian control
by 2010.

On December 28, 2005, a Russian Soyuz rocket fired from the old
Soviet Cosmodrome at Baikonur, Kazakhstan, carried the first Galileo
satellite into orbit—a launch received ecstatically in France, given a hearty
"well done" in Britain, and greeted with poorly disguised sour grapes in
the United States. As far as the air force is concerned, Galileo has truly
slipped the American leash. In September 2003, China joined the project,
promising to invest 230 million euros in it. In July 2004, Israel signed on;
India joined in September 2005; Morocco, Saudi Arabia, and South Korea
all affiliated with Galileo during the winter of 2005–6, each of them paying for the privilege. There was speculation that Argentina, Brazil, Chile,
Malaysia, Pakistan, and Russia also were considering becoming involved.[75]

The air force itself would be wise to start planning a transition to
Galileo instead of becoming paranoid over the prospect that many countries around the world may soon meet or exceed American space-based
navigational and guidance capabilities. For example, the U.S. military's
precision-guided Joint Direct Attack Munition (JDAM) GBU-31 bomb,
which has wreaked so much nonprecision carnage in Iraq, depends on the
GPS. Whether it will work with Galileo or whether the European Space
Agency will allow such a militaristic use of its satellites is not known.
According to the RAND Corporation, "A particularly glaring U.S. space
vulnerability is the constellation of Global Positioning System (GPS)
satellites, thanks to our extraordinary dependence on that system."[76]

Unfortunately for the United States and the prospects for peace, the
Air Force Space Command takes this dependency to mean that we must
actively defend the GPS and other military satellites by using antisatellite
(ASAT) weapons and other space-war devices. There are ways to prepare
for and protect against the inevitability of satellite sabotage or failure, but
the use of active military measures surely should not be among them.
About the only thing ASATs could do is create so much lethal debris in
orbital space as to make it useless for all nations for a very long time, perhaps permanently.

As of December 2005, there were approximately 800 active satellites of every sort in operation—exact numbers are not available since military secrecy hides a significant portion of the total American fleet. According to an estimate by the Union of Concerned Scientists, a Washington-based private watchdog organization, 413 of these satellites belong to American companies or the United States government. The Russians operate 87, the European Space Agency about 50, and the Chinese 34.[77] According to the Satellite Industry Association, revenue from both governmental and commercial customers for manufacturers and operators of satellites was $85.1 billion in 2000 and $97.2 billion in 2004, with the United States accounting for more than three-quarters of all spending.[78] Since 1998, there have been more commercial satellites in orbit than military ones, and the number of commercial launches each year has exceeded military launches. According to the Center for Defense Information, the U.S. military now uses privately owned commercial satellites for about 60 percent of its communications and that "dependence is growing."[79]

These commercial satellites do many useful things, most of them taken for granted and rarely thought of as related to satellites. Low Earth orbit, just 200 to 500 miles above the Earth's surface, is crowded with satellites reporting weather conditions, mapping the Earth's surface ("remote sensing"), sustaining the U.S. Space Shuttle, the International Space Station, and the Hubble Telescope, studying the size of the ozone hole in the atmosphere over Chile, photographing the damage done by the Southeast Asian tsunami or Hurricane Katrina, and transmitting financial and economic news around the world in real time. Satellites in low Earth orbit are so close to the planet, they must travel at very high speeds, usually about 17,000 miles per hour, so that gravity will not pull them back into the Earth's atmosphere.

Much farther out in space, the world's major television networks broadcast to their markets from large communications satellites in geosynchronous or geostationary orbits—abbreviated GEO—over the equator. These satellites orbit at the high altitude of 22,237 miles above sea level, where they are far enough from the Earth's gravitational pull to approximate the speed of Earth itself as it rotates on its own axis in each twenty-four-hour cycle (just over 1,000 miles per hour). This speed is, of course, much slower than the speed at which the Earth travels around the Sun (67,062 miles per hour). Flying at approximately the same speed that the Earth is turning on its axis, the satellite remains in the same position in relation to the Earth even though both are in constant motion.

In 1945, just as World War II was coming to an end but while London was still under attack from Nazi V-2 rockets fired from the Netherlands, the future science-fiction writer Sir Arthur C. Clarke calculated the height and speed required of a satellite to remain in the same place over the Earth. He published his findings in the magazine *Wireless World*. No´one took his idea seriously at the time, but twenty years later, on April 6, 1965, it became a reality with the launching of Intelsat I, also called "Early Bird," the first commercial geostationary communications satellite. There are today about thirty such communications satellites covering North America and more than a hundred orbiting the planet in different GEO locations. In 2002, the so-called Clarke Orbit, that is, the band where spacecraft can maintain a geosynchronous position with relation to the Earth, held over three hundred satellites of various kinds.[80] The fifteen U.S. early-warning satellites monitoring missile launches, for example, are almost entirely in GEO, which is quite crowded.[81] When a satellite finally wears out and ceases to function, scrupulous satellite operators have often provided small rockets and enough fuel to move them a few hundred miles higher into a cemetery orbit, but not all operators can or are willing to assume these costs.

One of the biggest communications satellites is the Department of Defense's Milstar, the size of a city bus, with electricity-generating solar panels as wide as the wingspan of a Boeing 747 jumbo jet. The six Milstars currently in orbit are the most secure of all the various communications satellites. They resist jamming and their electronics are hardened against the electromagnetic pulse that would accompany a nuclear attack.[82] In addition to being used for direct broadcasting, these communications satellites act as relay stations, bouncing telephone calls, TV images, Internet connections, and other signals from one part of the world to another.

Many satellite functions are quite mundane. As Richard DalBello, former president of the Satellite Industry Association, explains, "When you go to Wal-Mart to buy a pair of sneakers, the credit card goes up to the satellite, gets validated and approved. Then the same satellite tells Wal-Mart that it just sold a pair of sneakers at your neighborhood store, and Wal-Mart adjusts its inventory accordingly."[83] Our dependency on such capabilities can be starkly revealed when they are suddenly withdrawn. On May 19, 1998, the satellite Galaxy IV, owned by PanAmSat, was in geosynchronous orbit above Kansas. At 6:00 p.m. it suffered a failure of its onboard control system as well as all its backup systems and began to roll aimlessly. Some six hundred stations of the National Public Radio system, the CBS network, CNN's Airport Channel, the Chinese Television Network in Hong Kong, and the Soldiers' Satellite Network, which brings entertainment programs to the armed forces, were instantly knocked off the air. Many self-service gas stations found themselves unable to accept credit cards. Private business television networks operated by Aetna, Microsoft, 3M, and the Ford Motor Company shut down, as did the Ohio, Minnesota, and Texas state lotteries. Some thirty-five million personal pagers on the East Coast went dead, causing hospitals and obstetricians' offices to try frantically to reach doctors via telephone for emergency surgeries and unexpected baby deliveries.[84]

No one knows what happened to Galaxy IV—it seems likely that both the primary and backup onboard computers that navigate the spacecraft without ground intervention failed for unknown reasons. Nonetheless, it is air force doctrine that, until proved otherwise, we should assume that Galaxy IV was attacked by an antisatellite weapon operated by an unnamed hostile power.

Major General Daniel Darnell, head of the Air Force Space Command's Space Warfare Center at Schriever Air Force Base, has exhorted all satellite operators to assume that any disruption to their spacecraft is most likely a hostile strike.[85] "The first response when something goes wrong," he warns, "should be 'think possible attack.'" Actually, quite a number of events other than deliberate physical or electronic attack can cause a satellite to fail, including natural radiation emanating from galactic space (e.g., cosmic rays or solar storms), collisions with space debris, or technical malfunction.[86] The problem is that the air force has no way of knowing which of these things may have caused a particular failure. As the Center for Defense Information's Theresa Hitchens notes, "The Air Force does not have the capability at this time to ascertain on the spot whether any disruption of satellite operations is due to a malfunction, such as faulty software or space weather, or the result of some sort of deliberate interference or attack."[87] As usual, however, the military chooses to follow the worst-case scenario most useful for its future funding needs. As Lisbeth Gronlund, codirector of the Union of Concerned Scientists' Global Security Program, points out, its strategy for space combat is invariably "Fire, Aim, Ready" in that order.[88]

In an effort to "see" what is actually going on in space at any given time, the U.S. Air Force is working on "autonomous proximity operations"—orbital maneuvers that would allow satellites to inspect other satellites, diagnose malfunctions, and perhaps provide on-orbit servicing. The problem is that research in this area is devoted primarily to producing microsatellites, weighing less than one hundred kilograms, and nanosatellites, weighing less than ten kilograms, which the air force disguises to look like space debris and hopes to use to sneak up on other nations' satellites. These minisatellites would not, however, be on innocent inspection missions. They are designed to surround other satellites and photograph, jam, blind, or collide with them. Microsatellites are inherently dual-use and could function as lethal antisatellite weapons. The main U.S. stealth satellites are in the top-secret Misty series, first put into orbit in 1990, which, by 2005, had reportedly cost us $9.5 billion. Although the air force thought they were undetectable from Earth, the first one was spotted almost at once by amateur space observers in Canada and Europe.[89]

The latest innovation is an experimental microsatellite, XSS-11, that deploys tiny probes to inspect or service spacecraft in distress, according to the carefully worded air force publicity statement. It was launched from Vandenberg Air Force Base, California, on April 11, 2005. The plan is for the XSS-11 to remain in space for twelve to eighteen months and inspect six or seven spent rocket stages and dead U.S. satellites. Some space watchers have speculated that the XSS-11 is actually testing antisatellite concepts to disable enemy craft.[90]

Jeffrey Lewis of Harvard's Belfer Center for Science and International Affairs reports on two joint British-Chinese experimental microsatellites of fifty kilograms each, whose controllers were able to maneuver within nine meters of a Chinese target satellite. Lewis concludes, "If the Chinese were to conduct a proximity maneuver near a U.S. satellite, the reaction [in the Pentagon] would be apoplectic."[91] Nonetheless, Theresa Hitchens warns, "There will be a price to pay the first time a U.S. anti-satellite weapon shoots down an innocent Chinese communications satellite because a crucial widget on a U.S. satellite conked out due to faulty manufacturing processes."[92]

These problems will only get worse. In order to protect our nation's and others' space assets from the air force's hubris and incompetence, we must relearn how to cooperate with our fellow inhabitants of the planet and take the lead in crafting international agreements on the rules of the road in space, particularly treaties to control weapons in space. We need to agree, for example, that a country's technical means of observing and verifying what other nations are doing are never appropriate targets of anti-satellite or other kinds of space weapons. We should outlaw all weapons that are designed to destroy other nations' reconnaissance and surveillance satellites. This was the principle contained in the old Anti-Ballistic Missile Treaty, which we foolishly abandoned in accordance with the recommendations of the 2001 Rumsfeld space commission. The reason is that if one side blinds another, the country that is blinded is almost compelled to conclude that it is being set up for an attack and should therefore use everything it's got, including nuclear weapons, in retaliation.

The United States has greatly damaged the integrity of international law by refusing to be constrained by its norms, even though no nation needs international law more than we do. International law offers guidelines to acceptable behavior for all nations, rich and poor, and, since violations of the guidelines invite retaliation, it provides deterrence against illegal behavior. The current cluttering of key orbits with debris, for example, reflects a lack of cooperation and our own shortsighted imperialist arrogance. Without any rules on space debris, a poor state with few technical capabilities could decide to blind the United States by the active deployment of space garbage. Such a genuinely "rogue state" could, for instance, detonate a nuclear weapon in space, which is banned by the 1967 Outer Space Treaty but is actively discussed in every military headquarters around the world, particularly since the United States pays so little attention to treaty obligations. Such a detonation would not kill anyone and would not create a worldwide "nuclear winter," but its electromagnetic pulse would instantly fry the electronics in all orbiting satellites. Even more low-tech, a desperate state could simply send up a few rocket loads of gravel into low Earth orbit.[93] The resulting collisions would instantly level the global playing field: no more American smart bombs, no more electronic battlefields, no more global positioning systems, no more secure communications among troops in battle and commanders in rear areas. Instead of obtaining multilateral agreements that would ban such actions, the United States continues to waste its money building space-based antisatellite weapons.

Space weapons are not simply a strategic problem. They are both the cause and the result of several pathological developments in our political and economic system. The iron triangle of the air force, Congress, and the military-industrial complex, sanctified by the high-tech jobs it offers to American workers, is driving our country toward bankruptcy. For some, it is tempting to continue the lucrative practice of buying arcane space technologies that do not work—missile defenses, for example—simply because it keeps people employed. Meanwhile, our democracy is undercut by members of Congress who use the lavish "campaign contributions" they receive—bribes by any other name—to buy elections. The only public business these bought-and-paid-for congressmen attend to is providing a legal veneer for munitions makers' unquestioned access to the tax revenues of the government. The proper use of a vital human resource—the space we occupy in the universe—is a matter for profound philosophical deliberation. Space has also become, unfortunately, an arena for American hubris and one more piece of evidence that Nemesis is much closer than most of us would care to contemplate.

of the President that function solely to advise and assist the presi-
[de]nt also excluded all classified documents and nine types of informa-
[tion]—including national security information, confidential business
[infor]mation, matters of personal privacy, deliberations and decisions of
[fede]ral financial institutions, geological information (concerning mining
[an]d oil rights), and certain law enforcement records. The new law did not
[wo]rk very well. Many agencies simply failed to respond to FOIA requests
[an]d others dragged their bureaucratic feet interminably. In 1974, in the
[w]ake of revelations that President Nixon had illegally used the CIA, the
FBI, and the military to spy on the American people, Congress strengthened the act considerably. Nixon had even ordered his secret gang of personal thugs—"the plumbers"—to break into the office of the psychiatrist
of former Defense Department official Daniel Ellsberg seeking material
with which the White House could blackmail him.[6]

In an attempt to force the executive branch to comply with the law, the
1974 reforms required agencies to organize their archives in a standard
manner and hold them available for public scrutiny regardless of whether
or not a citizen ever asked. This ended the common practice of agencies
claiming that they could not provide information requested because their
archives were not adequately organized to do so. Donald Rumsfeld, then
President Gerald Ford's chief of staff, and Dick Cheney, Rumsfeld's
deputy, urged him to veto the act as "unworkable and unconstitutional."
Ford did as he was told, but Congress promptly overrode the veto.[7]

These amendments led to a great deal of litigation in court, making
the FOIA a far more formidable oversight instrument. In June 1995, while
in Tokyo, I had a conversation about the FOIA with former vice president
Walter Mondale, then ambassador to Japan. As a senator, he had been
deeply involved in the new law's passage. The law, he assured me, would
never have worked without the power of an applicant to go to court and
force the government to comply. For example, virtually all the information now publicly available on prisoner abuse, torture, and other criminal
acts by military men and women and CIA operatives at Abu Ghraib,
Guantánamo Bay, Bagram Air Base, and elsewhere came via FOIA
requests, first denied by government agencies and only fulfilled as a result
of a court order.[8]

The FOIA now depends almost totally on the courts for its viability, as
Bush administration officials have done their best to envelop the act in a

---

The Crisis of the American Republic

My administration has a job to do and we're going to do it. We will rid the
world of evildoers.

—PRESIDENT GEORGE W. BUSH,
September 16, 2001

The invasion of Iraq was a bandit act, an act of blatant state terrorism,
demonstrating absolute contempt for the concept of international law.
The invasion was an arbitrary military action inspired by a series of lies
upon lies and gross manipulation of the media and therefore of the public; an act intended to consolidate American military and economic control of the Middle East masquerading—as a last resort—all other
justifications having failed to justify themselves—as liberation. . . . We
have brought torture, cluster bombs, depleted uranium, innumerable
acts of random murder, misery, degradation and death to the Iraqi
people and call it "bringing freedom and democracy to the Middle East."

—HAROLD PINTER, the 2005 Nobel Prize Lecture in Literature,
Guardian, December 7, 2005

When America is no longer a threat to the world, the world will no longer
threaten us.

—HARRY BROWNE,
"What Has 'Victory' Achieved?"
Antiwar.com, January 11, 2002

As a goddess, Nemesis represents a warning that neither men and women
nor countries can indefinitely ignore the demands of reciprocal justice
and honesty. She is the spirit of retribution, a corrective to the greed and
stupidity that sometimes governs relations among people. America's most
famous interpreter of ancient Greek culture, Edith Hamilton, tells us that

Nemesis stands for "righteous anger."[1] If that is the case, we should welcome her arrival. For if we do not awaken soon to the wholesale betrayal of our basic political values and offer our own expression of righteous anger, the American republic will be as doomed as the Roman Republic was after the Ides of March that spring of 44 BC.

Several American presidents have been guilty of using excessive power during wartime. Abraham Lincoln suspended the right of habeas corpus; Woodrow Wilson had his "Red Scare" with the illegal jailing or deportation of people who opposed his intervention in World War I; Franklin Roosevelt conducted a pogrom against Americans of Japanese ancestry, incarcerating almost all of them in the continental United States in detention camps. In addition, there is no question that, from the earliest years of the republic to the 1990s, the United States witnessed a huge accretion of power by the executive branch, largely due to the numerous wars we fought and the concomitant growth of militarism. Nonetheless, the separation of powers, even if no longer a true balance of power, continued to serve as a check on any claims of presidential dominance.

When it comes to the deliberate dismantling of the Constitution, however, the events that followed the Supreme Court's intervention in the election of 2000 that named George W. Bush the forty-third president have proved unprecedented. Bush has since implemented what even right-wing columnist George Will has termed a "monarchical doctrine" and launched, as left-wing commentator James Ridgeway put it, "a consistent and long-range policy to wreck constitutional government."[2] In doing so, Bush has unleashed a political crisis comparable to the one Julius Caesar posed for the Roman constitution. If the United States has neither the means nor the will to overcome this crisis, then we have entered the last days of the republic.

James Madison, the primary author of our Constitution, considered the people's access to information the basic right upon which all other rights depend. This is the right that, from the moment George W. Bush entered the White House, his administration has most consistently attacked. Its implacable, sweeping claims to executive secrecy, which predate the "Global War on Terror," go a long way toward explaining why the press and the public have been so passive in the face of this imperial presidency. In 1798, in a resolution in the Virginia legislature defending the

first amendment against an act that Congress ... year, Madison denounced "a power [in the law] ... other, ought to produce universal alarm, because it ... right of freely examining public characters and me... communication among the people thereon, which ha... deemed the only effective guardian of every other righ... that if he can wrap his acts in a cloak of official secrecy, ne... nor the public will be able to exercise the slightest oversight.

"A popular government without popular information, or th... acquiring it," Madison later wrote, "is but a prologue to a f... tragedy, or perhaps both. Knowledge will forever govern ignoranc... people who mean to be their own governors must arm themselve... the power which knowledge gives."[4] In theory, given our Constitutio... should not need a Freedom of Information Act. Except for keeping... most sensitive details of military or financial operations secret, and on... until they have been carried out, we should enjoy easy access to information about the activities of our government. But in the late 1950s and early 1960s, Congressman John Moss (Democrat from California) became so frustrated by his inability to get accurate information out of the federal bureaucracy that he worked virtually single-handedly for years to push the Freedom of Information Act (FOIA) through Congress.

On July 4, 1966, President Lyndon Johnson signed it, expressing "a deep sense of pride that the United States is an open society in which the people's right to know is cherished and guarded." As Bill Moyers, Johnson's press secretary, later reported, "Well, yes, but what few people knew at the time is that LBJ had to be dragged kicking and screaming to the signing ceremony. He hated the very idea of the Freedom of Information Act; hated the thought of journalists rummaging in government closets; hated them challenging the official view of reality. He dug in his heels and even threatened to pocket veto the bill after it reached the White House. Only the courage and political skill of a Congressman named John Moss got the bill passed at all, and that was after a twelve-year battle against his elders in Congress who blinked every time the sun shined in the dark corridors of power."[5]

From the start the FOIA exempted from requests for disclosure the federal courts, the Congress (a big mistake), and parts of the Executive new web of secrecy and nondisclosure. The *San Francisco Chronicle*'s Ruth Rosen, in one of her columns, caught the crucial moment when this occurred, itself obscured by official secrecy, "The president didn't ask the networks for television time. The attorney general didn't hold a press conference. The media didn't report any dramatic change in governmental policy. As a result, most Americans had no idea that one of their most precious freedoms disappeared on October 12 [2001]."[9] On that day Attorney General John Ashcroft sent a memo to all federal agencies urging them to bring every excuse they could think of to bear in turning down Freedom of Information requests. He offered agency heads backing on this stance: "When you carefully consider FOIA requests and decide to withhold records, in whole or in part, you can be assured that the Department of Justice will defend your decisions unless they lack a sound legal basis." In marked contrast, his predecessor, Janet Reno, had advised all departments and agencies that they should honor FOIA requests so long as doing so caused "no foreseeable harm."[10]

The Bush administration subverted the FOIA in ways large and small. For instance, charges were raised to excessive levels for fulfilling FOIA requests even though the law stipulates that service fees should be minimal. In January 2005, the Justice Department typically informed People for the American Way, a watchdog organization critical of the government's record on civil rights and other issues, that it would be charged $372,999 for a search of the department's files and disclosure of 1,200 cases in which court proceedings against immigrants arrested and confined after 9/11 were conducted in secret.[11] Needless to say, small grassroots organizations cannot afford such expenses.

Three weeks after Ashcroft tried to shut down FOIA, President Bush made a tone-setting decision when it came to closing off the people's right to know. Back in 1974, at the height of the Watergate scandal, Congress seized President Nixon's records and tape recordings because it feared that the former president planned to destroy them. (On May 2, 1972, following the death of the longtime director of the FBI, J. Edgar Hoover, his personal secretary and lover, Clyde A. Tolson, had indeed destroyed decades of official and unofficial FBI records to keep Hoover's many illegal acts secret.) In light of these developments, in 1978, Congress passed the Presidential Records Act, making the papers of a former president federal property upon his leaving office. It required that such records be transferred to the

Archivist of the United States, who was ordered to open them to the public after no more than twelve years. The intent of the law was to lessen abuses of power under the veil of secrecy, or at least to disclose them in history books.

On November 1, 2001, just as a small portion of the Reagan administration's presidential papers was about to be opened to the public, President Bush issued Executive Order 13233 countermanding the Presidential Records Act.[12] It gave him (as well as former presidents) the right to veto requests to see his presidential records. Even if a former president wants his records released—as is the case with Bill Clinton—the order states that access will be granted only at the discretion of the sitting president in consultation with the former president, if still living. It has been widely speculated that Bush's intent was to protect his father, a former director of the CIA and Reagan's vice president, from being implicated in the crimes committed during the Iran-Contra affair by Reagan administration officials. Throughout the Iran-Contra investigation, George H. W. Bush argued that he had been "out of the loop" and therefore not involved in the complex illegal fund-raising for and support of the Nicaraguan Contras, who were trying to overthrow the Sandinista government. Reagan's records might have revealed just how far out of the loop he actually was.

As Thomas Blanton, executive director of the National Security Archive at George Washington University, observes, "The Presidential Records Act was designed to shift power over presidential records to the government and ultimately to the citizens. This [Executive Order] shifts the power back."[13] Historian Richard Reeves, author of *President Nixon: Alone in the White House* and *President Kennedy: Profile of Power*, comments, "Post-Nixon, presidential papers were no longer personal property. They belonged to the American people. So, now we live in a new historical reality."[14] The American Historical Association contends that Executive Order 13233 not only violated the 1978 act but functionally canceled the law by executive fiat and so "potentially threatens to undermine one of the very foundations of our nation." We still await a Supreme Court decision on whether the president can, through an executive order, or what is called a "signing statement," suspend or modify a law passed by Congress. So far, Bush has gotten away with it many times, and his two 2006 appointees to the court, John Roberts and Samuel Alito, are both believers in the "theory" of "unitary executive power."

Perhaps the most serious failure of the Supreme Court in this period was its refusal even to consider whether the Bush administration had the legal standing to round up well over a thousand foreigners in the United States in the wake of 9/11 and keep all details of their cases secret, including their names and the charges, if any, against them. We do not know whether these people were illegal aliens, visitors with tourist visas, permanent residents with Green Cards, or naturalized Americans. They were simply seized, incarcerated mostly in New York prisons, beaten by guards, and, after a lengthy time in jail, deported, usually for the most minor of offenses. Kate Martin of the Center for National Security Studies, comments, "We have a situation where the government arrested more than a thousand people in secret, and the courts let them get away with it. There is no accountability for the abuses, and secrecy allowed the abuses."[15] Not one of those arrested turned out to have the slightest connection to the 9/11 attacks.

The costs of such executive megalomania are high. As federal appellate judge Damon Keith wrote in his 2003 ruling against the Bush policy of holding hundreds of deportation hearings in secret, "Democracies die behind closed doors. . . . A government operating in the shadow of secrecy stands in complete opposition to the society envisioned by the Framers of the Constitution. When government begins closing doors, it selectively controls information rightfully belonging to the people. Selective information is misinformation."[16] The failure of the Supreme Court—and ultimately the public—to take notice of such outrages encouraged the Bush administration to assert ever more grandiose claims for its imperial presidency. According to New York University law professor Noah Feldman, "These claims add up to what is easily the most aggressive formulation of presidential power in our history."[17]

For some thirty years, a few Republican politicians from the Ford, Reagan, and Bush père administrations—including former president George H. W. Bush himself (and through him his son George W.), his secretary of defense, Dick Cheney, and Ford's secretary of defense, Donald Rumsfeld—have nursed grievances about the way Congress exposed illegal activities in the wake of Watergate, Vietnam, and Iran-Contra. They have never gotten over the public's demand that presidents should no longer go to war based on lies to Congress, such as the Vietnam-era Tonkin Gulf Resolution; that the CIA and the American military should be stopped from assassinating foreign leaders, such as President Ngo Dinh Diem of South Vietnam in 1963, and overthrowing governments that have done nothing to the United States, as they did in Chile in 1973; and that congressional oversight of our often incompetent and always deceitful intelligence agencies was long overdue.

Over the years, Dick Cheney has inveighed against President Ford's Executive Order 11905 of February 18, 1976, which stipulated that "No employee of the United States Government shall engage in, or conspire to engage in, political assassination"; the War Powers Act of 1973, which requires that the president obtain congressional approval within ninety days of ordering troops into combat; the congressional Budget Control and Impoundment Act of 1974, which was designed to stop Nixon and any other president from impounding congressionally mandated funds for programs they do not like; the Freedom of Information Act of 1966, which Congress strengthened in 1974; and the Intelligence Oversight Act of 1980, which set up the House and Senate select committees on intelligence. Similarly, in March 2005, former president George H. W. Bush, who headed the CIA from 1975 to 1977, spluttered at a conference on counterintelligence: "It burns me up to see the agency under fire." He was even more incensed that Congress had "unleashed a bunch of untutored little jerks" to investigate the CIA's involvement in domestic spying, assassinations, and other illegal activities and subsequently passed laws to prevent their recurrence.[18] Those "untutored little jerks" were the members of the Senate Select Committee to Study Governmental Operations with Respect to Intelligence Activities, chaired by Senator Frank Church, Democrat from Idaho, which issued its final report in 1976.

In January 2002, in an interview with *ABC News,* Cheney argued, "In thirty-four years, I have repeatedly seen an erosion of the powers and the ability of the president of the United States to do his job. One of the things that I feel an obligation on—and I know the president does too—is to pass on our offices in better shape than we found them."[19] But all of the legislation passed in the 1970s represented attempts to deal with crimes committed by government officials. Nonetheless, no president after Nixon has ever acknowledged the legitimacy of the War Powers Act, and most of these "limitations" on presidential power had been gutted, ignored, or violated long before Cheney became vice president. Bruce Fein, a constitutional scholar and former Reagan administration lawyer, calls them "museum pieces."[20] There is simply no evidence that, since the 1970s, there has been any real reduction in the powers of the presidency or that the Bush-Cheney government ever behaved as if it thought there were. "The vice president," noted Republican senator John E. Sununu, "may be the only person I know of who believes the executive has somehow lost power over the last thirty years."[21]

In pursuit of yet more power, Bush and Cheney have unilaterally authorized preventive war against nations they designate as needing "regime change," directed American soldiers to torture persons seized and imprisoned in various countries, ordered the National Security Agency to carry out illegal "data mining" surveillance of the American people, and done everything they could to prevent Congress from outlawing "cruel, inhumane, or degrading" treatment of people detained by the United States (acts that were, in any case, already illegal under both U.S. law and international agreements the United States had long ago signed and ratified). They have done these things in accordance with something they call the "unitary executive theory of the presidency."

This "theory" is, in fact, simply a bald-faced assertion of presidential supremacy in all matters relating to foreign affairs dressed up in legalistic mumbo jumbo. Its classic expression is contained in the August 1, 2002, "torture memo" conceived and written by a group of ultraconservative lawyers in the White House, Justice Department, and Vice President's office. Among them are John Yoo, a young, right-wing Korean-American scholar and a former law clerk for Supreme Court Justice Clarence Thomas, who served as a lawyer in the Justice Department's Office of Legal Counsel; Alberto Gonzales, then the White House's legal counsel; and David S. Addington, a former lawyer for the CIA, the Pentagon's general counsel when Cheney was secretary of defense, and then chief of staff in Cheney's office.[22]

The torture memo justified its extreme views by claiming that the commander-in-chief power even overrides U.S. laws: "In light of the president's complete authority over the conduct of war, without a clear statement otherwise, criminal statutes are not read as infringing on the president's ultimate authority in these areas." Ratified treaties, congressionally enacted statutes, and military orders prohibiting torture "must be construed as inapplicable to interrogations undertaken pursuant to his commander-in-chief authority. . . . Congress may no more regulate the president's ability to detain and interrogate enemy combatants than it may regulate his ability to direct troop movements on the battlefield." The same principle holds for "federal officials acting pursuant to the president's constitutional authority.... The Framers understood the [commander-in-chief] clause as investing the president with the fullest range of power," including "the conduct of warfare and the defense of the nation unless expressly assigned in the Constitution to Congress." That "sweeping grant" of power, the memo continued, is given because "national security decisions require the unity in purpose and energy in action that characterize the presidency rather than Congress."[23]

Yoo and company have concocted something that looks very much like an American version of the Chinese Communists' "Two Whatevers." These were the basic principles that prevailed during the years when the cult of Mao Zedong was ascendant: "We will resolutely uphold whatever policy decisions Chairman Mao makes; and we will unswervingly follow whatever instructions Chairman Mao gives." Substitute Bush for Mao and you get the idea. *Time* magazine contends that, according to the White House and the Justice Department, "The Commander in Chief's pursuit of national security cannot be constrained by any laws passed by Congress, even when he is acting against U.S. citizens."[24] Bruce Schneier, author of *Beyond Fear: Thinking Sensibly About Security in an Uncertain World,* sees an even more ominous development: "The president can define war however he chooses, and remain 'at war' for as long as he chooses. This is indefinite dictatorial power. And I don't use that term lightly; the very definition of a dictatorship is a system that puts a ruler above the law."[25] The implications for the constitutional separation of powers are thus grave, particularly since the unitary executive theory flies in the face of the Constitution itself.

As Dan Farber, a professor of law at the University of California, Berkeley, and author of *Lincoln's Constitution,* reminds us, "Constitutional law derives from the language of the Constitution, the original understanding, and two centuries of Supreme Court precedent. Often, these three are ambiguous or contradict each other, but not here. All three make it clear that the president must share power with Congress and the courts, in war as well as in peace."[26] Article 2 stresses without qualification that the president "shall take care that laws be faithfully executed." Many famous Supreme Court justices have emphasized, as Justices Felix Frank-furter and Hugo Black did in 1952, "The power to execute the laws starts and ends with the laws Congress has enacted." The Constitution explicitly gives Congress the power to declare war, to raise and support armies, to equip the navy, to call out the militia (today, the National Guard), and to "make rules for the Government and Regulation of the land and naval forces."

Perhaps the closest thing to malpractice in Yoo's theory is his failure to mention the most important legal precedent defining the balance of power between Congress and the president during wartime: the 1952 case *Youngstown Sheet and Tube Company v. Sawyer.*[27] During the Korean War, faced with the possibility of a strike that threatened to shut down the steel industry, President Harry Truman ordered the Department of Commerce to seize all steel plants and suspend the labor laws. The Supreme Court promptly declared that the president's commander-in-chief powers did not extend to areas in which Congress had passed legislation—in this case, the Taft-Hartley Act of 1947, which regulated strikes—and that he had exceeded his authority.

Concurring in the judgment and the opinion of the court, Justice Robert H. Jackson wrote, "[T]he Constitution did not contemplate that the title Commander-in-Chief of the Army and Navy will constitute [the president] also Commander-in-Chief of the country, its industries, and its inhabitants. He has no monopoly of 'war powers,' whatever they are. . . . His command power is not such an absolute as might be implied from that office in a militaristic system but is subject to limitations consistent with a constitutional Republic whose law and policy-making branch is a representative Congress. The purpose of lodging dual titles in one man was to insure that the civilian would control the military, not to enable the military to subordinate the presidential office. No penance would ever expiate the sin against free government of holding that a president can escape control of executive powers by law through assuming his military role." In the *Youngstown* case, both Justices Robert Jackson and Frank-furter, in their concurring opinions, quoted Justice Louis Brandeis's dissent in the 1926 case *Myers v. United States*: "The doctrine of the separation of powers was adopted by the Convention of 1787 not to promote efficiency but to preclude the exercise of arbitrary power. The purpose was, not to avoid friction, but by means of the inevitable friction incident to the distribution of the governmental powers among three departments, to save the people from autocracy."

Among the many instances in which George W. Bush has ignored his oath of office—"I will faithfully execute the office of President of the United States, and will to the best of my ability, preserve, protect, and defend the Constitution of the United States"—perhaps the most blatant has been the way he secretly authorized the National Security Agency (NSA), the country's leading cryptological and signals intelligence agency, to eavesdrop on Americans without a court-approved warrant. Such warrants are required by the Fourth Amendment to the Constitution and by the Foreign Intelligence Surveillance Act (FISA), which President Jimmy Carter signed into law on October 25, 1978.[28] Except in terms of a raw expansion of basic presidential powers, it is close to inexplicable why Bush chose to ignore the FISA law, since it would have readily facilitated virtually anything he wanted to do in the way of wiretapping. Enacted in the wake of revelations that the federal government had routinely, if illegally, tapped the telephones of people who opposed the war in Vietnam, the FISA law was anything but a strong reaffirmation of the prohibition against unreasonable searches and seizures in the Bill of Rights.

As its title indicates, the Foreign Intelligence Surveillance Act allows the FBI and the NSA to listen in on American citizens in order to collect intelligence, and it set up a secret court to issue warrants based on requests from the intelligence community. From its inception in 1979 through 2004, the FISA court issued 18,742 secret warrants while denying only four government requests.[29] The court was originally made up of seven federal judges appointed by the chief justice of the Supreme Court; the USA Patriot Act of 2001 expanded that number to eleven. The judges' identities are secret. They meet in total privacy behind a cipher-locked door in a windowless, bugproof, vaultlike room guarded twenty-four hours a day on the top floor of the Justice Department's building in Washington, D.C. Everything they do is "top secret."

The judges hear only the government's side. The court makes annual reports to Congress, normally just two paragraphs long, that give only the total number of warrants it has approved. Beyond that, there is no congressional oversight of the court's activities whatsoever. The law even allows emergency taps and searches for which a warrant can be issued retroactively if the government notifies the court within seventy-two hours. Compared with ordinary wiretaps, for which the government must provide a federal district court judge with evidence of "probable cause" that the person or persons under investigation are likely to commit a crime, the FISA process is weighted toward the government, not the citizen, and not surprisingly the secret court has authorized more warrants than all federal district judges combined.[30]

Nonetheless, immediately following 9/11, the president issued a secret executive order authorizing the National Security Agency to tap at will into the private communications of American citizens. Unknown bureaucrats at the NSA make the decisions about who is to be tapped without any supervision by a court or elected representatives of the people. When newspaper reporters got wind of what the president had done, the White House intervened to try to keep the information secret. On national security grounds, the *New York Times* was asked to sit for more than a year on the story of how the NSA was violating the law. Finally, on December 6, 2005, when publication was imminent, President Bush summoned the *Times*'s publisher Arthur Sulzberger Jr., and executive editor Bill Keller to the Oval Office and asked them to desist in the name of national security, the war on terror, and 9/11. But the president was unable to offer any sound legal basis for what he had done nor why the cover-up should continue. On December 16, 2005, a year late in terms of the public's right to know, the *New York Times* finally printed the story.[31] On December 20, one of the hitherto unknown FISA court judges, James Robertson, resigned in protest, a totally unprecedented action.

There is no obvious reason beyond trying to obtain pure power why the president chose to ignore FISA and go directly against an act of Congress. The syndicated columnist Paul Craig Roberts has speculated that Bush could not ask for warrants for the kinds of spying he wanted done because he had no legitimate reasons to offer even the lenient FISA court. Roberts suggests that he might have been using the spy apparatus of the U.S. government to influence the outcome of the 2004 presidential election or that he might have been collecting information on his Democratic Party opponents in order to blackmail them.[32] Former senior adviser to President Clinton and Washington bureau chief of Salon.com Sidney Blumenthal believes the administration simply had no probable cause for the NSA surveillance. The court, after all, must adhere to the law and cannot simply authorize surveillance because the president or an intelligence agency wants to eavesdrop on someone. It is also possible that the administration wanted to avoid the FISA court because what evidence it had supporting probable cause had been obtained by torture, which conceivably might cause the court to reject an application (although these days no one should count on it).[33]

Intelligence expert Thomas Powers, author of *Intelligence Wars: American Secret History from Hitler to Al-Qaeda,* has another theory entirely. He believes that the issue was not specific surveillance but the administration's desire to use the NSA to keep alive an ambitious Pentagon data-mining project called Total Information Awareness (TIA) after Congress (and the public) expressed outrage over its existence and in September 2003 ordered it stopped. TIA was the brainchild of John Poindexter, a former admiral and Ronald Reagan's national security adviser, who was convicted of seven felonies for his part in the Iran-Contra affair but was exonerated on appeal. A computer fanatic's ideal of "data mining," TIA, as Poindexter imagined it, was to compile everything that could be known about a vast range of individuals and then comb through such mountains of data for correlations that the government might find suspect. One of TIA's key collaborators was the National Security Agency, which supplied much of the data that went into its individual profiles.[34]

On November 14, 2002, the *New York Times*'s conservative columnist William Safire outlined the kind of data TIA sought: "Every purchase you make with a credit card, every magazine subscription you buy and medical prescription you fill, every web site you visit and e-mail you send or receive, every academic grade you receive, every bank deposit you make, every trip you book, and every event you attend—all these transactions and communications will go into what the Defense Department describes as a 'virtual centralized grand database.' "[35] Add to that all government information—passport applications, drivers' licenses, judicial and divorce records, IRS files, complaints by nosy neighbors, plus the latest hidden camera surveillance—and one has the perfect American computer version of Gestapo or KGB files.

There is growing evidence that in 2003 the TIA project was stopped in name only. The National Security Agency continued snooping and collecting data as before, while the analytical work was transferred to a new, totally secret agency inside the Pentagon known as the Counterintelligence Field Activity (CIFA). Its original specialty was illegally watching, photographing, and harassing peaceful public protests outside foreign and domestic military bases. According to Walter Pincus of the *Washington Post*, CIFA has "grown from an agency that coordinated policy and oversaw the counterintelligence activities of units within the military services and Pentagon agencies to an analytic and operational organization with nine directorates and ever-widening authority." It has become known as "the superpower of data mining within the U.S. national security community. . . . Since March 2004, CIFA has awarded at least $33 million in contracts to corporate giants Lockheed Martin, Unisys Corporation, Computer Sciences Corporation, and Northrop Grumman to develop databases that comb through classified and unclassified government data, commercial information, and Internet chatter to help sniff out terrorists, saboteurs, and spies."[36]

In 2005, CIFA reportedly "contracted with Computer Sciences Corp. to buy identity-masking software, which could allow it to create fake Web sites and monitor legitimate U.S. sites without leaving clues that it had been there." A former senior Pentagon official familiar with CIFA told Pincus, "They started with force protection from terrorists, but when you go down that road, you soon are into everything . . . where terrorists get their money, who they see, who they deal with." Because the National Security Agency is a major source of CIFA's data, that may have been one reason why Bush ordered the NSA to engage in surveillance of citizens completely outside the purview of the FISA court, which probably would not have approved open-ended data mining.[37]

One further way in which President Bush has shown his contempt for the Constitution is his use of what are called "signing statements." During the first six years of his presidency, Bush did not exercise his constitutionally authorized veto over a single piece of legislation passed by Congress, but in his first term alone, he issued 505 extraconstitutional challenges to various provisions of legislation that had been enacted by Congress.[38] Through "interpretive" statements issued at the time he signs them, the president disagrees with one or more provisions contained in the legislation and therefore reserves the right not to implement them. According to David Golove, a New York University law professor, "The signing statement is saying 'I will only comply with this law when I want to, and if something arises in the war on terrorism where I think it's important to torture or engage in cruel, inhuman, and degrading conduct, I have the authority to do so and nothing in this law is going to stop me.'"[39]

Many of these statements amount to illegal line-item vetoes. They often have the effect of nullifying legislation that has been passed by both houses of Congress and signed by the president. In 1998, in *Clinton v. New York,* the Supreme Court held that a line-item veto is unconstitutional because it violates "the Constitution's Presentment Clause. That Clause says that after a bill has passed both houses, but 'before it becomes a law,' it must be presented to the president, who 'shall sign it' if he approves, but 'return it'—that is, veto the bill, in its entirety—if he does not."[40] Bush's signing statements eliminate the possibility of the Congress overriding his veto since they take effect (whatever that might mean) after the bill has already become law, and they violate the first sentence of the Constitution's first article: "All legislative powers herein granted" belong to Congress. As the framers carefully explained, this means only the "Senate and House of Representatives"—not the president in the act of signing a bill into law.[41]

One of the most striking examples of the legal quagmire created by these signing statements lies in the 2006 Defense Appropriation Bill. On the initiative of Republican senator John McCain, who was himself tortured while a prisoner of war in Vietnam, the Senate added an amendment to the defense-spending authorization and called it the Detainee Treatment Act of 2005. It reads, "No individual in the custody or under the physical control of the United States government, regardless of nationality or physical location, shall be subject to cruel, inhuman, or degrading treatment or punishment," and it provides for "uniform standards" of interrogation. President Bush threatened to exercise his first veto over the whole Pentagon budget because of this amendment. Then he and Vice President Cheney lobbied Congress intensively in order to retain the Pentagon's and the CIA's "right" to the secret use of torture (although never termed torture, of course) without fear of domestic prosecution. When the Senate responded by passing McCain's torture ban by a veto-proof vote of 90–9, the White House turned to extralegal means to get what it wanted.[42]

On December 15, 2005, in a photo session at the White House, President Bush and Senator McCain shook hands and Bush announced that this landmark legislation would make it "clear to the world that this government does not torture." However, on Friday evening, December 30, when he actually signed the bill at his Crawford, Texas, ranch, Bush added a signing statement that essentially gutted McCain's amendment. It said that he would construe the new law "in a manner consistent with the constitutional authority of the president," that he would order whatever he deemed necessary in his war on terror, and that, as president "in a time of war," he was beyond any legal constraints. Elisa Massimino, the Washington director of Human Rights First, commented that "[t]he basic civics lesson that there are three coequal branches of government that provide checks and balances on each other is being fundamentally rejected by the executive branch."[43]

It is not clear how this muddled situation will ultimately be resolved, but its immediate costs are high. A former army interrogator at Abu Ghraib prison writes, "Those who serve in the prisons of Iraq deserve to know clearly the difference between legal and illegal orders. Soldiers on the ground need a commander in chief who does not seek strained legalisms that 'permit' the use of torture. . . . No slope is more slippery, I learned in Iraq, than the one that leads to torture."[44] As of mid-2006, none of President Bush's signing statements had been tested in court.

Moreover, it is not just the executive branch that has been tearing at the fabric of the Constitution. Through its partisanship, complacency, and corruption, Congress has done much to ensure that the crisis of the American republic will be fatal to democratic government. As constitutional specialist Noah Feldman writes, "For the last four years, a republican Congress has done almost nothing to rein in the expansion of presidential power. This abdication of responsibility has been even more remarkable than the president's assumption of new powers."[45] Al Gore, who served eight years in the House, eight years in the Senate, and presided over the Senate for eight years as vice president, observes, "The sharp decline of congressional power and autonomy in recent years has been almost as shocking as the efforts by the executive branch to attain a massive expansion of power. . . . Moreover, in the Congress as a whole—both House and Senate—the enhanced role of money in the re-election process, coupled with the diminished role for reasoned deliberation and debate, has produced an atmosphere conducive to pervasive institutionalized corruption. . . . It is the pitiful state of our legislative branch that primarily explains the failure of our vaunted checks and balances to prevent the dangerous overreach of the executive branch, which now threatens a radical transformation of the American system."[46]

I happen to be a registered voter in the Fiftieth Congressional District of California in northern San Diego county, where, in early 2006, our Republican representative for the previous fourteen years, Randy "Duke" Cunningham, received the longest sentence to a federal prison—eight years and four months—ever imposed on a member of Congress. Cunningham, a decorated Vietnam War pilot, confessed to pocketing $2.4 million, the largest bribe ever paid to a member of Congress. He had used his official positions on the Appropriations and Intelligence Committees to see that contracts worth millions of dollars went to defense manufacturers who had paid him off, and he did this primarily by adding classified earmarks to the Defense Appropriations bills and pressuring Pentagon officials to buy things they had made clear they did not want. The term "earmarks" is congressional jargon for spending by a lone representative, who surreptitiously tacks expenditures onto a larger appropriations bill that the House then passes without further scrutiny.

Well before the bribery charges were filed, I described Cunningham in the press as totally bought and paid for by the military-industrial complex.[47] However, I did so on the basis of published campaign contributions. It did not occur to me that, in selling his vote to munitions makers, as so many other members of Congress have done—including Cunningham's friend, neighbor in California's Fifty-second District, and chairman of the House Armed Services Committee, Republican representative Duncan Hunter—he was so stupid as to have actually accepted material bribes for his corrupt acts. If a member of Congress can claim there was no quid pro quo involved in accepting money from strangers, it is technically legal. Most members who want to line their pockets are content to wait and do so as lobbyists after retiring or being defeated. According to the Center for Responsive Politics, Hunter and Cunningham rank second and third among all members of Congress (first is Pennsylvania Democratic representative John P. Murtha) in terms of the total amount of money they have received from the defense industry.[48]

In buying Cunningham's influence, two San Diego–based defense contractors, Mitchell Wade, CEO of MZM Inc., which among other things provided Arabic translators for Abu Ghraib prison in Baghdad, and Brent Wilkes, CEO of ADCS Inc., supplied Cunningham with cash, a down payment and mortgage payments on a 7,628-square-foot mansion in an exclusive San Diego enclave, Persian rugs, antique French armoires, two yachts, a Rolls-Royce, and a college graduation party for his daughter.[49] In return, Cunningham arranged for $163 million in Pentagon contracts for MZM, which had not done much business with the Defense Department until Wade met him, and more than $90 million for Wilkes's company for converting old documents into computer-readable files. (Wilkes wanted to digitize the century-old archives dealing with the building of the Panama Canal, not exactly vital to the Global War on Terror and something Pentagon officials repeatedly insisted they did not need.) Senior correspondent for the *American Prospect* Laura Rozen notes, "Duncan Hunter [was] identified by a Defense Department Inspector General report—along with Cunningham—as actively intervening with the Pentagon to try to award a contract to a document-conversion company that had given him tens of thousands of dollars in campaign contributions for a program the Pentagon did not request or consider a priority."[50] Wilkes's technology was imported from Germany.

It is important to stress that the distinction in Congress between a bribe and a legal donation is a bit of sophistry intended to conceal the routine corruption of our elected representatives. As Bill Moyers has put it, "If [in baseball] a player sliding into home plate reached into his pocket and handed the umpire $1000 before he made the call, what would we call that? A bribe. And if a lawyer handed a judge $1000 before he issued a ruling, what do we call that? A bribe. But when a lobbyist or CEO [chief executive officer of a corporation] sidles up to a member of Congress at a fund-raiser or in a skybox and hands him a check for $1000, what do we call that? A campaign contribution."[51]

Brent Wilkes was more experienced at buying influence than Wade. He supplied private jet flights for House majority leader Tom DeLay and Republican Roy Blunt and became a "pioneer" in the Bush-Cheney 2004 reelection campaign by raising $100,000. From 1995 to 2005, Wilkes and his associates gave more than $840,000 to at least thirty-two congressional campaigns or their political action committees.[52] According to the Federal Election Commission, the recipients included Representative John Doolittle (Republican from California), total $82,000; Representative Randy Cunningham, $76,500; Representative Jerry Lewis (Republican from California), $60,000; Representative Tom DeLay (Republican from

Texas), $57,000; Representative Duncan Hunter, $39,200; Senator Larry Craig (Republican from Idaho), $29,000; Representative Jerry Weller (Republican from Illinois), $27,500; Representative Benjamin Gilman (Republican from New York), $25,843; Representative Roy Blunt (Republican from Missouri), $17,000; and Senator Lindsey Graham (Republican from South Carolina), $14,000.[53]

The culprits are not just Republicans. Consider the actions of the senators from Florida in 2006. In the 2006 federal budget, Republican senator Mel Martinez earmarked defense appropriations for Florida contractors worth $316 million. Since 2003, companies that received defense contracts made $33,000 worth of campaign contributions to Martinez. Democratic senator Bill Nelson, a member of the Armed Services Committee, obtained $916 million for defense projects, about two-thirds of which went to the Florida-based plants of Boeing, Honeywell, General Dynamics, Armor Holdings, and other munitions makers. Since 2003, Nelson has received $108,750 from thirteen companies for which he arranged contracts.[54]

Under such circumstances, it is still possible to imagine that some congressional votes in areas where money is flowing are not being influenced by campaign contributions, but only if the members are independently wealthy, and even then it is highly unlikely. There are, in addition, other ways to influence Congress, particularly through lobbying. The numbers of lobbyists, the amounts of money involved in lobbying, and the ties between the lobbying industry, the dominant Republicans in Congress, and the White House have all exploded in the Bush years. "Since Bush was elected," according to Bill Moyers, "the number of lobbyists registered to do business in Washington has more than doubled. That's 16,342 lobbyists in 2000 to 34,785 [in 2005]. Sixty-five lobbyists for every member of Congress."[55] In September 2005, Tom DeLay was forced to resign as majority leader of the House when he was indicted for channeling corporate contributions to politicians in Texas. He was the chief conduit of master lobbyist Jack Abramoff, who in January 2006 confessed to cheating his clients while spending lavishly on congressional junkets, meals, and campaign contributions. Some twenty-nine former staff members of DeLay's congressional office have left government service to accept positions as lobbyists in major Washington law firms, the largest number working for any member of Congress.

Typical of the DeLay-Abramoff operations was their lobbying for the Commonwealth of the Northern Mariana Islands. After World War II, these specks of land in the Pacific 5,625 miles west of San Francisco—the largest of which is the island of Saipan—became a United Nations trust territory, administered by the United States Department of the Interior. Under a scheme to make Saipan a sweatshop, the Interior Department exempted the islands from U.S. labor and immigration laws. There is no minimum wage on Saipan. Tens of thousands of Chinese women live in dormitories with no basic political rights; they are prohibited from marrying and are paid almost nothing. They work producing clothes with "Made in the USA" labels for companies like Levi Strauss & Co., the Gap, Eddie Bauer, Reebok, Polo, Nordstrom, Lord & Taylor, and Liz Claiborne, which are then shipped duty-free to the United States. The sweatshop operators, the biggest of whom are naturalized U.S. citizens of Chinese ancestry, paid Abramoff nearly $10 million, part of which he used to book congressmen and their "significant others" into luxury hotels and exclusive golf courses on Saipan, to ensure that Congress did not pass a minimum-wage law for the islands. Abramoff took DeLay and his wife there, and the congressman was moved to declare that the Marianas "represented what is best about America," calling them "my Galapagos."[56] Other major clients of the Abramoff-DeLay lobbying duo include gambling casinos on Indian reservations, Russian oil and gas interests, and the U.S. Family Network.

The mainstream press regularly refers to members of Congress as "lawmakers," but that phrase bears little relationship to what they actually do. An excellent example is the Foreign Operations bill for fiscal year 2005. At the time of passage, according to *Los Angeles Times* correspondent Ken Silverstein, it was "the biggest single piece of pork-barrel legislation in American history."[57] On November 17, 2004, a small group of senators and representatives from their respective appropriations committees folded into the bill funds for the Departments of Justice, State, Energy, Labor, Commerce, Education, Agriculture, Transportation, the Treasury, Interior, Veterans Affairs, Health and Human Services, and Housing and Urban Development, as well as the running expenses for the entire legislative and judicial branches. Around 12:15 a.m. on November 20, 2004, staff members, working frantically, made the 3,320-page bill available to "legislators" on the Web site of the House Rules Committee.

The House put it to a vote at approximately 4:00 p.m. in the afternoon of the same day and the Senate followed suit at 8:42 p.m. that evening. The legislation passed the House by a margin of 344 to 51 and the Senate by 65 to 30. It would have been a physical impossibility for any member to have read the entire piece of legislation in the time available, much less thought about what it involved. The bill included 11,772 separate earmarks worth a combined total of nearly $16 billion. Silverstein observes, "Of who added these grants, no public record exists."[58]

Earmarking of defense spending has more than tripled since fiscal year 1995, and the Department of Defense's black budget, which is secret from all citizens and virtually all members of Congress, was estimated at the end of 2005 at $28 billion per year: $14.2 billion for purchases of hardware and $13.7 billion in so-called research and development expenditures. According to Citizens Against Government Waste, in 1995 Congress approved 1,439 earmarked appropriations; in 2005, the number had risen to 13,998. Gordon Adams, director of security studies at George Washington University and a former White House budget director for national security, notes that members of such influential congressional committees as Intelligence and the Defense Subcommittees of the House and Senate Appropriations Committees "have a lot of power . . . and are sitting in a place where a lot of money flows. . . . There are huge opportunities here for politicians to tweak the system to their advantage. The smell of corruption is in the air."[59]

Franklin Spinney, for thirty years a budget analyst in the Pentagon, said in a discussion with Bill Moyers, "The military-industrial-Congressional complex is a political economy with a big *P* and a little *E*. It's very political in nature. Economic decisions, which should prevail in a normal market system, don't prevail in the Pentagon, or in the military-industrial complex. So what we have is a system that essentially rewards its senior players. . . . We have a term for it, it's a self-licking ice cream cone."[60] Moyers pointed out that pay for chief executive officers at Lockheed Martin went up from $5.8 million in 2000 to $25.3 million in 2002, at General Dynamics from $5.7 million in 2001 to $15.2 million in 2002, and at Northrop Grumman from $7.3 million in 2000 to $9.2 million in 2002.

Spinney explained that a main lobbying strategy of the military-industrial complex is to emphasize to members of Congress how many jobs are dependent on a particular contract being approved, rather than the usefulness or feasibility of a weapon. Lobbyists' letters and presentations to members of Congress always include maps showing precisely the communities that will be enriched by Pentagon spending and the funds they will receive.

Coming at it from a somewhat different political perspective is Winslow Wheeler, from 1996 to 2002 the senior analyst for national security on the Republican staff of the Senate Budget Committee and before that an aide to Senators Pete Domenici (Republican from New Mexico), Jacob Javits (Republican from New York), and Nancy Kassebaum (Republican from Kansas). After thirty years working on Capitol Hill, Wheeler retired and devoted himself to revealing the "systemic problems that reduce government to an exploitative system and make it possible for special interests to manipulate it at will."[61] He has documented how senators added $4 billion in useless "pork" projects to benefit their own states immediately after the 9/11 attacks, including Senator Robert Byrd (Democrat from West Virginia), who strongly opposed going to war against Iraq but nonetheless asked for funds to build an army museum in his home state. Senator Ted Stevens (Republican from Alaska), one of the stalwarts of the missile defense lobby because most of the ground-based interceptors are located in silos in his state, asked for post-9/11 funds to build parking garages (for automobiles, not missiles).

Wheeler's major study, *Wastrels of Defense: How Congress Sabotages U.S. Security,* was not brought out by a leftist or liberal publisher but by the Naval Institute Press.[62] He draws on his own experience to explain how dependent most members of Congress are on their staffs and how most staff officials spend their time inserting earmarks and add-ons to defense bills rather than actually trying to determine how the money of the people of the United States should be spent to achieve security. Between fiscal years 2001 and 2002, just as Wheeler's career in the Senate was coming to an end, so-called add-ons—that is, unrequested spending for the Pentagon—jumped from $3.3 billion to $5.4 billion, not including, in 2002, $583 million for thirty-two projects added at the last minute by the House-Senate Conference Committee for items neither requested by the Pentagon nor included in the House or Senate bills.[63] Wheeler presents numerous examples of how pork projects inserted into legislation to favor special interests undermined or took the place of serious defense projects. He notes that whereas defense appropriations bills in the 1980s might have had as many as two or three hundred pork items, in 2005 or 2006 a bill contains thousands. His argument is that after more than two centuries, the system of checks and balances built into our government by the Constitution no longer works.

If the corruption of the legislative branch were not enough to scuttle the separation of powers, the Congress regularly goes out of its way to bow down to the president. After the press revealed that the National Security Agency was illegally eavesdropping on the private conversations of American citizens and that President Bush had trashed the Foreign Intelligence Surveillance Act, the majority leadership in Congress introduced legislation that, in essence, would have retroactively forgiven him. As the *New York Times* editorialized, "Imagine being stopped for speeding and having the local legislature raise the limit so you won't have to pay the fine. It sounds absurd, but it's just what is happening to the 28-year-old law that prohibits the president from spying on Americans without getting a warrant from a judge. It's a familiar pattern. President Bush ignores the Constitution and the laws of the land, and the cowardly, rigidly partisan majority in Congress helps him out by rewriting the law he's broken."[64] A Congress that is indifferent to the separation of powers has given up its raison d'être as surely as the Roman Senate became a mere social club for old aristocrats paying obeisance to Augustus Caesar.

Similarly, even before President Bush undercut the McCain amendment to the Defense Appropriations Bill with his signing statement, Republican senator Lindsey Graham contributed another amendment that removed the federal courts' jurisdiction over Guantánamo prisoners who were hoping to challenge the legality of their detention. It states explicitly that "no court, justice, or judge shall have jurisdiction to hear or consider habeas corpus applications on behalf of those incarcerated by the Department of Defense in prisons at Guantánamo Bay, Cuba." The Senate passed this remarkably cruel piece of legislation by a vote of 49 to 42. It effectively repudiated the Supreme Court's 2004 decision in *Rasul v. Bush,* which gave non–U.S. citizens at Guantánamo the right to file claims based on habeas corpus in the federal courts. The legal scholar Brian Foley explains that habeas corpus forces the executive branch "to justify its detention of any person. It is a check for preventing the Executive from becoming too powerful. After all, an Executive that can jail anyone it dislikes, for as long as it likes, is a formidable power indeed."[65]

An authority on American use of torture over the years, Alfred W. McCoy, adds, "Senator McCain's now-compromised ban on cruel treatment of detainees was effectively eviscerated by Graham's denial of legal redress. To nullify the landmark Supreme Court ruling that Guantánamo is, in fact, American territory and so falls under the purview of U.S. courts, Graham also stipulated in the final legislation that 'the term "United States," when used in a geographic sense, does not include the United States Naval Station, Guantánamo Bay.' In this way, he tried once again to deny detainees any legal basis for access to the courts. In effect, McCain's motion more or less bans torture, but Graham's removes any real mechanism for enforcing such a ban."[66]

Senator Graham claimed that he was merely trying to increase the efficiency of the federal courts, that his amendment was necessary "to eliminate a blizzard of legal claims from prisoners that was tying up Department of Justice resources."[67] It is hard to imagine a lamer excuse for dishonoring such a well-established norm of American civil liberties. The Graham provision also explicitly gives the military officers who sit in judgment over Guantánamo prisoners in what the government calls "Combatant Status Review Tribunals" the right to use evidence obtained by torture. The effect of the law is, as Brian Foley argues, "to give the Executive unreviewable power. . . . A person can be captured, shackled, and sent to Guantánamo and never given a hearing. . . . He has no right to a hearing because he cannot enforce that right in a court. He can be tortured, because he cannot go to court to enforce a right not to be tortured."[68]

On June 29, 2006, the Supreme Court complicated these matters by declaring that the Guantánamo military commissions that Bush had created without congressional authorization were, in fact, unconstitutional. The case, *Hamdan v. Rumsfeld,* also repudiated the main provisions of Senator Graham's law. However, the justices voted 5–3, with Bush's new chief justice, John Roberts, not participating because he had ruled on the case as an appeals court justice, and the Republican Congress pledged to enact legislation that would allow Bush to proceed anyway with his drumhead courts.

The separation of powers that the Founders wrote into our Constitution as the main bulwark against dictatorship increasingly appears to be a dead letter, with the Congress no longer capable of asserting itself against presidential attempts to monopolize power. Corrupt and indifferent, the

Congress, which the Founders believed would be the leading branch of government, is simply not up to the task of confronting a modern Julius Caesar. As former representative Bob Barr, a conservative from Georgia, concludes, "The American people are going to have to say, 'Enough of this business of justifying everything as necessary for the war on terror.' Either the Constitution and the laws of this country mean something or they don't. It is truly frightening what is going on in this country."[69]

If the legislative branch of our government is broken—and it is hard to imagine how it could repair itself, given the massive interests that feed off it—the judicial branch is hardly less limited today in terms of its ability to maintain the balance. Even the Supreme Court's most extraordinary power, its ability to nullify a law as unconstitutional, rests on precedent rather than constitutional stipulation, and lower courts, increasingly packed with right-wing judges, have little taste for going against the prevailing political winds. For example, on February 16, 2006, U.S. District Court judge David Trager dismissed a suit for damages by a thirty-five-year-old Canadian citizen, Maher Arar, who in 2002 was seized by U.S. government agents at Kennedy Airport, New York, en route to Ottawa. Arar was shackled, hustled aboard a CIA airplane, and delivered to Syria, where he was tortured for ten months before being released. No charges were ever filed against him, and even his torturers declared that they had been unable to discover any evidence that might link him to a terror network. The case for compensation, not to mention an apology, seemed open and shut.

In dismissing Arar's suit, Judge Trager wrote that foreign policy and national security issues raised by the U.S. government were "compelling" and that such matters were the purview of the executive branch and Congress, not the courts. He acknowledged that in sending Arar to Syria, the U.S. government knew he would be tortured—the State Department had already publicly detailed the Syrians' capabilities and record as torturers. *New York Times* columnist Bob Herbert asked, "If kidnapping and torturing an innocent man is O.K., what's not O.K.?"[70]

The evidence strongly suggests that the legislative and judicial branches, having become so servile in the presence of the imperial presidency, have largely lost the ability to respond in a principled and independent manner. Could the people themselves restore constitutional government? A grassroots movement to abolish the CIA, break the hold of the military-industrial complex, and establish public financing of elections may be theoretically conceivable but is unlikely given the conglomerate control of the mass media and the difficulties of mobilizing our large and diffuse population.

It is also possible that, at some future moment, the U.S. military could actually take over the government and declare a dictatorship (though they undoubtedly would find a gentler, more user-friendly name for it). That is how the Roman Republic ended. But I think it unlikely that the American military will go that route. In recent years, the officer corps has become more "professional," as well as more political and more Republican in its sympathies, while the all-volunteer army has become an ever more separate institution in our society, its profile less and less like that of the general populace. Nonetheless, for the military voluntarily to move toward direct rule, its leaders would have to ignore their ties to civilian society, where the symbolic importance of constitutional legitimacy remains potent.

Rebellious officers might well worry about how the American people would react to such a move. Moreover, prosecutions of low-level military torturers from Abu Ghraib prison have demonstrated to enlisted ranks that obedience to illegal orders can result in their being punished, whereas officers go free. No one knows whether ordinary soldiers would obey clearly illegal orders to oust the elected government or whether the officer corps has sufficient confidence to issue such orders. For the time being at least, the highest medal for bravery and sacrifice in the American military is still the Congressional Medal of Honor, not the Victoria Cross, the Iron Cross, or the Order of Lenin. In addition, the present system already offers the military high command so much—in funds, prestige, and future employment via the military-industrial revolving door—that a perilous transition to anything like direct military rule would make little sense under reasonably normal conditions.

The likelihood is that the United States will maintain a façade of constitutional government and drift along until financial bankruptcy overtakes it. Of course, bankruptcy will not mean the literal end of the United States any more than it did for Germany in 1923, China in 1948, or Argentina in 2001–2. It might, in fact, open the way for an unexpected restoration of the American system, or for military rule, or simply for some new development we cannot yet imagine. Certainly, such a bank-ruptcy would mean a drastic lowering of our standard of living, a loss of control over international affairs, a process of adjusting to the rise of other powers, including China and India, and a further discrediting of the notion that the United States is somehow exceptional compared to other nations. We will have to learn what it means to be a far poorer nation and the attitudes and manners that go with it. As Anatol Lieven, author of *America Right or Wrong: An Anatomy of American Nationalism,* concludes, "U.S. global power, as presently conceived by the overwhelming majority of the U.S. establishment, is unsustainable. . . . The empire can no longer raise enough taxes or soldiers, it is increasingly indebted, and key vassal states are no longer reliable. . . . The result is that the empire can no longer pay for enough of the professional troops it needs to fulfill its self-assumed imperial tasks."[71]

On February 6, 2006, the Bush administration submitted to Congress a $439 billion defense appropriation budget for fiscal 2007. At the same time, the deficit in the United States' current account—the imbalance in the trading of goods and services as well as the shortfall in all other cross-border payments from interest income and rents to dividends and profits on direct investments—underwent its fastest-ever quarterly deteriora-tion.[72] In the fourth quarter of 2005, the deficit hit a staggering $225 bil-lion, up from $185.4 billion in the previous quarter. For all of 2005, the current account deficit was $805 billion, 6.4 percent of national income. In 2005, the U.S. trade deficit, the largest component of the current account deficit, soared to an all-time high of $725.8 billion, the fourth consecutive year that America's trade debts set records. The trade deficit with China alone rose to $201.6 billion, the highest imbalance ever recorded with any country. Meanwhile, since mid-2000, the country has lost nearly three million manufacturing jobs.[73]

To try to cope with these imbalances, on March 16, 2006, Congress raised the national debt limit from $8.2 trillion to $8.96 trillion. This was the fourth time since George W. Bush took office that it had to be raised. The national debt is the total amount owed by the government and should not be confused with the federal budget deficit, the annual amount by which federal spending exceeds revenue. Had Congress not raised the debt limit, the U.S. government would not have been able to borrow more money and would have had to default on its massive debts.

Among the creditors that finance this unprecedented sum, two of the largest are the central banks of China ($853.7 billion in reserves of dollars and other foreign currencies) and Japan ($831.58 billion), both of which are the managers of the huge trade surpluses these countries enjoy with the United States.[74] This helps explain why our debt burden has not yet triggered what standard economic theory would dictate: a steep decline in the value of the U.S. dollar followed by a severe contraction of the American economy because we could no longer afford the foreign goods we like so much. However, both the Chinese and Japanese governments continue to be willing to be paid in dollars in order to sustain American demand for their exports. For the sake of domestic employment, both countries lend huge amounts to the American Treasury, but there is no guarantee how long they will want or be able to do so.

According to Marshall Auerback, an international financial strategist, "Today, the U.S. economy is being kept afloat by enormous levels of foreign lending, which allow American consumers to continue to buy more imports, which only increases the bloated trade deficits."[75] We have become, in Auerback's terms, a "Blanche Dubois economy" (named after the leading character in Tennessee Williams's play *A Streetcar Named Desire*), heavily dependent on "the kindness of strangers." Unfortunately, in our case, as in Blanche's, there are not many strangers left willing to support our illusions.

Even a severe reduction in our numerous deficits (trade, governmental, current account, household, and savings) would still not be enough to save the republic, because of the unacknowledged nature of our economy—specifically our dependence on military spending and war for our wealth and well-being. Ever since we recovered from the Great Depression of the 1930s via massive governmental spending on armaments during World War II, we have become dependent on "military Keynesianism," artificially boosting the growth rate of the economy via government spending on armies and weapons.

"Keynesianism" is named for the English economist John Maynard Keynes, author of *The General Theory of Employment, Interest, and Money,* published in 1936, and other influential books. In his writings and his public career, Keynes developed a scheme to save capitalist economies from cycles of boom and bust as well as the severe decline of consumer spending that occurs in periods of depression. He was less interested in what causes these cycles or in whether capitalism itself promotes under-employment and unemployment, than in what to do when an inequitable distribution of income causes people to be unable to buy what their econ-omy produces. To prevent the economy from contracting, a development likely to be followed by social unrest, Keynes thought that the government should step in and, through deficit spending, put people back to work, even if this meant creating jobs artificially. Some of these jobs might be socially useful, but Keynes also favored make-work tasks if that proved necessary, simply to put money in the pockets of potential consumers. Conversely, during periods of prosperity, he thought government should cut spending and rebuild the treasury. He called his plan countercyclical "pump-priming."

During the New Deal in the 1930s, the United States tried to put Keynesianism into practice. Through various schemes the government attempted to restore morale—if not full employment.[76] These included "social security" to provide incomes for retired people; giving unions the right to strike (the Wagner Act); setting minimum wages and hours and prohibiting child labor; creating jobs for writers, artists, and creative people generally (the Works Projects Administration); financing the building of dams, roads, schools, and hospitals across the country, includ-ing the Triborough Bridge and Lincoln Tunnel in New York City, the Grand Coulee Dam in Washington, and the Key West Highway in Florida (the Public Works Administration); organizing projects for young people in agriculture and forestry (the Civilian Conservation Corps); and setting up the Tennessee Valley Authority to provide flood control and electric power generation in a seven-state area.

The New Deal also saw the rudimentary beginnings of a backlash against Keynesianism. Conservative capitalists feared, as the German political scientist and sociologist Jürgen Habermas has noted, that too much government intervention would delegitimate and demystify capi-talism as an economic system that works by allegedly quasi-natural laws. More seriously, too much spending on social welfare might, they feared, shift the balance of power in society from the capitalist class to the work-ing class and its unions.[77] For these reasons, establishment figures tried to hold back countercyclical spending until World War II unleashed a torrent of public funds for weapons.

In 1943, the Polish economist in exile Micha Kalecki coined the term "military Keynesianism" to explain Nazi Germany's success in overcoming the Great Depression and achieving full employment. Adolf Hitler did not undertake German rearmament for purely economic reasons; he wanted to build a powerful German military. The fact that he advocated governmental support for arms production made him acceptable to many German industrialists, who increasingly supported his regime.[78] For several years before Hitler's aggressive intentions became clear, he was celebrated around the world for having achieved a "German economic miracle."

Speaking theoretically, Kalecki understood that government spending on arms increases manufacturing and also has a multiplier effect on general consumer spending by raising workers' incomes. Both of these points are in accordance with general Keynesian doctrine. In addition, the enlargement of standing armies absorbs many workers, often young males with few skills and less education. The military thus becomes an employer of last resort, like the old Civilian Conservation Corps, but on a much larger scale. Increased spending on military research and the development of weapons systems also generates new infrastructure and advanced technologies. Well-known examples include the jet engine, radar, nuclear power, semiconductors, and the Internet, each of which began as a military project that later formed the basis for major civilian industries.[79] By 1962–63, military outlays accounted for some 52 percent of all expenditures on research and development in the United States. As the international relations theorist Ronald Steel puts it, "Despite whatever theories strategists may spin, the defense budget is now, to a large degree, a jobs program. It is also a cash cow that provides billions of dollars for corporations, lobbyists, and special interest groups."[80]

The negative aspects of military Keynesianism include its encouragement of militarism and the potential to create a military-industrial complex. Because such a complex becomes both directly and indirectly an employer and generator of employment, it comes to constitute a growing proportion of aggregate demand. Sooner or later, it short-circuits Keynes's insistence that government spending be cut back in times of nearly full employment. In other words, it becomes a permanent institution whose "pump" must always be primed. Governments invariably find it politically hard to reduce military spending once committed to it, particularly when munitions makers distribute their benefits as widely as possible and enlist the support of as many politicians as possible, as they have in the United States. In short, military Keynesianism leads to constant wars, or a huge waste of resources on socially worthless products, or both.

By the mid-1940s, everyone in the United States appreciated that the war boom had finally brought the Great Depression to an end, but it was never understood in Keynesian terms. It was a war economy. State expenditures on arms in 1944 reached 38 percent of gross domestic product (the sum total of all goods and services produced in an economy) or GDP, which seemed only appropriate given the nation's commitment to a two-front war. There was, however, a profound fear among political and economic elites as well as the American public that the end of the war—despite all the promises of future peacetime wonders like TVs, cars, and washing machines—would mean a return to economic hard times. Such reasoning lay, in part, behind the extraordinary expansion of arms manufacturing that began in 1947. The United States decided to "contain" the USSR and, in the early 1950s, to move from the production and use of atomic bombs to the building and stockpiling of the much larger and more destructive hydrogen bombs.

Between the 1940s and 1996, the United States spent at least $5.8 trillion on the development, testing, and construction of nuclear weapons alone. By 1967, the peak year of its nuclear stockpile, the United States possessed some 32,500 deliverable bombs, none of which, thankfully, was ever used. But they perfectly illustrate Keynes's proposal that, in order to create jobs, the government might as well decide to bury money in old mines and then pay unemployed workers to dig it up. Nuclear bombs were not just America's secret weapon but also a secret economic weapon. As of 2006, we still have 9,960 of them.

The Cold War contributed greatly to the country's sustained economic growth that began in 1947 and lasted until the 1973 oil crisis. Military spending was around 16 percent of GDP in the United States during the 1950s. In the 1960s, the Vietnam War sustained it at around 9 percent, but in the 1970s, strong economic competition from the free riders, Japan and Germany, forced a significant decline in military spending with a consequent U.S. decline into "stagflation" (a combination of stagnation and inflation).

The American response was a classic example of military Keynesianism—namely, Reaganomics. In the 1980s, President Reagan carried out a policy of large tax cuts combined with massive increases in defense spending allegedly to combat a new threat from communism. It turned out that there was no threat, only a campaign of fear-mongering from the White House bolstered by the CIA, which consistently overstated the size and growth of the Soviet armed forces during this period. The USSR was in fact starting to come apart internally because of serious economic imbalances and the deep contradictions of Stalinism. Reagan's policies drove American military expenditures to 6.2 percent of GDP, which in 1984 produced a growth rate for the economy as a whole of 7 percent and helped re-elect Reagan by a landslide.[81] During the Clinton years, military spending fell to about 2 percent of GDP, but the economy rallied strongly in Clinton's second term due to the boom in information technologies, weakness in the previously competitive Japanese economy, the government's more nationalistic support of the economy internationally, and serious efforts to reduce the national debt.

With the coming to power of George W. Bush and the launching of his Global War on Terror, military Keynesianism returned with a vengeance. According to Andrew Gumbel, a regular contributor to the *Independent* newspaper of London, during the second quarter of 2003, when the Iraq war was in full swing, some 60 percent of the 3.3 percent GDP growth rate was attributable to military spending.[82] In the U.S. budgets for the years between 2003 and 2007, defense occupied just over 50 percent of all discretionary spending by the government. This is money the president and Congress can actually appropriate, as distinct from mandatory spending in compliance with existing laws (for social security payments, medicare, interest on the national debt, and so on).

The official 2007 Pentagon budget is $439.3 billion—not including the costs of America's current wars. It essentially covers salaries and weapons—the funds for missile defense and other operations in outer space (between $7.4 billion and $9 billion a year since fiscal year 2002), new ships and submarines for the navy, and aircraft that were designed to fight the former Soviet Union's air force but that have been kept as active projects because of industry and air force lobbying. As Jonathan Karp of the *Wall Street Journal* observes, "Weapons spending has swelled faster than the overall Pentagon budget, soaring 43 percent in the past five years to $147 billion, with the majority of the funding going to programs conceived before 9/11. The estimated lifetime cost of the Pentagon's five biggest weapons systems is $550 billion, 89 percent more than the top-five programs were projected to cost in 2001."[83]

One of the absurdities of the Bush administration's defense appropriations is that the official defense budget has nothing to do with actual combat in Afghanistan and Iraq. We have built a fantastically high-tech military, but in order to use it, Congress has to appropriate separate annual "supplements" of around $120 billion a year. In the fiscal 2007 budget, the Congressional Research Service estimates that Pentagon spending will be about $9.8 billion per month for Operation Enduring Freedom and Operation Iraqi Freedom, or an extra $117.6 billion for the year.[84] As of 2006, the overall cost of the wars in Iraq and Afghanistan since their inception stood at about $450 billion.

To understand the real weight of military Keynesianism in the American economy, one must approach official defense statistics with great care. They are compiled and published in such a way as to minimize the actual size of the official "defense budget." The Pentagon does this to try to conceal from the public the real costs of the military establishment and its overall weight within the economy. There are numerous military activities not carried out by the Department of Defense and that are therefore not part of the Pentagon's annual budgets. These include the Department of Energy's spending on nuclear weapons ($16.4 billion in fiscal 2005), the Department of Homeland Security's outlays for the actual "defense" of the United States against terrorism ($41 billion), the Department of Veterans Affairs' responsibilities for the lifetime care of the seriously wounded ($68 billion), the Treasury Department's payments of pensions to military retirees and widows and their families (an amount not fully disclosed by official statistics), and the Department of State's financing of foreign arms sales and militarily related developmental assistance ($23 billion).

In addition to these amounts, there is something called the "Military Construction Appropriations Bill," which is tiny compared to the other expenditures—$12.2 billion for fiscal 2005—but which covers all the military bases around the world. Adding these non–Department of Defense expenditures, the supplemental appropriations for the wars in Iraq and Afghanistan, and the military construction budget to the Defense Appropriations Bill actually doubles what the administration calls the annual defense budget. It is an amount larger than all other defense budgets on Earth combined.[85] Still to be added to this are interest payments by the Treasury to cover past debt-financed defense outlays going back to 1916. Robert Higgs, author of *Crisis and Leviathan* and many other books on American militarism, estimates that in 2002 such interest payments amounted to $138.7 billion.[86]

Even when all these things are included, Enron-style accounting makes it hard to obtain an accurate understanding of our reliance on a permanent arms economy. In 2005, the Government Accountability Office reported to Congress that "the Pentagon has no accurate knowledge of the cost of military operations in Iraq, Afghanistan, or the fight against terrorism."[87] It said that, lacking a reliable method for tracking military costs, the army merely inserts into its accounts figures that match the available budget. "Effectively, the Army [is] reporting back to Congress what it had appropriated."

Joseph Stiglitz, the Nobel Prize–winning economist, and his colleague at Harvard Linda Bilmes have tried to put together an estimate of the real costs of the Iraq war. They calculate that it will cost about $2 trillion.[88] This figure is several orders of magnitude larger than what the Bush administration publicly acknowledges. Above all, Stiglitz and Bilmes have tried to compile honest figures for veterans' benefits. For 2006, the officially budgeted amount is $68 billion, which is absurdly low given the large number of our soldiers who have been severely wounded. We celebrate the medical miracles that allow some of our troops to survive the detonation of an "improvised explosive device" hidden in the Earth under a Humvee, but when larger numbers of soldiers who once might have died in such situations are saved, the resulting wounds, often including brain damage, require that they receive round-the-clock care for the rest of their lives.

We almost surely will end up repudiating some of the promises we have made to the men and women who have volunteered to serve in our armed forces. For instance, the government's medical insurance scheme for veterans and their families, called Tricare, is budgeted for 2007 at a mere $39 billion. But the future demands on Tricare are going to go off the chart. And we cannot afford them unless we radically reorient our economy. The American commitment to military Keynesianism and the nontransparent manner in which it is implemented have combined into a set of fatal contradictions for our country.

In *Blowback,* I set out to explain why we are hated around the world. The concept "blowback" does not just mean retaliation for things our government has done to and in foreign countries. It refers to retaliation for the numerous illegal operations we have carried out abroad that were kept totally secret from the American public. This means that when the retaliation comes—as it did so spectacularly on September 11, 2001—the American public is unable to put the events in context. So they tend to support acts intended to lash out against the perpetrators, thereby most commonly preparing the ground for yet another cycle of blowback. In the first book in this trilogy, I tried to provide some of the historical background for understanding the dilemmas we as a nation confront today, although I focused more on Asia—the area of my academic training—than on the Middle East.

The Sorrows of Empire was written during the American preparations for and launching of the invasions and occupations of Afghanistan and Iraq. I began to study our continuous military buildup since World War II and the 737 military bases we currently maintain in other people's countries. This empire of bases is the concrete manifestation of our global hegemony, and many of the blowback-inducing wars we have conducted had as their true purpose the sustaining and expanding of this network. We do not think of these overseas deployments as a form of empire; in fact, most Americans do not give them any thought at all until something truly shocking, such as the treatment of prisoners at Guantánamo Bay, brings them to our attention. But the people living next door to these bases and dealing with the swaggering soldiers who brawl and sometimes rape their women certainly think of them as imperial enclaves, just as the peoples of ancient Iberia or nineteenth-century India knew that they were victims of foreign colonization.

In *Nemesis,* I have tried to present historical, political, economic, and philosophical evidence of where our current behavior is likely to lead. Specifically, I believe that to maintain our empire abroad requires resources and commitments that will inevitably undercut our domestic democracy and in the end produce a military dictatorship or its civilian equivalent. The founders of our nation understood this well and tried to create a form of government—a republic—that would prevent this from occurring. But the combination of huge standing armies, almost continuous wars, military Keynesianism, and ruinous military expenses have destroyed our republican structure in favor of an imperial presidency. We are on the cusp of losing our democracy for the sake of keeping our empire. Once a nation is started down that path, the dynamics that apply to all empires come into play—isolation, overstretch, the uniting of forces opposed to imperialism, and bankruptcy. Nemesis stalks our life as a free nation.

History is instructive on this dilemma. If we choose to keep our empire, as the Roman Republic did, we will certainly lose our democracy and grimly await the eventual blowback that imperialism generates. There is an alternative, however. We could, like the British Empire after World War II, keep our democracy by giving up our empire. No more than the French and Dutch, the British did not do a particularly brilliant job of liquidating their empire, and there were several clear cases where British imperialists defied their nation's commitment to democracy in order to keep their foreign privileges. Kenya in the 1950s is a particularly savage example. But the overall thrust of postwar British history is clear: the people of the British Isles chose democracy over imperialism. For this reason, I can only regard Britain's willingness to join the United States in its invasion of Iraq as an atavistic response.

Britain's closing down its empire is one of its more admirable legacies. I do not share the nostalgia of contemporary Anglo-American writers who urge the United States to take up the "white man's burden" and follow in the footsteps of British imperialists. Instead, I have chosen as my role model a Japanese scholar and journalist, Hotsumi Ozaki, about whom I long ago wrote a biography. Ozaki was born in what was then the Japanese colony of Taiwan, and his early childhood was that of a little colonialist, being taken to school by rickshaw. As an adult, he was a prominent journalist and scholar in China, and he accurately foresaw that Japan's occupation of China would fail disastrously and lead to the blowback of the Chinese Communist revolution.

Ozaki tried to warn his own government about its misguided ventures. For his troubles he was hanged as a traitor by the Japanese government in the waning days of World War II. I hope not to meet a similar fate, but I am as certain as Ozaki was that my country is launched on a dangerous path that it must abandon or else face the consequences.

Notes

PROLOGUE: THE BLOWBACK TRILOGY

1. The CIA report is entitled *Clandestine Service History: Overthrow of Premier Mossadeq of Iran, November 1952–August 1953* (March 1954). The author is Donald N. Wilber. For the original typescript and a history of its declassification and publication, including the CIA's claim that the document had been destroyed and that no copy remained in existence, see, in particular, Malcolm Byrne, ed., "The Secret History of the Iran Coup, 1953," National Security Archive, Electronic Briefing Book no. 28, http://www.gwu.edu/~nsarchiv/NSAEBB/NSAEBB28/.

2. Elisabeth Bumiller, "Addressing Cadets, Bush Sees Parallel to World War II," *New York Times,* June 3, 2004.

3. "Bin Laden's Warning: Full Text," *BBC News,* October 7, 2001, http://news.bbc.co.uk/1/low/world/south_asia/1585636.stm. For a somewhat different translation, see "Bin Laden's Statement: 'The Sword Fell,'" *New York Times,* October 8, 2001.

4. Thomas Friedman, "No Mere Terrorist," *New York Times,* March 24, 2002. See also Ervand Abrahamian, "The U.S. Media, Huntington, and September 11," *Third World Quarterly* 24, no. 3 (2003), pp. 529–44; and a shorter version of the same essay in *Middle East Report,* Summer 2002, pp. 62–63.

5. John F. Harris, "God Gave U.S. 'What We Deserve,' Falwell Says," *Washington Post,* September 14, 2001; Oliver Burkeman, "Powell Attacks Christian Right," *Guardian,* November 15, 2002; John Sutherland, "God Save America," *Guardian,* May 3, 2004.

6. William M. Arkin, "The Pentagon Unleashes a Holy Warrior," *Los Angeles Times,* October 16, 2003; "Rumsfeld Defends General Who Commented on War, Satan," Associated Press, October 17, 2003; Douglas Jehl, "U.S. General Apologizes for Remarks About Islam," *New York Times,* October 18, 2003; Editorial, "For Religious Bigotry," *New York Times,* August 26, 2004.

7. Simon Jenkins, "Democrats Should Not Fight Fire with Fire," *Times* (London), September 12, 2001.

8. Mai Yamani, research fellow at the Royal Institute of International Affairs, "The Rise of Shi'ite 'Petrolistan,'" *Straits Times* (Singapore), March 5, 2004; Juan Cole, "The United States in Iraq and Shiite Islamic Politics" (speech, San Diego State University, April 19, 2005); Robin Wright, "Iraq Winners Allied with Iran Are the Opposite of U.S. Vision," *Washington Post,* February 14, 2005.

9. Army colonel Hy Rothstein, quoted by Seymour M. Hersh, "The Other War," *New Yorker,* April 12, 2004, p. 42.

10. Humberto Márquez, "Iraq Invasion the 'Biggest Cultural Disaster Since 1258,'" Antiwar.com, February 16, 2005; Ian Frazier, "Invaders: Destroying Baghdad," *New Yorker,* April 25, 2005.

11. Ronald Bruce St. John, "Iraq Blowback Is Global and Growing," Antiwar.com, December 11, 2004.

12. On the staggering costs of caring for our maimed and psychologically damaged veterans, see Ronald J. Glasser, "A War of Disabilities: Iraq's Hidden Costs Are Coming Home," *Harper's Magazine,* July 2005, pp. 59–62.

13. "Baghdad Burning," River Bend blog, May 7, 2004, http://www.riverbend blog.blogspot.com/.

14. Joanna Chung and Alex Halperin, "Arab Attitudes to U.S. Hardening," *Financial Times,* July 24–25, 2004.

15. "Millions Marched Against Bush's War," February 14–16, 2003, http://www .failureisimpossible.com/dosomething/0215.htm.

16. Shreffler's complete poem reads:

Neighborhood Girl

She's new to the neighborhood, her family just moved in
From Greece or somewhere, she's a great, tall, gawky girl
With braces and earrings and uneven skin:
Hormones and acne, her change is coming in,

And today, she's playing hooky. January fog.
Orange lights on the school zone sign beat out their tattoo
And caution the Homeland's socked-in morning rush
With their strobe-light samba: Condition Amber,

As she sits invisible, swinging her legs to the beat,
Perched up high on aluminum over
The uncanny Day-Glo of the key-lime fluorescence
That says: School at the top of this composition.

I see her and she lets me. I'm an old family friend:
Sometimes I play poker with her Aunt Erato.
Her name is Nemesis and she's just moved in,
She's new to the neighborhood, she's checking it out.

17. Micha F. Lindemans, "Nemesis," *Encyclopedia Mythica Online,* http://www .pantheon.org/articles/n/nemesis.html.

18. Richard Wagner, *Die Walküre,* act 2, scene 4.

1: MILITARISM AND THE BREAKDOWN OF CONSTITUTIONAL GOVERNMENT

1. Newsmax, "Tommy Franks: Martial Law Will Replace Constitution After Next Terror Attack," November 21, 2003, http://www.propagandamatrix .com/211103martiallaw.html.

2. Kevin Baker, "We're in the Army Now," *Harper's Magazine,* October 2003, p. 46.

3. Robert C. Byrd, "Congress Must Resist the Rush to War," *New York Times,* October 10, 2002.

4. Editorial, "Last Days of the Republic," *Berkshire Eagle* (Pittsfield, MA), October 12, 2002, http://www.mindfully.org/Reform/2002/Republic-Last-Days12oct02.htm.

5. Bill Winter, "The Monarchization of America Under Bush," Libertarian Party, October 29, 2004, http://nucnews.net/nucnews/2004nn/0410nn/041029nn.htm#680.

6. Adam Young, "War Gave Us Caesar," Ludwig von Mises Institute, October 12, 2004, http://www.mises.org/fullstory.aspx?Id=1642.

7. Robin Cook, "Bush Will Now Celebrate by Putting Fallujah to the Torch," *Guardian,* November 5, 2004.

8. Thomas E. Ricks, "Ex-Envoy Criticizes Bush's Postwar Policy," *Washington Post,* September 5, 2003.

9. Sonni Efron, "Diplomats on the Defensive," *Los Angeles Times,* May 8, 2003.

10. "President Addresses the Nation in Prime Time Press Conference" (White House, April 13, 2004), p. 8, http://www.whitehouse.gov/news/releases/2004/04/20040413-20.html.

11. Quoted by John Dillin, "To the Founders, Congress was King," *Christian Science Monitor,* January 20, 2005. See also Thomas E. Woods Jr., "Presidential War Powers," LewRockwell.com, July 7, 2005, http://www.lewrockwell.com/woods/woods45.html.

12. Lieutenant Colonel Charles J. Dunlap Jr., "The Origins of the American Military Coup of 2012," *Parameters* (U.S. Army War College Quarterly), Winter 1992–93, pp. 2–20; http://carlisle-www.army.mil/usawc/Parameters/1992/dunlap.htm, p. 6.

13. "Base Closure List Becomes Battleground," MSNBC.com, May 13, 2005, http://www.msnbc.msn.com/id/7834939/print/1/displaymode/1098/; Charles V. Peña, "Base Closing Blues," *Reason,* May 20, 2005, http://www.reason.com/hod/cp052005.shtml; Sheldon Richman, "Turning Off Government's Money Spigot," *Newsday,* May 31, 2005.

14. Hannah Arendt, *Responsibility and Judgment,* ed. Jerome Kohn (New York: Schocken Books, 2003), pp. 272–73.

15. James Madison, "Political Observations," April 20, 1795, http://www.reclaimdemocracy.org/quotes/madison_perpetual_war.html. Madison's statement on war continues: "[It should be well understood] that the powers proposed to be surrendered [by the Third Congress] to the Executive were those which the Constitution has most jealously appropriated to the Legislature. . . . The Constitution expressly and exclusively vests in the Legislature the power of declaring a state of war . . . the power of raising armies . . . the power of creating offices. . . . A delegation of such powers [to the President] would have struck, not only at the fabric of our Constitution, but at the foundation of all well organized and well checked governments. The separation of the power of declaring war from that of conducting it, is wisely contrived to exclude the danger of its being declared for the sake of its being conducted. The separation of the power of raising armies from the power of commanding them, is

intended to prevent the raising of armies for the sake of commanding them. The separation of the power of creating offices from that of filling them, is an essential guard against the temptation to create offices for the sake of gratifying favorites or multiplying dependents."

16. Gore Vidal, *Perpetual War for Perpetual Peace: How We Got to Be So Hated* (New York: Nation Books, 2002), pp. 22–40.

17. Michael J. Sullivan III, *American Adventurism Abroad: Thirty Invasions, Interventions, and Regime Changes Since World War II* (Newport, CT: Praeger, 2004). The two most complete and accurate compilations of modern American military operations abroad are William Blum, *Killing Hope: U.S. Military and CIA Interventions Since World War II* (Monroe, ME: Common Courage Press, 1995); and Clara Nieto, *Masters of War: Latin America and U.S. Aggression* (New York: Seven Stories Press, 2003). Also see Bernard Chazelle, "Anti-Americanism: A Clinical Study," September 2004, http://www.cs.princeton.edu/~chazelle/politics/antiam-print.html.

18. Minxin Pei and Sara Kasper, "Lessons From the Past: The American Record on Nation Building," Carnegie Endowment for International Peace, Policy Brief no. 24, May 2003; Roger Morris (a former member of the National Security Council staff), "Freedom, American Style," *Los Angeles Times,* April 23, 2003; Abid Aslam, "U.S. Selling More Weapons to Undemocratic Regimes That Support 'War on Terror,'" Common Dreams News Center, May 25, 2005.

19. See Richard Norton-Taylor, "Both the Military and the Spooks are Opposed to War in Iraq," *Guardian,* February 24, 2003, http://politics.guardian.co.uk/print/0,3858,4611927-103677,00.html. For a remarkably accurate, if fictional, treatment of how the CIA goes about overthrowing a regime that is no longer useful to the United States and installing a puppet government, see Henry Bromell, *Little America* (New York: Vintage, 2002).

20. Walter Karp (1934–1989), a theorist of republicanism and for a decade a contributing editor of *Harper's Magazine,* argues, "There is not a single modern American war which was forced upon the United States by compelling interest of any kind, yet every one of America's wars since 1898 the party oligarchs gave unmistakable signs of welcoming: by fabricating incidents, by carrying out secret provocations, by concocting far-fetched theories— 'dominoes' in one war, 'neutral rights' in another, 'collective security' in a third—to demonstrate an American interest not otherwise apparent and to hold up to the American people a foreign menace not otherwise menacing." See *Indispensable Enemies: The Politics of Misrule in America* (New York: Franklin Square Press, 1993), p. 264.

21. On secrecy in American overt and covert military activities abroad, see William M. Arkin, *Code Names: Deciphering U.S. Military Plans, Programs, and Operations in the 9/11 World* (Hanover, NH: Steerforth Press, 2005).

22. Andrew J. Bacevich, *The New American Militarism: How Americans Are Seduced by War* (New York: Oxford University Press, 2005), p. 2.

23. See, inter alia, John W. Dean, *Worse than Watergate: The Secret Presidency of George W. Bush* (New York: Warner Books, 2005); James Bovard, *The Bush Betrayal* (New York: Palgrave-Macmillan, 2004); Anthony Lewis, "One Liberty at a Time," *Mother Jones,* May–June 2004; Michael Lind, "How a Superpower Lost Its Stature," *Financial Times,* June 1, 2004; and Jim VandeHei, "GOP Tilting Balance of Power to the Right," *Washington Post,* May 26, 2005.

24. Hannah Arendt, *Eichmann in Jerusalem: A Report on the Banality of Evil* (New York: Viking, 1963). I have used the revised and enlarged edition, New York: Penguin, 1994.
25. Arendt, *Responsibility and Judgment,* p. 159.
26. Ibid., p. 160.
27. Ibid., p. xxix.
28. Ibid., p. 187.
29. Ibid., p. 160.
30. Mark Danner, "Abu Ghraib: The Hidden Story," *New York Review of Books,* October 7, 2004, p. 49. The most important book on the history of a distinctively American form of torture, developed by the CIA and employed throughout Afghanistan and Iraq, is Alfred W. McCoy, *A Question of Torture: CIA Interrogation, from the Cold War to the War on Terror* (New York: Metropolitan, 2006).
31. Seymour M. Hersh, "The Gray Zone: How a Secret Pentagon Program Came to Abu Ghraib," *New Yorker,* May 24, 2004, http://www.newyorker.com/fact/content/?040524fa_fact; John Shattuck, former assistant secretary of state for democracy, human rights, and labor, "On Abu Ghraib: One Sergeant's Courage a Model for U.S. Leaders," *Christian Science Monitor,* May 16, 2005.
32. Lawrence Smallman, "Rumsfeld Cracks Jokes, but Iraqis Aren't Laughing," Al Jazeera (English), April 12, 2003.
33. Michael Isikoff, "2002 Memo Reveals Push for Broader Presidential Powers," *Newsweek,* December 18, 2004.
34. "Gen. Richard Myers on 'Fox News Sunday,'" transcript, *Fox News,* May 2, 2004. Also see Gary Younge and Julian Borger, "CBS Delayed Report on Iraqi Prison Abuse After Military Chief's Plea," *Guardian,* May 4, 2004.
35. Statement of Secretary of State Condoleezza Rice, December 5, 2005, in "Rice Says United States Does Not Torture Terrorists," FindLaw, December 5, 2005, http://news.findlaw.com/scripts/printer_friendly.pl?page=/wash/s/20051205/20051205124753.html.
36. "Powell Discusses Future Roles of U.N.," Coalition on German TV, April 3, 2003," State Department transcript, http://www.usembassy.it/file2003_04/alia/A3040414.htm.
37. See George Hicks, *The Comfort Women: Japan's Brutal Regime of Enforced Prostitution in the Second World War* (New York: W. W. Norton, 1994); Yoshiaki Yoshimi, *Comfort Women: Sexual Slavery in the Japanese Military During World War II* (New York: Columbia University Press, 2000); Yuki Tanaka, *Japan's Comfort Women: Sexual Slavery and Prostitution during World War II and the U.S. Occupation* (New York: Routledge, 2002).
38. U.S. Air Force Pamphlet 14-210, February 1998. On the history of concepts like "collateral damage" and their uses as propaganda, see David Barsamian, interview with Noam Chomsky, "Collateral Language," *Z Magazine Online* 16, no. 7/8 (July–August 2003), http://zmagsite.zmag.org/Aug2003/barsamianpr0803.html.
39. "Geneva Conventions," *Encarta Online Encyclopedia,* 2005, http://encarta.msn.com/text_762529232__1/Geneva_Conventions.html. See also Anthony Gregory, "'Collateral Damage' as Euphemism for Mass Murder," LewRockwell.com, April 30, 2005, http://www.lewrockwell.com/gregory/gregory72.html.

40. Quoted by Sheldon Richman, "Iraqi Sanctions: Were They Worth It?" Future of Freedom Foundation, February 9, 2004. For a defense of the attitudes and policies of the Clinton administration, see Nancy Soderberg, *The Superpower Myth,* foreword by Bill Clinton (New York: John Wiley, 2005), pp. 204–7.

41. David Cortright, "A Hard Look at Iraq Sanctions," *Nation,* December 3, 2001.

42. Ramzi Kysia, "Biological Warfare in Iraq," Common Dreams News Center, August 21, 2002; Thomas J. Nagy, "The Secret Behind the Sanctions: How the U.S. Intentionally Destroyed Iraq's Water Supply," *Progressive,* August 2001, http://www.progressive.org/0801issue/nagy0901.html; James Bovard, "Iraq Sanctions and American Intentions: Blameless Carnage?" Future of Freedom Foundation, February 9, 2004. In his book *Terrorism and Tyranny* (New York: Palgrave-Macmillan, 2003), Bovard documents how the civilian infrastructure was deliberately targeted. Also see Anthony Arnove, ed., *Iraq Under Siege: The Deadly Impact of Sanctions and War,* 2nd ed. (Cambridge, MA: South End Press, 2003).

43. Barton Gellman, "Allied Air War Struck Broadly in Iraq; Officials Acknowledge Strategy Went Beyond Purely Military Targets," *Washington Post,* June 23, 1991.

44. Colonel John A. Warden III, "The Enemy as a System," *Airpower Journal* 9, no. 1 (Spring 1995), pp. 40–55, http://www.airpower.maxwell.af.mil/airchronicles/apj/warden.html.

45. Gellman, "Allied Air War."

46. International Committee of the Red Cross, International Humanitarian Law, full texts, http://www.icrc.org/ihl.nsf/WebCONVFULL!OpenView.

47. Jacob G. Hornberger, "Sanctions: The Cruel and Brutal War Against the Iraqi People," Future of Freedom Foundation, February 9, 2004.

48. Joy Gordon, "Cool War: Economic Sanctions as a Weapon of Mass Destruction," *Harper's Magazine,* November 2002, http://www.scn.org/ccpi/Harpers JoyGordonNov02.html.

49. Richman, "Iraqi Sanctions."

50. Gordon, "Cool War."

51. Hornberger, "Sanctions."

52. Cortright, "Hard Look"; Richard Garfield, "Morbidity and Mortality Among Iraqi Children from 1990 through 1998: Assessing the Impact of the Gulf War and Economic Sanctions," Columbia University Medical School, July 1999, http://www.nd.edu/~krocinst/ocpapers/op_16_3.pdf.

53. Richman, "Iraqi Sanctions." See also David Rieff, "Were Sanctions Right?" in *At the Point of a Gun: Democratic Dreams and Armed Intervention* (New York: Simon and Schuster, 2005), pp. 185–204.

54. William Rivers Pitt, "Stand and Be Heard," May 27, 2005, http://www.pdamerica.org/articles/news/stand-be-heard.php.

55. See Ellen Knickmeyer, "Iraq Puts Civilian Toll at 12,000," *Washington Post,* June 3, 2005, http://www.washingtonpost.com/wp-dyn/content/article/2005/06/02/AR2005060201098_pf.html; Associated Press, "Death from Insurgents," *San Diego Union-Tribune,* June 3, 2005; Michael Schwartz, "Why Immediate Withdrawal Makes Sense," TomDispatch.com, September 22, 2005, http://www.tomdispatch.com/indexprint.mhtml?pid =23549.

56. "Iraqi Civilian Casualties," United Press International, July 12, 2005, http://www.wpherald.com/print.php?StoryID=20050712-122153-5519r; Judith Coburn, "Unnamed and Unnoticed: Iraqi Casualties," TomDispatch.com, July 17, 2005, http://www.tomdispatch.com/index.mhtml?pid=6963; Neil Mackay, "Haditha: The Worst U.S. Atrocity Since Vietnam: Iraqi Women and Children Massacred by American Marines," *Sunday Herald,* June 4, 2006, http://www.sundayherald.com/print56107; Peter Beaumont and Mohammed al-Ubeidy, "U.S. Confronts Brutal Culture Among Its Finest Sons," *Guardian,* June 4, 2006.

57. William Langewiesche, "Letter from Baghdad," *Atlantic Monthly,* January–February 2005, p. 94.

58. Dahr Jamail, "Living Under the Bombs," TomDispatch.com, February 2, 2005, http://www.tomdispatch.com/index.mhtml?pid=2166.

59. "Burying the Bodies," *Harper's Magazine,* January 2002, p. 14.

60. Samir Haddad, "U.S. 'Fireballs' Threaten Iraqi Flora," Islam on Line, June 4, 2005, http://www.islamonline.org/English/News/2005-06/04/article05.shtml.

61. Derrick Z. Jackson, "The 'Tsunami' Victims that We Don't Count," *Boston Globe,* January 7, 2005; Patrick Cockburn, "Terrified U.S. Soldiers Are Still Killing Civilians with Impunity, while the Dead Go Uncounted," *Independent,* April 24, 2005; Christopher Dickey, "Body Counts: The Pentagon Secretly Keeps Track of Many Grim Statistics in Iraq," *Newsweek,* May 11, 2005, http://www.msnbc.msn.com/id/7818807/site/newsweek/print/1/displaymode/1098/; and Tom Engelhardt, "How Not to Count in Iraq: The Return of the Body Count," TomDispatch.com, May 23, 2005, http://www.tomdispatch.com/indexprint.mhtml?pid=2709. Anatol Lieven of the Carnegie Endowment for International Peace observes, "Since the war in Iraq began, U.S. forces have displayed their respect for the Iraqi civilians they came to liberate by failing even to keep count of the numbers they accidentally kill." See "A Second Chance to Learn the Lesson of Vietnam," *Financial Times,* June 8, 2004.

62. Alan Eisner, "U.S. Seen as Unaccountable in Iraqi Civilian Deaths," Reuters, May 3, 2005.

63. Cockburn, "Terrified U.S. Soldiers."

64. Robert Fisk, "Brace Yourself for Part Two of the War for Civilization," *Independent,* December 22, 2001.

65. Roland Watson, "U.S. Gunship Opened Fire on Afghan Wedding," *Times* (London), July 3, 2002, http://www.timesonline.co.uk/printFriendly/0,,1-3-345233,00.html; Alissa J. Rubin, "U.S. Raid on Afghan Village Prompts Afghans to Demand Changes in War Strategies," *Los Angeles Times,* July 15, 2002.

66. Anne Gearan, Associated Press, "Bush Rebuffs Karzai on Control of U.S. Troops in Afghanistan," *San Diego Union-Tribune,* May 23, 2005.

67. Les Roberts, Riyadh Lafta, Richard Garfield, James Khudhairi, and Gilbert Burnham, "Mortality Before and After the 2003 Invasion of Iraq," *Lancet* 364, no. 9448 (October 29, 2004), pp. 1857–64, summary, http://www.countthecasualties.org.uk/docs/robertsetal.pdf. See also Emma Ross, "Household Survey Sees 100,000 Iraqi Deaths," *Newsday,* October 29, 2004; "1,000 Iraqis Dying Each Month: Expert," *Daily Telegraph,* April 22, 2005.

68. Iraq Body Count Database, http://www.iraqbodycount.net/database/;
    Eisner, "U.S. Seen as Unaccountable."
69. Roberts, Lafta, Garfield, Khudhairi, and Burnham, "Mortality."
70. James Carroll, "Was the War Necessary?" *Boston Globe,* July 22, 2003;
    Douglas Jehl and Eric Schmitt, "Errors Are Seen in Early Attacks on Iraqi
    Leaders," *New York Times,* June 23, 2004; Jeremy Scahill, "The Other Bomb
    Drops," *Nation,* June 1, 2005.
71. Jeffrey D. Sachs, "Iraq's Civilian Dead Get No Hearing in the United States,"
    Daily Star (Lebanon), December 2, 2004, http://www.dailystar.com.lb/
    article.asp?edition_ID=10&article_ID=10594&categ_id=5. The best
    treatment of the social meaning of bombing and of how little "civilization"
    has affected the international law covering it is Sven Lindqvist, *A History
    of Bombing,* trans. Linda Haverty Rugg (New York: New Press, 2001). His
    main conclusion: "The laws of war protect enemies of the same race,
    class, and culture. The laws of war leave the foreign and the alien without
    protection."
72. Editorial, "A Failure of Leadership at the Highest Levels," *Army Times,* May
    17, 2004, http://www.armytimes.com/print.php?f=1-292925-2903288.php.
    See also Charles Aldinger, "Rumsfeld Criticized by Influential Military
    Paper," Reuters, May 10, 2004.
73. Edward Alden, Peter Spiegel, and Demetri Sevastopulo, "Chain of Command:
    Can Torture in Iraq Be Linked to the White House?" *Financial Times,* June
    17, 2004.
74. Quoted by Arendt, *Eichmann in Jerusalem,* p. 247.
75. Richard A. Clarke, *Against All Enemies: Inside America's War on Terror*
    (New York: Free Press, 2004), p. 24.
76. Timothy Garton Ash, "The Forward March of Liberty Has Been Halted—
    Even Reversed," *Guardian,* November 17, 2005, http://www.guardian.co.uk/
    print/0,3858,5334954-103677,00.html.
77. Richard A. Serrano, "Lindh Case Possible Sign of Abuse; Captors Instructed
    to 'Take Gloves Off' while Questioning," *Los Angeles Times,* June 9, 2004.
    Also see "A TomDispatch Interview with Mark Danner," TomDispatch.com,
    February 26, 2006, http://www.tomdispatch.com/index.mhtml?pid=63903;
    William Pfaff, "Torture: Shock, Awe, and the Human Body," *International
    Herald Tribune,* December 21, 2004, http://www.commondreams.org/
    views04/1221-30.htm.
78. Dave Lindorff, "A First Glance at Bush's Torture Show: John Walker Lindh
    Revisited," *Counterpunch,* June 5/6, 2004.
79. McCoy, *A Question of Torture*; and McCoy, "The Bush Legacy of Legalized
    Torture," TomDispatch.com, February 8, 2006, http://www.tomdispatch
    .com/index.mhtml?pid=57336.
80. Bob Woodward, *Bush at War* (New York: Simon & Schuster, 2002), pp. 76–77;
    Kenneth Roth, "The Law of War in the War on Terror," *Foreign Affairs* 83, no.
    1 (January/February 2004), pp. 2–7; "CIA Renditions of Terror Suspects Are
    'Out of Control': Report," Agence France-Presse, February 6, 2005; Douglas
    Jehl and David Johnston, "Rule Change Lets CIA Freely Send Suspects
    Abroad," *New York Times,* March 6, 2005; Jeffrey St. Clair, "The Road to
    Rendition: Torture Air, Incorporated," *Counterpunch,* April 9/10, 2005.

81. "U.S. Army Failed to Conduct Full Probe into Iraqi Torture Claims: Rights Group," Agence France-Presse, January 24, 2005; Matt Kelley, Associated Press, "U.S. Holds About 10,500 Prisoners in Iraq," *San Francisco Chronicle,* March 30, 2005; "U.S. and Iraq Lock Up Record Number of Suspects," Agence France-Presse, April 10, 2005; Sidney Blumenthal, "See No Evil," *Salon,* June 1, 2005, http://fairuse.1accesshost.com/news2/blumenthal-see-no-evil.html.

82. Matthew Rothschild, "Stripping Rumsfeld and Bush of Impunity," *Progressive,* July 2005, http://www.truthout.org/docs_2005/052805X.shtml. It should be noted that although the United States ratified the International Convention Against Torture in 1994, it tried during July 2002 to block the U.N.'s measures to create enforcement mechanisms but failed in the attempt. See Patrick Martin, "U.S. Seeks to Block Enforcement of Anti-Torture Treaty," World Socialist Web site, August 5, 2002, http://www.wsws.org/articles/2002/aug2002/tort-a05_prn.shtml. For key excerpts from the Convention Against Torture, see Philippe Sands, *Lawless World: America and the Making and Breaking of Global Rules from FDR's Atlantic Charter to George W. Bush's Illegal War* (New York: Viking, 2005), pp. 257–60.

83. The basic sources are Karen J. Greenberg and Joshua L. Dratel, eds., *The Torture Papers: The Road to Abu Ghraib* (New York: Cambridge University Press, 2005); Mark Danner, *Torture and Truth: America, Abu Ghraib, and the War on Terror* (New York: New York Review of Books, 2004); and Jeremy Brecher, Jill Cutler, and Brendan Smith, eds., *In the Name of Democracy: American War Crimes in Iraq and Beyond* (New York: Metropolitan Books, 2005). See also Katharine Q. Seelye, "A P.O.W. Tangle: What the Law Says," *New York Times,* January 29, 2002; Lisa Hajjar, "In the Penal Colony," *Nation,* February 7, 2005, pp. 23–30; Rachel Meeropol, ed., *America's Disappeared: Secret Imprisonment, Detainees, and the "War on Terror"* (New York: Seven Stories Press, 2005); and Rothschild, "Stripping Rumsfeld and Bush of Impunity."

84. Seymour M. Hersh, *Chain of Command: The Road from 9/11 to Abu Ghraib* (New York: HarperCollins, 2004), p. 51.

85. David Rose, "The Truth about Camp Delta," *Observer,* October 3, 2004, http://www.guardian.co.uk/print/0,3858,5030363-111575,00.html; David Rose, *Guantánamo: The War on Human Rights* (New York: New Press, 2004); Jane Mayer, "Outsourcing Torture," *New Yorker,* February 14, 2005; Bob Herbert, "Is No One Accountable?" *New York Times,* March 28, 2005. A *New York Times* editorial stated, "Report after report shows that a vast majority of those swept up in American anti-terrorism campaigns were innocent"; see "Self-Inflicted Wounds," *New York Times,* February 15, 2005. Also see Steve Crawshaw, "Torture Doesn't Work," *Prospect Magazine,* no. 122, May 2006, http://www.prospect-magazine.co.uk/printarticle.php?id=7440.

86. Editorial, "A Very Bad Deal," *New York Times,* October 8, 2004.

87. The basic source is Harlan K. Ullman and James P. Wade, *Shock and Awe: Achieving Rapid Dominance* (Washington, DC: National Defense University Press, 1996), http://www.ndu.edu/inss/books/books%20-%201996/Shock%20and%20Awe%20-%20Dec%2096/index.html (note that the military strategists who wrote this book misspell "blitzkrieg" throughout). See also

Susan Sontag, "Regarding the Torture of Others," *New York Times*, May 23, 2004.

88. Woodward, *Bush at War*, p. 96.

89. Naomi Klein, "Torture's Part of the Territory," *Los Angeles Times*, June 7, 2005. See also William Pfaff, "The Truth About Torture," *American Conservative*, February 15, 2005, http://amconmag.com/2005_02_14/print/articleprint1.html.

90. David Brooks, "The Age of Conflict: Politics and Culture after September 11," *Weekly Standard* 7, no. 8 (November 5, 2001).

91. Tim Golden, "After Terror, a Secret Rewriting of Military Law," *New York Times*, October 24, 2004.

92. "Working Group Report on Detainee Interrogations in the Global War on Terrorism: Assessment of Legal, Historical, Policy, and Operations Considerations," March 6, 2003, classified secret, "no foreign dissemination," http://www.yirmeyahureview.com/archive/documents/prisoner_abuse/detainee_interrogations_in_the_global_war_on_terrorism.htm. In regard to John Yoo, see also Maria L. La Ganga, "Scholar Calmly Takes Heat for His Memos on Torture," *Los Angeles Times*, May 16, 2005.

93. Karen J. Greenberg and Joshua L. Dratel, "Interrogating Donald Rumsfeld," TomDispatch.com, January 11, 2005, http://www.tomdispatch.com/index.mhtml?pid=2116.

94. Edward Alden, "Attempt to Find Legal Justification for Torture Leaves Lawyers Aghast," *Financial Times*, June 10, 2004; and Editorial, "Torturing the Law, if not Prisoners," *Financial Times*, December 8, 2004.

95. Sodei Rinjiro, "Remember in re Yamashita [327 US 1 (1946)]," *Japan Focus*, http://www.japanfocus.org/116.html. See also Andrew J. Bacevich, "Command Responsibility," *Washington Post*, June 28, 2005.

96. Human Rights Watch says that Rumsfeld may bear "command responsibility" for abuse in Iraq and asks that the United States name a special prosecutor to investigate his role. "Demand for Rumsfeld Abuse Inquiry," *BBC News*, May 24, 2005, http://news.bbc.co.uk/2/hi/americas/4475133.stm.

97. Hersh, "Gray Zone"; Arkin, *Code Names*, p. 321, s.v. "Copper Green."

98. Quoted by Dana Priest, "Spirited Debate Preceded Policies," *Washington Post*, June 23, 2004, http://www.washingtonpost.com/ac2/wp-dyn/A61942-2004Jun22?language=printer.

99. Josh White, "U.S. Generals in Iraq Were Told of Abuse Early, Inquiry Finds," *Washington Post*, December 1, 2004.

100. Sidney Blumenthal, " 'Abuse'? How About Torture?" *Salon*, May 6, 2004; Editorial, "Mr. Rumsfeld's Responsibility," *Washington Post*, May 6, 2004; Bob Herbert, "The Rumsfeld Stain," *New York Times*, May 23, 2005.

101. On the use of women in the armed forces as torturers, see Erik Saar, *Inside the Wire: A Military Intelligence Soldier's Eyewitness Account of Life at Guantánamo*, with Viveca Novak (New York: Penguin, 2005); Philip Kennicott, "A Wretched Picture of America," *Washington Post*, May 5, 2004; Marie Cocco, "Chain of Prisoner Abuse Starts at the Top," *Newsday*, May 24, 2005; Daniel Eisenberg and Timothy J. Burger, "What's Going on at Gitmo?" *Time*, June 6, 2005, pp. 30–31; Adam Zagorin and Michael Duffy, "Inside the Interrogation of Detainee 063," *Time*, June 20, 2005, pp. 26–33.

102. Quoted by Seymour M. Hersh, "Torture at Abu Ghraib," *New Yorker,* May 10, 2004, p. 43. For the text of General Taguba's report, see http://www.antiwar. com/article.php?articleid=2479. For the 279 photographs and 19 videos from the army's internal investigation of torture at Abu Ghraib, see Joan Walsh, "The Abu Ghraib Files," *Salon,* March 14, 2006, http://www.salon.com/news/abu_ghraib/2006/03/14/introduction/print.html.

103. "Gen. Richard Myers," *Fox News.*

104. Associated Press, "Army Probe Finds Abuse at Jail near Mosul," March 26, 2005.

105. Suzanne Goldenberg, "Former Guantánamo Chief Clashed with Army Interrogators," *Guardian,* May 19, 2004, http://www.guardian.co.uk/print/0,3858,4927249-111575,00.html; Peter Spiegel and Edward Alden, "Focus Back on General in Charge of Detention," *Financial Times,* June 10, 2004.

106. Dan Eggen and R. Jeffrey Smith, "FBI Agents Allege Abuse of Detainees at Guantánamo," *Washington Post,* December 21, 2004, http://www.washington post.com/ac2/wp-dyn/A14936-2004Dec20?language=printer.

107. Reuters, "Red Cross: Guantánamo Tactics 'Tantamount to Torture,'" November 30, 2004.

108. Rose, "Truth about Camp Delta."

109. Scott Higham, Josh White, and Christian Davenport, "A Prison on the Brink: Usual Military Checks and Balances Went Missing," *Washington Post,* May 9, 2004.

110. James Sturcke, "General Approved Extreme Interrogation Methods," *Guardian,* March 30, 2005, http://www.guardian.co.uk/print/0,3858,5158950-103550,00.html; Andrew Buncombe, "Green Light for Iraqi Prison Abuse Came from the Top," *Independent,* April 3, 2005, http://news.independent.co.uk/low_res/story.jsp?story=625909&host=3&dir=70.

111. Will Dunham, "U.S. General Urged 'Outer Limits' Iraq Interrogation," Reuters, May 2, 2006, http://www.alertnet.org/printable.htm?URL=/thenews/ newsdesk/N02295252.htm.

112. U.S. Department of Defense, Office of the Assistant Secretary of Defense (Public Affairs), "General Officer Assignments," news release no. 203–04, March 22, 2004; ibid., no. 1210–04, November 24, 2004; Gerry J. Gilmore, "Casey Takes Over Iraq Commander's Reins from Sanchez," American Forces Press Service, July 1, 2004; Reuters, "U.S. Replaces General Who Ran Prisons in Iraq," *ABC News,* November 24, 2004; Eric Schmitt and Thom Shanker, "Posts Considered for Commanders After Abuse Case," *New York Times,* June 20, 2005.

113. John Hendren, "4-Star Plans After Abu Ghraib," *Los Angeles Times,* October 15, 2004, http://www.truthout.org/docs_04/printer_101604I.shtml.

114. Dave Moniz, "Gen. Karpinski Demoted in Prison Scandal," *USA Today,* May 5, 2005.

115. Editorial, "Impunity," *Washington Post,* April 26, 2005. See also Editorial, "American Homicide," *Boston Globe,* March 29, 2005; Josh White, "Top Army Officers Are Cleared in Abuse Cases," *Washington Post,* April 23, 2005; Seymour Hersh, "The Unknown Unknowns of the Abu Ghraib Scandal," *Guardian,* May 21, 2005, http://www.guardian.co.uk/print/0,3858,5198906-103677,00.html.

116. Sonni Efron, "GOP Committee Targets International Red Cross," *Los Angeles Times*, June 15, 2005, http://fairuse.1accesshost.com/news2/latimes688
.html; Caroline Moorhead, "Speak No Evil," *Financial Times*, June 18–19, 2005.

117. Burton J. Lee III, "The Stain of Torture," *Washington Post*, July 1, 2005.

118. American Embassy, London, "Visit of President Bush to Northern Ireland, April 7–8, 2003," http://www.usembassy.org.uk/potus03/potus03c.html.

119. William R. Polk, introduction to *The Looting of the Iraq Museum, Baghdad: The Lost Legacy of Ancient Mesopotamia*, Milbry Polk and Angela M. H. Schuster, eds. (New York: Harry N. Abrams, 2005), p. 5. See also Suzanne Muchnic, "Spotlight on Iraq's Plundered Past," *Los Angeles Times*, June 20, 2005.

120. David Fromkin, *A Peace to End All Peace: The Fall of the Ottoman Empire and the Creation of the Modern Middle East* (New York: Owl Books, 1989, 2001), p. 450.

121. George Bush's address to the Iraqi people, broadcast on *Towards Freedom TV*, April 10, 2003, http://home.earthlink.net/~platter/speeches/030410-bush-tfreedom.html.

122. Office of the Undersecretary of Defense for Acquisition, Technology, and Logistics, Report of the Defense Science Board Task Force on Strategic Communication (Washington, DC: September 2004), pp. 39–40.

123. See Frank Rich, "And Now: 'Operation Iraqi Looting,'" *New York Times*, April 27, 2003; Eleanor Robson, "The Collection Lies in Ruins, Objects from a Long, Rich Past in Smithereens," *Guardian*, April 14, 2003, http://www. guardian.co.uk/arts/features/story/0,11710,936561,00
.html.

124. Robert Scheer, "It's U.S. Policy that's 'Untidy,'" *Los Angeles Times*, April 15, 2003; reprinted in "Books in Flames," TomDispatch.com, April 15, 2003, http://www.tomdispatch.com/index.mhtml?pid=578.

125. John F. Burns, "Pillagers Strip Iraqi Museum of Its Treasures," *New York Times*, April 13, 2003; Piotr Michalowski (University of Michigan), "The Ransacking of the Baghdad Museum Is a Disgrace," *History News Network*, April 14, 2003, http://hnn.us/articles/1386.html; Fiachra Gibbons, "The End of Civilization," *Guardian*, April 2, 2003, http://www.guardian.co.uk/arts/features/story/0,11710,927788,00.html.

126. Polk and Schuster, *Looting of Iraq Museum*, pp. 209–10; "Looters Trash Museum's Treasures," *Observer*, April 13, 2003, http://observer.guardian
.co.uk/international/story/0,,935762,00.html.

127. Mark Wilkinson, "Looting of Ancient Sites Threatens Iraqi Heritage," Reuters, June 29, 2005, http://famulus.msnbc.com/famulusintl/reuters06-29-050006.asp?reg=mideast&vts=62920051945. See also Matthew Bogdanos, *Thieves of Baghdad* (New York: Bloomsbury USA, 2005).

128. Polk and Schuster, *Looting of Iraq Museum*, pp. 23, 212–13; Louise Jury, "At Least 8,000 Treasures Looted from Iraq Museum Still Untraced," *Independent*, May 24, 2005; Stephen Fidler, "'The Looters Knew What They Wanted. It Looks Like Vandalism, but Organized Crime May Be Behind It,'" *Financial Times*, May 23, 2003; Rod Liddle, "The Day of the Jackals," *Spectator*, April 19, 2003, http://www.agitprop.org.au/nowar/20030419_liddle_ day_of_the_jackals.php.

129. Humberto Márquez, "Iraq Invasion the 'Biggest Cultural Disaster Since 1258,'" Antiwar.com, February 16, 2005, http://www.antiwar.com/ips/marquez.php?articleid=4859.

130. Robert Fisk, "Library Books, Letters, and Priceless Documents Are Set Ablaze in Final Chapter of the Sacking of Baghdad," *Independent,* April 15, 2003.

131. Polk and Schuster, *Looting of Iraq Museum,* p. 10.

132. Guy Gugliotta, "Pentagon Was Told of Risk to Museums; U.S. Urged to Save Iraq's Historic Artifacts," *Washington Post,* April 14, 2003; McGuire Gibson, "Cultural Tragedy in Iraq: A Report on the Looting of Museums, Archives, and Sites," International Foundation for Art Research, http://www.ifar.org/tragedy.htm. See also Jeremy Grant's interview with McGuire Gibson at the University of Chicago's Oriental Institute, "Hidden Gems and Unexpected Links," *Financial Times,* September 10–11, 2005.

133. Liddle, "Day of the Jackals"; Oliver Burkeman, "Ancient Archive Lost in Baghdad Blaze," *Guardian,* April 15, 2003, http://www.guardian.co.uk/international/story/0,,936943,00.html.

134. See James A. R. Nafziger, "Art Loss in Iraq: Protection of Cultural Heritage in Time of War and Its Aftermath," International Foundation for Art Research, http://www.ifar.org/heritage.htm.

135. Jonathan Steele, "Museum's Treasures Left to the Mercy of Looters, U.S. Generals Reject Plea to Protect Priceless Artifacts from Vandals," *Guardian,* April 14, 2003, http://www.guardian.co.uk/arts/news/story/0,11711,936557,00.html; Paul Martin, Ed Vulliamy, and Gaby Hinsliff, "U.S. Army Was Told to Protect Looted Museum," *Observer,* April 20, 2003, http://www.guardian.co.uk/print/0,3858,4651740-102275,00.html; Rich, "Operation Iraqi Looting"; Paul Martin, "Troops Were Told to Guard Treasures," *Washington Times,* April 20, 2003.

136. Said Arjomand, "Under the Eyes of U.S. Forces and This Happened?" History News Network, April 14, 2003, http://hnn.us/articles/1387.html. For the hypocrisy of marine colonel Matthew Bogdanos, who was put in charge of covering up or distracting from the failures of the American military to carry out its orders, see Christopher de Bellaigue, "Loot," *Granta,* no. 83 (Fall 2003), pp. 193–211. For Bogdanos's own attempt to conflate the looting in Iraq with the international trade in illegally obtained antiquities, see "The Terrorist in the Art Gallery," *New York Times,* December 10, 2005.

137. Ed Vulliamy "Troops 'Vandalize' Ancient City of Ur," *Observer,* May 18, 2003, http://observer.guardian.co.uk/print/0,3858,4671554-102275,00.html; Paul Johnson, *Art: A New History* (New York: Harper-Collins, 2003), pp. 18, 35; Polk and Schuster, *Looting of Iraq Museum,* p. 99, fig. 25.

138. "Tallil Air Base," GlobalSecurity.org, http://www.globalsecurity.org/military/world/iraq/tallil.htm.

139. Max Mallowan, *Mallowan's Memoirs* (London: Collins, 1977), p. 61.

140. Rory McCarthy and Maev Kennedy, "Babylon Wrecked by War," *Guardian,* January 15, 2005, http://www.guardian.co.uk/print/0,3858,5104058-103550,00.html.

141. Owen Bowcott, "Archaeologists Fight to Save Iraqi Sites," *Guardian,* June 20, 2005, http://www.guardian.co.uk/Iraq/Story/0,2763,1510061,00.html.

142. Zainab Bahrani, "The Fall of Babylon," in Polk and Schuster, *Looting of Iraq Museum*, p. 214. See also Bahrani, "Looting and Conquest," *Nation*, May 14, 2003, http://www.thenation.com/doc.mhtml?i=20030526 &s=bahrani.

143. Associated Press, "Hussein's Gazelles Feed Marine Base," *San Diego Union-Tribune*, April 19, 2003.

2: COMPARATIVE IMPERIAL PATHOLOGIES: ROME, BRITAIN, AND AMERICA

1. Cornel West is particularly interesting on the relationship between "prophetic Christians" and "Constantinian Christians." See his *Democracy Matters: Winning the Fight Against Imperialism* (New York: Penguin, 2004), pp. 146–69.

2. Robert C. Byrd, *The Senate of the Roman Republic* (Washington, DC: Government Printing Office, 1995), p. 41.

3. Anthony Everitt, *Cicero: The Life and Times of Rome's Greatest Politician* (New York: Random House, 2001), p. 67.

4. Michael Parenti, *The Assassination of Julius Caesar: A People's History of Ancient Rome* (New York: New Press, 2003), p. 191.

5. Ibid., p. 181.

6. Ibid., p. 221.

7. Ibid., p. 16.

8. Ibid., pp. 50, 204.

9. Tom Holland, *Rubicon: The Last Years of the Roman Republic* (New York: Doubleday, 2003), pp. 181–82.

10. Ibid., p. 8.

11. Patrick E. Tyler, "U.S. Strategy Plan Calls for Insuring No Rivals Develop," *New York Times*, March 8, 1992.

12. Paul Wolfowitz, "Remembering the Future," *National Interest*, Spring 2000, p. 36; David Armstrong, "Dick Cheney's Song of America: Drafting a Plan for Global Dominance," *Harper's Magazine*, October 2002, pp. 76–83.

13. Holland, *Rubicon*, p. 177.

14. Ibid., p. 167.

15. Ed Harriman, "Where Has All the Money Gone?" *London Review of Books*, July 7, 2005, pp. 3–7; Pratap Chatterjee, *Iraq, Inc.: A Profitable Occupation* (New York: Seven Stories Press, 2004).

16. For a map showing the "Tiber River," see James Sterling Young, *The Washington Community, 1800–1828* (New York: Columbia University Press, 1966), p. 67. Also see Byrd, *Senate of the Roman Republic*, p. 183.

17. Holland, *Rubicon*, pp. xv–xvi.

18. Ibid., p. xvii.

19. Everitt, *Cicero*, p. 12.

20. See, for example, Dana Priest, "The CinCs: Proconsuls to the Empire," in *The Mission: Waging War and Keeping Peace with America's Military* (New York: Norton, 2003), pp. 61–77.

21. Byrd, *Senate of the Roman Republic*, p. 50.

22. Holland, *Rubicon*, p. 21.

23. Parenti, *Assassination of Julius Caesar*, pp. 54–55.

24. Everitt, *Cicero*, p. 14.

25. Ibid., pp. 321–22.

26. Ibid., p. 11.
27. Holland, *Rubicon*, pp. 161–62.
28. Everitt, *Cicero*, pp. 126–27.
29. Suetonius, *The Twelve Caesars*, trans. Robert Graves (London: Penguin Books, 2003), p. 25.
30. Everitt, *Cicero*, pp. 16–17.
31. Byrd, *Senate of the Roman Republic*, pp. 111, 116.
32. Holland, *Rubicon*, p. 162.
33. Everitt, *Cicero*, p. 19.
34. Ibid., p. 45.
35. Suzanne Cross, "Gaius Marius, 157–86 B.C," http://heraklia.fws1.com/contemporaries/marius/.
36. Everitt, *Cicero*, p. 246.
37. Ibid., pp. 281, 296; Holland, *Rubicon*, p. 361; Parenti, *Assassination of Julius Caesar*, p. 201; Byrd, *Senate of the Roman Republic*, p. 34.
38. Everitt, *Cicero*, pp. 303–18.
39. Shasta Darlington, Reuters, "New Dig Says Caligula Was Indeed a Maniac," *San Diego Union-Tribune*, August 16, 2003.
40. On Nero's reputation, see Edward Champlin, *Nero* (Cambridge, MA: Harvard University Press, 2003).
41. Niall Ferguson, *Colossus: The Price of America's Empire* (New York: Penguin, 2004), p. 208. Also see Vivek Chibber, "The Good Empire: Should We Pick Up Where the British Left Off?" *Boston Review*, February–March 2005, pp. 30–34.
42. Niall Ferguson, *Empire: The Rise and Demise of the British World Order and the Lessons for Global Power* (New York: Basic Books, 2002), pp. xxi, x.
43. Max Boot, "The Case for an American Empire," *Weekly Standard*, October 15, 2001.
44. Review of Ferguson's *Colossus*, *Financial Times*, May 15–16, 2004.
45. See Mike Davis, *Late Victorian Holocausts* (London: Verso, 2001), pp. 7, 311–12.
46. Joshua Micah Marshall, "Power Rangers," *New Yorker*, February 2, 2004.
47. Bernard Porter, *The Absent-Minded Imperialists: Empire, Society, and Culture in Britain* (New York: Oxford University Press, 2005); Ronald Steel, *Pax Americana* (New York: Viking, 1967), pp. 16–17.
48. Bernard Porter, *Empire and Superempire: Britain, America and the World* (New Haven, CT: Yale University Press, 2006), p. 42.
49. Wikipedia, "Michael Ignatieff," http://en.wikipedia.org/wiki/Michael_Ignatieff; Peter C. Newman, "Q&A with Liberal Leadership Contender Michael Ignatieff," Macleans.ca, April 6, 2006, http://www.macleans.ca/topstories/politics/article.jsp?content=20060410_124769_124769; and Michael Ignatieff, "Lesser Evils," *New York Times Magazine*, May 2, 2004, http://www.ksg.harvard.edu/news/opeds/2004/ignatieff_less_evils_nytm_050204.htm.
50. Michael Ignatieff, "The Burden," *New York Times Magazine*, January 5, 2003; reprinted in various places under the title "The American Empire (Get Used to It)."
51. Michael Neumann, "Michael Ignatieff, Apostle of He-manitarianism," *Counterpunch*, December 8, 2003, which draws its quotations from Ignatieff's book

Empire Lite : Nation Building in Bosnia, Kosovo, Afghanistan (London: Vintage UK, 2003).

52. Ferguson, *Colossus,* p. 169; *Empire,* p. 267.

53. Quoted by Ferguson, *Colossus,* p. 220. Also see Roger Owen, *Lord Cromer: Victorian Imperialist, Edwardian Proconsul* (Oxford: Oxford University Press, 2004).

54. Quoted by Ferguson, *Empire,* p. 200.

55. Kevin Baker, "We're in the Army Now," *Harper's Magazine,* October 2003, p. 43.

56. Eric Foner, "The Lie that Empire Tells Itself," *London Review of Books,* May 19, 2005, p. 16.

57. Edward Said, "Jane Austen and Empire" (1990), in *The Edward Said Reader,* ed. Moustafa Bayoumi and Andrew Rubin (New York: Vintage Books, 2000), p. 349.

58. Hannah Arendt, *The Origins of Totalitarianism* (New York: Meridian, 1958), p. 216. The term comes from an unnamed British bureaucrat commenting on what was necessary to keep the population of India docile and under British control.

59. Quoted by Dinesh D'Souza, "In Praise of American Empire," *Christian Science Monitor,* April 26, 2002.

60. See John W. Dower, *Embracing Defeat: Japan in the Wake of World War II* (New York: W.W. Norton, 1999).

61. Foner, "Lie."

62. The most important compilation of such campaign names is Arkin, *Code Names.*

63. Quoted by Tony Stephens, "According to the White House this Action is Anything but War," *Sydney Morning Herald,* March 21, 2003, http://www .smh.com.au/articles/2003/03/20/1047749879550.html.

64. Sven Lindqvist, *"Exterminate All the Brutes": One Man's Odyssey into the Heart of Darkness and the Origins of European Genocide,* trans. Joan Tate (New York: New Press, 1996). Also see Tom Engelhardt, "The Cartography of Death," *Nation,* October 23, 2000.

65. Charles S. Maier, "An American Empire?" *Harvard Magazine,* November– December 2002, http://www.harvardmagazine.com/on-line/1102193.html.

66. Carl A. Trocki, *Opium, Empire, and the Global Political Economy: A Study of the Asian Opium Trade, 1750–1950* (London: Routledge, 1999). Also see Ferguson, *Empire,* p. 139; Yoshie Furuhashi, "A New Opium War," 2004, http://info.interactivist.net/print.pl?sid=04/12/11/2259233; James L. Hevia, "Opium, Empire, and Modern History," *China Review International* 10, no. 2 (Fall 2003); and John Richards, "The Opium Industry in British India," *Indian Economic and Social History Review* 39, no. 2–3 (2002), pp. 149–80. The classic studies are Maurice Collis, *Foreign Mud: Being an Account of the Opium Imbroglio at Canton in the 1830's and the Anglo-Chinese War that Followed* (New York: Knopf, 1947); and Alfred W. McCoy, *The Politics of Heroin* (Chicago: Lawrence Hill, 1991).

67. Arendt, *Origins of Totalitarianism,* pp. 183–84.

68. Davis, *Late Victorian Holocausts,* p. 292.

69. Ferguson, *Empire,* p. 22.

70. Lindqvist, *"Exterminate All the Brutes"*, pp. 81–88.
71. Ibid., p. 115.
72. Ferguson, *Empire*, p. 217.
73. Ibid., p. 219.
74. Ibid., p. 279.
75. P. J. Marshall, ed., *Cambridge Illustrated History of the British Empire* (Cambridge: Cambridge University Press, 1996), p, 373.
76. Ferguson, *Empire*, p. 169.
77. Katherine Bailey, "Edwina Mountbatten: India's Last Vicerine," *British Heritage*, April–May 2000, http://historynet.com/bh/blmountbatten/index.html.
78. Tapan Raychaudhuri, "British Rule in India: An Assessment," in Marshall, *History of the British Empire*, p. 367.
79. Marshall, *History of the British Empire*, pp. 371–72.
80. Editorial, "Promises, Promises," *New York Times*, August 22, 2005.
81. Anita Jain, "World Bank to Lend India $9bn to Help Improve Rural Areas," *Financial Times*, August 22, 2005.
82. See Walden Bello, *Dilemmas of Domination: The Unmaking of the American Empire* (New York: Metropolitan, 2005).
83. Ferguson, *Empire*, p. 304.
84. Ferguson, *Colossus*, p. 25.
85. John Gray, "The World Is Round," *New York Review of Books*, August 11, 2005, pp. 13–15.
86. Ferguson, *Empire*, p. 164.
87. Raychaudhuri, "British Rule in India," p. 363.
88. See Chalmers Johnson, "Whatever Happened to Globalization?" in *The Sorrows of Empire* (New York: Metropolitan Books, 2004), pp. 255–81; Johnson, *MITI and the Japanese Miracle* (Stanford, CA: Stanford University Press, 1982); Meredith Woo-Cumings, ed., *The Developmental State* (Ithaca, NY: Cornell University Press, 1999); and Johnson, "Economic Crisis in East Asia: The Clash of Capitalisms," *Cambridge Journal of Economics* 22, no. 6 (November 1998), pp. 653–61.
89. Davis, *Late Victorian Holocausts*, p. 295.
90. Karl Polanyi, *The Great Transformation: The Political and Economic Origins of Our Time* (1944; repr. Boston: Beacon Press, 1957), pp. 159–60; quoted by Davis, *Late Victorian Holocausts*, p. 10.
91. Ferguson, *Empire*, p. 314.
92. Thomas L. Friedman, *The Lexus and the Olive Tree* (New York: Farrar, Straus & Giroux, 1999), p. 381. The best study of globalization today is Manfred B. Steger, *Globalism: The New Market Ideology* (Lanham, MD: Rowman & Littlefield, 2002). Also see Jeff Faux, "Flat Note from the Pied Piper of Globalization," *Dissent*, Fall 2005, pp. 64–67.
93. Ferguson, *Colossus*, p. 196.
94. Ferguson, *Empire*, p. 302.
95. Marshall, *History of the British Empire*, pp. 372–73.
96. Caroline Elkins, *Imperial Reckoning: The Untold Story of Britain's Gulag in Kenya* (New York: Henry Holt, 2005), p. 11. Also see David Anderson, *Histories of the Hanged: Britain's Dirty War in Kenya and the End of Empire*

(London: Weidenfeld, 2005); Daphne Eviatar, "In Cold Blood," *Nation,* February 21, 2005; and Bernard Porter, "How Did They Get Away with It?" *London Review of Books,* March 3, 2005. An early study of Mau Mau had already discredited British propaganda that the insurgents were "heathen savages" and shown the revolt to have been in response particularly to set-tler land seizures. See Carl G. Rosberg Jr. and John Nottingham, *The Myth of Mau Mau: Nationalism in Kenya* (New York: Praeger, 1966).

97. Elkins, *Imperial Reckoning,* pp. xv–xvi.
98. Ferguson, *Empire,* p. xv.
99. Quoted by Andrew Gilmour, "How to Create Insurgents," *Spectator,* January 24, 2004.
100. Ferguson, *Colossus,* p. 221.
101. Eric Margolis, "George Bush's New Imperialism," *Toronto Sun,* August 4, 2002. The major work on this subject is Fromkin, *A Peace to End All Peace.* See also Karl E. Meyer, "Forty Years in the Sand: What Happened the Last Time Freedom Marched on Iraq," *Harper's Magazine,* June 2005, pp. 69–74.
102. The classic treatment is Khushwant Singh, *Mano Majra* (New York: Grove Press, 1956). Mano Majra is the name of a Punjabi village where Hindus and Muslims had lived in peace for hundreds of years until partition. Singh's novel has since been reissued under the title *Last Train to Pakistan.*
103. Raychaudhuri, "British Rule in India," pp. 366–67.
104. Ferguson, *Empire,* p. 297.
105. Arendt, *Origins of Totalitarianism,* pp. 503–4.

3: CENTRAL INTELLIGENCE AGENCY: THE PRESIDENT'S PRIVATE ARMY

1. Douglas Jehl, "Chief of CIA Tells His Staff to Back Bush," *New York Times,* November 17, 2004; David Wise, "Sycophant Spies," *Los Angeles Times,* November 21, 2004; Alexander Cockburn, "Politicize the CIA? You've Got to Be Kidding," *Nation,* December 20, 2004, p. 8.
2. Thomas Powers, "The Failure," *New York Review of Books,* April 29, 2004, p. 4.
3. Melvin A. Goodman, "Righting the CIA," *Baltimore Sun,* November 19, 2004.
4. See, among several references, the recollections of a CIA officer who actually heard Schlesinger's remark: Ray McGovern, "Cheney's Cat's Paw: Porter Goss as CIA Director," *Counterpunch,* July 6, 2004, http://www.counterpunch.org/mcgovern07062004.html.
5. See James Moore and Wayne Slater, *Bush's Brain: How Karl Rove Made George W. Bush Presidential* (New York: Wiley, 2004).
6. Scott Ritter, "A Silver Lining in Bush's New CIA Pick?" AlterNet, May 16, 2006, http://www.informationclearinghouse.info/article13063.htm.
7. Loch K. Johnson, *America's Secret Power: The CIA in a Democratic Society* (New York: Oxford University Press, 1989), p. 21.
8. See Willard C. Matthias, "An Assault upon the National Intelligence Process," in *America's Strategic Blunders: Intelligence Analysis and National Security Policy, 1936–1991* (University Park, PA: Pennsylvania State University Press, 2001), pp. 293–314.
9. Among the recommended books on the agency's past activities are William Blum, *Killing Hope: U.S. Military and CIA Interventions since World War II* (Monroe, ME: Common Courage Press, 1995); Steve Coll, *Ghost Wars: The Secret History of the CIA, Afghanistan, and Bin Laden from the Soviet Invasion*

to September 10, 2001 (New York: Penguin, 2004); Frederick H. Gareau, *State Terrorism and the United States* (Atlanta, GA: Clarity Press, 2003); Greg Grandin, *Empire's Workshop: Latin America, the United States, and the Rise of the New Imperialism* (New York: Metropolitan, 2006); Stephen Kinzer, *Overthrow: America's Century of Regime Change from Hawaii to Iraq* (New York: Henry Holt, 2006); John Kenneth Knaus, *Orphans of the Cold War: America and the Tibetan Struggle for Survival* (New York: Public Affairs, 1999); James Risen, *State of War: The Secret History of the CIA and the Bush Administration* (New York: Free Press, 2006); Frances Stonor Saunders, *The Cultural Cold War: The CIA and the World of Arts and Letters* (New York: New Press, 1999); Stephen Schlesinger and Stephen Kinzer, *Bitter Fruit: The Story of the American Coup in Guatemala,* expanded ed. (Cambridge, MA: Harvard University Press, 1999); Richard H. Schultz Jr., *The Secret War Against Hanoi* (New York: HarperCollins, 1999); and Paul Todd and Jonathan Bloch, *Global Intelligence: The World's Secret Services Today* (London: Zed Books, 2003).

10. Quoted by Johnson, *America's Secret Power,* p. 36.

11. William M. Arkin, "Secrecy Is the CIA's Stock in Trade, and the Agency's Hidden Weakness," *Los Angeles Times,* July 18, 2004; Nick Schwellenbach, "Government Secrecy Grows Out of Control," Common Dreams News Center, September 24, 2004, http://www.commondreams.org/views04/0923-05.htm; Dorothy Samuels, "President Bush Is Hard at Work Expanding Government Secrecy," *New York Times,* November 1, 2004; Kevin Freking, Associated Press, "Feds Increasingly Classify Documents," *ABC News,* July 2, 2005.

12. See, for example, Admiral Stansfield Turner [DCI, 1977–81], *Terrorism and Democracy* (Boston: Houghton Mifflin, 1991), pp. 27 ff.; Senator Daniel Patrick Moynihan, *Secrecy: The American Experience* (New Haven, CT: Yale University Press, 1998), pp. 8–9, 168–69; Mark Riebling, *Wedge: From Pearl Harbor to 9/11, How the Secret War Between the FBI and CIA Has Endangered National Security* (New York: Simon & Schuster Touchstone Books, 2002); Hersh, "Why the Government Didn't Know What It Knew," in *Chain of Command,* pp. 87–103.

13. For details, see Seymour M. Hersh, "Getting Out the Vote," *New Yorker,* July 25, 2005. Also see Hannah Allam and Warren P. Strobel, Knight Ridder News Service, "CIA Keeps Hold of Iraq's Intelligence Service in Turf War," *San Diego Union Tribune,* May 9, 2005; Gareth Porter, "The Coming Shi'ite Showdown," Antiwar.com, May 13, 2005; Patrick Cockburn, "Americans Accused of Interfering in Iraq Election," *Independent,* July 18, 2005.

14. Johnson, *America's Secret Power,* p. 43.

15. Bob Woodward, *Veil: The CIA's Secret Wars, 1981–87* (New York: Simon & Schuster, 1987), p. 49.

16. Johnson, *America's Secret Power,* p. 62.

17. Robert M. Gates, "The CIA and American Foreign Policy," *Foreign Affairs* 66 (Winter 1987–88), p. 227.

18. Johnson, *America's Secret Power,* p. 62. See also Harold P. Ford, *CIA and Vietnam Policymakers: Three Episodes, 1962–1968* (Washington: Central Intelligence Agency, 1998), pp. 86–104.

19. Senate Select Committee to Study Governmental Operations with Respect to Intelligence Activities (Church Committee), *Final Report,* 94th Cong. 2nd

sess. (Washington, DC: Government Printing Office, 1976), 1:78; Johnson, *America's Secret Power*, p. 64.

20. See Federation of American Scientists, Weapons of Mass Destruction, R-36/ SS-9 SCARP, http://www.fas.org/nuke/guide/russia/icbm/r-36.htm; and Fred Kaplan, "The Rumsfeld Intelligence Agency," *Slate*, October 28, 2002, http:// www.slate.com/toolbar.aspx?action=print&id=2073238.

21. Coll, *Ghost Wars*, p. 562.

22. McGovern, "Cheney's Cat's Paw."

23. See Clarke, *Against All Enemies*; Anonymous (Michael Scheuer), *Imperial Hubris: Why the West Is Losing the War on Terror* (Washington, DC: Brassey's, 2004); and Scheuer, "How Not to Catch a Terrorist," *Atlantic Monthly*, December 2004, pp. 50–52. See also Scheuer, "Why I Resigned from the CIA," *Los Angeles Times*, December 5, 2004.

24. Karen Kwiatkowski, "The New Pentagon Papers," March 10, 2004, http:// www.salon.com/opinion/feature/2004/03/10/osp_moveon/; "Karen Kwiatkowski: Archives," http://www.lewrockwell.com/kwiatkowski/ kwiatkowski-arch.html; Robert Dreyfuss and Jason Vest, "The Lie Factory," *Mother Jones*, January–February 2004, pp. 34–41; Marc Cooper, "Soldier for the Truth: Exposing Bush's Talking-points War," *LA Weekly*, February 20–26, 2004. Colonel Kwiatkowski also made an important contribution to Eugene Jarecki's documentary film *Why We Fight*, which won the gold medal at the 2005 Sundance Film Festival.

25. Joseph C. Wilson, "What I Didn't Find in Africa," *New York Times*, July 6, 2003, http://www.commondreams.org/views03/0706-02.htm; Wilson, "A Right-Wing Smear Is Gathering Steam," *Los Angeles Times*, July 21, 2004; Wilson, "Our 27 Months of Hell," *Los Angeles Times*, October 29, 2005; Neil Mackay, "Niger and Iraq: The War's Biggest Lie," *Sunday Herald*, July 13, 2003, http://www.sundayherald.com/print35264; Edward Alden, "Naming of Agent was Aimed at Discrediting CIA," *Financial Times*, October 25, 2003; James Risen, "How Niger Uranium Story Defied Wide Skepticism," *New York Times*, July 14, 2004; Ian Masters, "Who Forged the Niger Documents?" AlterNet, April 7, 2005, http://www.alternet.org/module/printversion/21704; Frank Rich, "Follow the Uranium," *New York Times*, July 17, 2005; Tom Hamburger and Peter Wallsten, "Top Aides Reportedly Set Sights on Wilson," *Los Angeles Times*, July 18, 2005; Matthew Yglesias, "Follow the Documents," *American Prospect Online*, July 19, 2005, http://www.prospect.org/web/ printfriendly-view.ww?id=10015.

26. Gary C. Schroen, *First In: An Insider's Account of How the CIA Spearheaded the War on Terror in Afghanistan* (Novato, CA: Presidio Press, 2005).

27. Melissa Boyle Mahle, *Denial and Deception: An Insider's View of the CIA from Iran-Contra to 9/11* (New York: Nation Books, 2005).

28. Quoted by Arthur Schlesinger Jr., "The Imperial Presidency Redux," *Washington Post*, June 28, 2003. Also see Mark Hubbard and Stephen Fidler, "No Smoking Gun: How Intelligence May Have Been Exaggerated, Misinterpreted, and Manipulated," *Financial Times*, June 4, 2003.

29. Douglas Jehl, "Ex-CIA Chief Nets $500,000 on Talk Circuit," *New York Times*, November 11, 2004.

30. Greg Miller, "Goss Isn't Done with Housecleaning at CIA," *Los Angeles Times*,

November 18, 2004; Douglas Jehl, "Director of Analysis at CIA Is the Latest to Be Forced Out," *New York Times,* December 29, 2004.

31. Spencer Ackerman, "Killing the Messenger," *Salon,* November 16, 2004.
32. Walter Pincus and Dana Priest, "Bush Orders the CIA to Hire More Spies," *Washington Post,* November 24, 2004.
33. Johnson, *America's Secret Power,* p. 106.
34. Thomas Powers, "Inside the Department of Dirty Tricks," *Atlantic Monthly,* August 1979, pp. 33–64.
35. Johnson, *America's Secret Power,* p. 107.
36. Powers, "Department of Dirty Tricks."
37. Peter Kornbluh, *The Pinochet File: A Declassified Dossier on Atrocity and Accountability* (New York: New Press, 2003, A National Security Archive Book), p. xvi.
38. The most important source is Kornbluh, *Pinochet File.* See also Peter Kornbluh, "The Chile Coup—The U.S. Hand," *iF Magazine.com,* October 25, 1998; John Dinges, "Pulling Back the Veil on Condor," *Nation,* July 24–31, 2000; Peter Kornbluh, "CIA Outrages in Chile," *Nation,* October 16, 2000; Diana Jean Schemo, "Kissinger Cool to Criticizing Junta in '76," *New York Times,* October 1, 2004; Associated Press, "Chile Torture Victims to Get Compensation," *New York Times,* November 29, 2004. On Kissinger's attempts to hide his role in the overthrow of Salvador Allende and the promotion of the Pinochet dictatorship, see Scott Sherman, "The Maxwell Affair," *Nation,* June 21, 2004; Sherman, "Kissinger's Shadow Over the Council on Foreign Relations," *Nation,* December 27, 2004; and Kenneth Maxwell, "The Case of the Missing Letter in Foreign Affairs: Kissinger, Pinochet, and Operation Condor" (Working Papers on Latin America, no. 04/05-3, David Rockefeller Center for Latin American Studies, Harvard University, 2004).
39. Kornbluh, *Pinochet File,* chap. 1, doc. 1.
40. Quoted by Kornbluh, "CIA Outrages."
41. Kornbluh, *Pinochet File,* pp. 18 and 510, notes 23 and 24; Powers, "Department of Dirty Tricks"; Johnson, *America's Secret Power,* p. 22.
42. Staff report of the Senate Select Committee to Study Governmental Operations with Respect to Intelligence Activities (Church Committee), *Covert Action in Chile, 1963–1973* (Washington: Government Printing Office, 1975), p. 15; Blum, *Killing Hope,* pp. 206–7.
43. Paul E. Sigmund, *The Overthrow of Allende and the Politics of Chile, 1964–1976* (Pittsburgh: University of Pittsburgh Press, 1977), pp. 35, 297; quoted by Blum, *Killing Hope,* p. 207.
44. Kornbluh, "Chile Coup"; Johnson, *America's Secret Power,* pp. 186, 197.
45. Blum, *Killing Hope,* p. 208.
46. Powers, "Department of Dirty Tricks"; Kornbluh, *Pinochet File,* p. 5.
47. Church Committee, *Covert Action in Chile,* p. 47; Blum, *Killing Hope,* p. 214.
48. NSSM (National Security Study Memorandum) 97, "Regarding Threats to U.S. Interests," c. August 11, 1970. See Kornbluh, *Pinochet File,* pp. 8–9.
49. Kornbluh, *Pinochet File,* chap. 1, doc. 12.
50. Ibid., p. 16.
51. Ibid., chap. 1, doc. 14.

52. Ibid., p. 30; Seymour M. Hersh, *The Price of Power: Kissinger in the Nixon White House* (New York: Summit Books, 1983), pp. 289–93.

53. Kornbluh, *Pinochet File,* p. 29.

54. Ibid., p. 113.

55. Larry Rohter, *New York Times,* "Report on Torture Forcing Chile to Rethink Its Past," *San Diego Union-Tribune,* November 28, 2004; Associated Press, "Chile Torture Victims to Get Compensated," *New York Times,* November 29, 2004; Peter Kornbluh, "Letter from Chile," *Nation,* January 31, 2005, pp. 22–24.

56. Kornbluh, *Pinochet File,* p. 324.

57. Ibid.

58. Dinges, "Pulling back the Veil."

59. See, inter alia, John Dinges and Saul Landau, *Assassination on Embassy Row* (New York: Pantheon, 1980); A. J. Langguth, *Hidden Terrors: The Truth About U.S. Police Operations in Latin America* (New York: Pantheon, 1978); John Dinges, *The Condor Years: How Pinochet and His Allies Brought Terrorism to Three Continents* (New York: New Press, 2004); Kornbluh, "CIA Outrages"; Francisco Letelier (son of Orlando Letelier), "My Case Against Pinochet," *Los Angeles Times,* December 17, 2004.

60. See, in particular, Philippe Sands, in "Pinochet in London," in *Lawless World: America and the Making and Breaking of Global Rules from FDR's Atlantic Charter to George W. Bush's Illegal War* (New York: Viking, 2005), pp. 23–45.

61. Timothy L. O'Brien and Larry Rohter, "U.S. and Others Gave Millions to Pinochet," *New York Times,* December 7, 2004; Adam Thomson, "Pinochet Stripped of Political Prestige," *Financial Times,* December 15, 2004; Kornbluh, "Letter from Chile."

62. George Crile, *Charlie Wilson's War: The Extraordinary Story of the Largest Covert Operation in History* (New York: Atlantic Monthly Press, 2003), p. 4; Johnson, *America's Secret Power,* p. 49.

63. Robert Michael Gates, *From the Shadows: The Ultimate Insider's Story of Five Presidents and How They Won the Cold War* (New York: Simon & Schuster, 1996), pp. 146–47.

64. Zbigniew Brzezinski, "Les Révélations d'un Ancien Conseiller de Carter: 'Oui, la CIA est Entrée en Afghanistan avant les Russes . . . ,' " *Le Nouvel Observateur* (Paris), January 15–21, 1998, trans. William Blum and David D. Gibbs in David D. Gibbs, "Afghanistan: The Soviet Invasion in Retrospect," *International Politics,* 37 (June 2000), pp. 233–46.

65. Quoted by Coll, *Ghost Wars,* p. 55.

66. Ibid., p. 92.

67. Ibid., pp. 93, 103–4, 112, 125.

68. Ibid., p. 60.

69. Ibid., p. 165.

70. Crile, *Charlie Wilson's War,* p. 338.

71. Quoted by Eric Konigsberg, "Washington's Sexual Awakening," *New York Magazine,* February 9, 1998.

72. Crile, *Charlie Wilson's War,* pp. 3, 12.

73. Ibid., pp. 40–42, 96.

74. Marcus Stern and Jerry Kammer, Copley News Service, "Cunningham Case:

A View into Political Pork Process," *San Diego Union-Tribune,* August 31, 2005. "Cunningham" in the title of this article refers to Randy "Duke" Cunningham, a former Republican congressman from California, who, like Wilson, was a member of both the Defense Appropriations Subcommittee and the Intelligence Oversight Committee of the House of Representatives. In 2006, Cunningham confessed to pocketing $2.4 million, the largest bribe ever paid to a member of Congress in U.S. history, and was sentenced to a long term in prison.

75. Richard Whittle and George Kuempel, *Dallas Morning News,* "Ex-lawmaker Accused of Arms Deal Kickbacks," *New Orleans Times-Picayune,* October 23, 1997; Crile, *Charlie Wilson's War,* pp. 210, 291–92, 460.

76. Quoted by Coll, *Ghost Wars,* p. 234.

77. Ibid., pp. 83–84.

78. Ibid., p. 144.

79. Ibid., p. 421.

80. Vernon Loeb, "CIA Fires Officer Over Embassy Bombing," *Washington Post,* April 9, 2000.

81. Quoted by Coll, *Ghost Wars,* pp. 394, 557.

82. Albert Bandura, "Moral Disengagement in the Perpetration of Inhumanities," *Personality and Social Psychology Review* 3, no. 3 (1999), pp. 193–209, at p. 195.

83. Quoted by Jane Mayer, "Outsourcing Torture," *New Yorker,* February 14, 2005, http://www.newyorker.com/printables/fact/050214fa_fact6.

84. See Bruce B. Campbell and Arthur D. Brenner, eds., *Death Squads in Global Perspective: Murder with Deniability* (New York: St. Martin's Press, 2000); Frederick H. Gareau, *State Terrorism and the United States: From Counterinsurgency to the War on Terrorism* (Atlanta, GA: Clarity Press, 2004).

85. See Tim Naftali, "Milan Snatch," *Slate,* June 30, 2005, http://www.slate.msn.com/toolbar.aspx?action=print&id=2121801; Congressional Record, Senate, "International Terrorism," March 15, 1989, p. S2538; U.S. Immigration and Customs Enforcement (ICE) Agency, Department of Homeland Security, "ICE Deports Terrorist Who Hijacked, Blew Up Airliner," news release, March 29, 2005.

86. Mayer, "Outsourcing Torture"; *CBS News,* "CIA Flying Suspects to Torture?" March 6, 2005, http://www.cbsnews.com/stories/2005/03/04/60minutes/main678155.shtml.

87. Ibid.

88. Dana Priest and Joe Stephens, "Secret World of U.S. Interrogation: Long History of Tactics in Overseas Prisons Is Coming to Light," *Washington Post,* May 11, 2004.

89. Douglas Jehl and David Johnston, "Rule Change Lets CIA Freely Send Suspects Abroad," *New York Times,* March 6, 2005.

90. Ibid.

91. Stephen Grey, "U.S. Accused of 'Torture Flights,' " *Times Online,* November 14, 2004, http://www.timesonline.co.uk/printFriendly/0,,1-524-1357699-524,00.html; *CBS News,* "CIA Flying Suspects to Torture?" Also see Amy Goodman's interview with Stephen Grey, "U.S. Operating Secret 'Torture Flights,' " *Democracy Now,* November 17, 2004, http://www.democracynow.org/article.pl?sid=04/11/17/1525208.

92. Ian Cobain, Stephen Grey, and Richard Norton-Taylor, "Destination Cairo: Human Rights Fears over CIA Flights," *Guardian*, September 12, 2005, http://www.guardian.co.uk/print/0,3858,5283268-105744,00.html.

93. Dan Bilefsky, "European Inquiry Says CIA Flew 1,000 Flights in Secret," *New York Times*, April 27, 2006, http://www.truthout.org/docs_2006/042706N.shtml; Jan Silva, "Probe of CIA Prisons Implicates EU Nations," Associated Press, June 7, 2006; Stephen Grey and Ian Cobain, "From Logistics to Turning a Blind Eye: Europe's Role in Terror Abductions," *Guardian*, June 7, 2006, http://www.guardian.co.uk/print/0,,329498686-110878,00.html; "Europeans 'Assisted CIA' with Abductions," *Financial Times*, June 8, 2006.

94. Quoted by Isabel Hilton, "The 800 lb Gorilla in American Foreign Policy," *Guardian*, July 28, 2004, http://www.truthout.org/docs_04/073104F.shtml.

95. Priest and Stephens, "Secret World."

96. See, inter alia, Dana Priest and Scott Higham, "At Guantánamo, a Prison Within a Prison; CIA Has Run a Secret Facility for Some Al-Qaeda Detainees, Officials Say," *Washington Post*, December 17, 2004; Dana Priest, "Long-Term Plan Sought for Terror Suspects," *Washington Post*, January 2, 2005; Priest and Stephens, "Secret World"; James Risen and Thom Shanker, "Saddam Enters Shadowy Realm of Foreign Detainees," *New York Times*, December 18, 2003; Inigo Gilmore and Robin Gedye, "Jordan 'Ghost' Jail Is Holding Senior al-Qaeda Leaders," *Telegraph* (London), October 14, 2004; *BBC News*, "Jordan Denies 'Secret U.S. Prison,'" October 14, 2004; Mayer, "Outsourcing Torture"; Jeffrey St. Clair, "The Road to Rendition: Torture Air, Incorporated," *CounterPunch*, April 9–10, 2005; Grey, "U.S. Accused of 'Torture Flights'"; Dana Priest, *Washington Post*, "CIA Holds Suspects in Secret Prisons," *San Diego Union-Tribune*, November 2, 2005; Dana Priest and Josh White, "Policies on Terrorism Suspects Come Under Fire," *Washington Post*, November 3, 2005; Editorial, "The Prison Puzzle," *New York Times*, November 3, 2005; Carlotta Gall, "Rights Group Reports Afghanistan Torture," *New York Times*, December 19, 2005; Reuters, "Poland Was Main CIA European Destination," December 9, 2005; Tom Walker and Sarah Baxter, "Revealed: The Terror Prison U.S. Is Helping Build in Morocco," *Sunday Times* (London), February 12, 2006.

97. Quoted by Adrian Levy and Cathy Scott-Clark, "[Afghanistan:] One Huge U.S. Jail," *Guardian*, March 19, 2005, http://www.guardian.co.uk/afghanistan/story/0,1284,1440836,00.html. See also Ken Silverstein, "U.S., Jordan Forge Closer Ties in Covert War on Terrorism," *Los Angeles Times*, November 11, 2005; Yossi Melman, "Jordanian Spy Agency Replaces Mossad as Key CIA Ally," *Haaretz* (Tel Aviv), November 12, 2005.

98. Mark Hosenball, "No Secrets: Eyes on the CIA," *Newsweek*, March 7, 2005, http://www.truthout.org/cgi-bin/artman/exec/view.cgi/37/9261/printer.

99. Stephen Grey, "U.S. Accused of 'Torture Flights'"; Dana Priest, "Jet Is an Open Secret in Terror War," *Washington Post*, December 27, 2004; Farah Stockman, "Terror Suspects' Torture Claims Have Mass. Link," *Boston Globe*, November 29, 2004; John Crewdson, "Mysterious Jet Tied to Torture Flights," *Chicago Tribune*, January 8, 2005. On Air America, see Alfred W. McCoy, *The Politics of Heroin: CIA Complicity in the Global Drug Trade* (Chicago:

Lawrence Hill Books, 1991); http://www.air-america.org/index.html; William M. Leary, "Supporting the 'Secret War': CIA Air Operations in Laos, 1955–1974," Central Intelligence Agency, *Studies in Intelligence,* Winter 1999–2000, http://www.cia.gov/csi/studies/winter99-00/art7.html.

100. See http://www.aahs-online.org/. Cf. Chalmers Johnson, "A Survey of Lockheed Orion History," *Journal of the American Aviation Historical Society* 1, no. 1 (June 1956), pp. 4–7; and ibid., "Thirty Years of Lockheed Vegas," 2, no. 1 (January–March 1957), pp. 1–35.

101. Priest, "Open Secret."

102. See, for example, http://www.airliners.net/; http://users.pandora.be/michel .vandaele/air1.htm; http://www.jetspotter.com/; http://www.planespotting .com/ (see also the links section on this Web site).

103. Seth Hettena, Associated Press, "Navy Secretly Contracted Jets Used by CIA," *San Francisco Chronicle,* September 24, 2005.

104. Ibid.

105. Tim Thursday, "CIA Torture Jet Sold in Attempted Cover Up," Independent Media Centre Ireland, December 9, 2004, http://www.indymedia.ie/news wire.php?story_id=67864&print_page=true; Crewdson, "Mysterious Jets."

106. Hettena, "Navy Secretly Contracted Jets."

107. Scott Shane, Stephen Grey, and Ford Fessenden, "Detainee's Suit Gains Support from Jet's Log," *New York Times,* March 30, 2005; Bob Herbert, "Torture, American Style," *New York Times,* February 11, 2005; Mayer, "Outsourcing Torture"; Hilton, "800 lb Gorilla."

108. Scott Shane, Stephen Grey, and Margot Williams, "CIA Expanding Terror Battle Under Guise of Charter Flights: Planes Owned by Shell Companies Move Suspects," *New York Times,* May 31, 2005.

109. Crewdson, "Mysterious Jets."

110. See "The Broken Promise," transcript, TV4 Monday, 17th May 2004," http://www.statewatch.org/news/2004/may/Sweden.pdf.

111. In addition to the TV4 transcript, see Grey, "U.S. Accused of Torture"; Stockman, "Torture Claims Have Mass. Link"; *CBS News,* "Flying Suspects to Torture"; Tim Reid, "Flight to Torture: Where Abuse Is Contracted Out," *Times Online,* March 26, 2005, http://www.timesonline.co.uk/printFriendly /0,,1-10889-1542390-10889,00.html; and Cobain, Grey, and Norton-Taylor, "Destination Cairo."

112. See Tom Engelhardt, "The CIA's La Dolce Vita War on Terror," TomDispatch .com, July 21, 2005, http://www.tomdispatch.com/indexprint.mhtml/?pid =7789.

113. Aidan Lewis, "Italy Judge Orders Arrest of 13 CIA Agents," Associated Press, June 24, 2005; Barbara McMahon, "Italians Hunt Covert CIA Snatch Squad," *Observer,* June 26, 2005; "European Warrant Issued for Arrest of CIA Agents," *Corriere della Serra* (Italy), June 27, 2005; Victor L. Simpson, "Italians Discuss Purported CIA Case," Associated Press, July 28, 2005; Simpson, "Italy to Seek Extradition of CIA Agents," Associated Press, June 28, 2005; John Crewdson and Alessandra Maggiorani, "Prosecutors in Italy File Request to Extradite 22 CIA Operatives," *Chicago Tribune,* November 10, 2005.

114. Craig Whitlock, "Europeans Investigate CIA Role in Abductions," *Washington Post,* March 13, 2005; John Crewdson and Tom Hundley, "Abducted Imam Aided CIA Ally," *Chicago Tribune,* July 3, 3005.

115. Daniel Williams, "Italy Probes Agency's Link to CIA in Cleric's Abduction," *Washington Post,* May 12, 2006.

116. Crewdson and Hundley, "Abducted Imam"; "Italy Asks U.S. to Explain CIA's Role in Kidnapping," *Bloomberg News,* June 30, 2005. Because of the involvement of Ramstein Air Base, the Germans are also investigating this abduction: "Deutsche Justiz ermittelt gegen US-Geheimdienst," *Spiegel Online,* November 12, 2005, http://www.spiegel.de/politik/deutschland/0,1518,384681,00.html.

117. Craig Whitlock, "Italians Detail Lavish CIA Operation," *Washington Post,* June 26, 2005; Tracy Wilkinson, "CIA Said to Leave Trail in Abduction," *Los Angeles Times,* June 26, 2005.

118. Simpson, "CIA Case"; "European Warrant," *Corriere della Serra.*

119. Tim Weiner, "Langley, We Have a Problem," *New York Times,* May 14, 2006.

120. Thomas Powers, "Spy vs. Spy," *New York Times,* May 10, 2006.

121. Quoted by Weiner, "Langley."

4: U.S. MILITARY BASES IN OTHER PEOPLE'S COUNTRIES

1. George Cahlink, "Pentagon Certifies Need for Base Closures," *Government Executive Magazine,* March 23, 2004.

2. See Laurence M. Vance, "The Problem with BRAC," LewRockwell.com, September 17, 2005.

3. See maps of the Roman and British Empires in "The Next American Empire," *Economist,* March 18, 2004.

4. Department of Defense, Office of the Deputy Undersecretary of Defense (Installations and Environment), *Base Structure Report,* Fiscal Year 2005, p. DOD–78.

5. Amy Holmes, "The Bases of Empire: The Impact of U.S. Military Installations on Germany and Turkey," Institute for Global Studies, Johns Hopkins University, February 19, 2004, pp. 7, 17–18.

6. Arkin, *Code Names,* pp. 6–7.

7. "Enough Time for Iraq to Implement UN Resolutions—[Foreign Minister Marwan] Muasher," *Jordan Times,* August 11, 2002; and Arkin, *Code Names,* pp. 4, 10.

8. Mark Sappenfield and Patrik Jonsson, "As Military Realigns Bases, the South Wins," *Christian Science Monitor,* May 16, 2005.

9. William M. Arkin, "War Plans Meaner, Not Leaner," *Los Angeles Times,* March 21, 2004.

10. Martin Sieff, "Analysis: Bush Pushes Global Force Reform," United Press International, November 25, 2003; Alan Bock, "Repositioning on the Titanic," Antiwar.com, August 20, 2004; David Isenberg, "Reshaping Washington's Global Footprint," *Asia Times,* August 20, 2004, http://www.atimes.com/atimes/Front_Page/FH20Aa01.html.

11. The White House, "President Speaks at Veterans of Foreign Wars Convention," http://www.whitehouse.gov/news/releases/2004/08/20040816-12.html.

dley Graham, "Commanders Plan Eventual Consolidation of U.S. Bases raq," *Washington Post*, May 22, 2005.
ristine Spolar, "14 'Enduring Bases' Set in Iraq," *Chicago Tribune*, March , 2004.
aham, "Eventual Consolidation."
ommission on Review of Overseas Military Facility Structure, *Report*, G13.
ee Engelhardt, "Bases, Bases Everywhere."
ee Global Security's Web site, http://www.globalsecurity.org/military/ acility/ iraq.htm, and http://www.globalsecurity.org/military/facility/ raq-intro.htm.
See Ariana Eunjung Cha, "Baghdad's U.S. Zone a Stand-In for Home," *Washington Post*, December 6, 2003.
Chris Hughes, "Exclusive: Billion Dollar Bunker," Mirror.co.uk, January 3, 2006, http://www.mirror.co.uk/printable_version.cfm?objectid=16541084& siteid=94762; Barbara Slavin, "Giant U.S. Embassy Rising in Baghdad," *USA Today*, April 19, 2006; Kevin Zeese, "They're Staying in Iraq," Antiwar.com, April 22, 2006; Charles J. Hanley, Associated Press, "Officials Mum on Huge U.S. Embassy," *Washington Times*, April 23, 2006, http://www .washington times.com/world/20060423-122454-5409r.htm; Daniel McGrory, "In the Chaos of Iraq, One Project Is on Target: A Giant U.S. Embassy," *London Times*, May 3, 2006, http://www.commondreams.org/cgi-bin/print .cgi?file=/ headlines06/0503-05.htm; Liz Sly, *Chicago Tribune*, "As Lavish U.S. Embassy Rises in Baghdad, Many Hard-up Iraqis Are Irked," *Arizona Star*, May 29, 2006.
6. Thom Shanker, "U.S. Retools Hussein Pleasure Palace as Camp Victory," *New York Times*, June 12, 2004.
57. See Hammer, "Digging In."
68. David R. Francis, "U.S. Bases in Iraq: Sticky Politics, Hard Math," *Christian Science Monitor*, September 30, 2004.
69. Global Security Organization, "Balad Air Base, Camp Anaconda," http:// www.globalsecurity.org/military/world/iraq/balad-ab.htm; Schmitt, "Pentagon Construction Boom"; Thomas E. Ricks, "Biggest Base in Iraq Has Small-Town Feel," *Washington Post*, February 4, 2006; Becky Branford, "Iraq Bases Spur Questions over U.S. Plans," *BBC News*, March 30, 2006; "U.S. Forces Planning for the Long Haul in Iraq," *Hindustan Times*, April 24, 2006.
70. Steve Liewer, "1st ID Readying New Iraq HQ," *Stars & Stripes*, November 10, 2004; Charles Aldinger, "U.S. Forces Leave Some Bases in North Iraq: General," Reuters, October 28, 2005; David Axe, "Seabees Buzz in to Build Up Bases," *Washington Times*, February 3, 2006.
71. Graham, "Eventual Consolidation."
72. See Brian Loveman, ed., *Addicted to Failure: U.S. Security Policy in Latin America and the Andean Region* (Boulder, CO: Rowman & Littlefield, 2006); and Greg Grandin, *Empire's Workshop: Latin America, the United States, and the Rise of the New Imperialism* (New York: Metropolitan Books, 2006).
73. Humberto Márquez, "Dutch Islands Caught Up in U.S.-Venezuela Friction," Antiwar.com, April 6, 2006.
74. John Lindsay-Poland, "U.S. Military Bases in Latin America and the Caribbean," *Foreign Policy in Focus, Policy Brief* 9, no. 3 (August 2004).

12. See Douglas J. Feith, Undersecretary of Defense for Policy, Department of Defense, *Strengthening U.S. Global Defense Posture*, Report to Congress, September 2004, http://www.defensecommunities.org/ResourceCenter/ Global_Posture.pdf.
13. "Pentagon to Close 35 Percent of Overseas Bases; 'Forward Operating Sites' to Replace Cold War-era Bases," Associated Press, September 23, 2004.
14. Jan Erickson and Leonard Tengco, "Congress Endangers Military Women's Health with Ban," National Organization for Women, May 28, 2003, http:// www.now.org/issues/military/052803ban.html?printable; Johnson, *Sorrows of Empire*, pp. 105–6.
15. Diana B. Henriques, "Temptation Near for Military's Problem Gamblers," *New York Times*, October 19, 2005.
16. Quoted by Michael T. Klare, "Imperial Reach: The Pentagon's New Basing Strategy," *Nation*, April 25, 2005, pp. 13–14.
17. Mark Mazzetti, "Pax Americana: Dispatched to Distant Outposts, U.S. Forces Confront the Perils of an Unruly World," *U.S. News & World Report*, October 6, 2003. Also see Eric Schmitt, "Pentagon Seeking New Access Pacts for Africa Bases," *New York Times*, July 5, 2003.
18. Commission on Review of Overseas Military Facility Structure, *Report to President and Congress*, Washington, DC, May 9, 2005, http://www.fas.org/ irp/agency/dod/obc.pdf, p. 7.
19. Edward Harris, Associated Press, "U.S. Green Berets Train Mali Troops to Guard Desert Interior Against Terrorists, Bandits," *San Francisco Chronicle*, March 17, 2004; Martin Plaut, "U.S. to Increase African Military Presence," *BBC News*, March 23, 2004; Michael Peel, "U.S. Urged to Turn Attention to Oil-Rich States in Africa," *Financial Times*, April 1, 2004.
20. Pepe Escobar, "The Algerian Connection," *Asia Times*, July 29, 2005; Commission on Review of Overseas Military Facility Structure, *Report*, pp. F11, F12, H11.
21. Vernon Loeb, "New Bases Reflect Shift in Military," *Washington Post*, June 9, 2003.
22. Mark Sappenfield, "Pentagon Stirs Tensions in Foreign Base Shuffle," *Christian Science Monitor*, August 1, 2005, http://www.csmonitor.com/2005/0801/ p02s01-usmi.htm.
23. Thomas Donnelly and Vance Serchuk, "Toward a Global Cavalry: Overseas Rebasing and Defense Transformation," *AEI National Security Outlook*, July 1, 2003, http://www.aei.org/include/pub_print.asp?pubID=17783.
24. David Morris, "Senators Seek to Shutter Overseas Military Bases," GovExec.com, April 29, 2003; Office of Senator Dianne Feinstein, "Senators Hutchison and Feinstein Introduce Legislation Creating an Overseas Military Base Commission," April 29, 2003; "S. 949, The Overseas Military Facility Structure Review Act," *Congressional Record* (April 29, 2003), p. S5495; Office of Senator Tim Johnson (Democrat from South Dakota), "Johnson Urges Study of Overseas Military Bases," May 2, 2003.
25. Commission on Review of Overseas Military Facility Structure, *Report*, p. M9.
26. Ibid., p. M7.
27. Ibid., p. M2.
28. Ibid.; Robert Burns, Associated Press, "Panel Urges Slow Return of Troops to Bases," *San Francisco Chronicle*, May 9, 2005.

29. William Pfaff, "U.S. Military Abroad: More Bases Won't Curb Terrorism,"
    International Herald Tribune, August 2, 2003.

30. Tom Engelhardt, "Bases, Bases Everywhere," TomDispatch.com, June 1, 2005,
    p. 4, http://www.tomdispatch.com/indexprint.mhtml?pid=3025; James
    Sterngold, "After 9/11, U.S. Policy Built on World Bases," *San Francisco
    Chronicle,* March 21, 2004.

31. Robin Wright and Ann Scott Tyson, "U.S. Evicted from Air Base in Uzbek-
    istan," *Washington Post,* July 30, 2005.

32. Raymond Whitaker, "A UK Diplomat Says Britain Is Part of a Worldwide
    Torture Plot," *Independent,* February 20, 2005; Grey, "U.S. Accused of
    'Torture Flights'"; Lutz Kleveman, "The New Great Game," *Guardian,*
    October 20, 2003; Will Dunham, "Pentagon Set to Pay Uzbekistan for Use
    of Air Base," Reuters, September 20, 2005.

33. See Christian Deitch (a former Peace Corps volunteer in Kyrgyzstan),
    "Kyrgyzstan: Democracy Stalled?" *Bulletin of the Atomic Scientists,* January–
    February 2005, pp. 16–17, 72; Justin Burke, "Kyrgyzstan Revolution: Be
    Careful What You Wish For," EurasiaNet, March 25, 2005; Ariel Cohen,
    "Kyrgyzstan's Tulip Revolution," *Washington Times,* March 27, 2005; Andrea
    Peters, "U.S. Money and Personnel Behind Kyrgyzstan's 'Tulip Revolution,'"
    World Socialist Web site, March 25, 2005; Simon Forrester, "Political Change
    in Kyrgyzstan," INTRAC: International NGO Training and Research Centre,
    April 25, 2005 (the writer is a member of the INTRAC Representative Office
    in Bishkek, the capital of Kyrgyzstan); Martin Sieff, United Press Interna-
    tional, "U.S. Bases Face Flak," *Washington Times,* July 16, 2005.

34. Ann Scott Tyson and Robin Wright, "Crackdown Muddies U.S.-Uzbek Rela-
    tions," *Washington Post,* June 4, 2005; "Uzbekistan Restricts U.S. Military's
    Use of Air Base," Agence France-Presse, June 15, 2005; Vince Crawley,
    "Uzbekistan Sets January Deadline for Withdrawal from Base," *Air Force
    Times,* August 1, 2005; "U.S. Confirms Uzbek Base Departure," *BBC News,*
    September 27, 2005; Will Dunham, "U.S. Pulls Out of Uzbekistan Base After
    Eviction," Reuters, November 21, 2005.

35. Bruce Pannier, "Kyrgyzstan: Bishkek Presents New Air-Base Terms to U.S.-
    Led Coalition," Radio Free Europe/Radio Liberty, January 25, 2006; "Kyr-
    gyzstan Reportedly Wins Massive Rent Hike for U.S. Base," Radio Free
    Europe/Radio Liberty, February 15, 2006; Isabel Gorst, "U.S. Facility Faces
    Eviction from Kyrgyzstan," *Financial Times,* May 19, 2006; "Kyrgyzstan:
    Negotiations Over U.S. Base End Inconclusively," Radio Free Europe/Radio
    Liberty, June 1, 2006.

36. Stephen Graham, "U.S. Army to Leave 13 Bases in Germany," Associated
    Press, July 29, 2005. See also Steve Liewer, "Building Continues as if the U.S.
    Is Staying in Germany: Army Spending Millions to Upgrade Bases Bound for
    German Hands," *Stars & Stripes,* September 6, 2005.

37. Commission on Review of Overseas Military Facility Structure, *Report,*
    pp. F7, F8.

38. Bertrand Benoit, "U.S. Bases Undermine Sovereignty, Says Lafontaine,"
    Financial Times, August 29, 2005.

39. "Last Spanish Combat Troops Leave Iraq," *MSNBC,* April 27, 2004, http://
    www.msnbc.msn.com/id/4845463/; Michael R. Gordon, "A Pentagon Plan
    to Sharply Cut G.I.'s in Germany," *New York Times,* June 4, 2004.

40. Tracy Wilkinson, "Sardinia Says It's Time for the
    Los Angeles Times, July 17, 2005; Brian Wingfield,
    That Aids Nuclear Subs," *New York Times,* Novemb

41. Kent Harris, "Life Isn't Just Sun and Sand for Soldie
    Italy," *Stars & Stripes,* May 12, 2002; Richard Owen,
    Discovery of Huge U.S. Munitions Base," *Times Onli*
    "Anti-War Protesters Block U.S. Military Train in Ital
    Presse, February 23, 2003; "Italian Protests Block Arm
    February 24, 2003.

42. Liza Porteus, "Pentagon Ponders Overseas Military Shi
    2003; Associated Press, "U.S. to Take Over Bases in Rom
    December 6, 2005.

43. Steve Liewer, "Plans Slow for Base Closures in Europe,"
    December 8, 2003; Oana Lungescu, "U.S. Briefs Allies on
    BBC News, December 8, 2003; William J. Kole, Associated
    Base Focus of Secret Prison Probe," *Guardian,* November

44. Holmes, "Bases of Empire," p. 9.

45. Judy Dempsey, "U.S. Rejects German Calls to Withdraw Nu
    New York Times, May 3, 2005.

46. For details on the Echelon espionage network, see Johnson,
    Empire, pp. 165–67. See also Holmes, "Bases of Empire."

47. Mark Landler, "After 60 Years, the Yanks Fly Out, Leaving Jus
    New York Times, October 21, 2005. See also Jim McDonald, A:
    "U.S. Hands Historic Rhein-Main Air Base to Germany after
    Diego Union-Tribune, October 11, 2005.

48. See, in particular, Office of the Undersecretary of Defense for A
    Technology, and Logistics, *Report of the Defense Science Board T
    Strategic Communication* (Washington, D.C.: September 2004).

49. Peter J. Katzenstein, *A World of Regions: Asia and Europe in the A
    Imperium* (Ithaca, NY: Cornell University Press, 2005), pp. 3, 246-

50. Ibid., p. 245.

51. Karen Kwiatkowski, "Our Inscrutable Iraq Policy: Why We Did It,
    to Do Now, and What Happens Next," LewRockwell.com, October
    p. 3.

52. Joshua Hammer, "Digging In: If the U.S. Government Doesn't Plan
    Occupy Iraq for Any Longer than Necessary, Why Is It Spending Bill
    Dollars to Build 'Enduring' Bases?'" *Mother Jones,* March–April 2005

53. Commission on Review of Overseas Military Facility Structure, *Repor*
    p. G7.

54. Quoted by Bradley Graham, "Iraq, Afghan Commitments Fuel U.S. A
    Construction," *Washington Post,* September 17, 2005. See also Tom Eng
    hardt, "Can You Say 'Permanent Bases'? The American Press Can't," Ton
    Dispatch.com, February 14, 2006, http://www.tomdispatch.com/index
    .mhtml?pid=59774.

55. Quoted by Sam Graham-Felsen, "Operation: Enduring Presence," AlterN
    July 28, 2005, http://www.alternet.org/module/printversion/23755.

56. Eric Schmitt, "Pentagon Construction Boom Beefs Up Mideast Air Bases,"
    New York Times, September 18, 2005.

57. Hammer, "Digging In."

58. Bra
    in

59. Ch
    23

60. G

61. C
    p

62. S

63. S
    f

64.

65.

75. Mary Donohue and Melissa Nepomiachi, "Washington Secures Long-Sought Hemispheric Outpost, Perhaps at the Expense of Regional Sovereignty," Council on Hemispheric Affairs, July 20, 2005.

76. Michael Flynn, "What's the Deal at Manta?," *Bulletin of the Atomic Scientists,* January–February 2005, pp. 23–29.

77. On private military companies, see Johnson, *Sorrows of Empire,* pp. 140–49.

78. Lindsay-Poland, "U.S. Military Bases."

79. Larry Luxner and Douglas Engle, "The Arabs of Brazil," *Saudi Aramco World,* September–October 2005, pp. 18–23.

80. *CIA Factbook,* s.v. Paraguay, http://www.odci.gov/cia/publications/factbook/geos/pa.html.

81. Jeffrey Goldberg, "In the Party of God: Hezbollah Sets Up Operations in South America and the United States," *New Yorker,* October 28, 2002, http://www.newyorker.com/printables/fact/021028fa_fact2.

82. Ibid.; Jessica Stern, "The Protean Enemy," *Foreign Affairs,* July–August 2003.

83. Quoted by Goldberg, "Party of God."

84. Letter from Ambassador Rubens Barbosa, "Triborder Dispute," *Foreign Affairs,* January–February 2004. Also see Kenneth Rapoza, "The New Fakers: State Department Undercuts the *New Yorker*'s Jeffrey Goldberg," *Counterpunch,* May 14, 2003.

85. Quoted by Kenneth Rapoza, "U.S. Inroads into South America Raise Alarm," *Washington Times,* October 25, 2005.

86. Charlotte Elmer, "Spotlight on U.S. Troops in Paraguay," *BBC News,* September 28, 2005; Kelly Hearn "U.S. Military Presence in Paraguay Irks Neighbors," *Christian Science Monitor,* December 2, 2005.

87. Alejandro Sciscioli, "U.S. Military Presence in Paraguay Stirs Speculation," Antiwar.com, August 4, 2005.

88. Benjamin Dangl, "What Is the U.S. Military Doing in Paraguay?" Information Clearing House, August 4, 2005; Rapoza, "U.S. Inroads."

89. Kevin Gray, Reuters, "Paraguayans Uneasy over U.S. Presence," *San Diego Union-Tribune,* September 27, 2005.

90. Quoted by Sciscioli, "U.S. Military Presence."

91. Dangl, "U.S. Military."

92. Marcela Valente, "Presence of U.S. Troops Upsets Paraguay's Partners," Antiwar.com, August 9, 2005.

93. "Mexico Ratifies War Crimes Tribunal Treaty," Associated Press, October 28, 2005; "4 Nations that Won't Sign Deal with U.S. Risk Aid Loss," *Miami Herald,* December 18, 2004. See also Razl Zibechi, "The Installation of a U.S. Military Base in Paraguay: A Wedge in Mercosur," Agencia Latinoamericana de Informacion (ALAI), November 29, 2005, http://www.globalresearch.ca/index.php?context=viewArticle&code=ZIB20051129&articleId=1363.

5: HOW AMERICAN IMPERIALISM ACTUALLY WORKS: THE SOFA IN JAPAN

1. For the text of the Japan-U.S. Security Treaty, see U.S. Forces Japan, http://usfj.mil/references/treaty1.html.

2. The Japan SOFA can be found at http://www.niraikanai.wwma.net/pages/archive/sofa.html. Most publicly disclosed SOFAs, including the SOFA with the Republic of Korea (July 1966), are available in *United States Treaties and*

Other Agreements (arranged by Treaties and Other International Acts Series [TIAS] Number) (Washington, DC: Department of State, Distributed by the Superintendent of Documents, Government Printing Office, annual), s.v. "TIAS 6127."

3. T. D. Flack, "South Korea Refusing Return of U.S. Bases 'As-Is'; General Bell: New Standards Exceed SOFA Agreements," *Stars & Stripes,* June 7, 2006, http://stripes.com/articleprint.asp?section=104&article=37688.

4. "Kadena Noise Pollution Suit Stirs Up Residents in Atsugi, Yokota," *Asahi Shimbun* (Tokyo), February 18, 2005; "U.S. Military Fails to Pay Compensation Despite SOFA's '75%' Clause; Ignores Requests for Payment," *Tokyo Shimbun,* February 18, 2005 (Tokyo press reports are in Japanese).

5. Keiichi Inamine, "The Anger of Okinawa Residents Is Magma Ready to Explode," *Ronza,* October 2003.

6. Wikipedia, "Girard Incident," http://en.wikipedia.org/wiki/Girard_Incident.

7. "The Presidential Papers of Dwight David Eisenhower, Letter to Dorothy Girard," June 13, 1957, http://eisenhowermemorial.org/presidential-papers/second-term/documents/200.cfm; "The Girard Case," *Time,* July 22, 1957, http://time-proxy.yaga.com/time/archive/printout/0,23657,862596,00.html.

8. See, for example, the case of Lieutenant Colonel Martha McSally, the highest-ranking female pilot in the air force, who took the Defense Department to court for requiring her to wear an *abaya*—the total body covering devout Saudi women put on in public—when off base in Saudi Arabia. She claimed this was an unconstitutional infringement on her rights, and she won. See Johnson, *Sorrows of Empire,* p. 241.

9. Quoted in "Girard Case," *Time.*

10. "Only the Removal of U.S. Bases Can Ensure the End of U.S. Military Crimes," *Japan Press Weekly,* July 18, 2005, http://www.politicalaffairs.net/article/view/1506/1/109?PrintableVersion=enabled.

11. Wikipedia, "Status of Forces Agreement," http://en.wikipedia.org/wiki/Status_of_forces_agreement.

12. "Girard Case," *Time.*

13. U. S. Department of State, "Backgrounder: Status of Forces Agreements," April 12, 1996, http://194.90.114.5/publish/press/security/archive/april/ds2_4-15.htm.

14. William Arkin, "U.S. Air Bases Forge Double-Edged Sword," *Los Angeles Times,* January 6, 2002.

15. There are so many military bases in Japan and in Okinawa, the total numbers are open to dispute. According to the Pentagon's 2005 *Base Structure Report,* there are 111 installations in Japan as a whole and 39 in Okinawa prefecture. These numbers are surely accurate, but there are anomalies—for example, the *Base Structure Report* includes Futenma Air Base under Camp Smedley D. Butler, one of the Marine Corps' key bases on the island, along with 15 other sites. I have chosen to use the conservative count of 88 bases for Japan as a whole and 37 for Okinawa based on the careful calculations in *Mainichi Shimbun,* August 6, 2004, eve. ed; *Tokyo Shimbun,* October 15, 2005; and Kelly Dietz, Ph.D. candidate, sociology, Cornell University, and the Futenma-Henoko Action Network, "Okinawa Update," October 2005.

16. Global Security Organization, "U.S. Forces, Japan," www.globalsecurity.org/

military/agency/dod/usfj.htm; Thom Shanker, "Okinawans Ask Rumsfeld to Thin Out Troops," *New York Times,* November 17, 2003; U.S. Department of Defense, Washington Headquarters Services, Directorate for Information, Operations, and Reports, *Worldwide Manpower Distribution by Geographical Area,* September 30, 2004, http://web1.whs.osd.mil/DIORCAT.HTM#M05.

17. Toshiya Hoshino (Osaka University) and Takashi Nawakami (Takushoku University), "Future of U.S. Bases in Japan and Force Transformation in Okinawa," *Sekai Shuho,* April 26, 2005.

18. See U.S. Forces, Japan, "Agreed Minutes to the Agreement Under Article VI of the Treaty of Mutual Cooperation and Security Between Japan and the United States of America, Regarding Facilities and Areas and the Status of United States Armed Forces in Japan," http://usfj.mil/references/sofa.html.

19. See Chalmers Johnson, ed., *Okinawa: Cold War Island* (Cardiff, CA: Japan Policy Research Institute, 1999); and Johnson, *Blowback,* chap. 2.

20. On these issues, see Shigemitsu Dando, *Japanese Criminal Procedure,* trans. B. J. George Jr. (South Hackensack, NJ: Fred B. Rothman & Co., 1965); Chalmers Johnson, *Conspiracy at Matsukawa* (Berkeley: University of California Press, 1972); David T. Johnson, *The Japanese Way of Justice: Prosecuting Crime in Japan* (New York: Oxford University Press, 2002).

21. Thom Shanker, "U.S. and Japan Discuss Transfer of American Rape Suspect," *New York Times,* July 6, 2001.

22. "Inamine Meets Rumsfeld: Perception Gap Not Closed Despite Direct Appeal on Base Issues," *Asahi Shimbun,* November 17, 2003.

23. "Okinawa Governor Urges Rumsfeld to Reduce U.S. Bases," *Japan Today,* November 20, 2003, http://www.japantoday.com/e/?content=news&id= 279127; Shanker, "Thin Out Troops."

24. David Allen, "Friend of Accused Testifies in Rape Trial on Okinawa," *Stars & Stripes,* November 10, 2001.

25. "Japanese Parliament Panel Seeks Review of U.S. Forces Pact," Agence France-Presse, July 10, 2001.

26. Shanker, "U.S. and Japan Discuss Transfer."

27. Sheila K. Johnson, "Another Okinawa Outrage," *Los Angeles Times,* July 8, 2001; and Johnson, "Blame Misplaced in Okinawa Rape Case," *Japan Times,* August 2, 2001.

28. "Airman Gets 32 Months for Rape in Okinawa," *Japan Times,* March 29, 2002; Howard W. French, "Airman's Rape Conviction Fans Okinawa's Ire Over U.S. Bases," *New York Times,* March 29, 2002; Komako Akai, "Woodland Convicted of Rape, Sentenced to 32 Months in Japanese Prison," *Stars & Stripes,* March 28, 2002.

29. "Attempted Rape Incident in Okinawa: U.S. Military Suspect's Statement: 'I Was Seduced,'" *Tokyo Shimbun,* December 9, 2002; Ministry of Foreign Affairs, "Statement by Minister for Foreign Affairs Yoriko Kawaguchi Concerning Charges Against a U.S. Marine Major of Attempted Rape," December 3, 2002, http://www.mofa.go.jp/announce/announce/2002/1203.html; "U.S. Officer Named in Rape Bid on Filipina in Japan," Agence France-Presse, December 5, 2002; "U.S. Suspect in Rape Case 'Intoxicated,'" Kyodo, December 8, 2002; and "Criminal Case Involves Officer," *Okinawa Times Weekly,* December 7, 2002.

30. "USMC Major Charged with Attempted Rape in Okinawa," *Asahi Shimbun,* December 4, 2002; Elaine Lies, "Japan Calls for Crackdown on U.S. Military Crime," Reuters, December 4, 2002.

31. Teruaki Ueno, "U.S. Refuses to Hand Over Marine in Japan Rape Case," Reuters, December 5, 2002; "Attempted Rape in Okinawa: U.S. Refuses to Turn Over Suspected U.S. Serviceman," *Asahi Shimbun,* December 6, 2002.

32. "Police Raid Home of Accused Marine," Associated Press, December 7, 2002.

33. "MOFA [Ministry of Foreign Affairs] Expresses Regret to U.S. Envoy," *Asahi Shimbun,* December 4, 2002; "Foreign Minister Kawaguchi to Ask for Improvement in SOFA Operation to Allow Handing Over of U.S. Military Personnel Even in 'Attempted' [Rape] Incidents," *Mainichi Shimbun,* December 6, 2002; "Attempted Rape in Okinawa: Prime Minister Says Pre-indictment Turnover of Suspect Unnecessary," *Yomiuri Shimbun,* December 7, 2002; "Japan Won't Press for Marine Rape Suspect," *Japan Times,* December 7, 2002; "U.S. Rejection of the Handover of U.S. Marine Major Exposes U.S. Upper Hand Regarding SOFA; Japan Must Conduct National Debate by Taking Okinawa's Voice to Heart," *Yomiuri Shimbun,* December 17, 2002.

34. "Japanese Court Seeks Arrest of U. S. Marine," Associated Press, December 3, 2002; "Japan Protests Over Alleged Rape Attempt," Agence France-Presse, December 3, 2002; "Okinawa Prefectural Assembly Adopts Resolution Protesting U.S. Refusal to Hand Over Marine Corps Major," *Asahi Shimbun,* December 11, 2002; "Governors Call for Revision to SOFA," *Japan Times,* February 13, 2003.

35. "Japan Prosecutors Indict U.S. Marine on Rape Attempt," Reuters, December 19, 2002; "Marine Handed Over to Local Authorities over Attempted Rape," *Nihon Keizai Shimbun,* December 20, 2002.

36. The text of the petition is available at http://www2.gol.com/users/coynerhm/maj_michael_j_brown_v_usa.htm. It was filed in Washington, D.C., on the logic that George W. Bush is the petitioner's commander in chief and he resides in Washington.

37. "Free Major Brown" Web site, http://www.majorbrown.org/major_brown.htm. As of June 2006, his Web site had disappeared from the Internet.

38. "U.S. Serviceman's Attempted Rape Case in Okinawa: Victim Testifies in Court, 'I Wanted to Withdraw My Complaint,'" *Nihon Keizai Shimbun,* May 14, 2003.

39. "U.S. Marine Accused of Attempted Rape Is Granted Bail," Kyodo, May 17, 2003; Hiroshi Matsubara, "Detention Process Questioned," *Japan Times,* September 21, 2001.

40. David Allen, "Japanese Court Dismisses Motion to Disqualify Panel in Brown Case," *Stars & Stripes,* October 23, 2003; Allen, "Japan's High Court Rejects Brown Appeal," *Stars & Stripes,* November 16, 2003.

41. "Judicial Friction Seen over SOFA: USMC Major Consistently Asserts Innocence in Attempted Rape," *Asahi Shimbun,* July 16, 2003.

42. "Marine in Okinawa Gets Suspended Sentence for Attempted Molestation," Kyodo, July 9, 2004; David Allen, "Brown Convicted of 'Attempted Indecent' Act," *Stars & Stripes,* July 10, 2004.

43. David Allen, "Convicted on Okinawa, Marine Brown in Trouble in States," *Stars & Stripes,* October 9, 2005; "Marine Acquitted of Attempted Rape in Okinawa Arrested in U.S. on Abduction Charge," *Japan Today,* October 9,

2005, http://www.japantoday.com/e/tools/print.asp?content=news&id=
351579; Curtis Johnson, "Kidnapping Defendant Due Back this Week,"
Herald-Dispatch (Huntington, West Virginia), October 19, 2005; "Accused
Kidnapper in Court," WTRF-TV, October 20, 2005, http://www.wtrf.com/
story.cfm?func=viewstory&storyid=6049&catid=43; Curtis Johnson,
"Kidnapping Suspect Returns," *Herald-Dispatch*, October 21, 2005; Johnson,
"$75,000 Bond Set in Kidnapping Case," *Herald-Dispatch*, November 1,
2005; David Allen, "Brown Free on $75,000 Bond; Banned from W. Virginia
until Hearing," *Stars & Stripes*, November 10, 2005.

44. "Endless Crimes Involving U.S. Servicemen Fuel Fear in Okinawa," *Asahi
Shimbun*, June 17, 2003.

45. "U.S. Marine Held in New Okinawa Rape Case," *CNN.com.*, June 12, 2003;
"Okinawa Prefectural Police Questioning U.S. Marine on Voluntary Basis on
Charges of Assaulting 19-year-old Woman," *Nihon Keizai Shimbun*, June 12,
2003; "U.S. Serviceman Questioned in Okinawa on Charge of Rape Amid
Loud Calls for 'Review of SOFA,' " *Tokyo Shimbun*, June 13, 2003; "U.S.
Envoy Expresses Regret," *Asahi Shimbun*, June 13, 2003; Mark Oliva, "Oki-
nawa Police Continue to Investigate Marine," *Stars & Stripes*, June 15, 2003;
Saikazu Nakamura, "Sexual Assault Incident in Okinawa: Arrest Warrant for
U.S. Serviceman Issued," *Mainichi Shimbun*, June 16, 2003, eve. ed.; Ministry
of Foreign Affairs, "Statement by Minister for Foreign Affairs Yoriko
Kawaguchi Concerning Alleged Rape Resulting in Injury Committed by
a U.S. Marine Lance Corporal," June 16, 2003, http://www.mofa.go.jp/
announce/announce/2003/6/0616.html; "Government Asks U.S. at Joint
Committee to Turn Over U.S. Marine Rape Suspect to Japan Before Indictment," *Nihon Keizai Shimbun*, June 17, 2003; "U.S. Marine Rape Incident:
Chief Cabinet Secretary Asks U.S. Ambassador to Turn the Suspect Over
to Japanese Side," *Asahi Shimbun*, June 18, 2003; "Marine Sentenced to Jail
for Rape," Reuters, September 14, 2003.

46. "Drunk U.S. Base Worker Kills Man in Okinawa Car Crash," *Mainichi Daily
News*, March 17, 2003; David Allen and Chiyomi Sumida, "Two Americans
in Custody After Incidents on Okinawa," *Stars & Stripes*, May 7, 2003; "Five
U.S. Marines Arrested over Series of Incidents in Okinawa," *Tokyo Shimbun*,
June 1, 2003. On the history of Koza, see Okinawa-shi Heiwa Bunka Shinko-
ka, ed., *Koza: Hito, Machi, Koto* [*Koza: People, Town, Events*] (Okinawa-shi:
Okinawa-shi Yakusho, 1997).

47. "Governor Inamine's Nationwide Pilgrimage to Form Alliance to Force
Central Government to Move on Revision of the Japan-U.S. Status of
Forces Agreement," *Asahi Shimbun*, June 14, 2003; "Inamine Asks Ishihara
for Cooperation on SOFA Revision," *Tokyo Shimbun*, June 14, 2003.

48. "SOFA: U.S. Hints at Refusing Suspect Turnover," *Asahi Shimbun*, July 3, 2003.

49. "Judicial Friction Seen over SOFA," *Asahi Shimbun*, July 16, 2003.

50. "Talks on SOFA Legal Procedures," *Sankei Shimbun*, July 4, 2003; Yoichi
Toyota, "SOFA Talks: Japan, U.S. Confront over Official Presence at Police
Questioning of U.S. Military Suspects," *Tokyo Shimbun*, July 12, 2003.

51. Editorial, "SOFA Revision Needed After All," *Asahi Shimbun*, June 20, 2003;
"SOFA Talks to Focus on Interpreter, Lawyer; U.S. Stresses Human Rights in
New Rules," *Asahi Shimbun*, June 20, 2003; "Japan, U.S. Meet over GI Justice,"
Christian Science Monitor, June 30, 2003; David Allen and Chiyomi Sumida,

"Japanese Leaders Want Comfier SOFA," *Stars & Stripes,* July 21, 2003; Hiroyuki Sato, "SOFA Talks: Japan-U.S. Views Remain at Odds," *Asahi Shimbun,* July 26, 2003; "SOFA: Government to Allow U.S. Officials to Be Present During Questioning of U.S. Suspects by Japanese Police," *Sankei Shimbun,* July 30, 2003; Taro Kono (Liberal Democratic Party member of the House of Representatives), "If the U.S. Is Asking More of Japan, Will the U.S. Tread More Lightly in Turn?" *Christian Science Monitor,* August 1, 2003; "U.S., Japan Disagree on Justice for Troops," Reuters, August 1, 2003; "Inability to Reach Agreement on SOFA Assurances Will Affect the Japan-U.S. Alliance," *Nihon Keizai Shimbun,* August 3, 2003.

52. Robert Burns, "Rumsfeld Holds Range of Talks in Tokyo," Associated Press, November 16, 2003.

53. Editorial, "Crash of U.S. Helicopter in Okinawa," *Mainichi Shimbun,* August 18, 2004.

54. Editorial, "Government Should Give Up Henoko Plan for Futenma Transfer," *Asahi Shimbun,* April 26, 2005; David McNeill, "People Power: Have Okinawan Protests Forced Tokyo and Washington to Rethink Their Base Plan?" *Japan Focus,* September 27, 2005, http://japanfocus.org/article.asp?id=407; Sarah Buckley, "Okinawa Base Battle Resolved," *BBC News,* October 26, 2005; Gavan McCormack, "Okinawa and the Revamped U.S.-Japan Alliance," *Japan Focus,* November 15, 2005, http://japanfocus.org/article.asp?id=449.

55. "U.S. Copter Crashes on Campus; Local Ire Raised," *Japan Times,* August 14, 2004; James Brooke, "Ginowan Journal," *New York Times,* September 13, 2004; "Okinawa, U.S. Helicopter Accident: Back to Square One," *Mainichi Shimbun,* September 29, 2004.

56. "Helicopter Crash in Okinawa: Local Police Investigation Stymied without Agreement of U.S. Forces," *Tokyo Shimbun,* August 15, 2004; "Probe into U.S. Helicopter Crash in Okinawa," *Asahi Shimbun,* September 7, 2004. For photos of the crash site and an eyewitness account, see Darrell Y. Hamamoto, "Imperial Bird-Droppings: A First-hand Report on the U.S. Military Helicopter Accident in Okinawa," *JPRI Critique* 11, no. 6 (November 2004), http://www.jpri.org/publications/critiques/critique_XI_6.html.

57. "The U.S. Military: Unyielding Vested Interests; Helicopter Crash in Okinawa; the Reason Behind the Refusal of an On-site Inspection," *Tokyo Shimbun,* August 20, 2004; "U.S. Military Crash in Okinawa Reignites Debate on SOFA Issue," *Mainichi Shimbun,* August 26, 2004.

58. See note 18 above.

59. *Asahi Shimbun,* August 31, 2004.

60. "Refusal of an On-Site Inspection," *Tokyo Shimbun;* "U.S. Military Unwilling to Let Japan Independently Investigate Okinawa Helicopter Crash," Associated Press, February 18, 2005.

61. "Japan-U.S. SOFA: 'No Longer Meets the Needs of the Times,' Still Keeps Privileges for U.S. Troops," *Asahi Shimbun,* August 10, 2005.

62. Takehiko Kambayashi, "U.S., Japan Agree to Troop Drawdown," *Washington Times,* September 24, 2004.

63. "U.S. Copter Crash Attributed to Poor Maintenance," *Asahi Shimbun,* October 6, 2004; "Maintenance Error Found to Have Caused U.S. Marine Corps Chopper Crash in Okinawa," *Mainichi Shimbun,* February 18, 2005.

64. See Ted Galen Carpenter, "President Bush's Muddled Policy on Taiwan," CATO Institute, Foreign Policy Briefing, No. 82, March 15, 2004.

65. See, inter alia, Chalmers Johnson, review of *Gold Warriors: America's Secret Recovery of Yamashita's Gold,* by Sterling and Peggy Seagrave, *London Review of Books,* November 20, 2003, pp. 3–6; " 'Rape of Nanjing' Comic Draws Ire," Reuters, October 14, 2004; Anthony Faiola, "Scandals Force Out Japanese TV Chief: Critics Say Network Bowed to Pressure to Soften Controversial WWII Program," *Washington Post,* January 26, 2005.

66. Norimitsu Onishi, "Ad Man-Turned-Priest Tackles His Hardest Sales Job," *New York Times,* February 12, 2005; David Pilling, "Unbowed: Koizumi's Assertive Japan Is Standing Up Increasingly to China," *Financial Times,* February 14, 2005.

67. Yoshibumi Wakamiya, "Zero Fighters in Chongqing and Pearl Harbor; Yasukuni's War Criminals as Martyrs?" *Japan Focus,* December 6, 2004, http://japanfocus.org/182.html; Koji Uemura, Mayumi Otani, and Yudai Nakazawa, "Chinese Soccer Fans Jeering at Japanese," *Mainichi Shimbun,* August 6, 2004; Jim Yardley, "In Soccer Loss, a Glimpse of China's Rising Ire at Japan," *New York Times,* August 9, 2004.

68. Bryan Bender and Shane Green (*Boston Globe*), "U.S. Signals Rethink on Bases Overseas," *Sydney Morning Herald,* November 27, 2003; and "U.S. Force Realignment: Okinawa's Burden Alleviation Expected to Be Small," *Nihon Keizai Shimbun,* November 27, 2003.

69. "U.S. Military Transformation Plan: Aims to Strengthen Base Functions with Allies," *Asahi Shimbun,* August 6, 2004; "U.S. Military Realignment Plan: Host Municipalities Strongly Against U.S. Military Realignment Plan; U.S. Frustrated with Japan's Elusive Attitude," *Asahi Shimbun,* August 7, 2004.

70. "USAFJ's Yokota HQ May Disappear; 'GHQ' for USFJ to Be Moved to Zama," and "Transformation of U.S. Forces in Japan: Less Weight to Be Given to Defense of Japan; Building Strategic Center for Launching Attacks in Middle East and Other Locations," *Tokyo Shimbun,* July 29, 2004.

71. Peter Alford, "U.S. Nuclear Carrier Hits War Nerve," *Australian,* October 29, 2005; David Pilling, "Japan to Overturn Nuclear Taboo by Having U.S. Carrier Based in Port," *Financial Times,* October 29–30, 2005; Robert Burns, Associated Press, "Nuclear-Powered Ship to Be Based in Japan," *San Francisco Chronicle,* December 2, 2005.

72. "USFJ to be Vested with Own Command Right," *Yomiuri Shimbun,* July 20, 2004.

73. "Rumsfeld Cancels Japan Visit Due to Base Row," *Herald News Daily,* October 6, 2005, http://www.heraldnewsdaily.com/stories/news-0081930.html; David Pilling, "U.S. Anger at Pace of Japan Defense Talks," *Financial Times,* October 26, 2005.

74. "World Navies Top 15," http://www.deagel.com/forums/world-navies-top-15_62.aspx.

75. "Constitution Survey Shows 77% Oppose Changing Article 9," *Japan Times,* May 4, 2006.

76. "Realigning U.S. Military in Japan for War Not 'Defense,'" *Japan Press Weekly,* no. 2454, November 12, 2005.

77. "Government Considering Accepting Transfer of U.S. Army Command to Camp Zama and Flexibly Interpreting 'Far East Clause' in Security Treaty," *Mainichi Shimbun,* October 17, 2004; "U.S. Troops to Be Under Local Command Outside Far East," *Nihon Keizai Shimbun,* January 9, 2005; Chalmers Johnson "No Longer the 'Lone' Superpower: Coming to Terms with China," *JPRI Working Paper,* no. 105, March 2005, http://www.jpri.org/publications/workingpapers/wp105.html.

78. "Defense Agency, Koizumi's Aides at Odds Over Futenma Relocation," *Nihon Keizai Shimbun,* March 21, 2005; Anthony Faiola, "U.S. Agrees to Relocate Marines on Okinawa," *Washington Post,* October 27, 2005; "Futenma Relocation Issue: Japan with Proposal for Partial Land-Reclamation Plan at Camp Schwab; Hopes to Resolve Issue with New 'Trump Card,' but the Key Is Persuading U.S.," *Yomiuri Shimbun,* October 13, 2005.

79. "Talks Break Down on USFJ Realignment; Washington Urges Tokyo to Break Impasse under Premier's Initiative," *Sankei Shimbun,* September 30, 2005; "Japan, U.S. at Odds over Futenma Relocation; Defense Agency Raps U.S. Government's Sea-based Heliport Proposal," *Nihon Keizai Shimbun,* October 4, 2005.

80. "Futenma Relocation: U.S. Can't Wait, Japan Fumbling for a Solution," *Asahi Shimbun,* February 25, 2005; "Interview with U.S. Consul General to Okinawa Thomas Reich on the USFJ Realignment Interim Report," *Okinawa Times,* November 30, 2005; David McNeill, "U.S. Military Retreats over Japanese Base after Protests by Islanders," *Independent,* October 27, 2005; Jeff Schogol, "U.S. Agrees to Move 7,000 Marines from Okinawa to Guam; Change Will Be Implemented over the Next Six Years," *Stars & Stripes,* October 31, 2005.

81. David Allen and Chiyomi Sumida, " 'It's Done,' Rumsfeld Says of Troop Realignment Agreement for Okinawa," *Stars & Stripes,* November 5, 2005; "USFJ Realignment, Local Hurdles: All 55 Base-Hosting Municipalities Opposed to Realignment Plans," *Nihon Keizai Shimbun,* November 10, 2005.

82. "USFJ Realignment: No Progress in Coordination; Local Governments Watching Okinawa," *Nihon Keizai Shimbun,* November 22, 2005.

83. Masaaki Gabe, "USFJ Realignment: Government Held Accountable for Base-Hosting Burdens," *Mainichi Shimbun,* November 20, 2005.

84. "Full Text of Government Policy to Implement U.S. Force Realignment in Japan," *Mainichi Shimbun,* May 31, 2006; "Japan to Pay $6 Billion to Move U.S. Marines to Guam," *Asahi Shimbun,* April 25, 2006, http://japanfocus.org/article.asp?id=585.

85. David McNeill, "Anger in Okinawa as U.S. Airman Faces Child Sex Charges," *Independent,* July 5, 2005; "Surprised, Dumbfounded, and Angered at the Statement by the U.S. Embassy Official 'Trivializing the Issue' of a U.S. Airman Molesting a Little Girl," *Ryukyu Shimpo,* July 6, 2005; "Okinawa Assembly Passes Resolution Protesting Molestation Case Involving U.S. Serviceman," *Asahi Shimbun,* July 7, 2005; "U.S. Air Base Imposes Late-Night Curfew Following Alleged Groping of Japanese Schoolgirl," Associated Press, July 8, 2005; Simon Montlake, "U.S. Military Rape Case Tests Philippine President," *Christian Science Monitor,* November 10, 2005; James Hookway,

Wall Street Journal, "Rape Allegation Against Marines in Philippines Raises Furor," *San Diego Union-Tribune*, November 23, 2005; Reuters, "Four U.S. Marines Charged with Rape," *CNN.com*, December 27, 2005; Chris Hogg, "Japan Jails U.S. Sailor for Murder," *BBC News*, June 2, 2006.

6: SPACE: THE ULTIMATE IMPERIALIST PROJECT

1. Federation of American Scientists, "Address to the Nation on National Security by President Ronald Reagan, March 23, 1983," http://www.fas.org/spp/starwars/offdocs/rrspch.htm.

2. The best book on Reagan's Star Wars is Frances FitzGerald, *Way Out There in the Blue: Reagan, Star Wars, and the End of the Cold War* (New York: Simon & Schuster, 2000).

3. Tim Weiner, "Air Force Seeks Bush's Approval for Space Arms," *New York Times*, May 18, 2005, http://www.commondreams.org/cgi-bin/print.cgi?file=/headlines05/0518-02.htm.

4. Walter Pincus, "Pentagon Has Far-Reaching Defense Spacecraft in Works," *Washington Post*, March 16, 2005, http://www.washingtonpost.com/ac2/wp-dyn/A38272-2005Mar15?language=printer.

5. Alexander Zaitchik, *New York Press* 17, no. 52 (December 28, 2004), http://www.nypress.com/print.cfm?content_id=11848.

6. General Habiger, quoted by Bradley Graham, "Interceptor System Set, But Doubts Remain: Network Hasn't Undergone Realistic Testing," *Washington Post*, September 29, 2004; Philip Coyle, "Is Missile Defense on Target?" *Arms Control Today*, October 2003.

7. Richard Drayton, "Shock, Awe, and Hobbes Have Backfired on America's Neocons," *Guardian*, December 28, 2005. Drayton is the author of *Nature's Government: Science, Imperial Britain, and the "Improvement" of the World* (New Haven, CT: Yale University Press, 2000).

8. Michelle Ciarrocca and William D. Hartung, *Axis of Influence: Behind the Bush Administration's Missile Defense Revival* (New York: Arms Trade Resource Center, World Policy Institute, July 2002), pp. 13–14.

9. William D. Hartung, Frida Berrigan, Michelle Ciarrocca, and Jonathan Wingo, "Tangled Web 2005: A Profile of the Missile Defense and Space Weapons Lobbies" (New York: Arms Trade Resource Center, World Policy Institute, 2005), p. 4.

10. Ciarrocca and Hartung, *Axis of Influence*, p. 10. Bradley Graham of the *Washington Post* discusses the role of Boeing and Lockheed Martin engineers in influencing the conclusions of the commission. See his *Hit to Kill: The New Battle over Shielding America from Missile Attack* (New York: Public Affairs, 2001), pp. 43–44.

11. Center for Security Policy, "Now That It's U.S. Policy to Defend America Against Missile Attack, Let the Debate Be Joined As to the Optimal Way to Do So," Decision Brief 99-D 37 (March 18, 1999); John Isaacs, "Missile Defense: It's Back," *Bulletin of the Atomic Scientists* 55, no. 3 (May–June 1999), pp. 26–28.

12. Phil Jones, "Clinton Calls for Time," *CBS News*, September 1, 2000, http://www.cbsnews.com/stories/2000/09/01/national/printable229850.shtml.

13. Report of the Commission to Assess United States National Security Space

Management and Organization, Washington, DC, January 11, 2001, http://www.defenselink.mil/pubs/space20010111.html, pp. 13, 16.

14. Michael Dobbs, "How Politics Helped Redefine Threat," *Washington Post,* January 14, 2002, http://www.washingtonpost.com/ac2/wp-dyn/ A40780-2002Jan13?language=printer.

15. Demetri Sevastopulo, "Concern Over Keeping the Final Frontier Demilitarized," *Financial Times,* September 13, 2005.

16. Quoted by Weiner, "Air Force Seeks Bush's Approval."

17. Quoted by Jack Kelly, "U.S. the Leader in War Plans for Space," *Pittsburgh Post-Gazette,* July 28, 2003.

18. Quoted by Hannah Middleton, "Star Wars: The Armed Wing of Globalization," Australian Anti-Bases Campaign Coalition, http://www.anti-bases.org/nmd/ armed_wing_of_globalisation.htm.

19. U.S. Air Force, *Counterspace Doctrine,* Doctrine Document 2-2.1, August 2, 2004, http://www.dtic.mil/doctrine/jel/service_pubs/afdd2_2_1.pdf; Bryan Bender, "Pentagon Eyeing Weapons in Space," *Boston Globe,* March 14, 2006.

20. Theresa Hitchens, "Weapons in Space: Silver Bullet or Russian Roulette?" Center for Defense Information, April 18, 2002, http://www.cdi.org/missile-defense/spaceweapons.cfm, p. 10.

21. Quoted by Leonard David, "What Should U.S. Military Do in Space?" *MSNBC,* June 17, 2005, http://www.msnbc.msn.com/id/8258501/print/1/ displaymode/1098/.

22. Quoted by Mike Moore, "Space Cops: Coming to a Planet Near You," *Bulletin of the Atomic Scientists* 59, no. 6 (November–December 2003), p. 50. Dolman is the author of *Astropolitik: Classical Geopolitics in the Space Age* (London: Frank Cass, 2002).

23. The most complete account of this era is Philip Taubman, *Secret Empire: Eisenhower, the CIA, and the Hidden Story of America's Space Espionage* (New York: Simon & Schuster, 2003). On the subject of the "missile gap," Taubman writes, "In September [1959], the Agency had reported in a major study of Soviet missiles that 'we believe it is now well established that the USSR is not engaged in a "crash" program for ICBM development.' The assessment, reflecting the figures [Allen] Dulles had given to the Armed Services Committees in January 1959, estimated that just a handful of intercontinental missiles—around ten—might already be operational or nearly so. By that standard, the Air Force estimate of one hundred Russian missiles seemed wildly overblown, and inspired primarily by a desire to stampede Congress into fattening the Air Force budget. But because the U-2 flights were so secret, Dulles couldn't cite the photographic evidence in his Senate testimony," p. 296. See also Jeffrey T. Richelson, *Spying on the Bomb: American Nuclear Intelligence from Nazi Germany to Iran and North Korea* (New York: W. W. Norton, 2006), pp. 128–30.

24. The only reference to space debris in the air force's *Counterspace Doctrine* is: "Environmental monitoring includes the characterization and assessment of space weather (i.e., solar conditions) on satellites and links, terrestrial weather near important ground nodes, and natural and man-made phenomena in outer space (i.e., orbital debris). . . . Operators must be able to differentiate between natural phenomena interference and an intentional attack on a

space system in order to formulate an appropriate response." U.S. Air Force, *Counterspace Doctrine,* p. 21.

25. Theresa Hitchens, "Space Debris," *CDI Fact Sheet,* August 2005, http://www .space4peace.org/articles/debris_facts.htm.

26. From Ride's speech at Stanford University, April 10, 2002. Quoted by Joel Primack, "Pelted by Paint, Downed by Debris," *Bulletin of the Atomic Scientists* 58, no. 5 (September–October 2002), pp. 24–25. See also Dawn Levy, "Anti-Satellite Weapons Testing Would Have 'Disastrous' Effects, Ride Says," *Stanford Report,* April 17, 2002.

27. Primack, "Pelted by Paint."

28. Richard Stenger, "Scientist: Space Weapons Pose Debris Threat," *CNN.com,* May 3, 2002.

29. Members of the Council on Foreign Relations Study Group on Space Weapons (Bruce M. DeBlois, Richard L. Garwin, R. Scott Kemp, and Jeremy C. Marwell), "Space Weapons: Crossing the U.S. Rubicon," *International Security* 29, no. 2 (Fall 2004), pp. 52, 64, 83.

30. Hitchens, "Weapons in Space," p. 11.

31. "Space-Based Missile Interceptors Could Pose Debris Threat," DefenceTalk .com, September 14, 2004.

32. James Clay Moltz, "Space Weapons or Space Arms Control," Center for Nonproliferation Studies, April 15, 2002, http://cns.miis.edu/pubs/week/ 020415.htm.

33. Leonard David, "U.S.-China Space Debris Collide in Orbit," Space.com, April 16, 2005, http://www.space.com/news/050416_debris_crash.html.

34. Ciarrocca and Hartung, *Axis of Influence,* p. 12.

35. Christopher Hellman, "Funding Request for Ballistic Missile Defense," Center for Defense Information, February 4, 2002, http://www.cdi.org/ issues/budget/FY03bmd-pr.cfm.

36. For General Bell's testimony, see Norimitsu Onishi, "U.S. Confirms Test of Missiles Was Conducted by North Korea," *New York Times,* March 9, 2006.

37. "U.S. Dismisses Call to Destroy N. Korean Missile," *NBC News,* June 22, 2006, http://www.msnbc.msn.com/id/13481845/print/1/displaymode/ 1098/; Terence Hunt, "U.S. Says Missile Defense System Limited," Associated Press, June 22, 2006, http://www.chron.com/disp/story.mpl/ap/world/ 3992279.html.

38. See, for example, Hitchens, "Weapons in Space," p. 10; Jeff Sallot, "Arms Experts Issue Missile Defense Alert," *Globe and Mail* (Toronto), December 7, 2004; David Pugliese, "U.S. Won't Rule Out Waging War in Space, General Says," *Ottawa Citizen,* February 21, 2005. In February 2006, Air Force Lieutenant General Henry Obering, head of the Missile Defense Agency, said to the press that he intended to put the entire batch of forty scheduled interceptors into Alaskan silos: "We can take those forty interceptors and turn them into an ability to counter much more complex threat[s]." Martin Sieff, "Congress Gives $150m Boost to Alaska ABM Deployment," United Press International, February 7, 2006.

39. On China's reaction to the GMD, see Nicole C. Evans, "Missile Defense: Winning Minds, Not Hearts," *Bulletin of the Atomic Scientists* 60, no. 5 (September–October 2004), pp. 48–55.

40. Victoria Samson, "Remember the Anti-Missile Missile? Forget It," Center for Defense Information, January 4, 2006, http://www.cdi.org/friendlyversion/printversion.cfm?documentID=3244&from_page=../program/document.cfm.

41. Charles Piller, "Little Room for Error in Catching a Missile," *Los Angeles Times,* December 25, 2004.

42. David Stout and John H. Cushman Jr., "Defense Missile for U.S. System Fails to Launch; Setback for Interceptor," *New York Times,* December 16, 2004; "Two Successive Failures Reflect Vulnerabilities in U.S. Missile Defense Effort," Agence France-Presse, February 15, 2005; Rachel D'Oro, Associated Press, "Missile Test Failures Sideline Progress at Alaska's Fort Greely," *Anchorage Daily News,* January 6, 2006, http://www.adn.com/news/alaska/ap_alaska/v-printer/story/7338986p-7251040c.html.

43. Robert Gard, "The Pathetic State of National Missile Defense," Center for Arms Control and Non-Proliferation, Washington, DC, February 2, 2005.

44. Coyle, "Is Missile Defense on Target?" See also Walter C. Uhler, "Missile Shield or Holy Grail?" *Nation,* January 28, 2002, pp. 25–29.

45. See, inter alia, Richard J. Newman, "Space Watch, High and Low," *Air Force Magazine,* July 2001, http://www.afa.org/magazine/July2001/0701SBIRS.asp; Federation of American Scientists, "Space-Based Infrared System," October 2003, http://www.fas.org/spp/military/program/warning/sbir.htm; Tara Copp, "Giant Globe Radar Another Piece in Missile Defense System," Scripps Howard News Service, September 10, 2003; Missile Defense Agency, "Fact Sheet: Sea-Based X-Band Radar," September 2005; "Sea-Based X-Band Radar Begins Transport Operation Through Straits of Magellan," Spacewar.com, November 14, 2005, http://www.spacewar.com/news/abm-05zp.html. For a photo of the X-band radar at sea on its oil rig, see the Boeing advertisement opposite page 4, *National Journal,* February 4, 2006.

46. See FitzGerald, *Way Out There,* pp. 408–11.

47. Evans, "Missile Defense"; Geoffrey Forden, "Laser Defenses: What If They Work?" *Bulletin of the Atomic Scientists* 58, no. 5 (September–October 2002), pp. 49–53.

48. Miranda Priebe, "Airborne Laser: Overweight and Oh-so-late," *Bulletin of the Atomic Scientists* 59, no. 3 (May–June 2003), pp. 18–20.

49. Quoted by Michael Clark and Victoria Samson, "A Look at the Troubled Development of the Airborne Laser," Center for Defense Information, March 15, 2005, http://www.cdi.org/pdfs/ABL-031505.pdf.

50. See Taubman, *Secret Empire,* pp. 305–7.

51. Coyle, "Is Missile Defense on Target?" See also Uhler, "Missile Shield."

52. "Rumsfeld Says Missile Shield Will Soon Have 'Modest Capacity,'" Agence France-Presse, December 23, 2004.

53. Bradley Graham, "Panel Faults Tactics in Rush to Install Antimissile System," *Washington Post,* June 10, 2005; Editorial, "Star Wars' Political Bull's-Eye," *New York Times,* June 24, 2005; Martin Sieff, "BMD Focus: DOD Space Buys Leak Billions," United Press International, July 19, 2005, http://www.wpherald.com/print.php?StoryID=20050719-042857-1423r; Sieff, "Ballistic Missile Defense: The Test of Reality," United Press International, July 26, 2005, http://www.wpherald.com/print.php?StoryID=20050726-123729-8313r; Sieff, "Ballistic Missile Defense: Shortfalls in Space," United Press

International, August 2, 2005, http://www.wpherald.com/print.php?Story ID=20050802-024235-8315r; Sieff, "Ballistic Missile Defense: Space Defense Budget Mess," United Press International, October 6, 2005, http://www .wpherald.com/print.php?StoryID=20051006-021655-4516r.

54. "U.S. Gives Up on Upgrading Missile Defense," United Press International, October 13, 2005, http://www.wpherald.com/print.php?StoryID=20051013-044213-8370r.

55. Lisbeth Gronlund, "Fire, Aim, Ready," *Bulletin of the Atomic Scientists* 61, no. 5 (September–October 2005), pp. 67–68, http://www.thebulletin.org/ print.php?art_ofn=so05gronlund.

56. Scott Ritter, "Rude Awakening to Missile-defense Dream," *Christian Science Monitor,* January 4, 2005, http://www.csmonitor.com/2005/0104/p09s02-coop.html.

57. Uhler, "Missile Shield"; David E. Sanger and Michael Wines, "With a Shrug, a Monument to Cold War Fades Away," *New York Times,* June 14, 2002; Evans, "Missile Defense"; "Russia Deploys New Set of Strategic Nuclear Missiles," *Pravda* (Moscow), December 24, 2005, http://newsfromrussia. com/main/2005/12/24/70454.html; Natural Resources Defense Council, "Russian Nuclear Forces, 2006," *Bulletin of the Atomic Scientists* 62, no. 2 (March–April 2006), pp. 64–67.

58. Ciarrocca and Hartung, *Axis of Influence,* p. 33.

59. Quoted by Toby Eckert, Copley News Service, "Bribery Admission Spotlights Favoritism; 'Earmarking' Has Grown in Congress," *San Diego Union-Tribune,* December 3, 2005.

60. Hartung, Berrigan, Ciarrocca, and Wingo, "Tangled Web 2005"; John Isaacs, "An Indefensible Budget," *Bulletin of the Atomic Scientists* 61, no. 3 (May/ June 2005), p. 22.

61. Theresa Hitchens, "Bad Time to Invest in U.S. Missile Defense Program" (speech, Royal United Services Institute's International Missile Defense Conference, London, November 2–3, 2005), Center for Defense Information, January 9, 2006; Hartung, Berrigan, Ciarrocca, and Wingo, "Tangled Web 2005"; Editorial, "Dream-Filled Missile Silos," *New York Times,* April 1, 2004.

62. Richard F. Kaufman, "The Folly of Space Weapons," *TomPaine.com,* June 15, 2005, http://www.tompaine.com/print/the_folly_of_space_weapons.php; Lawrence S. Wittner, "Bush's Maginot Line in the Sky," *History News Network,* May 10, 2004, http://hnn.us/articles/printfriendly/5026.html.

63. David Wood, Newhouse News Service, "Pentagon's 'Black' Budgets Ripe for Corruption," *San Diego Union-Tribune,* December 2, 2005.

64. Ciarrocca and Hartung, *Axis of Influence.*

65. Bill Moyers, "Inside the Pentagon," *Now,* transcript, Public Broadcasting Service, December 5, 2003, http://www.pbs.org/now/transcript/transcript 245_full.html.

66. See Ken Silverstein, "Huntsville's Missile Payload," *Mother Jones,* July–August 2001.

67. Quoted by Mike Moore, "Space War—Now We're Jammin!" *Bulletin of the Atomic Scientists* 61, no. 2 (March/April 2005), pp. 6–8; Donna Miles, "Iraq Jamming Incident Underscores Lessons about Space," American Forces Press Service, September 15, 2004, http://www.defenselink.mil/news/Sep2004/ n09152004_2004091510.html.

68. George Smith, "Weapon of the Week: The Ruski Jammer," *Village Voice,* January 22–28, 2003.

69. Moore, "Space War."

70. Federal Aviation Administration, "Satellite Navigation," http://gps.faa.gov/ GPSbasics/index.htm; Wikipedia, "Global Positioning System," January 18, 2006, http://en.wikipedia.org/wiki/Gps.

71. David Whitman, "Keeping Our Bearings: The Coming War over the Global Positioning System," *U.S. News & World Report,* October 21, 2002, pp. 72–73.

72. For further details and a survey of GPS, see Morag Chivers, "Differential GPS Explained," ESRI, http://www.esri.com/news/arcuser/0103/differential 1of2.html.

73. "President Clinton: Improving the Civilian Global Positioning System (GPS)," May 1, 2000, http://clinton3.nara.gov/WH/EOP/OSTP/html/ 0053_4.html.

74. Jennifer Lee, "Europe Plans to Compete with U.S. Satellite Network," *New York Times,* November 26, 2001; European Space Agency, "What Is Galileo?" March 17, 2005, http://www.esa.int/esaNA/GGGMX650NDC_index_2 .html; Jonathan Amos, "Europe's Galileo Project," *BBC News,* December 28, 2005; Daniel Clery, "Find Yourself with Galileo: Europeans Will Not Have to Rely on the U.S. Military," *Financial Times,* March 10, 2006.

75. Wikipedia, "Galileo Positioning System," January 18, 2006, http://en .wikipedia.org/wiki/Galileo_positioning_system; George Parker and John Thornhill, "European Navigation Satellite a Challenge to the U.S.," *Financial Times,* December 29, 2005.

76. Benjamin S. Lambeth, *Mastering the High Ground: Next Steps in the Military Uses of Space* (Santa Monica, CA: The RAND Corp., 2003), p. 103.

77. Katherine Shrader, "U.S. Has More Satellites in Orbit than Other Countries," Associated Press, December 9, 2005.

78. Hitchens, "Weapons in Space"; Satellite Industry Association, "SIA Releases Satellite Industry Report," press release, Long Beach, CA, June 6, 2005.

79. Philip E. Coyle and John B. Rhinelander, "Drawing the Line: The Path to Controlling Weapons in Space," *Disarmament Diplomacy,* no. 66 (September 2002); Hitchens, "Weapons in Space."

80. "The 1945 Proposal by Arthur C. Clarke for Geostationary Satellite Communications," http://lakdiva.org/clarke/1945ww/.

81. Thomas Graham Jr., "Space Weapons and the Risk of Accidental Nuclear War," *Arms Control Today,* December 2005, http://www.armscontrol.org/act/ 2005_12/Dec-spaceweapons.asp.

82. "Yugoslavia—Afghanistan—Iraq: The Satellite Wars," *Space Today Online,* http://www.spacetoday.org/Satellites/YugoWarSats.html.

83. Jack Kelly, "U.S. the Leader in War."

84. "Satellite's Death Puts Millions Out of Touch," *USA Today,* May 21, 1998; Caron Carlson, "What Went Wrong? High Costs Don't Support Benefits," *Wireless Week,* May 25, 1998, http://www.wirelessweek.com/article/CA4355. html?spacedesc=; Boeing Integrated Defense Systems, "Galaxy IV Specifications," http://www.boeing.com/defense-space/space/bss/factsheets/601/ galaxy_iv/galaxy_iv.html; Lambeth, *Mastering the High Ground,* p. 104. Environmental and weather satellites are threatened by a shortage of money

as military demands crowd out civilian and scientific projects. See Matt Crenson, Associated Press, "Budgets Imperil Environmental Satellites," *ABC News*, March 10, 2006, http://abcnews.go.com/US/print?id=1693735.

85. From *Air Force Magazine*, January 2005, quoted by Theresa Hitchens, "Worst-Case Mentality Clouds USAF Space Strategy," Center for Defense Information, February 14, 2005, http://www.cdi.org/friendlyversion/ printversion.cfm?documentID=2885.

86. Lambeth, *Mastering the High Ground*, p. 104.

87. Hitchens, "Worst-Case Mentality." Members of the Council on Foreign Relations Study Group on Space Weapons write, "The quality of available information about what is going on in space—so-called space situational awareness—is currently one of the United States' most urgent space security shortcomings." *International Security* (Fall 2004), p. 56.

88. Gronlund, "Fire, Aim, Ready," pp. 67–68.

89. Patrick Radden Keefe, "A Shortsighted Eye in the Sky," *New York Times*, February 5, 2005; Jeffrey Richelson, "The Spy Satellite So Stealthy that the Senate Couldn't Kill It," National Security Archive, Washington, DC, December 14, 2004; Walter Pincus, "Spy Satellites Are Under Scrutiny," *Washington Post*, August 16, 2005. The leading authority on codes, special access projects, and the black budget, William Arkin, notes that "Misty" is a very black code word indeed. All he can say about it is "Possible code word for possible stealth reconnaissance satellite." See *Code Names*, p. 426.

90. Justin Ray, "Minotaur Rocket Launches U.S. Military Spacecraft," *Spaceflight Now*, April 11, 2005, http://www.spaceflightnow.com/minotaur/xss11/. Giuseppe Anzera comments, "XSS-11 is in fact specifically designed to disturb other states' military reconnaissance or communications satellites." See "The Pentagon's Bid to Militarize Space," *Power and Interest News Report (PINR)*, August 17, 2005, http://www.pinr.com/report.php?ac =view_printable&report_id=347&language_id=1.

91. Jeffrey Lewis, International Network of Engineers and Scientists Against Proliferation, "Space Weapons in U.S. Defense Planning," *Bulletin* 23 (n.d., c. 2004), http://www.inesap.org/bulletin23/art03.htm.

92. Hitchens, "Worst-Case Mentality."

93. According to Leonard David, some poor nations are talking about "debris-creating weapons." See "The Clutter Above," *Bulletin of the Atomic Scientists* 61, no. 4 (July–August 2005), pp. 32–37. On the effects of a nuclear explosion in space, see Department of Defense, Defense Threat Reduction Agency, *High Altitude Nuclear Detonations Against Low Earth Orbit Satellites* (Washington, DC: April 2001); Nick Schwellenbach, "EMPty Threat?" *Bulletin of the Atomic Scientists* 61, no. 55 (September/October 2005), pp. 50–57. Schwellenbach is writing about the electromagnetic pulse that is released by all nuclear explosions.

7: THE CRISIS OF THE AMERICAN REPUBLIC

1. Edith Hamilton, *Mythology* (1940; repr., New York: Mentor Books, 1953), p. 88.

2. George F. Will, *Washington Post*, "Having the President Observe the Law," *San Diego Union-Tribune*, February 16, 2006; James Ridgeway, "The Bush

Family Coup," *Village Voice,* December 30, 2005. See also Federation of American Scientists, Project on Governmental Secrecy, "Confronting the White House's 'Monarchical Doctrine,'" *Secrecy News,* February 16, 2006.

3. James Madison, "Virginia Resolutions," December 21, 1798, http://press-pubs. uchicago.edu/founders/documents/amendI_speechs19.html.

4. James Madison, from a letter to W. T. Barry, August 4, 1822, http://www .matisse.net/files/madison.html.

5. "Bill Moyers on the Freedom of Information Act," *Now,* Public Broadcasting Service, April 5, 2002, http://www.pbs.org/now/printable/transcript_ moyers4_print.html.

6. See Daniel Ellsberg, *Secrets: A Memoir of Vietnam and the Pentagon Papers* (New York: Viking, 2002); and Johnson, Review of Ellsberg, *Secrets,* in *London Review of Books,* February 6, 2003, pp. 7–9, http://www.lrb.co.uk/v25/ n03/print/john04_.html.

7. James Bovard, "Uncle Sam's Iron Curtain of Secrecy," Future of Freedom Foundation, August 1, 2005, http://www.fff.org/freedom/fd0504c.asp.

8. Jeremy Brecher and Brendan Smith, "War Crimes Made Easy: How the Bush Administration Legalized Intelligence Deceptions, Assassinations, and Aggressive War," TomDispatch.com, December 6, 2005, p. 3, http://www .tomdispatch.com/index.mhtml?pid=41419.

9. Ruth Rosen, "The Day Ashcroft Censored Freedom of Information," *San Francisco Chronicle,* January 7, 2002, http://www.commondreams.org/ cgi-bin/print.cgi?file=/views02/0108-04.htm.

10. Quoted by Brecher and Smith, "War Crimes Made Easy." See also Adam Clymer, "Bush Expands Government Secrecy," *New York Times,* January 3, 2003.

11. Bovard, "Uncle Sam's Iron Curtain."

12. Wikipedia, "Executive Order 13233," February 12, 2006, http://en.wikipedia .org/wiki/Executive_Order_13233.

13. Quoted in Editorial, "An Executive Order Hiding Presidential Papers," *San Francisco Chronicle,* November 11, 2001.

14. Federation of American Scientists, "Statement of Richard Reeves on Presidential Records," April 11, 2002, http://www.fas.org/sgp/congress/2002/ 041102reeves.html.

15. Quoted by Bovard, "Uncle Sam's Iron Curtain."

16. Ibid.

17. Noah Feldman, "Who Can Check the President?" *New York Times Magazine,* January 8, 2006, p. 55.

18. Quoted by Ridgeway, "Bush Family Coup."

19. Quoted by Caroline Daniel, "Cheney Leads Fight for Presidential Power," *Financial Times,* December 14, 2005.

20. Quoted by Linda Feldmann, "Tug of War over Presidential Powers," *Christian Science Monitor,* December 22, 2005, http://csmonitor.com/2005/ 1222/p01s03-uspo.htm.

21. Quoted by Thomas E. Woods Jr., "All the President's Power," *American Conservative,* January 30, 2006, http://www.amconmag.com/2006/2006_ 01_30/print/coverprint.html.

22. R. Jeffrey Smith and Dan Eggen, "Gonzales Helped Set the Course for Detainees," *Washington Post,* January 5, 2005; Daniel, "Cheney Leads Fight"; Jane Mayer, "The Memo: How an Internal Effort to Ban the Abuse and

Torture of Detainees Was Thwarted," *New Yorker,* February 27, 2006, http:// www.newyorker.com/printables/fact/060227fa_fact. For texts of the memo and other documents, see Human Rights First, "U.S. Government Memos on Torture and International Law," http://www.humanrightsfirst.org/ us_law/etn/gov_rep/gov_memo_intlaw.htm.

23. Quoted by Dana Milbank, "In Cheney's Shadow, Counsel Pushes the Conservative Cause," *Washington Post,* October 11, 2004. There are altogether four Yoo memos available to the public that assert a dictatorial power for the president: (1) September 21, 2001, arguing that 9/11 allowed the president to take "measures which in less troubled conditions could be seen as infringements of individual liberties"; (2) September 25, 2001, in which Yoo says Congress could not put "limits on the president's determinations as to any terrorist threat, the amount of military force to be used in response, or the method, timing, and nature of the response. These decisions, under our Constitution, are for the president alone to make"; (3) January 9, 2002, a Yoo memo saying that the Geneva Conventions did not apply to American prisoners even though ratified treaties are, according to the Constitution, the "supreme law of the land"; and (4) the Torture Memo of August 1, 2002. See Sidney Blumenthal, "The Law Is King," *Salon,* December 22, 2005, http://fairuse.1accesshost.com/news2/blumenthal-lawking.html. For a detailed analysis of the executive branch's defense of torture, see Tom Engelhardt, "George Orwell Meet . . . Franz Kafka," TomDispatch.com, June 13, 2004, http://www.tomdispatch.com/index .mhtml?pid=1494.

24. Massimo Calabresi, "Wartime Power Play," *Time,* February 5, 2006.

25. Bruce Schneier, "Unchecked Presidential Power," *StarTribune.com,* December 21, 2005, http://www.startribune.com/dynamic/mobile_story .php?story=5793639.

26. Dan Farber, "The Case Against Presidential Supremacy," *San Diego Union-Tribune,* January 15, 2006.

27. 343 US 579; Mayer, "The Memo."

28. For details of the FISA, see Johnson, *Sorrows of Empire,* pp. 295–98.

29. See Electronic Privacy Information Center, "Foreign Intelligence Surveillance Act Orders, 1979–2004," http://www.epic.org/privacy/wiretap/stats/ fisa_stats.html.

30. Paul Craig Roberts, "A Criminal Administration," Antiwar.com, January 2, 2006.

31. James Risen and Eric Lichtblau, "Bush Lets U.S. Spy on Callers Without Courts," *New York Times,* December 16, 2005. See also Aziz Huq (School of Law, New York University), "At the NSA, the Enemy Is Us," *TomPaine.com,* March 2, 2006, http://www.tompaine.com/articles/2006/03/02/at_the_nsa_ the_enemy_is_us.php.

32. Roberts, "Criminal Administration."

33. Blumenthal, "Law Is King."

34. Thomas Powers, "The Biggest Secret," *New York Review of Books,* February 23, 2006, pp. 9–12.

35. Quoted by Amy Goodman, "Total Information Awareness Lives On Inside the National Security Agency," *Democracy Now,* February 27, 2006, http://www.democracynow.org/print.pl?sid=06/02/27/1519235.

36. Walter Pincus, "Pentagon's Intelligence Authority Widens," *Washington Post,*
    December 19, 2005, http://www.washingtonpost.com/wpdyn/content/
    article/2005/12/18/AR2005121801006_pf.html. See also Tom Engelhardt,
    "Proliferation Wars in the Intelligence Community," TomDispatch.com,
    May 30, 2006, http://www.tomdispatch.com/index.mhtml?pid=87452.

37. Shane Harris, "TIA Lives On," *National Journal,* February 23, 2006; John W.
    Dean, "Why Should Anyone Worry about Whose Communications Bush
    and Cheney Are Intercepting If It Helps to Find Terrorists?" FindLaw.com,
    February 24, 2006, http://writ.corporate.findlaw.com/dean/20060224.html;
    Shane Harris, "Signals and Noise," *National Journal,* June 17, 2006, http://
    news.nationaljournal.com/articles/0619nj1.htm.

38. John W. Dean, "The Problem with Presidential Signing Statements: Their
    Use and Misuse by the Bush Administration," FindLaw.com, January 13,
    2006, http://writ.findlaw.com/dean/20060113.html.

39. Quoted by Charlie Savage, "Bush Could Bypass New Torture Ban," *Boston
    Globe,* January 4, 2006, http://www.truthout.org/docs_2006/printer_
    010406A.shtml. See also Savage, "Bush Challenges Hundreds of Laws,"
    Boston Globe, April 30, 2006, http://www.boston.com/news/nation/
    washington/articles/2006/04/30/bush_challenges_hundreds_of_laws/.

40. Dean, "Presidential Signing Statements."

41. Aziz Huq, "Constitutional License," *TomPaine.com,* January 24, 2006,
    http://www.tompaine.com/print/constitutional_license.php.

42. See Alfred W. McCoy, "Why the McCain Torture Ban Won't Work," *Tom
    Dispatch.com,* February 8, 2006, http://www.tomdispatch.com/index
    .mhtml?pid=57336.

43. Quoted by Savage, "Bush Could Bypass Torture Ban."

44. Anthony Legouranis, "Tortured Logic: What I Learned as a Military
    Interrogator in Iraq," *New York Times,* February 28, 2006.

45. Feldman, "Who Can Check the President?"

46. Al Gore, "U.S. Constitution in Grave Danger," January 16, 2006,
    http://www.truthout.org/docs_2006/printer_011606Y.shtml.

47. See Chalmers Johnson, "The Military-Industrial Man," TomDispatch.com,
    September 14, 2004, http://www.tomdispatch.com/index.mhtml?pid=1818;
    and "My Congressman Stands for Money, Not for Me—And, What's Even
    Worse, There's No Way I Can Get Rid of Him," *Los Angeles Times,* September
    26, 2004.

48. Matt Kelley and Jim Drinkard, "Secret Military Spending Gets Little Over-
    sight," *USA Today,* November 8, 2005; Paul Sisson, "Defense Dollars for
    Everyone," *North County Times* (San Diego), July 17, 2005, p. E5.

49. Onell R. Soto, "Rep. Cunningham Resigns; Took $2.4 Million in Bribes,"
    San Diego Union-Tribune, November 29, 2005; Soto, "Feds Seek 10 Years for
    Cunningham," *San Diego Union-Tribune,* February 18, 2006; Finlay Lewis,
    Jerry Kammer, and Joe Cantlupe, "Contractor Admits Bribing Cunningham,"
    San Diego Union-Tribune, February 25, 2006.

50. Laura Rozen, " 'Duke' of Deception," *American Prospect,* February 2006,
    http://www.prospect.org/web/printfriendly-view.ww?id=10816.

51. Bill Moyers, "Restoring the Public Trust," *TomPaine.com,* February 24, 2006,
    http://www.tompaine.com/articles/2006/02/24/restoring_the_public_trust
    .php.

52. Matt Kelley and Jim Drinkard, "Contractor Spends Big on Key Lawmakers," *USA Today,* November 20, 2005.

53. Dean Calbreath, "The Power of Persuasion: Poway Businessman Brent Wilkes Funneled Campaign Donations to Key Lawmakers as He Tried to Build a Defense Empire," *San Diego Union-Tribune,* February 5, 2006.

54. Wes Allison and Anita Kumar, "Fla. Senators Get Funds for Military Companies, Many of Them Donors," *St. Petersburg Times* (FL), March 11, 2006.

55. Moyers, "Restoring the Public Trust."

56. Ibid. Also see Larry Margasak and Sharon Theimer, Associated Press, "Dollar Trail from D.C. to Islands," *CBS News,* May 3, 2005; Rep. George Miller (Democrat from California), "New Developments—Abramoff, DeLay, and the Northern Mariana Islands," May 6, 2005, http://www.house.gov/george miller/marianasupdate.html; Dennis Cook, Associated Press, "Controversial Lobbyist Had Close Contact with Bush Team," *USA Today,* May 6, 2005, http://www.usatoday.com/news/washington/2005-05-06-abramoff-bush_ x.htm; Eamon Javers, "Op-Eds for Sale," *Business Week,* December 15, 2005; Byron York, "Hillary, Saipan, Sweatshops, Campaign Cash—and Abramoff," *National Review,* March 10, 2006.

57. Ken Silverstein, "The Great American Pork Barrel," *Harper's Magazine,* July 2005, http://www.harpers.org/TheGreatAmericanPorkBarrel.html.

58. Ibid.

59. Quoted by David Wood, Newhouse News Service, "Pentagon's 'Black' Budgets Ripe for Corruption," *San Diego Union-Tribune,* December 2, 2005. Also see Dan Morgan, "Classified Spending On the Rise," *Washington Post,* August 27, 2003; Drew Brown, "Classified Military Spending Reaches Highest Level Since Cold War," Knight Ridder Newspapers, May 19, 2006.

60. Moyers, "Inside the Pentagon." See also William D. Hartung, "Dick Cheney and the Power of the Self-Licking Ice Cream Cone," in *How Much Are You Making on the War, Daddy? A Quick and Dirty Guide to War Profiteering in the Bush Administration* (New York: Nation Books, 2004), pp. 23–43.

61. Winslow T. Wheeler, "How Congress Sacrifices Readiness for Pork," *Counterpunch,* January 24, 2006; Emanuel Pastreich, "Rebels Within the U.S. Federal System," Center for Defense Information, January 10, 2006.

62. Annapolis, MD: Naval Institute Press, 2004.

63. Center for Defense Information, "Fiscal Year 2001 Add-Ons: Congress's Unrequested Spending for the Pentagon," July 28, 2000, http://cdi.org/issues/budget/add-ons01.html; Center for Defense Information, "Fiscal Year 2002 Add-Ons," January 16, 2002, http://www.cdi.org/issues/budget/add-ons02-pr.cfm.

64. Editorial, "Kabuki Congress," *New York Times,* March 6, 2006. See also Editorial, "The Death of the Intelligence Panel," *New York Times,* March 9, 2006.

65. Brian Foley, "Playing with Fire: Congress and Executive Power," *Jurist,* January 9, 2006, http://jurist.law.pitt.edu/forumy/2006/01/playing-with-fire-congress-and.php.

66. McCoy, "McCain Ban Won't Work."

67. Quoted by Eric Schmitt, "Senate Approves Limiting Rights of U.S. Detainees," *New York Times,* November 11, 2005.

68. Foley, "Playing with Fire."

69. Quoted by Woods, "All the President's Power."

70. Bob Herbert, "The Torturers Win," *New York Times,* February 20, 2006.

71. Anatol Lieven, "Decadent America Must Give Up Imperial Ambitions," *Financial Times,* November 29, 2005.

72. Louis Uchitelle, "U.S. and Trade Partners Maintain Unhealthy Long-Term Relationship," *New York Times,* September 18, 2004; Christopher Swann, "U.S. Deficit Data Fuel Anxieties on Dollar," *Financial Times,* March 15, 2006.

73. Martin Crutsinger, "U.S. Trade Deficit Hits All-Time High," Associated Press, February 10, 2006.

74. Keith Bradsher, "China Passes Japan in Foreign Exchange Reserves," *New York Times,* March 29, 2006.

75. Marshall Auerback, "What Could Go Wrong in 2005?" TomDispatch.com, January 22, 2005, http://www.tomdispatch.com/index.mhtml?pid=2141.

76. See the discussion by Doug Dowd, "U.S. Military Expenditures: Beneficial or Harmful? Or, Who Benefits and Who Pays?" *State of Nature,* Winter 2006, http://www.stateofnature.org/milex.html. See also Robert B. Reich, "John Maynard Keynes: His Radical Idea that Governments Should Spend Money They Don't Have May Have Saved Capitalism," *Time,* March 29, 1999, http://www.time.com/time/time100/scientist/profile/keynes.html.

77. Wikipedia, "Permanent Arms Economy," February 10, 2006, http://en .wikipedia.org/wiki/Permanent_arms_economy.

78. Andrew Gumbel, "How the War Machine Is Driving the U.S. Economy," *Independent,* January 6, 2004.

79. Wikipedia, "Military Keynesianism," February 5, 2006, http://en.wikipedia. org/wiki/Military_Keynesianism; Michael Kidron, "A Permanent Arms Economy," *International Socialism* 1, no. 28 (Spring 1967), http://www .marxists.org/archive/kidron/works/1967/xx/permarms.htm.

80. Ronald Steel, *Temptations of a Superpower* (Cambridge, MA: Harvard University Press, 1995), p. 61.

81. See John L. Boies, *Buying for Armageddon: Business, Society, and Military Spending Since the Cuban Missile Crisis* (New Brunswick, NJ: Rutgers University Press, 1994).

82. Gumbel, "War Machine"; Fred Kaplan, "The Military's Bloated Budget," *Slate,* September 12, 2003.

83. Jonathan Karp, "Pet Projects Prevail in U.S. Military-Spending Boom," *Wall Street Journal,* June 16, 2006.

84. Jeff Bliss, "U.S. War Spending to Rise 44% to $9.8 Billion a Month, Report Says," Bloomberg.com, March 17, 2006, http://truthout.org/docs_2006/ printer_031706B.shtml.

85. Winslow T. Wheeler, "A Tutorial on How to Find the Real Numbers: Just How Big Is the Defense Budget?" *Counterpunch,* January 19, 2006.

86. Robert Higgs, "The Defense Budget Is Bigger than You Think," The Independent Institute, January 18, 2004, http://www.independent.org/newsroom/ article.asp?id=1253.80; Doug Dowd, "U.S. Military Expenditures"; Walter Adams and James W. Brock, *The Bigness Complex: Industry, Labor, and Government in the American Economy,* 2nd ed. (Stanford, CA: Stanford University Press, 2004).

87. Ann Scott Tyson, "Defense Spending Is Overstated, GAO Report Says," *Washington Post,* September 22, 2005.

88. Linda Bilmes and Joseph Stiglitz, "The Economic Costs of the Iraq War: An Appraisal Three Years After the Beginning of the Conflict," National Bureau of Economic Research (Working Paper 12054, February 2006), http://www2.gsb.columbia.edu/faculty/jstiglitz/download/2006_Cost_of_War_in_Iraq_NBER.pdf.

Acknowledgments

Sheila K. Johnson, who has her Ph.D. in anthropology from the University of California, Berkeley, spent endless hours in conversation with me about this book, and she carefully edited my first draft. As my wife of forty-nine years, she obviously knows where I'm coming from.

Tom Engelhardt is the founder and editor of *TomDispatch.com*, "a regular antidote to the mainstream media" and a project of the Nation Institute. He is also the editor of all three books of the Blowback Trilogy—*Blowback, The Sorrows of Empire*, and *Nemesis*—for Metropolitan Books. I am indebted to him for his intelligence, integrity, and support for the American Empire Project, which he helped create.

Sandra Dijkstra, my literary agent, and her assistant Taryn Fagerness have worked miracles in having my books published in over a dozen languages around the world.

The poet John Shreffler, of Brookline, Massachusetts, dedicated to me his conception of the arrival of Nemesis in the United States.

Several close friends have helped me with comments, articles, suggestions, and conversations about this book. They are Dr. Kozy Amemiya, one of our country's pioneer researchers on Okinawa, and her husband, Thomas Royden, avocado and palm grower; Dr. Barry Keehn of Los Angeles, an equally talented psychologist and political scientist; Drs. Maricler and Alfredo Antognini, exiles from the "dirty war" in Argentina and major contributors to the world of painting; Dr. Patrick Lloyd Hatcher, lieutenant colonel U.S. Army (ret.) and a longtime colleague; Professor Yoshihiko Nakamoto of Shizuoka University, Japan. My geriatric cat, Mof, a Russian blue, helps keep me cheerful.

Index

About the Author

CHALMERS JOHNSON, president of the Japan Policy Research Institute, is the author of the award-winning *Blowback* and *The Sorrows of Empire*. A frequent contributor to *Harper's Magazine*, the *London Review of Books*, and the *Nation*, he appears in the 2005 prizewinning documentary film *Why We Fight*. He lives near San Diego.

The American Empire Project

In an era of unprecedented military strength, leaders of the United States, the global hyperpower, have increasingly embraced imperial ambitions. How did this significant shift in purpose and policy come about? And what lies down the road?

The American Empire Project is a response to the changes that have occurred in America's strategic thinking as well as in its military and economic posture. Empire, long considered an offense against America's democratic heritage, now threatens to define the relationship between our country and the rest of the world. The American Empire Project publishes books that question this development, examine the origins of U.S. imperial aspirations, analyze their ramifications at home and abroad, and discuss alternatives to this dangerous trend.

The project was conceived by Tom Engelhardt and Steve Fraser, editors who are themselves historians and writers. Published by Metropolitan Books, an imprint of Henry Holt and Company, its titles include *Hegemony or Survival* by Noam Chomsky, *The Sorrows of Empire* by Chalmers Johnson, *Crusade* by James Carroll, *How to Succeed at Globalization* by El Fisgón, *Blood and Oil* by Michael Klare, *Dilemmas of Domination* by Walden Bello, *War Powers* by Peter Irons, *Devil's Game* by Robert Dreyfuss, *In the Name of Democracy*, edited by Jeremy Brecher, Jill Cutler, and Brendan Smith, *Imperial Ambitions* by Noam Chomsky, *A Question of Torture* by Alfred McCoy, *Failed States* by Noam Chomsky, and *Empire's Workshop* by Greg Grandin.

For more information about the American Empire Project and for a list of forthcoming titles, please visit *www.americanempireproject.com*.